The Good Wife's

astes que k

A brie petit

que bous er

A presenx

songneuser

diligence 7

comme bou

sacre conseil ce croy je bien que le brie. En

comme en fais secoro que pour lamour de

The Good Wife's Guide

LE MÉNAGIER DE PARIS

A MEDIEVAL HOUSEHOLD BOOK

Translated, with Critical Introduction, by

GINA L. GRECO & CHRISTINE M. ROSE

CORNELL UNIVERSITY PRESS

ITHACA AND LONDON

First published 2009 by Cornell University Press
First printing, Cornell Paperbacks, 2009

Printed in the United States of America

The Library of Congress Cataloging-in-Publication Data may be found on the last page of this book.

Cornell University Press strives to use environmentally responsible suppliers and materials to the fullest extent possible in the publishing of its books. Such materials include vegetable-based, low-VOC inks and acid-free papers that are recycled, totally chlorine-free, or partly composed of nonwood fibers. For further information, visit our website at www.cornellpress.cornell.edu.

Cloth printing   10 9 8 7 6 5 4 3 2 1
Paperback printing 10 9 8 7 6 5 4 3 2 1

FRONTISPIECE:
Le Ménagier MS A, Paris, Bibliothèque nationale de France, fonds français 12477, fol. 1. Small image before the beginning of the text ("Chiere seur . . .") of a man and woman conversing.

TO GAETANO AND JOHN

Contents

Preface

This project began when Christine Rose decided to teach *Le Ménagier de Paris* in a "Medieval Women" class. She discovered that Eileen Power's 1928 *Goodman of Paris* translation was out of print and permission to photocopy it for the class could not be obtained. No alternative translation provided a substantial representative section of the book. When Gina Greco, a friend and a meticulous Old French scholar, agreed to collaborate on a scholarly English translation, it seemed incredibly fortuitous, and we began the long trek through the text. We feel especially qualified to partner in this undertaking and are blessed by how our training in palaeography and languages complement one another. It has been a most satisfactory collaboration in every way.

Impetus to finish the translation came from academic colleagues who heard Rose's conference papers on *Le Ménagier de Paris* and inquired when a translation might appear, since they found it a crucial text for medieval studies. We appreciated and took seriously the comments and questions we received, especially from Polish colleagues at Adam Mickiewicz University in Poznan and Professors Jacek Fisiak, O.B.E., and Liliana Sikorska, who arranged two outstanding symposiums where Rose had the opportunity to discuss her research on the text. As the volume gradually took shape, the tasks were divided, with Greco as the primary translator of Middle French, and Rose in charge of the introduction, notes, and rendering the text into readable and interesting modern English. But there was indeed much crossover in our duties. We were not prepared to love the book as much as we did, and do, despite its darker aspects. While the last parts of the translation and introduction were refined, Greco was in Burkina Faso, Africa, on a Fulbright grant, and then in Angers, France, and the files flew through cyberspace between there and Seattle and Portland. While one translator slept, the other was probably working on *Le Ménagier*. Each version of our translation traveled back and forth multiple times for fine-tuning, astonishing us with the wonder and the ease of the partnership from opposite ends of the earth and with the wealth of electronic aids found at Portland State and the University of Washington libraries, as well as on the Worldwide Web.

We strove to make sure that the translation not stray from the exact sense of the Middle French. Correct readings of crucial terms cropped up in many and diverse places, including databases of medieval cookbooks and Old French dictionaries; French equestrian clubs; farmers' markets in France; websites on cow anatomy, falconry, horse dentistry; books of penitential reading; and, of course, old-fashioned haunting of libraries. We consider this work as continuing and improving upon the efforts of those scholars who have explored this text over the years, its popularity long hampered by the lack of an English translation and still stalled by the fact that Baron Pichon's edition remains the sole resource for three sizable sections of the text. From his edition in 1846, to Georgine E. Brereton and Janet M. Ferrier's in 1981, to Brereton, Ferrier, and Karin Ueltschi's in 1994, we had before us the various notes and choices for what a reading might be, many of which we rejected, but these were inestimable guides to getting it right, and we benefited from both correct and inexact readings. Our readers can fruitfully consult Brereton-Ferrier and Pichon for expanded explanatory notes to the text, most of which we did not reproduce here. The English translations—Power's and the few excerpts—piecemeal as they are, helped us narrow down some issues, and the cookbook in particular, with its arcane terminology, was mightily aided by the number of reference books, recipe books, and websites on medieval cookery that abound, some of which included material from *Le Ménagier*. Studying manuscripts A and C in the Bibliothèque Nationale in Paris was enormously valuable, although the work of Pichon and Brereton-Ferrier was generally accurate, and few questions about manuscript readings were not answered by their notes. We have every confidence in the faithfulness of our translation to the author's book. At times, we have given his narrator a more interesting vocabulary than the text provides, but we have remained true to the sense. Through our translation we endeavor to join a conversation that explores medieval female behavior and those writings that proscribed and prescribed how women (and men) were to conceptualize their place in society and their subjectivity, while attending to what the social and personal consequences of such a literature might be. We hope that the introduction will foster further study and enjoyment of this text by scholars and students, as well as situate the book in its cultural moment and milieu.

While the matter of the book may seem amusing or outrageous in its strictures against female freedom and its advocacy of absolute obedience to the husband, such a program of restraint of females is not a relic of some medieval past but forms part of the fabric of Western civilization and was a widespread ethos in the United States until recent times. (One might propose that female suffrage in the United States and Europe was one of the agents of change, but even since then, the belief in the rightness of female obedience has had its proponents.) Such a system, which, as Elizabeth Cady Stanton wrote in the 1848 Seneca Falls "Declaration of Sentiments," involves "a history of repeated injuries and usurpations on the part of man toward women, having in direct object the establishment of an absolute tyranny over her," continues to exist as the cultural norm of some sects, regimes, and regions. Though readers may find this antique French husband inconsequential as he consciously strains to advocate control of the behavior or reading of obstreperous medieval women, we must not allow our distance from this system to lull us into discounting its cultural power and gravity as an agenda of female oppression. Despite the fact that the authorized version of "good" female and wifely behavior in the Middle Ages was often at odds with the derelictions of the "bad" women displayed in stereotyped stories and probably in actual medieval life, the models for virtue in women were taken seriously, it seems. Such a system of control of women as we see in *Le Ménagier* had then—and has now—real costs for women and society. Perhaps, along with the young wife, we might both love and fear such a man as the narrator, and the work he presents may elicit a complicated aesthetic response in the reader. In this book, for our consideration, reside both scary stuff and fun stuff: rules to follow (with threats of punishment, both present and in the hereafter) and work to do, but also useful tips, agreeable stories, and good things to eat. For ourselves, neither of us has attempted any of the feats of gastronomy mentioned herein, or taken to heart any of the advice on how to be "good" wives.

✳ ✳ ✳

For their encouragement and affection, we thank first our parents, Beryl and Claude Greco, and Marjorie and Lloyd Rose, and our brothers and sisters in our own childhood *ménages*: Kenneth, Joseph, and Douglas Rose; Aimée Schafer, Matthew, Marc, and Stephen Greco. Our husbands, Gaetano DeLeonibus and John Coldewey, to whom we dedicate this volume, were always positive and wise about our work, while Elena and Sophia DeLeonibus and Christopher and Devin Coldewey tolerated our scholarly projects woven into their childhoods, yet have survived splendidly. We love them all. So many teachers and colleagues have been our models, inspirations, and supporters, and we are in their debt. This book could not have come to pass without the intellectual generosity, inspiration, and friendship of Sheila Delany, to whom Christine Rose owes a profound debt of gratitude. Likewise, Gina Greco could not have spent as much time with the manuscripts without the unstinting hospitality and friendship of Hana Rottman throughout the years. We thank also from our past education, and gratefully count among our present (and departed) friends and mentors:(CR) F. Donald Logan, Charles Lionel Regan, Peter Carafiol, Paul G. Remley, John M. Ganim, Ralph Hanna III, Laurie A. Finke, Paul Giles, G. Robert Stange, Sylvan Barnet, John M. Fyler, Georgia Ronan Crampton, Sister Anne Cyril Delaney, A. S .G. Edwards, Michel-André Boissy, Raymond Biggar, C. Warren Hollister, Elizabeth A. Robertson, Larry D. Benson, Harriet Spiegel, Charlene Rogers, Christine Thompson, Linda Dow Ferguson, Diane Carmody Wynne, and—most of all—Eileen D. Hardy, the best of friends; (GG) Karl D. Uitti, Carleton Carroll, Sandra Rosengrant, Sylvie Rottman, Karen Carr, Elisabeth Jacquier, Rhonda Case, Gretta Siegel,

Debora Schwartz, Laura Zinker, Peter DeLeonibus, and for their assistance—so vital to the completion of the project—Beverly Mangold and Wendy de Charnacé. Thanks to our astute copyeditor Susan Tarcov, to Karen Popp for cheering us on, to our editor Teresa Jesionowski, and to Peter Potter, Editor-in-Chief of Cornell University Press, for his faith in the enterprise.

Portland State University provided essential computer support as well as Faculty Development funds granted to both Rose and Greco, resulting in valuable research and travel opportunities that fostered our work. The P. S. U. Library, especially through Sharon Elteto, Janet Wright, and Linda Absher, and the University of Washington libraries, offered stalwart aid in our research. The Department of English at the University of Washington has kindly granted Rose Visiting Scholar privileges over the years, enabling her to access a greater range of research material, as well as to enjoy the benefits of intellectual exchange with scholars there. The Department of Foreign Languages and Literatures of Portland State University readily arranged for Greco to spend a crucial trimester in France. Jim DeWalt, head of the Rare Book Department of the Free Library of Philadelphia, conveyed important information about the *Chemin* poem manuscript there. M. Luc Deitz of the Bibliothèque Nationale of Luxembourg kindly took the time and effort to help us identify the *Le Ménagier* manuscript in that collection by sending much-appreciated photocopies. Kathleen Blake furnished Christine Rose with dozens of hours of valuable collegial conversation *en plein air*, and the work benefited immeasurably from these discussions. Steve Jones, D.V.M., and his "horse sense" helped us through the veterinary matters herein. Ava Rose was our in-house greyhound expert and muse. Our colleagues and students at Portland State University constantly enrich our lives.

Gina L. Greco and Christine M. Rose

Maid to Order The Good Wife of Paris

> This book will provide you with a great advantage, since other
> women never had such a guide.—*Le Ménagier de Paris*

The Book: Backgrounds, Narrator, Genre, Sources

In the closing years of the fourteenth century someone carefully compiled a
large book in French, addressed to a fifteen-year-old bride and narrated in the
voice of her husband, an aging wealthy Parisian bourgeois. This book aimed at
teaching her the moral attributes, duties, and conduct befitting a wife of her station in society, and provided for her use and that of her household many practical texts such as gardening instructions, over 380 recipes, menus for feasts, tips on
choosing servants, advice about keeping fleas out of bedclothes, medical care for
horses, and directions for raising and training hawks. This Parisian man of means
and status feels that owing to his wife's youth, she may require such instruction
on womanly conduct and her household responsibilities as she begins her married life with him. Other medieval texts of household books, conduct manuals, or
hunting treatises resemble this book in some ways, but none provide just such a
comprehensive program of education, framed as the matter this young wife needs
to know. The work's unique and delightful contents of prose and poetry, treatises and recipes, morals and menus prove the narrator correct in his assessment
that indeed no other woman ever had "such a guide," since it is the only surviving medieval book with this amalgamation of instructional materials.

In his book, the husband narrator notes in passing what might be indications
of his connections to the court of the duke of Berry, and in the course of this
manual we discover that he has a large house in Paris itself, as well as a country
estate and a farm. He possesses a staff of servants, stables, farm animals, mews,
ample gardens in town, and fields in the countryside for hunting and farming. The
book contains one of the most interesting and important medieval conduct books
for women, as well as a treasure trove of cookery and other homemaking tips. In
its details can be found a literary recreation of the material and intellectual culture in an affluent Parisian domestic setting during the late Middle Ages and an
ongoing contemplation of the complex negotiation that constituted medieval
marriage.

We present here the first complete modern English translation of that anonymously authored medieval householder's book generally known as *Le Ménagier*

de Paris—which means *The Parisian Household Book*—probably compiled in 1392–94. The manual may be a sincere didactic treatise from an actual husband, but our working assumption considers it a "literary" creation. For clarity, our discussion differentiates between the *author* who compiled the book and the *narrator* who performs the text in the voice of the aged husband. The text, assembled from many sources, depicts the husband-narrator taking upon himself the duty of educating his bride about how to be a good and proper wife. In fact, "good" (*bon* and its variations) is a fundamental term in the work, and the author uses it to mean myriad things that in modern English have different equivalents, synonyms, and ethical valences, making it a vexed word for translators (see "Translation Protocols" below). Although *Le Ménagier* has in the past primarily been admired for its antique horticultural and culinary matter, we see the heart of the book as the moral treatise and the theme of the work as the absolute obedience the householder demands of his wife in all her actions. The husband-narrator declares that he has created this manual for his young wife for the salvation of her soul and the smooth running of their household. But above all, it seems, he desires his own happiness in a prosperous, bountiful, and peaceful residence with an obedient spouse attending to his needs, overseeing the management of his home, and guaranteeing his good name. In addition, and significantly, he seeks the praise of his young wife's next husband for having taught her well. His book reflects the manners and mores of its age and reveals the desiderata for a "good" wife along with providing directions for a plenteous array of delicious food for his table and a comfortable home with compliant servants, hawks, hounds, and wife.

This compilation survives in three fifteenth-century manuscripts, related but not exact copies of one another. What's more, an early sixteenth-century paper manuscript of *Le Ménagier* recently came to our attention in Luxembourg's Bibliothèque Nationale (MS I: 95), which attests to the work's continued popularity over the next century.[1] That this late text was handwritten, though the printing

---

1. The four extant manuscripts are: (A) Paris, Bibliothèque nationale de France (BnF), fonds français 12477 (fifteenth century, with Burgundian ducal connections; slightly later than MS B); (B) Brussels, Bibliothèque royale, 10310–10311 (fifteenth century); (C) Paris, BnF, nouvelles acquisitions françaises 6739 (late fifteenth century, appears to be a copy of MS A). According to Georgine E. Brereton and Janet M. Ferrier, MS A is the closest to the common source of the three (*Le menagier de Paris*, ed. Brereton and Ferrier, with a foreword by Beryl Smalley [Oxford, 1981] [hereafter cited as BF]). Unknown to Brereton-Ferrier and Pichon, in addition to A, B, and C, an early sixteenth-century manuscript of the work exists, Luxembourg, Bibliothèque nationale du Luxembourg MS I:95 (ancien numéro 19) (360 f.), a codex associated with the family of Count de Lalaing. Little more is known of its provenance. M. Luc Deitz, Curator of Manuscripts and Rare Books at the Luxembourg National Library, assisted our provisional identification of this handsomely written manuscript by providing images of the manuscript. After the scribal explicit fol-

press was available, may indicate that the Luxembourg work was copied specially for a single elite client and that the market for it was not robust enough for a printer to take it on as a paying venture. None of the manuscripts show hard wear or any evidence, through stains or mistreatment, of being consulted—despite the contents—in a kitchen, garden, mews, or stable. Although they are attractive, well-preserved manuscripts, they lack lavish programs of illustrations, revealing themselves poor cousins to other more splendid Burgundian manuscripts, appearing indeed as if they were reference reading rather than objets d'art.

The text of *Le Ménagier* was edited and published for the first time in 1846 as a "traité de morale et d'économie domestique" by Baron Jérôme Pichon.[2] The work's scholarly edition is by Georgine E. Brereton and Janet M. Ferrier,[3] and there is a Middle French/modern French facing-page version, based on the Brereton-Ferrier edition, by Karin Ueltschi.[4] The Brereton-Ferrier edition omits three lengthy sections of the text: the tale of Griselda (1.6); the tale of Prudence and Melibee from Renard de Louens's version of Albertanus of Brescia's story (1.9); and the poem by Jacques Bruyant (c. 1324), *Le Chemin de povreté et de richesse* (The Way of Poverty and Riches) (2.1). They justify these exclusions by

---

low four more folios of recipes. At the time this translation was going to press, we were unable to examine MS I:95 in person, but we plan to discuss it in a future article. BF describe MSS A, B, and C in some detail in their introduction, xii–xviii. We examined MSS A and C at the BnF and have relied on the catalogue of the ducal library and BF for information on B. See the entry for MS B by Tania Van Hemelryck in *La Librairie des ducs de Bourgogne: Manuscrits conservés à la Bibliothèque royale de Belgique*, vol. 2, *Textes didactiques*, ed. Bernard Bousmanne, Frédérique Johan, and Céline van Hoorebeeck (Turnhout: Brepols, 2003), 164–69. The first modern editor, Baron Jérôme Pichon (*Le Ménagier de Paris, Traité de morale et d'economie domestique composé vers 1393 par un bourgeois Parisien*, 2 vols. [Paris: Société des Bibliophiles François, 1846–47; reprint, Geneva: Slatkine, 1982][hereafter cited as Pichon]), feels MS C may have belonged to a woman, Marguerite, the wife of Pierre or Rene de Roubais, in the fifteenth century. Roubais was a member of the household of the duke of Burgundy. Pichon judges the narrator to be over fifty from references to his witnessing events in 1358 or 1359 (I, 149, n.1) and the date of the work's composition to be c. 1394 (I, xix–xxiii).

2. This edition has helpful historical notes. BF call Pichon "select and often high-handed" in the emendations he makes to his texts and the readings he chooses (xxi). Pichon is at present the only source for editions of the Griselda, Melibee, and *Chemin* texts included in the *Le Ménagier de Paris* miscellany. We checked his texts of these three sections against MS A for our translation. See "Translation Protocols."

3. Our work has benefited from the introduction and explanatory notes, as well as the competent edition of the Middle French. The base text in BF is MS A, BnF, fonds français 12477, with variants noted from B and C.

4. *Le Mesnagier de Paris*, ed. Georgina [sic] E. Brereton and Janet M. Ferrier, translation and notes by Karin Ueltschi (Paris: Livre de Poche, 1994) (hereafter cited as BF/Ueltschi).

treating these sections as not the original work of the author/compiler, and therefore not an essential part of the book. Thus, their edition presents an incomplete version of the work, but beyond that, their text feels disordered and misrepresented because they privilege the sections the author seems to have composed himself over those he borrowed directly from other writers and redactors. The Ueltschi modern French translation includes all three texts omitted in Brereton-Ferrier but has relegated the *Chemin* poem to an appendix. Pichon's 1846 edition is the basis of Ueltschi's modern French translation of the Griselda and Melibee stories, while her edition reproduces Pichon's edition of the *Chemin* poem without translating it. In fact, however, these borrowings of the long narrative and poetic excursions are essential to the author's project, and it is clear that any historically and culturally responsible translation should incorporate them. Accordingly, all three neglected sections—Griselda, Melibee, and *Chemin*—are integrated into our text at their original locations within the extant manuscripts A, B, and C to echo the initial conception of the work by its author/compiler. We translate these pieces into modern English for the first time as part of this undertaking to supply a complete English text.

Portions of *Le Ménagier de Paris* appeared in an early twentieth-century English translation, Eileen Power's *The Goodman of Paris* (1928).[5] Power substantially abridged and bowdlerized the text and rendered the prose into a consciously archaic English style. Our translation presents the complete book as it must have existed for its earliest readers, that is, in a form approximating the way that its first readers—the young wife included?—encountered it, since the manuscripts we

5. Eileen Power, *The Goodman of Paris* (London: Routledge, 1928; reprint, London: Boydell, 2006)(hereafter cited as Power). Power uses antiquated English diction to capture the flavor of a medieval text. She has abridged her translation in both large and small ways. Some of her excisions are bowdlerizations of sexual materials (in the Seven Deadly Sins section and other places) or the antifeminine rants of the narrator; she excluded two of the large pieces the author copied from his sources (the *Chemin* poem and the tale of Melibee). As the first English translation, it is an unarguably fine beginning. In some instances Power has made judicious translation decisions, which we have at times adopted. A small selection of *Le Ménagier* was translated by Tania Bayard as *A Medieval Home Companion: Housekeeping in the Fourteenth Century* (New York: Harper Perennial, 1991). Snippets of the text appear translated in a few anthologies of medieval contexts, such as Emily Amt, *Women's Lives in Medieval Europe: A Sourcebook* (New York: Routledge, 1993). Some recipes and culinary information from *Le Ménagier* are included in books on medieval cookery: D. Eleanor Scully and Terence Scully, *Early French Cookery: Sources, History, Original Recipes and Modern Adaptations* (Ann Arbor: University of Michigan Press, 2002); Odile Redon, Françoise Sabban, and Silvano Serventi, with a foreword by Georges Duby, *The Medieval Kitchen: Recipes from France and Italy,* trans. Edward Schneider (Chicago: University of Chicago Press, 1998); and Constance Hieatt and Sharon Butler, *Pleyn Delit: Medieval Cookery for Modern Cooks* (Toronto: University of Toronto Press, 1979).

follow seem to be copies of some lost original. Thus we include those selections the author regarded so highly and thought so useful for a wife's education that he copied them wholesale into his volume from other sources. From culinary collections such as Taillevent's *Viandier*—or he may have remembered very well from his own life—the author provides menus from aristocratic dinner parties and recipes for exotic medieval dishes. The narrator says of Jacques Bruyant's 2,626-line poem *Le Chemin de poverté et de richesse*: "Because I have no wish to mutilate his book, or extract a fragment or excerpt it from the rest, and likewise because it is all of a piece, I help myself to the whole to reach the only point that I desire" (2.1.5). We consider this sentiment akin to our own endeavor not to tinker with the book's contents and, however sprawling or prolix some of the materials might seem, to honor the intent of the author (and our readers) by presenting it in its entirety. Considering this compelling text as a whole is crucial to historicizing reading practices, understanding the author's purposes and the late medieval audience's actual reading matter, and noting what they cared to preserve for use in their households. Such verbose didactic texts would have been considered valuable, entertaining, and uplifting by a medieval audience.[6] And our modern audience should find it interesting as well, for example, to observe how deftly the later sections of the text reflect and expand themes and motifs begun in the moral treatise of section 1. It is apparent that the author envisioned the work as the husband's whole system of household orderliness that stretched from his wife, to his kitchen, to his stables, mews, and gardens.

Gathered, as the husband-narrator indicates, from his reading and his own experience for his wife's reference and that of his household, the volume offers readers a vivid picture of the home life of this couple. From what he tells us in the prologue, his plan was to divide the material into three "distinctions" (sections) —the first, on the moral life of a good wife; the second, on domestic management and cookery; and the third, on games and amusements with which the wife should be familiar as part of her hostessing duties.

Section 1, with nine articles, comprises a long moral treatise on the ideals of womanly behavior. The narrator explains to his young wife in the prologue that this initial material "teaches you how to attain God's love and the salvation of your soul, and also to win your husband's love and to give yourself, in this world, the peace that should be found in marriage. And because these two things, salvation of the soul and the contentment of your husband, are the the two most impor-

6. Indeed, that it was read as such by its original audience is supported by parallels between *Le Ménagier* and Antoine de la Sale's *Jehan de Saintré*, a didactic work composed approximately fifty years after *Le Ménagier*. Gina L. Greco, "Court Values in Jehan de Saintré," paper delivered at the International Congress on Medieval Studies, Kalamazoo, MI, May 7, 2006.

tant things that exist, they are placed first." Articles 1.1 and 1.2 comprise exhortations to piety and prayers, modest dress, and control of the gaze. An explanation of the Mass, the examination of conscience and confession, and the Seven Deadly Sins with their corresponding virtues makes up article 1.3. Wifely chastity is the topic of article 1.4; wifely fidelity, article 1.5; wifely obedience, including the story of Griselda, article 1.6; care of the husband's person, article 1.7; care of the husband's secrets and reputation, article 1.8. The final piece in this section, article 1.9, about a wife's responsibility for good counsel and for keeping her husband from sin or folly, incorporates the story of Melibee and Prudence. Section 2, with five articles, primarily concerns household management. But this section begins with the allegorical poem *Le Chemin de povreté et de richesse,* which recapitulates much of the moral instruction and dramatizes how to attain wealth through virtue and hard work (2.1). The remainder of this section has articles on gardening (2.2); the hiring of and conduct toward servants and the choosing and medical care of horses (2.3); the purchase of food, planning of dinners and courses, and menus of actual feasts (2.4); and an elaborate cookbook of ordinary household fare as well as cuisine for festive occasions (2.5). This matter, says the narrator, "instructs you on how to increase the prosperity of the household, gain friends, preserve your possessions, and make those misfortunes attendant upon old age easier for you to bear" (prologue, ¶ 6).

According to the prologue, section 3 was destined to have three articles treating "pleasant enough games and amusements to help you socialize with company and make conversation," but it is now incomplete in the extant MSS. Its first article was to describe parlor games for indoor amusement, dice, and chess—this part is now lost or was never finished according to his plan. The third article, a book of riddles and arithmetic games, is now also missing. The second article, the only surviving part of this third planned section, is a treatise on raising and hunting with hawks; it has been inserted into section 2 in all the MSS, following a treatise on horses (2.3). We have placed it there in this translation to reflect its position in the extant early manuscripts, but have labeled it "3.2" adhering to the plan outlined in the prologue. So, as we have inherited it from the fourteenth century, via the three fifteenth-century manuscript witnesses, the book is divided into only two sections—a moral treatise on female conduct and a group of instructional materials on domestic management and cooking. Moral goodness (section 1) and practical skills (section 2) comprise the two essential dimensions of the training of a wife in this manual.

While the 1928 Power translation privileges the "Mrs. Beeton" aspect of the text's garden and culinary instruction, we see the heart of the book as the moral treatise, and in fact the work's theme emerges as the unquestioning obedience that the householder—and by inference all husbands of his class—requires of his wife. Oddly, even the Library of Congress classification system militates against focusing on the moral treatise, placing the Pichon and the Brereton-Ferrier editions in the "TX" section —with cookbooks![7] Interestingly, Power's choice of title, *The Goodman of Paris,* provides a clue to her reading of the text, which finds the narrator avuncular, benevolent, even doting, and focuses on him. And, in their introduction, Brereton and Ferrier characterize the narrator as "kindly" and encouraging of his wife.[8] One can surely find this sentiment in the text, yet we are less sanguine about his geniality given his often strident insistence on wifely subservience in all things. The benevolent tone at the outset is belied by the manner in which the moral treatise of section 1 piles on exhortations to submission, illustrating the violence visited upon wives who disobey.[9] Indeed, we find the wife-as-reader a significantly more intriguing "character" or silent presence in the text, and a potential site of resistance to the strictures within. Perhaps the title might reasonably be *The Goodwife of Paris.*

Submission to the husband as a Christian obeys God is the model to be inculcated. The sections lessoning the wife on estate management, for example, reflect the surveillance and tight control the householder wants to have over his spouse and minions, his vegetables, his horses, his dogs and his birds.[10] Haughtiness or

---

7. Nicole Crossley-Holland, in *Living and Dining in Medieval Paris: The Household of a Medieval Knight* (Cardiff: University of Wales Press, 1999), also focuses on the "alimentary typology" aspect of *Le Ménagier* (7). Using the book as her primary source, Crossley-Holland describes life in medieval Paris, and in particular how such a household as that described in *Le Ménagier* might have been ordered. This quirky book explains the physical set-up of medieval houses of this class, the types of gardens and vegetables, and the accuracy of the recipes and offers other valuable details of Parisian life in the fourteenth century.

8. Crossley-Holland, too, considers the author to be the narrator, and deems him to have "gifts of elegance, kindness and concern for others" (*Living and Dining in Medieval Paris*, 2) with a "gentle courtesy and freshness that must have delighted the young wife" (10).

9. A most nuanced discussion of the relationship of violence and aesthetics in medieval representations, and audience responses to this complex issue, is Jody Enders's "A Polemical Introduction" to *The Medieval Theater of Cruelty* (Ithaca: Cornell University Press, 1999), 1–24.

10. See Christine M. Rose, "What Every Goodwoman Wants: The Parameters of Desire in *Le Ménagier de Paris / The Goodman of Paris,*" *Studia Anglica Posnaniensia* 38 (2002): 394–410. This essay explores the system of household surveillance imbedded in the book and shows that the moral and physical domestication of a wife is analogous to the taming of the hawks, animals, and plants the author so lavishly describes. The next husband, the entire household, and the young wife herself are all implicated in overseeing the wife's obedience. Some portions of this introduction have been adapted from this article. The editor of *Studia Anglica Posnaniensia,* Professor Jacek Fisiak has graciously granted us permission to use this material, as well as portions of Rose's plenary address to the Medieval English Studies Symposium held in Poznan in November 2006, "Glossing Griselda in a Medieval Conduct Book: *Le Ménagier de Paris,*" in *Medieval English Mirror,* 4 (2008): 81–103.

waywardness on the part of servants, or by his hawks or dogs, is vanquished by firm training. The narrator's manual gives advice to the young wife and to the others he includes in his audience on how to know and choose a *good* hunting dog, a *good* horse, a *good* hawk, *good* meat and vegetables, *good* servants, and, always, how to identify a *good* wife. The exempla in *Le Ménagier*'s moral treatise continually reinforce the notion that a disobedient wife is a sinful and unseemly wife. The ideal "good" wife models the humble and patient Griselda, whose story appears in the moral treatise in the section on obedience (1.6). This selfless long-suffering female always assents to her husband's will, whatever he asks—even if it represents emotional or physical violence to herself. The tale of Griselda acts as the centerpiece of the moral treatise. As the paradigmatic wife of the whole book, the ultra-obedient Griselda is recalled in each anecdote about wifely behavior and echoed in the later sections on domestic management. Even as the narrator borrows the story from a contemporary source, Philippe de Mézières via Petrarch and Boccaccio, he augments it with some of his own ideas on wifely obedience. Accordingly, he gives Griselda a long speech not found in his source about bearing with patience the ordeals to which her husband subjects her. The tale depicts Griselda schooled incredibly harshly by her husband, Walter—as indeed, by inference, might be the young wife-addressee of the treatise. The householder's literate young wife is adjured to read of this ideal wife and her behavior and take this text to heart. Aspects of Griselda's fictional husband, the tyrant Marquis Walter, are recreated in the character of the husband-narrator himself, as well as in the shallow, ego-driven husbands he provides for his young wife to study in his exempla and in his supposed real-life associates. In the final moments of the tale, Walter is beatifically ready to reembrace the Griselda he tormented, knowing she will assent to and forgive it all. Likewise, the narrator rhetorically turns to his wife and assures her he neither desires nor finds himself worthy to school his new bride harshly even as he has been furnishing stories of the ominous consequences of insubordination. In other words, he dissociates himself from Walter, while performing Walter's character at every opportunity in his wife's guidebook. We offer a fuller discussion of Griselda's singular importance to the book in a separate section below.

A woman who learned all the book had to teach would be, by medieval standards, a most accomplished chatelaine and hostess, as well as a moral, obedient, and attentive wife. *Le Ménagier de Paris* must also have appealed to medieval audiences interested in discovering how wealthy families conducted their spiritual and conjugal lives and managed their complicated *ménage,* not to mention the array of menus to refer to, admire, and perhaps reproduce in their own milieu. As either a text detailing the "lifestyles of the rich and famous" or a work validating their own moral and culinary tastes, a late-medieval audience would have found much to approve of in this compendium of moral rectitude, wifely order-liness, conspicuous consumption, and expensive partying. The narrator asks his wife here and there to economize and watch the tradesmen's prices, but there is no denying the display of the household's affluence and the considerable cost of even the spices needed to create the foodstuffs for the dinners described. Know-ing that a wife of this estate in society had such expectations for her behavior would have made the work's moral instruction a benchmark for others to aspire to. The text offers training in domestic tasks that a wife of her class should be able to perform, like hiring servants, dealing with tradesmen, preserving roses in win-ter, airing furs, or buying pork.

The two goals of a secure family life—achieving salvation and creating a sta-ble *polis* and social structure—are articulated in the instructions the husband provides for his wife's tuition in how to be a "good" wife. In the prologue and en-suing treatises, the tone is of fatherly admonishment, both coercive and avuncu-lar. He fashions himself principally as a tutor in manners and morals, as a kind of household priest, interested in the religious education and proper develop-ment of his wife's soul. He gives pride of place in his handbook to the treatise on praying, conducting religious devotions, and examining the conscience (1.1–1.3), no doubt derived from one of the many *manuels des pécheurs* available in the French vernacular during the period. These first three treatises (called "articles") concern the young woman's spiritual life and provide catechistic instruction. Later parts instruct her on taking care of a husband's bodily needs (1.7); keeping his secrets (1.8); being devoted to him (1.5); choosing his servants (2.3); and over-seeing the preparation of his meals (2.5). In sum, the husband-narrator dauntingly portrays himself as incarnating all available patriarchal structures: father, hus-band, chaplain, supervisor, feudal lord.

But the young wife is not his only audience. Later, he addresses a piece of the manual on choosing horses and treating their ailments (2.3) to the household's steward, Jehan, and suggests that the young wife's companion/governess, Dame Agnes the Beguine, might benefit from reading some portions of the work on do-mestic management. But by far the most remarkable of the audiences created within the text is the young wife's *next* husband, whom the older man wishes to impress with his wife-training skills—and clearly with his learning, wide read-ing, and moral rectitude. This wife comes complete with an owner's manual. By seeking the potential future husband's praise and approbation, the narrator con-structs a homosocial bond between them, with the remade woman as the sign of the transfer of power and honor from one to the other. Thus, the continuance of the cultural model perpetrated by the first husband is secured; further, the wife is instructed to indoctrinate her own children—from either husband—accord-ing to the book's precepts of female obedience to male authority. In many intriguing elisions, the narrator displaces the notion of his bride's obeying *him* to her obedience to the husband-that-will-be. He writes, for example:

> Thus, dear one, I repeat, you must be obedient to your future husband, for it is through good obeisance that a wise woman obtains her husband's love and, in the end, receives from him what she desires. Similarly, I can assert that if you act arrogantly or disobediently, you destroy yourself, your husband, and your household. (1.6.11)

This platitude presents a paradox encoded in the model for marriage that the *Ménagier* narrator proposes: in the end the wife may get her way, but only by consenting to be dominated. Predictably, perhaps, the book's lessons on obedience reinscribe a patriarchal feudal structure, one that closely restricts women's speech and chastity, for women to internalize and for men to attempt to enforce.

Virtually everyone writing on *Le Ménagier* has accepted its author as who he claims to be, a wealthy elderly Parisian married to a fifteen-year-old, since he begins his prologue: "My dear, because you were only fifteen years old the week we were married, you asked that I be indulgent about your youth and inexperience until you had seen and learned more."[11] But it is more useful to consider him an "author" with an authorial persona, the "narrator," who has a "literary" plan for his work. In so doing we avoid the trap of accepting the literary as *literal*.

In section 2 and what would have been section 3, the author gives voice to this educated man well acquainted with the running of substantial city and country households, with lands, gardens, farm animals, laborers, housemaids, and varlets. It may be that the handbook was read and copied as a conduct manual for women and a domestic management reference, but it is also artfully shaped, especially, as we have indicated, the framing of the Griselda story within the whole treatise on obedient wives. The manual simultaneously allows us to observe in this narrative the tension in medieval society between what wives and loyal sub-

---

11. Crossley-Holland (*Living and Dining in Medieval Paris*) assumes the narrative voice to be the "author" and attempts to ascertain through internal evidence of dates, people, and places mentioned just what the identity of the householder-author might have been. She settles on Guy de Montigny, a knight in the service of the duke of Berry. The evidence provided is unconvincing, but intriguing. Nevertheless, her work remains a helpful resource for the study of the domestic management sections of the text. Pichon feels the narrator was a bureaucrat with some expertise in military finance, or in the judiciary or city government, which might account for his vocabulary or rhetorical style. BF call him "the author" but do not separate his literary persona of the husband from his authorial nature. They do see him as the person who he says he is. And, of course, we cannot say this is not so, only that it is not a valid assumption at the outset. Roberta L. Krueger also notes an author/narrator division in "Identity Begins at Home: Female Conduct and the Failure of Counsel in *Le Menagier de Paris*," *Essays in Medieval Studies* 22 (2005): 21–39.

jects should be (submissive) and what they surely sometimes were (malcontent and uppity). One senses at times in the moral treatise that the narrator's experience of the behavior of real wives disproves the authorities he uses continually to buttress his advocacy of female submission. Queer theory has shown that even as the reinscription of "key cultural orthodoxies works to uphold their status on the one hand, so does it expose their fragility: for gender and sexual norms to *remain* norms they need to be 'performed' continually."[12] The narrator urges his wife to see the world divided along the lines of good and evil. He constrains his subject matter as he seeks to constrain his wife, and imposes an order and a moral reading on the batch of diverse exempla he collects that the unruly tales often threaten to shrug off.

The book's contents are all about management: the management of a wife's body and soul and her duties toward her husband, the management of the home and garden. It advances from dictating the inner life of her soul to dictating her outward behavior, and thence to the manner in which the wife's household reflects her regulated nature, which in turn reflects well on the husband. However genial the narrator's tone may be in places, his moral and domestic tuition infantilizes the woman and reifies her as a sort of domestic animal in need of obedience training and surveillance, while also paradoxically insisting on her position as the mistress of this complicated household whom others must obey.[13] As we have noted, the last planned section on leisure pastimes is incomplete in all extant manuscripts. The missing disquisitions on games and riddles might have been a happy addition for scholars, but it would not disturb the dark contours of this picture of a wife in charge of the pleasure of others. The wife needs to know games in order to entertain her husband and his guests. The hawking treatise, although it was slated to appear in the section on amusements, does not indicate that the sport gives much pleasure but rather details the drudgery of hand-rais-

12. Lynne Pearce, "Popular Romance and Its Readers," in *A Companion to Romance: From Classical to Contemporary,* ed. Corinne Saunders (Malden, MA: Blackwell, 2007), 536.

13. The complex situation of the medieval aristocratic wife as estate manager yet subservient is explored by Christine de Pizan in her *Treasury of the City of Ladies,* especially in book 2, chapter 10. *A Medieval Woman's Mirror of Honor: The Treasury of the City of Ladies,* trans. Charity Cannon Willard, ed. Madeleine Pelner Cosman (New York: Persea, 1989). See also, although primarily citing evidence from upper-class English estate documents, Rowena B. Archer, "'How ladies . . . who live on their manors ought to manage their households and estates': Women as Landholders and Administrators in the Later Middle Ages," in *Woman Is a Worthy Wight: Women in English Society, c. 1200–1500,* ed. P. J. P. Goldberg (Wolfboro Falls, NH: Sutton, 1992), 149–81. Archer attempts to frame what it might really have been like to be a woman of property, and to explore the gap between didactic theory and actual practice of women managing their lands and money.

ing baby hawks, keeping the fledglings warm, catering to their decidedly fragile personalities and appetites, and extends to examining their droppings for indications of their health. Their hunting training, too, is labor-intensive, requiring enormous patience. The hawks, like the women depicted in some of the exempla from the moral treatise, can be wayward and unpredictable and must be tamed to work for their master. Women might be understood in this text as resembling hawks on a tether, trained to be eager to return to the glove. In this work, manners, morals, recipes and housekeeping details, horses, dogs, hawks, gardens, and women are associated and integrated to portray a wife as a domestic animal or garden plant, raised and tamed by the master to ensure his contentment.

In the moral treatise women are, indeed, repeatedly compared to animals, especially to dogs, because of their loyalty, and to horses, bred to the bridle and docile with proper schooling. Wives, it suggests, should emulate examples of many faithful animals, such as the dog the narrator himself saw at Niort who guarded his master's grave, and another dog named Macaire who avenged his master's death. Like beasts or pets, women too must learn to love their masters and mates:

> Regarding domestic animals, witness that a greyhound, mastiff, or small dog, whether it is walking on the road, at table, or in bed, always stays closest to the person from whom he takes his food and neglects and is distant and timid with all others. If the dog is far off, he always has his heart and eye on his master. Even if his master beats him and casts stones at him, the dog follows him, wagging his tail and fawning before his master to appease him. (1.5.28)

And, to continue the comparison of women with animals, he notes that

> beasts have the sagacity to love completely and be friendly with their owners and benefactors, keeping their distance from others. So much more should women, with God-given sense and reason, have perfect and solemn love for their husbands. (1.5.33)

Portraying women with equine metaphors, as in Ovid's *Art of Love,* is an ancient trope, so we are not surprised by the book's recurring imagery of woman-as-horse.[14] The points of a good horse include, it seems, what medieval men found attractive in women and horses alike. A horse should have

---

14. The word *harridan* actually originates from *haridelle* the Middle French word for a worn-out workhorse, a "lene, ill-favored jade." Randle Cotgrave, *A Dictionarie of the French and English Tongues* (London, 1611), <http://www.pbm.com/~lindahl/cotgrave/> (hereafter cited as Cotgrave). This reference from Maureen Dowd's *Are Men Necessary? When Sexes Collide* (New York: Putnam, 2005), 116.

16 characteristics. That is, three qualities of a fox: short, upright ears; a good stiff coat; and a straight bushy tail; 4 of a hare: that is, a narrow head, great attentiveness, nimbleness, and speed; four of an ox: that is, wide, large, and broad *herpe* [chest]; a great belly; large protruding eyes; and low joints; three of an ass: good feet, a strong backbone, and gentleness; 4 of a maiden: a handsome mane, a beautiful chest, fine-looking loins, and large buttocks. (2.3.20)

The recipes for ordinary or elaborate dishes and the menus for lavish aristocratic parties in section 2 may recall the medieval concern for reading as eating—*ruminatio*—where the digested book becomes part of the reader. Thus, the book is a "recipe" for a good wife, a recipe for a husband's pleasure. The treatise on wifely behavior (section 1) inscribes a transformative model whereby the wife assimilates the text by imitating the feminine virtues described therein and turning away from the *exempla in malo* of bad women—of which there are many. The author wants his wife to read, to chew on—he often directs her to think about this or that—to digest, to *become* the book, to be morally good and fiscally prudent with his resources, treating him well in his body, keeping fleas out of his house, sparing him from wifely obstreperousness and ill-nature, and easing his mind of threats to his reputation. Reinforcing this association of eating and the book, the author connects women with gluttony and sins of the mouth in his section on spiritual management and confession (1.3). In the course of his manual, the author rehearses familiar misogynistic platitudes about women: women talk too much, cannot keep secrets, are easily led astray and lustful, have poor judgment of the characters of others without men's tutelage, aspire by nature to ascendancy, and tend to evil. Echoing medieval stereotypes, the narrator everywhere essentializes the nature of "women" and indeed that of "husbands," too; this manual naturalizes the brutality of men while blaming women for it, placing the severest strictures against women's anger—righteous or not.

Lest we present the book as a harsh and uninviting regimen, we hasten to point out that it is fascinating and filled with engaging details. The style of the text is spirited, especially in section 1, the moral treatise, where the narrator recounts many lively as well as pointedly grim moralizing stories. He uses threats, cajolements, anecdotes, and exempla to convince his wife to be obedient to him—or the husband she will have after him. Significantly, the narrator displays to us (and the next husband) that his wife can read, and in fact he not only encourages her to read this book but also proffers other edifying works in French from his own collection, "the Bible, the *Golden Legend,* the Apocalypse, the *Life of the Fathers,* and various other good books in French that I possess, and that you are free to take at your pleasure"(1.3.118)—a gesture interesting in itself as a marker of the education Parisian women of her class might have achieved. He expects her to read and appreciate poetry, since he includes in his book a didactic poem he greatly admires, *The Way of Poverty and Riches* (*Le Chemin de povreté et de richesse*). That poetry was an ordinary part of such a bourgeois compendium is noteworthy. The wife must also have been able to write, since he directs her to write letters to her husband in private and instructs her on other sorts of things to record. The book might have provided a one-volume condensed version of the average, educated, secular medieval Frenchman's library. Such a library probably included a Bible, a psalter, a book of Gospels, a collection of the epistles, several collections of sermons, pious treatises, some breviaries, collections of songs, books of courtly and popular poems, several works on land and feudal rights, books of recipes for medicinal potions and other practical matters, a volume on horses, and one on the hunt.[15] These texts were primarily in the vernacular. Thus, as the narrator's opinion of women's intellect was none too adulatory (see 2.1.1), he made for the young wife a library *in parvo*. Perhaps she might be more inclined to read this abbreviated version of a library and at a later date turn with profit to the originals for more information. Or it may be this was all he could hope his child-wife would be able to tolerate or absorb because, as we see from some of his comments to her, he is quite worried that she will be cross with him for setting her the task of reading the book and enacting all his instructions.

The desired result of her studying his voluminous book—about being submissive, pious, amusing to his guests, socially adept, as well as conversant with his practical instructions for gardening, cookery, and ordering his household for his comfort and good reputation—should be the perfect wife. But this amounts to a tall order: she must be both a submissive helpmeet and the female CEO of a wealthy and extensive domestic establishment. In fact, the narrator has qualms in several places in the text that he has overburdened his wife with details about her duties. As he begins the second section of his book, on practical household matters, he reports these misgivings:

> My dear, I must say that I am filled with distress over whether to end my book here or to continue, because I fear that I may bore you. It is worrisome that I may be taxing you with so much that you might consider me unreasonable. I would be most ashamed if you were afraid that you could not accomplish what my instructions demand and were in despair of ever being able to bear the heavy burden of all my advice. (2.1.1)

He adds, in ironic deference to her inherent female weakness, that he may have assigned her an unworkable task,

15. See Bousmanne, Johan, and van Hoorebeeck, *La Librairie des ducs de Bourgogne*, 2: 20.

[f]or neither you nor any other woman could retain it all. So first I wish to consider the amount of instruction I have given you, and what part of it is indispensable, and whether I should entrust you with additional material, and how much, or if there really already is more to do than you are capable of, in which case I will help you. (2.1.1)

But he mitigates her task by explaining that she does not bear sole responsibility for the work she oversees, but primarily for delegating and organizing the workers:

you must be in charge of yourself, your children, and your belongings. But in each of these things you can certainly have assistance. You must see how best to apply yourself to the household tasks, what help and what people you will employ, and how you will occupy them. In these matters, you need take on only the command, the supervision, and the conscientiousness to have things done right, but have the work performed by others, at your husband's expense. (2.1.3)

Nonetheless at the beginning of section 2, after these remarks recapitulating what lessons he has dispensed for her tutelage, in a kind of turnabout, he rationalizes his verbosity and the plethora of instructions by observing that, after all, it is not so much to learn.

Well, you can see from what has gone before, my dear, that really you must not complain. You are hardly overburdened, and have only the obligations rightly belonging to you, which should be pleasant, such as serving God and taking care of your husband's person, and in a nutshell, that is all. (2.1.4)

A bit later, since he still has doubts about her patience, before commencing the treatise on horses (2.3), he decides to give her a break, remarking: "Now, at this moment I want to allow you to rest or be merry and will address you no more while you amuse yourself elsewhere." He then turns his attention to Master Jehan, the chief steward, and furnishes him with advice on purchasing and caring for horses.

Notwithstanding the stern restrictions on female behavior, *Le Ménagier de Paris* depicts a family and a household where the home is a moral refuge from the outside world. This outer realm is pictured as often alien, unruly, and morally dangerous.[16] Yet, it is intriguing that the work nowhere acknowledges the actual

16. See Steven A. Epstein, "The Medieval Family: A Place of Refuge and Sorrow," in *Portraits of Medieval and Renaissance Living: Essays in Memory of David Herlihy*, ed. Samuel K. Cohn Jr. and Steven A. Epstein (Ann Arbor: University of Michigan Press, 1996), 151.

danger of the turbulent political times that the author must have experienced. No mention of war, invaders, brigands, or pestilence invades the serenity of the wife's domestic arrangements. Paris is seemingly safe from strife, where husbands are away from home only on business, not at war, and wives may safely go hawking in the countryside. In the world of the text the wife's peace will be disturbed only by her own ill-chosen words or actions. The husband fears marauding from without less than wifely disrespect from within. Companions must be selected carefully, says the husband-narrator, since so many men and women one might meet are unfit and lead trivial or even immoral lives.

> Many dangers have come from overmuch talk, especially when speaking with arrogant or strong-tempered people or persons of the court or lords. Above all, refrain from conversing with such folk, and if by chance they should speak to you, it will be wise of you, and indeed it is crucial, to avoid them, withdrawing sensibly and courteously. (1.8.1)

> Most of all, steer clear of swaggering and idle young men who live beyond their means and who, possessing no land or lineage, become dancers. Refrain also from consorting with courtiers of great lords, and don't mix with any men or women with reputations for leading trivial, amorous, and licentious lives. (1.5.1)

Who is and who is not admitted to the inner circle of their set, then, is determined by clear rules. There are signals too for making sure that everyone recognizes that you are from a respectable household, and ways of differentiating yourself by dress from those who are not respectable:

> Before leaving your chamber or home, be mindful that the collar of your shift, of your camisole, or of your robe or surcoat does not slip out one over the other, as happens with drunken, foolish, or ignorant women who do not care about their own honor or the good repute of their estate or of their husband, and go with open eyes, head appallingly lifted like a lion, their hair in disarray spilling from their coifs, and the collars of their shifts and robes all in a muddle one over the other. They walk in mannish fashion and comport themselves disgracefully in public without shame, quite saucy. When spoken to about it, they provide an excuse for themselves on the basis of diligence and humility, saying that they are so conscientious, hardworking, and charitable that they have little thought for themselves. But they are lying: they think so highly of themselves that if they were in honorable company, they would not at all want to be less well served than the sensible women of equal rank, or have fewer salutations, bows, reverences, or compliments than the others, but rather more. On top of that, they are not worthy of it since they are ignorant of how

to maintain the honor, not only of their own estate, but that of their husband and their lineage, on whom they bring shame. (1.1.10)

The medieval home in the text represents a center for clean, practical care of people, animals, and plants. Yet apparent in the contents of *Le Ménagier* is a tension between the authority residing in the husband alone and the concept of the family as a site of love between husband and wife, a strain that ran throughout discussions on marriage by the medieval church.[17] Some conflict between the idea of the household as refuge (for the husband) and as prison (for the young wife) might certainly also be inferred from the text before us.

Heir to such works as John Balbi's *Catholicon* (1286), a popular medieval work in which a secular lettered man might find answers to interpretation of the Bible and other matters and which he mentions in his text, the *Le Ménagier* narrator seems to reflect on Balbi's etymological exploration of the word *maritus* (husband) in composing his book of instructions. The *Catholicon*'s entry on this word includes much that seems incarnated in the text of this household book. Selecting a husband entailed caring about four things: *virtus* (manly virtue), *genus* (family), *pulchritudo* (beauty), and *sapientia* (wisdom), with wisdom as the most important of the four.[18] Choosing a wife, one had to care about *pulchritudo*, *genus*, *divitie* (riches), and *mores* (morals). In his definition of *mulier* (wife), Balbi notes that "the virtue of the husband is greater and that of the wife less" (*virtus viri est maior et mulieris minor*). The wife is weak with respect to the husband (*debilis respectu viri mulier sub domino est*) because of the guilt of Eve and not by the nature of the woman (*hoc accidit ex culpa non est natura*).[19] Georges Duby describes the twelfth-century notion of the ideal woman, which does not seem too far from what *Le Ménagier* advocates. The qualities of twelfth-century womanly perfection were *pia filia, morigera conjunx, domina clemens, utilis mater*:

Until she married she was a dutiful [*pia*] daughter; she accepted the husband chosen for her. Her destiny being that of a wife, she then became what all wives

17. Alcuin Blamires, *Woman Defamed and Women Defended: An Anthology of Medieval Texts* (Oxford: Oxford University Press, 1992) and *The Case for Women in Medieval Culture* (Oxford: Oxford University Press, 1997), provide useful excerpts of these writings on marriage and women.

18. Material on Balbi's *Catholicon* is from Epstein, "Medieval Family," 160ff., and reflects conventional wisdom on marriage. Balbi's work is derivative of Isidore of Seville's *Etymologiae* (sixth century) and Papias's *Vocabulista* (c. 1050)—see the comprehensive *Catholic Encyclopedia* entries on these authors. Balbi's words resemble Bartholomaeus Anglicus's notions from his *De proprietatibus rerum* (c. 1250), and Eustache Deschamps's fourteenth-century *Miroir de mariage*. For pertinent excerpts of Bartolomeus and Deschamps in translation, see Robert Miller, *Chaucer: Sources and Backgrounds* (Oxford: Oxford University Press, 1977), 385–91.

19. Epstein, "Medieval Family," 161–62.

should be: meek, obedient, *morigera*. But she was also a *domina*, or a mistress of a household, endowed with considerable power. . . . But . . . [s]he was relegated to an ancillary position, like the Virgin standing beside Christ as he sat in the seat of judgment; and there she was *clemens,* indulgent, introducing a little kindness into the seigniorial office. . . . Did motherhood, then, give her some authority at last? No, as a mother she had to be *utilis*—"useful" to whom? To other men, to her own sons.[20]

The husband-narrator voices the tradition he himself inherited, and his book provides not only instruction to the wife on how to hold up her end despite her moral weakness but also evidence for such established views of marriage. His book might also be considered, as might other books of this genre, an extended gloss on the maxims and instructions in the biblical book of Proverbs. Solomon-like, the author writes his own advice tome.

Contexts: Conduct Books and Household Books

When we investigate the conduct the author holds up for approval and explore the manner in which he expresses his instructions, this bourgeois Parisian book reveals what woman's desire was educated to be and, concomitantly, what men were led to desire in women. Conduct books are vital to understanding literature about women and their roles in medieval society. Often, and with unintentional irony, such works feature male writers addressing a female audience on comportment. The variety of medieval works we call "conduct books" for women include texts such as Christine de Pizan's *Treasury of the City of Ladies, The Book of the Knight of the Tower, How the Good Wijf Tauȝt Hir Douȝtir, The Thewis of Gud Women,* the *Miroir des bonnes femmes,* the *Speculum dominarum,* Mézières's *Le Livre de la vertu du sacrement de mariage,* various female saints' lives, and pastoral marriage manuals. Such works range from directions for pious conduct and table manners, to catalogues of examples of good and bad women, to advice for wives or even nuns, as in the *Ancrene Wisse* and the texts of the Katherine Group. Authors of such texts ordinarily direct female readers to remake themselves, advocating chastity, silence, and compliance, while castigating female anger for its danger to male hegemony. Sometimes called "advice books" or "courtesy books," such texts offer intriguing cultural markers for understanding medieval audiences—their expectations of female behavior, their social interactions, their desire for political stability, and their

---

20. *The Knight, the Lady and the Priest: The Making of Modern Marriage in Medieval France,* trans. B. Bray (New York: Pantheon, 1983), 234. Quoted in Laurie A. Finke, "Towards a Cultural Poetics of the Romance," *Genre* 22 (Summer 1989): 115.

tastes in literature.[21] The good woman/wife and the bad are pervasive themes in late medieval conduct or advice literature. Enormously revealing indicators of the collective self, conduct books construct and witness female subjectivity. Thus, however trite or ephemeral these texts about manners and behavior may seem, books of conduct for women in the Middle Ages need to be attended to for their roles in shaping social reality, educating women (and men) in their socially approved desire, and reproducing the dominant ideology. These texts seek to inscribe what is desirable in a woman in order that she may receive social approbation and attract a socially approved male. Such works, however, also imply another aspect of desire—the subject who desires the object of desire. Men are conditioned to desire a particular type of woman. Handbooks like these, then, continually reproduce male and female norms of desire. Conduct books for women offer clear instances of the means Western culture has developed to create and regulate desire. If redefining female desire revises the basis of sexual relations, then this redefinition of desire affects the basis of political power, since, as Lynn Staley and others have demonstrated, changes in marital and familial relations inevitably have profound effects upon the official institutions of state.[22]

21. Among recent discussions of conduct books, see Carolyn P. Collette, "Chaucer and the French Tradition Revisited: Philippe de Mézières and the Good Wife," in *Medieval Women: Texts and Contexts in Late Medieval Britain. Essays for Felicity Riddy,* ed. J. Wogan-Browne and R. Voaden et al. (Turnhout: Brepols, 2000), 151–68, and "Heeding the Counsel of Prudence: A Context for the *Melibee,*" *Chaucer Review* 29 (1995): 337–49. See also Rose, "What Every Goodwoman Wants," and the valuable essay collection *Medieval Conduct,* ed. Kathleen Ashley and Robert Clark (Minneapolis: University of Minnesota Press, 2001). Ashley's essay in that volume, "The *Miroir des bonnes femmes*: Not for Women Only?" 86–105, and her "Medieval Courtesy Literature and Dramatic Mirrors of Female Conduct," in *The Ideology of Conduct,* ed. Nancy Armstrong and Leonard Tennenhouse (New York: Routledge, 1987), 25–38, explore the role of conduct literature in medieval culture. The various theoretical underpinnings for the genre and growth of literature of conduct are discussed in Norbert Elias, *The Civilizing Process: The History of Manners and State Formation and Civilization,* trans. Edmund Jephcott (Oxford: Blackwell, 1994); Jorge Arditi, *A Genealogy of Manners* (Chicago: University of Chicago Press, 1998); and Jonathan Nicholls's chapters 1–4 and appendices in *The Matter of Courtesy: Medieval Courtesy Books and the Gawain-Poet* (London: D. S. Brewer, 1985). Lynn Staley's *Languages of Power in the Age of Richard II* (University Park: Pennsylvania State University Press, 2005) has an important discussion of the significance of conduct books in late medieval social structures, 265–338. Conduct books were also composed for men, but by and large the books for men concerned courtly manners and knightly behavior and were aristocratic in content, and of course they did not include antimale sentiment the way conduct manuals for women encode antifeminist sentiment for women to internalize, nor did they advocate absolute obedience to a spouse. For some of these masculine courtesy books, see Nicholls.

22. Staley, *Languages of Power.* See also Ashley, "Medieval Courtesy Literature."

Such texts baldly display the moral training of medieval authors and audiences, who breathed in the atmosphere of the tenets of prudent or wayward female conduct depicted in these manuals. Conduct books prescribe women's behavior in their home and spiritual lives, indicating proper aspirations for their futures. Medieval women and men read and were read to from these volumes. They ordered them from booksellers; they commissioned manuscript—and later print—editions and translations of them, such as William Caxton's fifteenth-century *Book of the Knight of the Tower*.[23] In a literary representation of one such manual, Chaucer's clerk Jankyn reads to the Wife of Bath from his *Book of Wicked Wives* and incites not only her ire but an incident of domestic violence with his depictions of the wiles and wickedness of women, to the point where she tells of tearing a page from that book in outrage and being struck a blow in return.[24] Like the body of the Church with Christ as its head, the medieval household appears in conduct books with the husband as its lord and master. The long tradition of the Aristotelian concept of marriage as a friendly relationship between unequal partners obtained.[25] The importance of honor—of the husband, the family, the group—is regularly stressed. Female misbehavior brings dishonor; good manners reflect decent moral lives. Marital peace helped preserve national peace, quell discord, and confirm alliances, so social harmony was generated from domestic harmony.[26] Marriage manuals of the period, a variety of conduct book, corroborated women's natural inferiority and subordinate position, dictating that women were to help their husbands achieve salvation through their own example and counsel, while husbands' duties were to instruct and correct their wives.[27] Husbands, as part of their moral responsibility, were directed to repress their

23. William Caxton, *The Book of the Knight of the Tower*, ed. M. Y. Offord, Early English Text Society, S.S. 2 (London: Oxford University Press, 1971).

24. For a lineup of what misogynist texts Jankyn read to infuriate the Wife of Bath, see *Jankyn's Book of Wikked Wyves*, ed. Ralph Hanna III and Traugott Lawler, using materials collected by Karl Young and Robert Pratt (Athens: University of Georgia Press, 1997). The Wife of Bath's Prologue in the *Canterbury Tales* (ll. 788–96) contains the scene of the assault by and on the book. References to Chaucer are to *The Riverside Chaucer*, ed. Larry D. Benson, 3rd ed. (Boston: Houghton-Mifflin, 1987).

25. Sylvana Vecchio, "The Good Wife," in *A History of Women: Silences of the Middle Ages*, vol. 2, ed. Christiane Klapisch-Zuber (Cambridge: Harvard University Press, 1992), 111. Vecchio's chapter contains relevant information about medieval marriage, especially regarding how the Church began to extol its virtues in the later Middle Ages.

26. Ibid., 109.

27. Ibid., 117. Aristotle's *Economics*, a wellspring of these marital manuals, considered teaching the wife a conjugal duty of the husband (119). See also Sharon Farmer, "Persuasive Voices: Clerical Images of Medieval Wives," *Speculum* 61, no. 3 (1986): 517–43.

wives' taste for vain ornamentation and frivolity. Thirteenth- through fifteenth-century literature was rife with husband-teachers of home economics and moral education.[28] But of course this was a literature of control more than edification. From all the evidence of their use as source materials for other works, and by virtue of their circulation and preservation, works on female conduct were taken seriously.

As a "household book," *Le Ménagier de Paris* has clear generic ties not only to the conduct book but also to those late-medieval codices in which bourgeois families collected texts and formed anthologies for the education primarily of the female members of the household.[29] Felicity Riddy reminds us that in English the word "household," uncommon until the 1380s, designated a collection of people linked to a place; they were not necessarily relatives, but were co-located, and household books instructed servants as well as female family members, as in the English poem *How the Good Wijf Tauȝt Hir Douȝtir*.[30] Concern for the wife's duty

28. David Aers finds that "the kitchen, its resources, and the work done there existed within networks of power, chains of command, and financial resources dominated by men." Despite the obvious presence of women in the domestic arrangements involving the kitchen, what power there was in these social contexts was held by men. Answering Caroline Bynum's argument of the empowering of medieval women through their role as food preparers (*Holy Feast and Holy Fast: The Religious Significance of Food to Medieval Women* [Berkeley: University of California Press, 1987]), Aers goes on to say, "There can be no adequate understanding of social relations in kitchens and around the preparation of food if we abstract these from the social networks and sources of power within which they exist and have their being. . . . What Bynum calls a 'woman's world' was never an autonomous domain." The resources were at all levels controlled by men, and thus the schooling of the wife in *Le Ménagier* is appropriately done by the person in charge of the home's largesse, the husband. David Aers and Lynn Staley, *The Powers of the Holy: Religion, Politics, and Gender in Late Medieval English Culture* (University Park: Pennsylvania State University Press, 2004), 30–31.

29. On household books, see Julia Boffey, "Bodleian Library, MS Arch. Seldon. B.24 and the Definitions of the 'Household Book,'" in *The English Medieval Book*, ed. A. S. G. Edwards et al. (London: British Library, 2000), 125–34. Katherine J. Lewis, in "Model Girls? Virgin-Martyrs and the Training of Young Women in Late-Medieval England," in *Young Medieval Women*, ed. K. Lewis, N. Menuge, and K. Phillips (New York: St. Martin's Press, 1999), 25–46, discusses books containing legends of virgin-martyrs as models for women to be staunch in their chastity, preserving their good name and that of their family. Lewis notes that many household books in England that include the life of Saint Katherine, for example, were owned by the aristocracy, gentry, and wealthy urban mercantile families whose interests were served by having the saint's life in their books, since Katherine was noted as an educated woman who learned at her father's behest. She was a household manager, yet her ultimate authority was her father, a model that women who had to cope in the absence of the male householder could internalize (35).

30. Riddy, "Looking Closely: Authority and Intimacy in the Late Medieval Urban Home," in *Gendering the Master Narrative: Women and Power in the Middle Ages,* ed. Mary C. Erler and

to teach her servants appears as well in *Le Ménagier*. Wealthy families—for book-making was expensive—often bound together collections of prayers, recipes, medicinal remedies, and gardening instructions.[31] Together with these materials, some volumes also preserved heuristic texts or treatises about proper female deportment, including chaste female saints' lives, tracts on salvation, instructions on modest dress, anecdotes about "good" or "bad" wives, and marital how-tos such as appear in *Le Ménagier*. Many of Chaucer's works are bound into such upper-class household miscellanies.[32] The sorts of texts found together, secular or sacred, storybook or instructional matter, provide evidence of their interpretation by early manuscript owners and indicate their role as behavioral blueprints for young women of means in late-medieval Europe. The literature of female conduct, with its assumed ability to produce socially approved change in women, can also be read as a literature about political authority, its creation and maintenance. These books, as noted by Kathleen Ashley, fostered upward mobility, as many conduct books written for bourgeois women seek to model their behavior along aristocratic lines. The *Le Ménagier de Paris* narrator repeatedly enjoins his wife to remember their social status and estate, and neither to aspire to be of higher status by giving herself airs or spending, dressing, or eating too lavishly, nor to consort with individuals below them in social rank, which would mar his reputation forever.

One of the *Le Ménagier* compiler's main authorities was Philippe de Mézières's *Le Livre de la vertu du sacrement de mariage* (1384–89), a conduct work the author clearly admired for its views on wives and morality.[33] Mézières, an influential personage in medieval France, a trusted counselor to Charles V, and an important

Maryanne Kowaleski (Ithaca: Cornell University Press, 2003), 212–28. See also Riddy's "Mother Knows Best: Reading Social Change in a Courtesy Text," *Speculum* 71, no. 1 (1996): 66–86.

31. One such English book is the *Tollemache Book of Secrets*, filled with a variety of useful household texts resembling those in *Le Ménagier*, including a treatise on angling, materials on hawks, ink making, horticultural treatises such as Nicholas Bollard's fourteenth-century *On the Growing and Grafting of Trees*, culinary terms and sauces appropriate for certain dishes, etc. See *The Tollemache Book of Secrets: A Descriptive Index and Complete Facsimile with an Introduction and Transcriptions together with Catherine Tollemache's Receipts of Pastery, Confectionary & c*, ed. Jeremy Griffiths, completed by A. S. G. Edwards (London: Roxburgh Club, 2001).

32. See John M. Manly and Edith Rickert, eds., *The Text of* The Canterbury Tales, *Studied on the Basis of All Known Manuscripts*, 8 vols. (Chicago: University of Chicago Press, 1940), for the tables of contents of manuscripts containing Chaucer's *Canterbury Tales*.

33. Philippe de Mézières, *Le Livre de la vertu du sacrement de mariage*, ed. Joan B. Williamson (Washington, DC: Catholic University of America Press, 1993). There is no English translation of this probable source of *Le Ménagier*'s tale of Griselda.

figure in the reign of Charles VI, in 1389 proposed a ban at court of all poets except those using moral or religious themes.[34] This censorious and conservative tone seems to be carried over into the work of the *Le Ménagier* author, who might have been approved of by a bluestocking like Christine de Pizan, his contemporary, who certainly insisted that literary texts have a highly moral and unambiguous nature so as not to induce any readers to sin through misinterpretation.[35]

Despite her advocacy of education for women and her faith in their abilities as manageresses, Christine's words offer just such an exordium to wives as appears in *Le Ménagier*. She addresses women, in what might be considered the "retraction" in the final section of *The City of Ladies* (1405), counseling them to bear with trying husbands, even wife beaters, in hopes of turning those husbands again to virtue, since marriage offers an opportunity to attain salvation, a common enough theme among pastoral manuals and the Church Fathers:

> And to you ladies who are married, do not scorn being subject to your husbands, for sometimes it is not the best thing for a creature to be independent. . . .
> Those women with peaceful, good, and discreet husbands who are devoted to them, praise God for this boon, which is not inconsiderable, for a greater boon in the world could not be given them. And may they be diligent in serving, loving, and cherishing their husbands in the loyalty of their heart, as they should, keeping their peace and praying to God to uphold and save them. And those women who have husbands neither completely good nor completely bad should still praise God for not having the worst and should strive to moderate their vices and pacify them, according to their conditions. And those women who have husbands who are cruel, mean, and savage should strive to endure them while trying to overcome their vices and lead them back, if they can, to a reasonable and seemly life. And if they are so obstinate that their wives are unable to do anything, at least they will acquire great merit for their souls through the virtue of patience. And everyone will bless them and support them.[36]

The *Le Ménagier de Paris* narrator, too, presents for his readers the thorny, contradictory model of marriage encoded in much literature for women of the

34. Sheila Delany cites this event in "'Mothers to Think Back Through': Who Are They? The Ambiguous Example of Christine de Pizan," in *Medieval Texts and Contemporary Readers,* ed. Laurie A. Finke and Martin B. Shichtman (Ithaca: Cornell University Press, 1987), 193.

35. Christine de Pizan's literary career coincided with the composition of *Le Ménagier,* and her work might reveal traces of her familiarity with that book. On her notions of literary theory, see her contribution to the "querelle de la Rose" in, for example, *Medieval Women's Visionary Literature,* ed. Elizabeth Alvilda Petroff (Oxford: Oxford University Press, 1986), 340–46.

36. *City of Ladies* 3.19.2, from *The Book of the City of Ladies,* trans. Earl Jeffrey Richards (New York: Persea, 1982), 255.

period. The model of the "good" woman and wife is a paradoxical one, with Griselda as its prime illustration. The tyrannous husband chooses a saintly wife, a woman who has contractually agreed to be dominated, even as she is also meant to be a mate, lover, and helpmeet. An unachievable task is set here for a wife—only a saint could interiorize this model, and surely the conduct book urges sainthood upon women. Traces of the complex model surface in Chaucer's *Wife of Bath's Tale* where the hag cedes "maistrie" (mastery) to the knight-rapist and pleases him in all things, becoming the submissive woman of his dreams. A wife must somehow manage to be an equal partner in loving, with some say in running the home, and at the same time contractually subjugated by her husband, subject to male oppression and even violence.

One of the many marriages and "good" and "bad" wives examined in section 1, the union of Melibee and his wife Prudence (1.9) continues and complicates the discussion of the wedded state. This story, like the tale of Griselda, illustrates a household run by an unpredictable tyrant. Melibee is ireful, reckless, and vengeful, whereas Griselda's Walter shows himself cruel and capricious in employing his power over the subject members of his household and his polis. But both husbands provide further variations upon the *Le Ménagier* author's motif of the autocratic and angry husband who must be placated by wifely obedience and patience. The scenario of both stories shows the household as the site of tyranny and the wife's single-handed struggle to cope. Melibee and Prudence's narrative is derived from Renaud de Louens's French version of Albertanus of Brescia's 1246 Latin prose treatise *Liber consolationis et consilii*, with Boethian connections. This work was also notably adapted by Chaucer for one of the two tales he assigns himself, as the narrator of the *Canterbury Tales*, to tell on the Canterbury journey. Prudence seems clearly to have been a popular exemplum of moderation and peacemaking, although both Chaucer and the *Le Ménagier* author include the tale in contexts that invite us to resist interpreting the tale as just a treatise on wifely excellence.[37] All the same, both the *Le Ménagier* narrator and Chaucer's Host Harry Bailly find that interpretation of Prudence sufficient. After hearing the tale, Bailly proclaims that the tale is not instructional for him but relevant to his wife: "She ys nothyng of swich pacience / As was this Melibeus wyf Prudence" (*Melibee*

37. See William Askins, "*The Tale of Melibee*," in *Sources and Analogues of The Canterbury Tales*, vol. 1, ed. Robert M. Correale and Mary Hamel (Cambridge: D. S. Brewer, 2003), 321–408. The criticism on Chaucer's *Melibee* is copious, but three of the best recent readings of the tale are Stephen G. Morse, "Apply Yourself: Learning While Reading the *Tale of Melibee*," *Chaucer Review* 38, no. 1 (2003): 83–97; David Wallace's "Household Rhetoric: Violence and Eloquence in *The Tale of Melibee*," in *Chaucerian Polity: Absolutist Lineages and Associational Forms in England and Italy* (Stanford: Stanford University Press, 1997), 212–46; and Lee Patterson, "'What Man Artow?' Authorial Self-Definition in the *Tale of Sir Thopas* and the *Tale of Melibee*," *Studies in the Age of*

ll. 1895–96). The topic of 1.9 and of the account of Melibee, states the *Le Ménagier* narrator, is wifely counsel, "to be wise when your husband acts foolishly, as young or imprudent people often do, and to dissuade him gently and sensibly from his follies."

The story commences in the context of a vendetta; during the absence of the young nobleman Melibee, his home is assailed by his enemies, with his daughter and wife severely beaten. Upon his return to discover this outrage against himself, Melibee vows instant and utter revenge on the attackers. He gathers his courtiers and toadies around him, and they too cry for war. But Prudence admonishes him against hasty vengeance by means of a lengthy and most rational argument analyzing his sorrow and rage. While marshaling dozens of Christian and pagan sources as her evidence, she attempts to convince the hotheaded Melibee of the wisdom of postponing an attack and deliberating with appropriate wise counselors on how to make peace with his enemies. After extensive schooling by his wife, Melibee learns not so much to be a peacemaker (he remains irascible up to the end) as to seek his wife's advice before entering into a course of action bound for serious consequences. The story, as it is framed and interpreted by the narrator, concerns a learned but self-effacing wife's duty to deter her husband from harming himself and others owing to rashness, to keep him from wrong and sinful acts, to help him make good decisions—in fact to be "prudent." Prudence is a properly subservient and respectful wife to Melibee, who finally capitulates to her logic and proposes a treaty with those who have injured him. Melibee learns to moderate his impulsiveness and listen to reason, not necessarily to become reasonable himself, but to choose wiser counsel.

The tale fits well into the program of advice for wives offered in *Le Ménagier*, since it demonstrates that Prudence is after all right; however, she makes it look as if Melibee himself makes overtures of reconciliation to those who bear him enmity. David Wallace characterizes the medieval story as a "handbook for go-betweens," concerning strategies for those who must speak with powerful men.[38] Prudence supports Melibee and indeed is the cool head of reason, despite her

---

Chaucer 11 (1989): 117–75. Morse proposes that the tale focuses on the act of reading, calling it "an elaborate process of refining judgment" (88). Patterson locates the story in the advice-for-princes genre, and yet it displays a kind of prudential wisdom that might be appropriate instruction for children or women (149). He sees Melibee as becoming a "submissive son to a domineering mother" (Prudence), who infantilizes him by offering sound bites of accepted knowledge (158). These readings help to contextualize the tale within *Le Ménagier*'s program of education for the young wife and future audiences and justify including this sententious piece in a book for the education of a young woman or women, who need to mollify angry and irascible spouses at every turn.

38. Wallace, *Chaucerian Polity*, 221.

own injuries, teaching him about turning the other cheek, about his flawed perceptions of situations, and about the proper use of his wealth and power. Like Jehanne le Quentine (another exemplum in 1.9), she covers up for her husband's mistakes, yet she does so not with hidden acts of generosity but through canniness and powerful logic and an endless store of pertinent examples from the Old and New Testaments, the Church Fathers, classical poets, rhetoricians, and sages to convince him to modify his behavior. Her learning seems wide-ranging (although perhaps mainly consisting of common schoolbook sententiae), allowing her ample rhetorical ammunition in her quest to prevent Melibee from self-destruction through ire and vengefulness. Like Griselda, she is patient, constant to her convictions, and faithful to her lord. Yet Prudence works persistently on Melibee's blindness to reason and leading him calmly with wise speeches until her good judgment dawns on him and he learns to consult her. Not only are there dozens of excellent moral adages for the reader to contemplate in this digest of wisdom, but Prudence models the wife who, like Griselda, acts as a peacemaker in her home and in her world at large. Prudence is loquacious, the way some of the "bad" wives presented in the book are. Though she is voluble, her words are wise and pertinent to her husband's good, and they get to the core of the issues at hand—offsetting the garrulous, nagging, and empty-headed female speech the narrator elsewhere condemns.

A particularly gruesome example from the section on wifely humility and obedience (1.6) concerns the ubiquitous tyrannical husband figure in yet another context; it describes a young wife whose elderly husband was not solacing her sexually.[39] Ironically, the author prefaces his anecdote by saying that the story of an old man with a young wife is not far-fetched "because of course you will scarcely see a man so old that he does not willingly take a young wife." The girl's mother admonishes her not to take a lover: "'Daughter,' said the mother, 'if you did it, your husband would treat you incredibly harshly. For certainly there is no greater vengeance than that of an old man.'" Notwithstanding, the wife tests the old man's capacity for anger by chopping down his favorite fruit tree, slaying his favorite greyhound, and, at the last, embarrassing him by overturning the table full of food and drink at a feast he gives for prominent citizens of the realm. Exacting a cruel revenge, the husband tells her she must be a victim of "bad blood" for her outrageous behavior and has her bled. Lying near death from blood loss, she agrees with her mother that she should have heeded the advice about an old man's penchant for revenge. In its details resembling the household described in Le Ménagier—there, too, we hear of fruit trees, greyhounds, and feasting—this

39. The author adapts this story from the *Tentamina* in *The Seven Sages of Rome* (BF, xxxviii). See the edition by Karl Brunner, Early English Text Society 191 (Oxford: Oxford University Press, 1933).

dark tale perhaps points to a grave subtext of the book: beware of this old man and his appearance of paternalism. He may forgive you some indiscretions, but he is vigilant and owns your body and your blood.

The *Le Ménagier* narrator cites scriptural authority for the "natural" law of female submission to the male. Several other anecdotes show that a wife may under no circumstances displease or defy her husband or there will be punishment of a particularly nasty sort, such as being displaced in her husband's bed by more "obedient" chambermaids or disreputable women, to her public shame. And men, it seems, enjoy trying a wife's obedience as they would a sport. In the tract on wifely obedience (1.6), the narrator remarks, when reminding his wife to be submissive, that it is a facet of husbandly amusement to try his wife:

> [M]y dear, be assured that it is necessary that human nature take enjoyment in something. Even the poor, the powerless, the sick or languishing, or those on their deathbeds feel and seek pleasure and joy, as do, for even greater reason, those who are in good health. Some people find gladness only in hunting or hawking. Others enjoy playing instruments; yet others swimming, dancing, singing, or jousting, each finding delight according to his condition. Even you seek your entertainment in diverse ways. Therefore, if your husband imagines that he would find happiness in your service or obedience, as I described above, then serve and content him. (1.6.43)

Any larger medieval audience, with worldly and mercantile concerns as well as conservative politics and spiritual probity, expected in a conduct book precisely such a recipe for a good wife and a harmonious household, where the husband is content. While Eileen Power finds in the *Le Ménagier* narrator sympathy, tenderness, and the "mellow sadness of an autumn evening,"[40] the tone of the narrator is at best fatherly—but we must recall he was not her father; at worst threatening, reminding us of the surveillance that Michel Foucault ascribes to Jeremy Bentham's model of the Panopticon prison, with everyone watching everyone else, leading to the interiorization of such scrutiny.[41] The education of a wife in this book reifies management and surveillance, which she, as well as those around her, must interiorize.

Le Ménagier de Paris displays the husband's capital as well, organized with his inheritance of spiritual and moral precepts for his wife in a kind of moral ledger book. A businesslike approach to the construction of his legacy and of his wife's life, the book represents concrete documentation of his moral and culinary code,

40. Power, *Goodman of Paris*, 3.
41. Michel Foucault, *Discipline and Punish: The Birth of the Prison*, trans. Alan Sheridan (New York: Vintage, 1995), 223.

like a ledger where debits and credits are registered. In fact, he uses images of the "tally" in his book, arguing that the wife must not trust her own or her tradesmen's memories, that life is smoother if all accounts are written down, if one makes bargains and keeps records. The narrator invests in the labor of writing his book in order to obtain the returns he desires: the "good" wife with practical skills and an orderly household. Images of profit and loss abound; the language of economics, of men wagering, shows this bourgeois authorial voice to be deeply concerned with commerce, money, and goods. The book manifests itself in its details as a secular, class-specific document. Designed for pious learning, entertainment and the sociopolitical education of a class, the book participates in the resurgence of edifying vernacular works fostered in the late fourteenth century by Charles V, produced by such highly placed figures as Mézières, Christine de Pizan, and Evart de Conty.[42] Conduct literature of the Anglo-French cultural matrix in the fourteenth century, of which Le Ménagier forms a part, discusses the moral life of the married woman as a key to social and political harmony. We turn now to the story of Griselda—the lynchpin of the codex—to explore the framing of the tale and its interpretation within the context of the household book, the nature of the audience that the book's compiler might have assumed for such a tale, and the model of marriage that audience experienced.

Glossing the Tale of Griselda: The Model Wife and Marriage in Le Ménagier de Paris

The story of Griselda is central to the theme and content of this householder's book. In fact, her tale of wifely submission was admired and recounted by other medieval authors as well, first by Boccaccio in Italian, then by Petrarch in Latin. In short order, the tale was redacted into English by Chaucer and into French by Christine de Pizan and others, including Philippe de Mézières, whose work was likely the closest source for the author of Le Ménagier and who described his heroine as the "miroir des dames mariees, la noble marquise de Saluce"—the model

42. Alastair Minnis discusses Evart de Conty's (fl. 1330–1405) commentary on Livre des Eschez amoureux moralises. He notes the highly moral nature of Evart's advice to young courtiers on the proper conduct of a marriage and how to bring up children and manage servants. Magister Amoris: The Roman de la Rose and Vernacular Hermeneutics (Oxford: Oxford University Press, 2001), 30. Examining a magnificent manuscript (BnF, fonds français 9197, XV c.) of the Livre des Eschez at the BnF at the same time one handles the two BnF MSS of Le Ménagier, one cannot help but be struck by the extravagant opulence of the former and the utilitarian appearance of the latter two. It is clear that the gorgeously illuminated Echez manuscript's target audience was a courtly one not concerned with the kitchen matters or social climbing as the Le Ménagier audience must have been. The Le Ménagier manuscripts, while large and clearly written, were far less fashionable family accessories.

wife.[43] How are we to account for the diverse interpretations this tale has received in the past—in particular, for its use in *Le Ménagier*'s moral treatise on ideal female conduct? Lee Patterson challenges us to find literary meaning in terms of the history of reading by examining and reconstructing the experiences of differing groups of readers.[44] The *Le Ménagier* author frames and interprets the story of

43. See *Livre de la vertu,* 356. Christine de Pizan depicts her Griselda, who appears first briefly in *The City of Ladies* (2.2.2) as a loving, loyal daughter, earning merit for honoring her parent. Later, the long story of Walter and Griselda in Christine's work follows the tales of bad rulers Nero, Galba, Otho, and Vitellius, and Griselda refutes women's alleged weakness and inconstancy, since she is "strong in virtue" (2.50.1; Richards ed., 170). At least eight versions of the tale of Griselda, more or less related, were extant in the fourteenth century. See J. Burke Severs, *The Literary Relationships of Chaucer's* Clerk's Tale (New Haven: Yale University Press, 1942; rpt. Hamden, Conn.: Archon Books, 1972). Severs notes that several details in the *Clerk's Tale* are likely from *Le Ménagier* and not another French source, and he posits that Chaucer indeed knew the text. Boccaccio's tale provides the literary genesis of the story, with its roots in folktales of the Patience group of the Cupid/Psyche genre (Severs, 5). In this early folk matter, an otherworldly being requires his mortal mate to take a vow of silence or enjoins her to superhuman emotional control (never to shed a single tear, etc.). The demands of the other-world creature, whose supernatural laws are not understood by mere mortals, seem weird and arbitrary. The folktale elements make some of Walter's cruel behavior coherent, although Boccaccio casts his Gualteri not as godlike but as obnoxious. Petrarch's Latin rereading and rewriting of Boccaccio's tale for his own male clerkly audience forms the basis for yet more literary redactions of Griselda's trials in late-fourteenth-century France, among them Mézières's *Le Livre de la vertu*; an anonymous prose translation of Petrarch, *Le Livre Griseldis,* and *Le Ménagier de Paris.* Scholars settle more or less upon Petrarch and *Le Livre Grisildis* as Chaucer's sources, acknowledging that he may also have seen Boccaccio's version as well as that of *Le Ménagier.* For the notion that the story may have been new to much of Chaucer's audience, who may not have known the other versions, see Larry Scanlon, "What's the Pope Got to Do with It? Forgery, Didacticism, and Desire in the *Clerk's Tale,*" *New Medieval Literatures* 6 (2003): 129–65. See also Collette, "Chaucer and the French Tradition Revisited"; Charlotte P. Morse, "The Exemplary Griselda," *Studies in the Age of Chaucer* 7 (1985): 51–86; Anne Middleton, "The Clerk and His Tale: Some Literary Contexts," *Studies in the Age of Chaucer* 2 (1980): 121–50; Lesley Johnson, "Reincarnations of Griselda: Contexts for the *Clerk's Tale?*" in *Feminist Readings in Middle English Literature: The Wife of Bath and All Her Sect,* ed. Ruth Evans and Lesley Johnson (London: Routledge, 1994), 195–220.

For the versions of the story extant in Chaucer's era (and that of the author of *Le Ménagier,* his contemporary), see the section on the *Clerk's Tale* by Thomas J. Farrell and Amy Goodwin in Correale and Hamel, *Sources and Analogues of the Canterbury Tales,* 1: 101–67, esp. Goodwin's section, "The Griselda Story in France," 130–67. Correale and Hamel update Severs's work. On Christine de Pizan's version of Griselda, see Roberta L. Krueger, "Uncovering Griselda, Christine de Pizan, 'une seule chemise,' and the Clerical Tradition: Boccaccio, Petrarch, Philippe de Mézières, and the Ménagier de Paris," in *Medieval Fabrications: Dress, Textiles, Clothwork, and Other Cultural Imaginings,* ed. Jane Chance (New York: Palgrave Macmillan, 2004), 71–88.

44. *Negotiating the Past* (Madison: University of Wisconsin Press, 1987), 116.

patient Griselda as his thematic center within the discussion of wifely obedience in the moral treatise in article 1.6. Because he has compiled his manual for an audience whose taste for *moralitas* may require that Griselda's meaning not be in debate, his treatment of the exemplum assures Griselda of a singular meaning as the obedient wife and perfect self-controlled woman. The author, that is, may shape his narrative voice to cater to a prudish, literal-minded audience and to provide them with the *moralitas* they expect from his text. Looking at *Le Ménagier* in the context of Chaucer's adaptation of the Griselda tale and considering just how it diverges from Chaucer's version reveals that medieval readers were not homogeneous, and some perhaps, using a phrase from Vladimir Nabokov, required only "the ornamentation of the commonplace"—their own ideas, social class, and mores tricked out in fancy phrasing—to make them satisfied with a book.[45] Notwithstanding, it is difficult to refrain from also sensing in the *Le Ménagier*'s narrator's text a kind of anxiety about controlling his narrow meaning, and in this conflict between irony and didacticism lies its appeal as a narrative performance and a complex literary achievement about gender relations in the later Middle Ages.

While he adds his own numerous glosses interpreting the Griselda story after he tells it, as does Chaucer's Clerk in his *Canterbury Tales* version, where the Clerk multiplies Griselda's meaning, in *Le Ménagier* the narrator's glossing leads inexorably to the picture of the ideal wife as Griselda. In fact, the entire codex constructs a Griselda for the Parisian home: a woman of self-control, moral probity, piety, stalwart loyalty to her mate, humility, temperance, chastity, and patience, colored by Boethian fatalism. Orderliness, too, continues to be a theme stressed in the whole book and Griselda's tale. The narrator exhorts the teenaged wife-as-audience to be Griselda-like in her desire for the contentment of her husband above her own will and for the common good over self. It is a conservative moral agenda, well suited to an audience whose tastes ran to books on manners and piety, books that ensure peace in the home and the polis.[46]

The *Le Ménagier* avatar of Griselda locates the story's message as the necessity of the virtuous wife's self-control and prudence, and her submission to the will

45. Vladimir Nabokov, *Lectures on Literature,* ed. Fredson Bowers (New York: Harcourt Brace, 1980), 2.

46. Artifacts from the courts of the dukes of Burgundy during the late Middle Ages, courts associated with at least two of the extant manuscripts of *Le Ménagier,* overwhelmingly reveal their taste in art to be religious and sober, as is their taste in books. See, for example, Stephen Fliegel et al., eds., *Art from the Court of Burgundy: The Patronage of Phillip the Bold and John the Fearless, 1364–1419,* exhibition catalogue, Cleveland Museum of Art / Musee des Beaux-Arts of Dijon (Cleveland: Cleveland Museum of Art, 2004). Lynn Staley considers the Burgundian court's use of the well-run household as an important metaphor for the rule of Charles V. See *Languages of*

of her husband as the pattern for both an ideal Christian relationship with God and a stable society that obeys its superiors. Mézières's redaction of Griselda was intended to endorse the virtue of self-mastery and to extol the docile wife, while maintaining the orderly hierarchy of class and gender boundaries.[47] Significantly, as noted above, the Le Ménagier author inscribes in his book the always-paradoxical medieval model for marriage, where the wife makes a pact to be dominated, though her role must confusingly also include that of lover and business partner. The tale of the patient, lowborn woman, emotionally tormented by her aristocratic husband, presents cruel Marquis Walter testing Griselda's faithfulness to her vow of submission to him in marriage. Before their marriage, she vowed never to gainsay him or to "grucche" (Chaucer's term, Clerk's Tale, l. 354) at any mistreatment. The story pits mother-love uncomfortably against the oath to a husband and political superior and asks Griselda to put the common good —as her husband misrepresents it to her—over self, to cast aside her love of her children and her own desires and allow Walter, as she believes, to murder their children and later revoke their marriage in order to wed a woman of a higher estate. All of this she does without a "grucche."[48]

Chaucer's strategy is to employ conventional conduct literature materials unconventionally when his Clerk strives to obfuscate and complicate Griselda's interpretation by glossing Griselda at the end of the tale he tells and in his Envoy in contradictory ways. While participating in the locutions of Griselda as the ideal

---

Power, where Staley analyzes some of the conduct manuals of the period as encouraging political stability and class distinctions. The ducal library contained dozens of didactic works, such as La Somme le Roi of Laurent du Bois, Le Livre du chevalier de La Tour Landry of Geoffrey de La Tour Landry, De regimine principum of Giles of Rome (in French), Le Petit Jean de Saintré of Antoine de La Sale, and L'Instruction d'un jeune prince of Gilbert de Lannoy. Many of the didactic works in the ducal library catalogue are sources for matter in Le Ménagier. See Bousmanne, Johan, and van Hoorebeeck, La Librairie des ducs de Bourgogne, vol. 2, Textes didactiques.

47. Aers and Staley, Powers of the Holy, 247. Aers and Staley note that in 1395 Mézières wrote to Richard II, wishing him a wife like Griselda. He wants Richard to have such a woman, "for the furtherance of peace in Christendom and the comfort of your royal personage." See Letter to King Richard II, ed. and trans. G. W. Coopland (New York: Barnes and Noble, 1976), 42, 115; quoted in Susan Crane, The Performance of Self: Ritual, Clothing, and Identity during the Hundred Years War (Philadelphia: University of Pennsylvania Press, 2002), 191 n. 83. Richard himself, according to Froissart's Chronicles, wanted a very young wife so that, "he can form her according to his wishes and guide and train her in English ways." Jean Froissart, Chronicles, trans. Geoffrey Brereton (New York: Penguin, 1978), 408.

48. Collette notes that in de Mézières's version of Griselda, "the compulsion to civic harmony drives her submission, as much as her promise to Walter. . . . she chooses between her will and the public good" ("Chaucer and the French Tradition Revisited," 165).

wife, Chaucer's version obscures that significance through the Clerk's display of the possibilities of what Griselda can mean, saying in his Envoy that no one could find such a woman: "Grisilde is deed and eek hire pacience" (*Clerk's Tale*, l. 1177). His performance of the multiplicity of meanings for the exemplum shows how unsustainable such narrow readings as conduct books offer are and highlights how much is at stake in deciphering the tale's inconsistencies and incoherencies. In the end, the Clerk proposes disobedience, dissembling, and obstreperousness for wives as a curative to the exemplum's ostensible moral of patience and submission.[49] But exactly where he stands on the issue remains unclear as he rhetorically undercuts each "moral" he proffers. In Chaucer's hands, the tale's failure at closure reflects a very clerk-ly understanding of how complex a thing it is to take a vow or read a text, or be a medieval wife.[50] Proper exegesis of the tale, for the Clerk, means that there are no easy answers and no easy way to live. While surely conscious of how Griselda's story might be construed in a conduct book, Chaucer's courtly and educated audience is invited to question that use of her story and the position of Griselda as the ideal Christian wife. The Clerk complicates the allegoresis of the tale and finally seems to acknowledge that women might not find Griselda's example desirable or even understandable in terms of how "real" lives are lived. But the question of wifely obedience (and how to interpret the tale) remains unresolved. Where the conduct book generically, and *Le Ménagier* in particular, asks the wifely audience to transform herself to resemble the submissive Griselda, the Clerk initiates a debate about the nature of vows and the human inability completely to live up to such words when the context is exchanged for an incoherent one—such as when your husband murders your children and demands that you not complain. The Clerk asks us to intellectualize this pointedly emotional tale full of unreconciled dichotomies, divorcing our response to the pathos of the mother's abandonment of her children's welfare and the father's emotional coldness and violence to the mother of his children from our awareness of the nature of vows and sacrifices, which might actually involve such hard kinds of choices.

Where Chaucer's Clerk may invite his audience to ponder Griselda's signifi-

49. See Joseph Grossi, "The Clerk vs. the Wife of Bath: Nominalism, Carnival, and Chaucer's Last Laugh," in *Literary Nominalism and the Theory of Reading Late Medieval Texts*, ed. Richard J. Utz, Medieval Studies 5 (Lewiston, NY: Edwin Mellen Press, 1999), 147–78.

50. This insight comes from Mark Miller's persuasive exploration of vows and the nature of Griselda's piety in his paper "The *Clerk's Tale* and the Scandal of the Unconditional," New Chaucer Society, Glasgow, 2004. Notable recent readings of Griselda are Carolyn Dinshaw, *Chaucer's Sexual Poetics* (Madison: University of Wisconsin Press, 1989), 132–55; Andrea Denny-Brown "*Povre* Griselda and the All-Consuming *Archwyves*," *Studies in the Age of Chaucer* 28 (2006): 77–115; and David Wallace, in *Chaucerian Polity*, 261–98.

cance, the *Le Ménagier* narrator dictates to his audience the confining (and comforting) way in which his text's Griselda is to be understood. Narrowly deciphered by the *Le Ménagier* narrator, Griselda seems a touchstone for defining the society's central and conservative values about marriage and gender roles. The narrator delivers on this expectation by reading his Griselda invariably: whatever your husband requests you to do, it is right for you to obey, since your relationship to him is as man's to God. It necessitates absolute obedience on peril of sin, or, as appears in the narrative, pain and violence. For a late medieval audience whose taste ran to *moralitas* in their reading, the *Le Ménagier* narrator makes the literary *literal*. Chaucer wryly depicts such a reader, Harry Bailly, the Host on the Canterbury pilgrimage, who calls Griselda's story a "legende"—used in Middle English most often to refer to a saint's life[51]—and reads it literally as an exemplum of obedience he wishes his wife would follow, just as he does with the story of Prudence: "By Goddes bones, / Me were levere than a barel ale / Me wyf at hoom had herd this legende ones!"[52] Such a readership, unperturbed by gray areas of fictional interpretation, stresses well-defined moral precepts to enforce the notion of female submission. The problem—and the humor of Harry's remark—arises from his inability to enforce wifely obedience in his home. Since no one remotely resembling Griselda resides there, he says he despairs of his wife's taking the lesson to heart. Conduct book readers, perhaps like Harry, wanted their Griselda pointedly situated in a heuristic context that emphasized piety, public morality, behavior appropriate to their class, fitting exercise of temporal power, and a proper attitude toward riches. Yet Chaucer reveals the human condition: that society, while operating according to black and white rules, consistently provides gray areas that must be negotiated. In contrast, the *Le Ménagier* narrator strains to interpret his book with no ambiguities for the wife/audience to ponder.

For, at issue in *Le Ménagier,* especially in article 1.6, is the injunction to the wife to absorb the contradictory nature of medieval marriage that the narrator sets out for her. Early in the treatise he tells her that a wife must be "obedient, by which is understood to your husband and to his commandments, whatever they be, whether they be made in earnest or in jest, or require you to do something strange, or whether they concern trivial or important matters; because all things must be considered important by you since it will be your husband who will have commanded them" (1.6.2), and "God commands women to be subject to their

---

51. Helen Cooper, *Oxford Guides to Chaucer: The Canterbury Tales,* 2nd ed. (Oxford: Oxford University Press, 1996), 188.

52. *Clerk's Tale,* ll. 1212b–1212d. These lines occur in twenty-two manuscripts and appear after the envoy in most of the manuscripts that preserve it. The stanza may have been canceled by Chaucer once he connected the Merchant's tale to the Clerk's with the repetition of the final "wepe" and "waille" (l. 1212) in the first line of the Merchant's Prologue.

husbands as to . . . their leader, and obey their orders large and small" (1.6.6). Here, though, is how the narrator envisions the good marriage:

> In God's name, I believe that when two good, virtuous people are married, all other loves outside of each other are remote and forgotten. It seems to me that when they are in each other's presence, they look at each other more than at others, playfully tweak one another, press close, and do not willingly recognize or speak to anyone besides each other. And when they are separated, they think of each other, saying in their hearts, "When I see him, I will do this for him, say this to him, ask him about this." All their private pleasures, their dearest desires, and their perfect joys are satisfied in pleasing and obeying the other. But if they don't love each other, then they don't value obedience and reverence any more than does the average couple, which is, in most cases, not much. (1.6.26)

These competing discourses within the book itself—the companion/equal partner marriage versus the husband-dominated marriage, appear side by side without irony. Of Griselda and Walter, says the narrator, "[n]o one could perceive that in these two people there was more than one mind, and that single mind and will was the husband's." Even after Walter wrenches their infant daughter from her mother's arms, on the pretext of murdering her, they continued in a "loving and peaceful life." As for Griselda, "[s]he who had freely chosen, after careful consideration and reflection, to submit herself and all that was hers to her lord's will steeled herself and, fortified, decided that she would wait for any orders that her husband, to whom she had submitted herself, might issue." The narrator provides Griselda with a Magnificat-like speech of acceptance of Walter's will. He speaks of her vanquishing the wrath or sorrow in her nature in order to give up first her daughter, then her infant son, although it "pierced her entrails." It becomes virtuous to sacrifice her children to the whims of her husband and lord. If a marriage is a partnership, then the wife should be able to reprimand the husband as he may her; but the Griselda model of the good wife shows that women who "grucche" lack virtue.

Loving obedience is the Christian model for the relationship of man to God, but Walter and some of the husbands the *Le Ménagier* narrator provides in his other exempla are of decidedly unangelic character and display positive wickedness in what they demand of their wives, such as toleration of adultery or physical abuse. For medieval conduct book readers, however, the husband serves as God's representative, so that even when the wife feels upset and finds his request blatantly wrong or ridiculous, he must be obeyed. The narrator invokes biblical authority and analogy. If wives become too dominant and neglect being dutiful, they are compared to Lucifer, and they will be "felled with one stroke, by their husbands' rightful will" (1.7.8). He provides Old Testament illustrations of the good wife, as do other writers, such as the author of the *Miroir des bonnes femmes*.[53] After recounting the story of Leah and Rachel who shared Jacob as husband, and who, he feels, lived together in harmonious polygamy, the narrator fulminates on the character of women of his own time:

> How many women today would do that and would live so peaceably that when one would have the husband, the other would not pout or grouse? But even worse, for by God I think that today they would slap each other! O God! What good and holy women they were! It isn't for nothing that these words are recalled in the wedding blessing: *Sit amabilis ut Rachel viro, prudens ut Sarra, sapiens ut Rebecqua.* (1.5.24)[54]

As part of the series of indignities, tests, and cruelties—which include convincing her that he acts for the good of the realm—Walter repudiates Griselda, taking back her fine wardrobe and returning her nearly naked to her humble former life. Even at that, Griselda herself bids women to obey their husbands. In a speech original with this work, reinforcing her submission and humility, and even her pleasure in it, Griselda declares that Walter

> had good cause to do all that he wished with her, who was bound by duty to suffer and bear it. They could see that she was not distressed about it. She admonished them for the love of God to love their husbands loyally and wholeheartedly and to serve and honor them with all their might, since they could in the end achieve no greater good or higher renown than in that way.

The exemplum teaches that obedience to the husband as to God is ultimately rewarded, since Griselda is restored to her husband, her aristocratic status, her deluxe clothes, and her children in the end, however disturbing it all feels to us. The author makes it clear that to Griselda, basking in Walter's approval and later having her children back compensates for all the pain he caused her. In his glossing of the tale, the narrator sidesteps the allegory that Petrarch provides about gaining virtue by obeying God and insists on Griselda's relevance to contemporary wives and their behavior.

Indeed, there are several uneasy resemblances between the wife-audience of

---

53. From the early fourteenth century. See John L. Grigsby, "*Miroir des bonnes femmes*: A New Fragment of the *Somme le Roi* and a *Miroir des bonnes femmes*, a Hitherto Unnoticed Text," *Romania* 80 (1961): 447–60 and 82 (1962): 458–81, for a summary of the text.

54. The narrator reveals himself to be a bad reader here, or at least to foster bad reading in his audience, since the biblical story he has just recounted *is* one of jealousy, rancor, and disharmony between Leah and Rachael, despite what he asserts. This insight thanks to Thaddeus Tsohantaridis.

Le Ménagier and the heroine of the exemplum, not the least being the surveillance and scrutiny of her by her husband and household. In his prologue, the narrator proposes that he writes his book to offer his young wife "la paix que l'en doit avoir en mariaige" (marital peace), the salvation of the soul, and the peace/comfort of the husband "la paix du mary." Similarly, in Griselda's tale, Walter, when deciding to marry at his subjects' insistence, states that he will marry if God grants him a wife he can live with in the peace and quiet necessary for his salvation: "je puisse vivre en paix et en repos expédient à mon salut."[55] Like Griselda, the *Le Ménagier* wife seems to have no strong father figure to protect her. Described in the prologue as a well-born orphan, she finds refuge with a husband who wants to mold her into a Griselda, private, concealed, submissive, decked in the clothes he dictates, enclosed in his own garden and household. Like Griselda, she too could be sent back, but to an even bleaker former home, for she is parentless. If she were to transgress, says the narrator, "that sort of behavior, of course, would not be excused by the fact, which I know well, that you are of nobler lineage than I. For, by God, the women of your family are so virtuous that on their own, without any prompting from me, they would correct you harshly if they heard of such unacceptable behavior from me or anyone else" (prologue, 3). He softens this statement by assuring her that he has confidence in her good intent, remarking that his book is also destined for the instruction of her future daughters. The wisdom he provides her will lead to enhancement of her own reputation and his: "The more you are knowledgeable, the more respect you will receive, and the more your parents, myself, and the others who raised you will be praised" (prologue, 4). Like Griselda, she is supposed to take on the role of an experienced lady boss, to run the manor in his absence; like Walter, the narrator takes charge of the opulence of her clothing, warning his wife how (and how not) to dress to assure his good reputation, as in 1.1, where she is warned about donning fashionable garments that would be too ostentatious for their social class.

Two other parallels to the Griselda story within *Le Ménagier* are worth noting. Just as Walter insinuates that he has an authentic papal dispensation (which he does not) to prove he can divorce Griselda, the narrator also asserts authenticity, apparent when he takes pains to cite his examples as genuine.[56]

> On this subject, I will tell you a piteous and astonishing tale, which provokes sympathy. I know a woman from a bourgeois family of distinction who is married to a good man, and they are both decent creatures, an irreproachable couple with two beautiful young children. (1.6.25)

55. BF/Ueltschi, 26 (first two quotations), 196.
56. Scanlon says Petrarch locates Griselda's authenticity "in her impossibility" ("What's the Pope Got to Do with It?" 160).

Le Ménagier also models the Walter-Griselda pattern of consensual marriage, important to canon law in the Middle Ages.[57] Jarringly reminiscent of the wedding bargain in the tale, the husband-narrator of *Le Ménagier* recalls in his prologue how he organized their marriage and his wife's behavior by means of a contract. He reminds his wife:

> You expressly promised to listen carefully and to apply yourself wholeheartedly to preserving my contentment and love for you . . . , beseeching me humbly in our bed, as I recall, that for the love of God I not rebuke you harshly in front of either strangers or our household, but that I admonish you each night, or on a daily basis, in our bedroom, and that I remind you of your errors or foolishness of the day or days past and that I chastise you, if I should want to. You said that you would not fail to improve yourself according to my teaching and correction, and you would do everything in your power to behave according to my wishes. (Prologue, 1)

Thus, he writes the book to school her in private, as she has requested, rather than disgrace her in public. The young wife, Griselda-like, learns submission, and the husband can tyrannically—and contractually—provide opportunities to deploy this virtue.

When, subsequent to his Griselda tale, the narrator proceeds directly into explication, he decodes the tale specifically as Harry Bailly reads Chaucer's Clerk's Grisilde. But, unlike the Clerk's, his glosses do not confuse or challenge his reader, merely overwhelm her. The young wife-as-audience is impeded from any interpretation of her own by the avalanche of immediate and monolithic glossing of the material. He wants his wife to be in awe, to wonder at Griselda and the other incredibly virtuous and selfless wives he depicts, and to emulate them. His first gloss offers that Petrarch told the tale not only to move women to be patient and uncomplaining about the tribulations from their husbands but

> to show that since God, the Church, and reason require that they be obedient, and since their husbands will that they have so much to suffer, to avoid worse they must submit themselves in all things to the will of their husbands and endure patiently all that their husbands require. . . . Thus, it is all the more reasonable that men and women suffer patiently the tribulations that God . . . sends them. . . . one must always forbear and return to . . . the love of the . . . eternal, and everlasting God, through the example of this poor woman, . . . without distinction or learning, who suffered so much for her mortal friend. (1.6.9)

57. Scanlon, on consensual marriage, ibid., 136–37.

Providing himself with plenty of scriptural justification, the narrator insists that the tale concerns the importance of just such absolute obedience to husbandly authority as a facet of divine authority. Unsurprisingly, the narrator reminds his readers that medieval women are insolent and subject to men because of Eve. And Griselda redeems Eve's sin, as the Blessed Virgin has:

> Think about how much He loved the Virgin Mary for her obedience. Recall the obedience and deeds of Abraham, . . . who purely because of a command did such great and awful things without asking why. Consider Griselda, what things she bore and endured in her heart, without inquiring about the reason. One can perceive no cause or shadow of a cause, no future profit and no need to act as she did, only her husband's will, both dreadful and terrible. Nor did she ask him for any justification or, indeed, say a word about it. . . . 500 years after her death, we still read of her goodness! (1.6.28)

He does include an odd disclaimer that his own young wife need not fear testing by him, because she outranks him in class, making him unworthy of exact obedience from her, and he regrets the cruelty of the tale: "And I apologize if the story contains excessive accounts of cruelty, in my opinion more than is fitting, and I don't believe it was ever true. But the story is thus, and I must not amend or change it, for someone wiser than I compiled and recounted it" (1.6.10). He has no comments on Griselda's own brand of excessiveness other than wonder and praise.

Although he alleges that the wife is not implicated in his lesson of Griselda as the model of obedience—we saw that he earlier proposed an ideal marriage where the partners are equal—ironically and confusingly, the narrator expands on that tale with numerous *exempla in malo* that construct the ideal wife as exactly like Griselda. Either he cannot escape the generic expectations of the conduct book format, or he cannot help but reveal himself as a kind of Walter, setting for his wife a grim task under his tutelage. Anecdote piles upon anecdote following the Griselda exemplum, illustrating the necessity of female acquiescence in great and trivial matters, with female rebelliousness, arrogance, slyness, and pride as the sources of great ill to themselves and others. Obedience to the husband is required, whether his wishes are erratic or jesting, strange or inconsequential. Compliance, even with an injunction to a wrong act, would be praiseworthy in a wife, he says, because submission to the husband outweighs other considerations. The bourgeois conduct book thus enacts the Walter-Griselda oppression, disallowing questioning of its authority. Obedience to the text-as-husband is required, with his the only authorized exegesis. The book's ideal woman accepts domestic violence and emotional abuse as part of the natural order of male dominance. Griselda's tale, explains the narrator, manifests that "benefits come to a woman who is obedient to her husband" (1.6.8).

Submission is required as well to public opinion. The work evinces a deep unease about what others will think of him if his wife misbehaves in public. More than once he brings up a husband's adultery as a consequence of a wife's disobedience. Men, it seems, take pleasure in compliance. If they do not find it in their own homes, they find another woman more inclined to obey, and thus bring shame upon their wives through their infidelities. A wife must present a façade to the world about how authority in their marriage operates, he says: "to show her obedience and to maintain her honor, she should not speak a word, because it would seem to people who would hear it that the husband was accustomed to giving his wife an account of his reasons" (1.6.19). The woman, like Dorigen in Chaucer's *Franklin's Tale,* might be allowed some measure of sway at home behind closed doors, but to society at large she is never to appear dominant.

A further anecdote-as-gloss following the Griselda exemplum in *Le Ménagier* tells of a woman who actually has a contract (*cedule*) with her husband as to her duties toward him (1.6.11–12). The couple had been wrangling, and "like fools they exchanged accusations, and the wife maintained such bitter acrimony against her husband—who, in the beginning, as it so happened, had not instructed her carefully." Friends have to intervene in the dispute "to avoid a scandal" and keep the peace: "Out of pride, the wife would accept no alternative but, on the one hand, that all of her rights be written down, point by point, with all of the obligations she owed her husband, and, on the other hand, that her husband's rights and obligations to her also be clearly listed." This wife "narrowly guarded her rights as listed in the document," and the husband had to summon his patience for "he had set about to correct her too late." When the husband later falls into a deep ditch and shouts to her for help, she consults her contract, and "since her document did not mention the current situation," she walks away, leaving him in peril. The local lord rescues the husband, and on being informed of the wife's behavior, he has her captured—and burnt! Evidently, the husband's failure to school her properly causes this woman's treason, and the exemplum admonishes the audience of the book that the behavior molding must be conducted early and often. Confusingly, this woman reads her marriage contract literally, as Griselda does, and merits punishment, whereas Griselda gains praise for her exact reading. Perhaps the lesson is that women need to be directed how to read and men need to teach them well. The dangers of the contract and sticking to the letter of the law, as Griselda does, surface in the exemplum, providing an *exemplum in malo* of literal reading of any text, if the result is female dominance. Yet the narrator surely wants his wife/audience to read his book literally. Both stories put forward instances of abuse of contracts, but Walter's abuse evokes spiritual perfection in a woman, while the woman of independent will threatens the system and must be extinguished (granted, she is not a nice person). The paradox reflects once more that central inconsistency of the medieval marital model, the equal-yet-dominated woman. Moreover, it also suggests that the narrator is not, as he would like to be, in full control of his text or, perhaps, his wife.

The *Le Ménagier* narrator attempts to contain Griselda's tale just as his whole book works to create and maintain order in his household and beyond. She is the counterexample to what he sees as bad tendencies in female deportment. His library *in parvo* provides all this wife needs to carry on his values and that of his class. Lynn Staley sees in this work an anxiety about transmitting principles to the next generation, to turn his wife away from the mercantile city values and fashions toward order and purity within the home.[58] This book also functions as a manual on power relations in the bourgeois household, showing the strains of emulating the upper classes while preserving one's own honor and estate. But writing about what home life should be is not equivalent to actually producing that reality. The book's tone at once stridently advocates female subservience and showcases defiant women, whose stories are often the best, some of whom in fact do seem to get the better of their men. Self-abasing women can achieve merit at home, however, gaining the high moral ground through their goodness. Hence the example of Jehanne le Quentine, who reclaimed her husband from an adulterous liaison with a poverty-stricken girl by furnishing the girl with money and clean laundry for her husband's comfort and shaming him through her selflessness to return to her and his home (1.9). It is a vicious circle: women are exhorted to patience; their patience leads men to test them; the testing leads to their domination by men. The whole structure of male dominance built up by the conduct manual is a fragile one. As Chaucer's Clerk's Envoy suggests, wedded men must dominate or be dominated, a problem articulated in *Le Ménagier*. There is no question where the narrator stands on this matter.

Because *Le Ménagier* illustrates that most women are unlikely Griseldas, female attempts at emulating her in the face of their own marital subservience are

---

58. Staley, *Languages of Power*, 280, 295. Staley scrutinizes *Le Ménagier* in her chapter "French Georgics and English Ripostes," where she discusses the differences between French and English conversations about power. She focuses on the origins of French household management/wifely management treatises in the pseudo-Aristotle's *Economics*, which figures the political community as a household to be ordered, and "the household as a kind of monarchical kingdom whose borders need to be very carefully guarded" (268–69). Contained in *Economics* (book 2) is a conduct book for a young wife, who must obey her husband in patience and realize that household duties are holy, with the good order of the household dependent upon the quality of the instruction the husband gives to his wife. The husband is construed as a benign powerful monarch, like Charles V's construction of himself during his reign, says Staley (269). Staley argues, most convincingly, that *Le Ménagier* written about fourteen years after the death of Charles V, harks back to the orderly hierarchical world of Charles V in a less stable age.

all the more heroic. Thus the domestic arena offers opportunities for martyr-like trials of Griseldian forbearance. Women would be, according to the pious logic of such a tale, *lucky* to have tyrannous and impossible husbands such as Walter, so that, by transcending his arbitrary cruelty with patience, they could become more spiritually perfect, a situation, as we have noted earlier, that Christine de Pizan also envisions. The *Le Ménagier* narrator thereby efficiently provides the opportunity for flawlessness in a wife by fashioning himself and other husbands he seems to know of as wife "testers" like Walter. He portrays in his book a community zealous to uncover whose wife is "bad," who shames her husband, by recounting a number of tests of wives, where husbands wager on whose wife is the most obedient (1.6.27, 33, etc.). Since scripture authorizes the "natural" law of female submission to the male, the author excuses husbands who try their wives, comparing them to God, who tested Adam and Eve, or Lot and his family, out of love. Without Walter's tests, Griselda could not display her exemplary piety. These tests would be impossible without Walter's dominance in their marriage. But Walter can tyrannize only because he is no ordinary husband, subject to his wife's displays of discontent, such as the examples of bad wives in *Le Ménagier* depict. In this model of Griselda, then, it is better for a husband to be extraordinarily trying, since through this ordeal a wife can display her prudence and patience and grow in these virtues.

Janet Ferrier notes that the long poem copied into the *Le Ménagier* text, *Le Chemin de povreté et de richesse,* contains an antifeminist diatribe, adding that this "odd choice" seems "unlike" the narrator's "own views" on the value of wifely counsel, in direct opposition to Prudence's story.[59] However, the commingling in *Le Ménagier* of antifeminism with disclaimers that valorize certain ideal women epitomizes the narrative voice. Despite illustrations of good fictional women like Griselda or Prudence, one leaves the moral treatise section feeling it is more a *Legend of Bad Women,* and so many of the bad wives he has heard of are local French women. This manual naturalizes the brutality of men while blaming women for it and disallows women's anger. Men in the book are angry or potentially angry all the time. The author/narrator evinces discomfort in asserting male dominance in marital relations, yet he assures us it is the only way to peaceful domiciles, marital accord, and female perfection. Those like Eileen Power who find the *Le Ménagier* author avuncular fail to register the competing discourses within the book that, even as they seek to deny the kind of multiplicity of meanings for Griselda that Chaucer's Clerk's Envoy displays, underline Griselda's and women's complex subjectivity and position in society. While the *Le Ménagier*

59. "'Seulement pour vous endoctriner': The Author's Use of Exempla in *Le Menagier de Paris,*" *Medium Aevum* 48 (1979): 79.

author seems to close down meanings by his insistence on Griselda's exemplary saintly status for his reader(s) to emulate, his glosses on the tale, multiplying and rereading Griselda for his wife, keep the problem of dominance in medieval marriage in the foreground. Griselda's value lies in her consent to be dominated.[60] Marriage necessitates male-female consent; nevertheless, males must have dominance for a happy marriage; therefore, women must agree to this way of life. Both models of marriage obtain in *Le Ménagier* in an edgy tension—the lip service to a relatively equal partnership and injunctions to imitate a submissive wife of a dominant husband. Negotiating these two models seems the sword bridge over which the young wife and *Le Ménagier*'s later audiences must find their way.

The *Le Ménagier* narrator attempts through glossing to influence the reception of his anecdotes, especially in the article on obedience (1.6). The tyranny of the text prevails over the imagined audience, who is prevented from "identifying" with any of the bad women or their motives, either by fright at what happens to them (burning, bleeding, etc.) or by the threat of society's disapprobation. The fifteenth-century Middle English conduct poem *How the Good Wijf Tauȝt Hir Douȝtir* provides schooling for just such a quintessentially patient wife, advising her to placate her husband, "Meekely þou him answere, And not as an attirling [shrew], / And so maist þou slake his mood, And ben his dere derlynge" (ll. 41–42).[61]

In the fifteenth century patience became the "supreme public virtue," and the story of Griselda, along with *Melibee* and other of Chaucer's serious works such as *The Parson's Tale*, are frequently acclaimed by fifteenth century poets as moral and political works. "Griselda's patience . . . is exalted as a model of behavior rather than censured for submission to the monstrous Walter."[62] The inclusion of the story of Griselda as well as that of Melibee in such a manual as *Le Ménagier*, designed for the smooth and peaceful operation of a household, and exhorting women to be pacific reconcilers, is no accident. Nonetheless, as Sylvana Vecchio notes, peacemaking was not a specific positive quality in a medieval woman, but rather peacemaking arises from a woman's docility and capacity for submission.[63] Accord in the home between husband and wife, using the *Le Ménagier* author's

60. Scanlon, "What's the Pope Got to Do with It?" of the *Clerk's Tale*.

61. *How the good wijf Tauȝt Hir Douȝtir,* in *The Babees Book,* ed. Frederick J. Furnivall, Early English Text Society, O.S. 32 (London: Oxford University Press, 1868; reprint, Millwood, N.Y.: Kraus, 1990), 38.

62. David Lawton, "Dullness in the Fifteenth Century," *ELH* 54, no. 4 (1987): 780. Lawton suggests of England that the fifteenth century "offered a uniquely inauspicious set of circumstances in which to announce the preeminence of peace and patience as public virtues; yet this, with few exceptions, is what fifteenth century poets do, in the tradition of Chaucer and Gower" (781). The emphasis on "reconciliation rather than vengeance . . . is ubiquitous in the fifteenth century." 782.

63. Vecchio, "Good Wife," 109.

analogy of the inner/outer conduct of life, led to peace in the political and international spheres and in the cosmos. Griselda's story of the hardworking selfless woman, unconcerned with material goods and social status, confirms much of the heuristic message of the other parts of the text. Reading Griselda literally, then, leads to the "good" life.

Irony and didacticism occupy the "same indeterminate discursive space" for the *Le Ménagier* author, who recounts his tales and emends the sources with a sense of their shape, appeal, and instructive function.[64] While he writes ostensibly for those audiences who like their literature literal, the gray areas and indeterminacy of marital relations in late medieval society irrupt from his text nonetheless. The narrative presents cruel, fallible, and corrupt husbandly figures in an imperfect world, along with a contradictory model for women's emulation —a woman contractually consenting to be submissive to someone she must also love as an equal partner. The *Le Ménagier* author—who may indeed never have had a young wife to educate but who, like Petrarch,[65] considered a young wife the best option for a compliant companion and smooth-running household, and a good topic for a book—represents a cultural marker important to his time and genre. He reinvents the conduct book as a gloss on the figure of Griselda, both didactic and ironic, showcasing the problem of women and the conundrum of the consent to be dominated. This conduct book does not merely repeat the clichéd standards for obedient women. Its artful embracing of the Griselda story and the other wonders it contains should furnish it with more claims on our attention.

64. Scanlon, of Chaucer's *Clerk's Tale,* "What's the Pope Got to Do with It?" 161, 165.

65. Petrarch's letters (*Familiares* 22.1, September 11, 1362) note his preference for a young wife that can be molded into what the older man wishes. "It is best to select a young virgin from a distant community. . . . For a noble maiden, devoted to you from an early age and distanced from her people's flatteries and old women's gossipings, will be more chaste and humble, more obedient and holy; quickly casting off her girlish frivolity, she will don the seriousness of a married woman. In short, whether a virgin or a widow, once she joins you in the nuptial bed, hearing, seeing and thinking of you alone, she will be transformed into your image alone and will adopt your ways." Quoted in Wallace, *Chaucerian Polity,* 274–75.

Translation Protocols

We base our translation on the Brereton-Ferrier Middle French edition, checked against the manuscripts as necessary, and the 1846 edition by Pichon. Pichon began his project with MS C, yet was fairly free with the addition of readings from the other MSS. Brereton-Ferrier use MS A. We have also consulted the partial English translation by Eileen Power and the modern French translation by Karin Ueltschi in a facing-page arrangement with Brereton-Ferrier. We have numbered our paragraphs to correspond to the numbering in the Brereton-Ferrier/Ueltschi edition for ease of reference.

Our goal is to provide a readable translation that does not transgress the register of the original Middle French text. This register is formal by modern standards—for instance, the husband uses the formal mode of address with his wife —but this form of address and register were general practice in a bourgeois family at the turn of the fourteenth century, and even through the early part of the twentieth century for upper bourgeois families. The level of formality thus reflects typical familial discourse of this class and is no way archaic. The author tends to employ clear and ordinary vocabulary. Since all the audiences of this text, of course, are fictional, this notion has influenced our diction and word choices. By that we mean that the primary fictional audience is a fifteen-year-old medieval woman who can read. Even if the text were written for an actual wife, her presence in the text is an authorial construct. One would not expect her husband to use overly complex terms to her, considering the average vocabulary of a teenager and his opinions on women's intellectual resources. Nonetheless, we must remember another fictional audience—the next husband, for whom without doubt the narrator would show off his erudition. In addition, there are the Beguine Dame Agnes and Jehan the steward who need to read sections of the book, as well as those future children of the wife who the author feels will benefit from the book's teachings. Of course, our *real* readers, and most likely the author's larger audience in his Parisian society and later, are not all fifteen-year-old girls and surely have substantially more skills and richer vocabularies. Thus, we have not found it imperative to restrict ourselves to the simplest constructions and synonyms.

To render the text accessible in modern English, we punctuate according to modern English principles, adjusting in many places the sentence divisions and punctuation of the edited Middle French text. Since the register of the Middle French text is generally simple and clear, we made primarily minor stylistic emendations; but we did eliminate some few elements of Middle French that may sound awkward to a modern reader. For example, the tendency to provide pairs of synonyms can seem otiose in modern English; thus in some cases we have dropped one of the synonyms. But because doublets were a feature of late medieval English prose (one has only to look at Caxton's *The Book of the Knight of the Tower* of 1483, another conduct book for women, to see how prevalent this rhetorical feature was),[1] we have retained many of the doublets that add clarity of meaning and are faithful to the French style, especially when the single term seems inadequate or unemphatic, or when preserving the second term adds to the dignity of the expression in the way we conceive the narrator might sermonize to the young wife. Use of the doublet might be said to be characteristic of this narrator's otiose style, wanting to ensure that his young wife understands exactly what he means, giving her two words where one might do.

At times we have added more precise conjunctions, when English logic demands it, since in modern English as well as modern French, conjunctions are often more accurately distinguished than in late medieval French, which frequently uses the less specific *et.* In the few cases where no modern English equivalent exists for a Middle French term, we retain the original term and gloss it in a note. We kept the Latin *item,* which announces the next item in a list, since it does not impede the reader's understanding. Other Latin terms are also retained and glossed, since it is significant that the wife would understand such minor Latin phrases as a matter of course. Where the manuscripts (and editions) use roman numerals, we have substituted arabic numerals; where numbers are spelled out, we do likewise. Many of the uncommon cooking terms in section 2 have rare or old-fashioned English equivalents. When such equivalents exist, we use them, but for clarity we provide a glossary of terms used in the menus and recipes.

We have translated as prose the Middle French poem *Le Chemin de povreté et de richesse* included in article 2.1 of the codex, a 2,626–line allegorical dream-vision in couplets that the narrator inserts to reinforce his moral message of how to find happiness in marriage. Ours is the first published modern English translation of this didactic poem.[2] The Middle French octosyllabic couplets can be rendered more sensible and readable by using English prose, since English is so rhyme-poor and our poetic talents so thin. We strove to preserve the matter and abundant charms (although there are scholars who scoff at the poetry as amateurish) of the original while rendering it in a shorter space through eliminating some repetitive language required by the poetic meter and rhyme. No twentieth-

1. Offord, in Caxton, *Book of the Knight of the Tower,* xxx–xxxii.
2. In 1506 Wynkyn de Worde printed an English translation of a French adaptation of the poem. See below, article 2.1, n. 1.

century editorial or critical treatment of *Le Ménagier* has actually considered this poem an integral part of the book, and we hope to remedy this neglect. The story of Melibee (1.9) is also here translated into modern English for the first time directly from MS A with some aid from Pichon's edition. It was daunting to be translating into English a tale whose most notable English translator was Chaucer. We avoided using his wonderful work except at the very end to check the sense of some disputed passages. To judge by the obvious variants, his source text was not the same one as the *Ménagier* author used.

The word that most needed our attention was the insistent use of the forms of *bon* (good) by the narrator in the instructions to his wife. He has shaped his book to the end that his wife be "good," but the senses in which he employs the term are assorted, requiring scores of different English terms to render the connotations throughout the work. To keep from the tedious and imprecise repetition of "good," we have often made judgments about just what "good" the narrator had in mind and translated accordingly. The narrator's sententiousness is not affected by a more precise rendering of his demands for his wife's "good"-ness. Our task was complicated, however, by considering the medieval reader, possibly such a young woman as the narrator suggests as his audience. We have, as is inevitable in any translation, narrowed the interpretive possibilities of "good" by qualifying many of the occasions of its use and substituting a synonym, thus indicating to the reader our idea of what "good" means in this or that instance. Since the task of the reader was to transform herself into a "good" wife, it behooved her, possibly, to ponder in each occurrence of the term just what kind of "good" was being discussed: benefit, luck, right behavior, tasty, satisfying, etc.—it was the most thumbed page in our thesaurus. Her interpretive task was to consider the ramifications of how to be "good" and to decode just what the narrator meant her to learn by ruminating on "good" where it appears in her manual. After all, she was supposed to *become* the book by digesting it. So her exegetical duty may have been to ascertain meaning where there were only signposts, turning over the narrator's words in her mind. For example, when the husband says, "On my soul, I believe that there is no other witchcraft than doing good, and you cannot enthrall a man any better way than by pleasing him" (1.7.2), the expansive "good" is "good deeds" as well as flirtation, sexual intimacies, cooking and cleaning, and solicitous attention to the well-being of the body of the husband—among other things. Consequently, if we have done any disservice to the text by flattening its ambiguities, we hope we have made up for it by expanding and clarifying for our readers the notion of a "good" wife that constitutes the main theme of the work.

The Good Wife's Guide
Le Ménagier de Paris
A Medieval Household Book

¶ Prologue

1. My dear,[1] because you were only fifteen years old the week we were married, you asked that I be indulgent about your youth and inexperience until you had seen and learned more. You expressly promised to listen carefully and to apply yourself wholeheartedly to preserving my contentment and love for you (as you so prudently said following advice from, I do believe, someone more wise than yourself), beseeching me humbly in our bed, as I recall, that for the love of God I not rebuke you harshly in front of either strangers or our household, but that I admonish you each night, or on a daily basis, in our bedroom, and that I remind you of your errors or foolishness of the day or days past and that I chastise you, if I should want to.[2] You said that you would not fail to improve yourself according to my teaching and correction, and you would do everything in your power to behave according to my wishes. That pleased me so much, and I praised and thanked you for what you said, and I have since remembered it often.

2. Rest assured, my dear, that to my knowledge all that you have done since our marriage, and all that you will do with good intentions, has been and is proper, and continues to be and will ever be pleasing to me. Your youth excuses you from being always wise and will naturally pardon you in all things that you do with the intentions of being good and not offending me. Understand that it doesn't displease me, but rather pleases me, that you tend roses, raise violets, make garlands of them, and also that you dance and sing. I would like you to continue such activities among our friends and our equals—it is only natural and appropriate that a girl spend her adolescence in such pursuits, as long as you don't desire to frequent parties or dances of high-ranking lords, because that would not be appropriate to your rank or mine.

3. As for all the many grand things that you said you would willingly do for me if you knew how and that you asked me to teach you, know, my dear, that it is enough for me that you treat me as your good neighbors or relatives, who are of our same rank, treat their husbands. Consult them first about this, then

---

1. The Middle French reads "chiere seur," yet in modern English usage a fond husband would not call his wife "sister," but rather "dear," even with a considerable difference in their ages.

2. The first thing "conceived" in this marital bed was this book, a literary offspring of the older man, inspired by the girl. The book is to be internalized and carried within the young wife and to bear fruit in her obedience and proficiency in household duties.

follow their advice, more or less, as you please. Having a sense of you and your good intentions, I am not so presumptuous as to find your services insufficient, provided that you are not deceitful, scornful, or disdainful. That sort of behavior, of course, would not be excused by the fact, which I know well, that you are of nobler lineage than I. For, by God, the women of your family are so virtuous that on their own, without any prompting from me, they would correct you harshly if they heard of such unacceptable behavior from me or anyone else. But I don't have any worries about you; I am confident of your honorableness.

4. Although, as I said, it is not appropriate for me to ask much of you for myself, I would nonetheless desire that you have a real understanding of virtue, honor, and duty, not so much for my sake, but so that you can better serve another husband, if you have one after me, or so that you might more ably instruct your daughters, friends, or others, if you wish and if they need it. The more you are knowledgeable, the more respect you will receive, and the more your parents, myself, and the others who raised you will be praised. For your honor and love, and not for ministering to my needs (for only common service, or less, is appropriate for me), and because I have tender compassion for you who have for so long been without father and mother, any nearby kinswomen, or anyone else from whom you could seek advice concerning your private needs, except myself, for whom you have been removed from your family and birthplace, I have often and repeatedly wondered if I could find an easy and general introduction that could guide you in your efforts and work. Then you could teach yourself, without burdening me with the task described above. In the end, it seems to me that if your affection is really as you have shown to me in such well-intentioned words, the lessons can be accomplished in the following manner: I will write and give you general instructions in three sections containing nineteen principal articles.

5. The first of the three sections teaches you how to attain God's love and the salvation of your soul, and also to win your husband's love and to give yourself, in this world, the peace that should be found in marriage. And because these two things, salvation of the soul and the contentment of your husband, are the two most important things that exist, they are placed first in this book. This first section contains 9 articles.

6. The second section instructs you on how to increase the prosperity of the household, gain friends, preserve your possessions, and make those misfortunes attendant upon old age easier for you to bear. This section contains 6 articles.

7. The third section treats pleasant enough games and amusements to help you socialize with company and make conversation. This section contains three articles.

8. Section 1:

The first article speaks of how to address and thank Our Lord and His Blessed Mother upon waking and rising, as well as how to attire yourself appropriately and then make your confession.

9. The second article treats having appropriate companions accompany you when going to church, selecting a seat, behaving properly, hearing Mass, and going to confession.

10. The third article charges you to love God and His Blessed Mother, to serve them continually, to place yourself in their grace and maintain this state.

11. The fourth article teaches you about remaining continent and living chastely, following the example of Susanna, Lucretia, and others.

12. The 5th article shows that you should love your husband, be it me or another, after the example of Sarah, Rebecca, and Rachel.

13. The 6th article instructs you to be humble and obey your husband, following the examples of Griselda, of the woman who would not rescue her husband from drowning, of the Mother of God who responded *fiat*, of Lucifer, of . . . of the puis,[3] of the bailiff of Tournai, of the men of the cloth and husbands, of Madame d'Andresel, of the people of Chaumont and the lady from Rome.

14. The 7th charges that you be attentive to and care for your husband well.

15. The 8th, that you keep his secrets, following the examples of Papirius, the woman who laid eight eggs, the woman from Venice, the woman who returned from Santiago de Compostela, and the lawyer.

16. The 9th and last article shows that if your husband tries to wander or strays from the virtuous path, you are to bring him back, not with harshness, but gently, wisely, and humbly, as in the stories of Melibee and Dame Jehanne la Quentine.

17. Section 2:

The first article instructs that you take care of your household, with diligence, perseverance, and regard for your work. Take pains to find pleasure in your duties, and I will do the same so that we will reach the castle that is spoken of.[4]

18. The second article informs you so that, at the least, you may enjoy and have some knowledge of horticulture and gardening, grafting in the proper season, and keeping roses in winter.

19. The third article explains how to choose varlets, doormen, handymen, or other strong men to do the heavy work that must be done throughout the day. In

---

3. The ellipsis indicates a lacuna in the MSS at this point.

4. In the poem *Le Chemin de pauvreté et de richesse* that the author includes later in his volume, the castle is the allegorical Castle of Riches.

addition, you will need to understand about dealing with farm laborers, as well as tailors, shoemakers, bakers, pastry makers, and so forth. You will especially need to be acquainted with how to put your varlets and chambermaids to work: sifting and winnowing grain; cleaning, airing, and drying garments; attending to the sheep and horses; storing and conserving wines, etc.

20. The fourth article is written so that you, as sovereign mistress of your house, may know how to order dinners, suppers, dishes, and courses and be informed about meat and poultry, as well as about spices.

21. The 5th article is presented so that you know how to order, organize, talk about, and have prepared all sorts of pottages, stews, sauces, and other dishes. *Idem*[5] how to provide nourishments for sick people.

22. Section 3:

The first article in this section concerns curious amusements based on the luck of dice, rooks, or kings.

23. The 2nd article acquaints you with how to raise hawks and teach them to hunt.

24. The third article is about other puzzles concerning counting, plus numbering puzzles that require skill to solve or to guess.

---

5. Latin: "the same."

Introductory Note to Articles 1.1–1.3

The first three articles explain the religious aspect of life for the young wife. She is instructed in prayers, behavior, the ritual content of the Mass, and, at most length, the kinds of sin and the manner of making a confession, along with the virtues to remedy the Seven Deadly Sins. The author used a number of recognizable sources in putting together the information in these articles. Brereton-Ferrier's and Pichon's notes cite those of the author's borrowings, often unacknowledged, that can be attributed to specific religious texts, but they cannot pin down the source of many of the author's quotations or reference texts, and such an effort would require enormous expertise in the array of devotional works widely available to the French layman of the period. Even then, the true source may not have survived, or the author may have cobbled together his work from what he read and knew. Certainly, devotional books explaining the Mass were commonplace items in a household such as the narrator describes as his own, and even in homes of modest circumstances during the late Middle Ages. Books of hours or other collections of prayers could have provided the author with his texts concerning devotions, and the description of the Mass that appears in the early paragraphs of article 1.3 might have its origin in any one of the many commentaries on the liturgy written for the laity of the period.[1] His general familiarity with the Bible is obvious, yet his versions of biblical stories are often not traceable to any Bible available at the time, or any collection of Bible stories such as Petrus Comestor's *Historia scholastica* and its several French adaptations, called generally *Bible historiale* (see article 1.5, note 1). The author may have inserted them from memory, or from some as yet undiscovered source, and used them as evidence to point to his moral message. The material in article 1.3 on sins and virtues, which the young woman was to avail herself of in examining her conscience in preparation for confession, has its closest source in *La Somme le Roy* (1279) of Friar Laurent d'Orléans from the court of Philip the Bold.[2] Toward the end of this article, especially in the paragraphs describing the virtues, the author has garbled and abridged some of Laurent's work.

1. See BF introduction (xxx–xxxix) on the biblical and literary sources of section 1.

2. The fourteenth-century English translation is *The Book of Vices and Virtues: A Fourteenth Century English Translation of the* Somme le Roi *of Lorens D'Orléans,* ed. W. N. Francis, Early English Text Society, O.S. 217 (Oxford: Oxford University Press, 1942).

He telescopes and transposes the discussion, rendering it unrecognizable and fairly confusing unless you have the *Somme* to hand as a lengthy supplement to this text—which, indeed, the young wife may have had. The narrator invites her to consult other works in his library that he provides for her further instruction, should she care to, and if God prompts her (1.3.118).

This treatise, like the one on hawking, feels rushed toward its end. Perhaps, as he says in paragraph 2.1.1, the narrator is a little guilty at overwhelming the girl with so many injunctions about her moral and practical life, and so he hits what he considers the high points of the *Somme le Roy*'s notions of vice and virtue. Article 1.3 makes sense generally, as one would expect in a compendium of moral instruction for youth, without providing chapter and verse of his prolix source full of sermons and specifics. Since there were several abridged versions of the *Somme* available in the fourteenth century, our text may have originated in one of these, such as the *Livre de sagesse,* or other versions noted by W. N. Francis.[3] But as yet a direct source has eluded scholars. Brereton-Ferrier and Pichon do not use scribal error too often to explain mistakes in their exemplars, and we offer that excuse in a few places, and in general, as a possibility for obvious misreadings, since manuscripts A, B, and C are related to one another and to a lost original that may have been miscopied.

3. See ibid., xxvii–xxviii.

¶ 1.1 *Prayers and Orderly Dress*

1. The beginning and the first article of the first section treats prayer and arising. You must arise in the morning—and morning means, with regard to the subject we are treating here, Matins.[1] For just as we country folk describe the day as from dawn to night, or from sunrise to sunset, clerks who are more subtle say that is the artificial day, and that the natural day is 24 hours long, and begins at midnight and ends at the following midnight. So that is why I explained that morning refers to Matins. I mention it because the Matins bell rings then to wake up the monks to say the Matins and praise God, and not at all because I wish to imply that you, dear one, or any married women, must get up at that hour. But I do want to have pointed it out, so that at the hour that you hear the Matins ringing, you praise and hail Our Lord with some greeting or prayer before you fall back to sleep. To this purpose, proper orisons or prayers are included below. For either the hour of Matins or at daybreak, I have written down two prayers for you to address to Our Lord, and two others for Our Lady, appropriate to say when waking up or arising from bed.

2. First, here follows the midnight prayer. In saying it, you thank Our Lord for granting, through his grace, that you may live up to that moment. You will pray in this way:

3. *Gracias ago tibi, Domine Deus omnipotens, qui es trinus et unus, qui es semper in omnibus, et eras ante omnia, et eris per omnia Deus benedictus per secula, qui me de transacto noctis spacio ad matutinales horas deducere dignatus es. Et nunc queso, Domine, ut donas michi hunc diem per tuam sanctam misericordiam sine peccato transire quatenus ad vesperum. Et semper tibi, Domino Deo meo, refferre valeam actiones graciarum. Per Christum Dominum nostrum. Amen.*

4. In French that means: "Lord God Almighty, Who are one in three persons, Who were, are, and will be in all things God, blessed through the ages, I give You thanks that You deigned to lead me from the beginning of this night to the morning hours. And now I beg that, in Your holy mercy, You sanction me to cross this

---

1. Here and elsewhere in the text, the narrator refers to the medieval way of noting time by the liturgical "hours," the sequence of prayers said by the consecrated religious and many lay people at specific times of the day. The hours are: Matins (night or daybreak prayer), Lauds (dawning); Prime (6 a.m.); Terce (9 a.m.); Sext (noon); None (3 p.m.); Vespers (end of daylight); Compline (evening/close of day); Vigils (nocturnal).

day without sin, in such a way that in the evening I can thank You again, adore You, and greet You as my Lord and my God."

5. *Item*, the other prayer to Our Lord follows: *Domine sancte, Pater omnipotens, eterne Deus, qui me ad principium huius diei pervenire fecisti, tua me hodie salva virtute ut in hac die ad nullum declinem mortale peccatum, ne ullum incurram periculum; sed semper ad tuam justiciam et voluntatem faciendam omnis mea actio tuo moderamine dirigatur. Per Christum.*

6. In French that means: "Lord God Almighty and Eternal Father, Who has allowed me to reach the beginning of this day, by Your holy power, protect me from all danger, so that I may turn away from any mortal sin and that by Your gentle moderation my thoughts may be directed to do Your holy justice and will."

7. *Item*, the two prayers to Our Lady follow: *Sancta Maria, mater domini nostri Iesu Christi, in manus filii tui et in tuas commendo hodie et omni tempore animam meam, corpus meum, et sensum meum. Custodi me, Domini, a cunctis viciis, a peccatis, et a temptacionibus diaboli; et ab eis libera me, Domine Iesu Christe, et adiuva me. Dona michi sanitatem anime et corporis. Dona michi bene agere et in isto seculo recte vivere et bene perseverare, et omnium peccatorum meorum remissionem concede. Salva me, Domine, vigilantem, custodi me dormientem ut dormiam in pace et vigitem in te, Deus meus. Amen.*

8. In French, that means: "Mary, Holy Mother of Jesus Christ, I commend my soul, my body, and my mind, today and for all time, into the hands of you and your Blessed Son. Lord, preserve me from all vices, from all sins, and from all temptation by the devil, and deliver me from all dangers. Lord, sweet Jesus Christ, help me and give me health of soul and body. Give me the desire to do good, to live justly in this world, and to persevere. Grant me remission of all my sins. Lord, protect me while awake, guard me while asleep, so that I may sleep in peace and awake in You in the glory of Paradise."

9. The other prayer to Our Lady follows in French: "O steadfast hope, Lady Protectress of all who place their trust in you, glorious Virgin Mary, I beg you now that in that hour when my eyes will be so heavy from the shadows of death that I will not be able to see the light of this world, or able to move my tongue to pray to you or call to you, when my miserable heart that is so weak will tremble for fear of the enemies from hell, and will be so anxiously frightened that all the members of my body will melt in sweat because of the painful anguish of death, then, most gentle and precious Lady, deign to look on me in pity and to help me, to have with you the company of angels and also the knighthood of Paradise, so that the devils, agitated and terrified by your succor, cannot have any glimmer, presumption, or suspicion of evil against me, or any hope or power of removing me from your presence. Rather, instead, most gentle Lady, may it please you then to remember the prayer that I make to you now, and receive my soul in your

blessed faith, into your care and protection, and present it to your glorious Son to be vested in the robe of glory and accompanied to the joyous feast of the angels and all the saints. O Lady of the angels! O gate of Paradise! O Lady of the patriarchs, of the prophets, the apostles, the martyrs, the confessors, the virgins, and of all the saints! O morning star, more resplendent than the sun and whiter than snow! I join my hands and lift my eyes and bend my knees before you, tender Lady, in the name of the joy you had when your holy soul departed from your body without dread or fear and was carried in the presence of the singing angels and archangels, and presented to your glorious Son, who received it to dwell in eternal joy. I pray that you may rescue me and come before me in that hour of dread when death will be so near. Lady, be a comfort and refuge to my soul. Protect it carefully, so that the cruel enemies of hell, who are so terrifying to behold, may not accuse me of the sins that I have committed. Rather, let these sins first through your prayer be forgiven me, and by your Blessed Son erased. May my soul be presented by you, tender Lady, to your Blessed Son, and by your prayer attain eternal repose and joy never ending."

10. You can say these prayers at Matins or when you awake in the morning, or at both times, or while getting up and dressed, or after dressing—all are fine times as long as it is before breaking fast and addressing other business. But since I mentioned getting dressed, I wish to speak here a little bit about clothing. About which, my dear, know that if you choose to behave according to my advice, you will consider and pay attention to our status and our means, attiring yourself with respect to the estate of your family and mine, amongst whom you will mingle and dwell each day. Make sure that you dress decently without introducing new fashions and without too much or too little ostentation. Before leaving your chamber or home, be mindful that the collar of your shift, of your camisole, or of your robe or surcoat does not slip out one over the other, as happens with drunken, foolish, or ignorant women who do not care about their own honor or the good repute of their estate or of their husband, and go with open eyes, head appallingly lifted like a lion, their hair in disarray spilling from their coifs, and the collars of their shifts and robes all in a muddle one over the other. They walk in mannish fashion and comport themselves disgracefully in public without shame, quite saucy. When spoken to about it, they provide an excuse for themselves on the basis of diligence and humility, saying that they are so conscientious, hardworking, and charitable that they have little thought for themselves. But they are lying: they think so highly of themselves that if they were in honorable company, they would not at all want to be less well served than the sensible women of equal rank, or have fewer salutations, bows, reverences, or compliments than the others, but rather more. On top of that, they are not worthy of it since they are ignorant of how to maintain the honor, not only of their own estate,

but that of their husband and their lineage, on whom they bring shame. Be careful then, my dear, that your hair, your headdress, your kerchief, your hood, and the rest of your garments be neatly and simply arranged, so that anyone who sees you will not be able to laugh or mock you. Instead, make yourself an example of good order, simplicity, and respectability to all others. This should suffice for this first article.

¶ 1.2 *Behavior and Attire in Public*

The second article.

1. The second article instructs that when traveling to town or church you should be suitably accompanied according to your estate, by that I mean by gentlewomen, and avoid suspect company. Never approach or allow in your company dishonorable women. When walking in public keep your head upright, eyes downcast and immobile. Gaze four *toises*[1] straight ahead and toward the ground, without looking or glancing at any man or woman to the right or left, or looking up, or in a fickle way casting your gaze about in sundry directions,[2] nor laugh nor stop to speak to anyone on the street. Once you arrive at the church, select as private and solitary a place as you can. Situate yourself in front of a beautiful altar or statue and remain there without changing places or moving about, holding your head straight, constantly moving your lips in orisons and prayers. Also, keep your eyes continuously on your book or on the face of the statue, without looking at man or woman, a painting or anything else, and without hypocrisy or affectation. Focus your thoughts on heaven and pray with your whole heart, and in such manner attend Mass every day and go to confession often. If you act and persevere in this way, honor and great benefit will come to you. What is said above must suffice for this beginning, for the good gentlewomen who will keep you company will provide you with sterling examples, as much by their deeds as by their teaching. The virtuous, wise, and worthy old priests to whom you will confess and the natural good sense that God has given you will guide you and fill in the remainder of this second article.

---

1. A toise is about six feet.

2. Middle French uses here a vocabulary of inconstancy—*changier, muablement,* words so often associated with the weaknesses of women—to express how the young wife should not direct her gaze wantonly.

¶ 1.3 *The Mass, Confession, the Vices and Virtues*

The third article.

1. The third article teaches that you must love God and maintain yourself in His grace. In that regard, in the evening or at Vespers I advise you to cease all activities without delay and refrain from drinking or eating, except a little bit, and remove yourself from all worldly thoughts, and find a private, solitary place and remain there, walking to and fro, far from others, thinking only of hearing Mass early the next morning. Afterward, make a heartfelt, full, and well-considered confession of all your sins to your confessor. And because these two things—hearing Mass and confession—are to some extent different, we will speak first about Mass and then about confession.

The Mass[1]

2. Concerning Mass, my dear, know that the Mass has several formal rituals in a precise order that should be explained to you. First, after the priest has put on his vestments, and said his *Confiteor,* he commences Mass with the *Introit,* the beginning or entry of the Mass, during which each man and woman must direct his thoughts inward and avoid thinking of any worldly thing he has ever seen or heard. For when men or women are in church to hear the divine service, their hearts must not stray to their home, or the fields, or other worldly place. They must dwell not on temporal things but exclusively on God Himself and pray to Him devoutly.

3. After the *Introit* is sung or said, *Kyrie eleison, Christe eleison* is repeated 9 times to signify that in Paradise there are nine orders or hierarchies of angels. Some from each order come to Mass—not all of them, but a part of each. Each person must pray to these holy angels that they may intercede for him to Our Lord, saying: "O you holy angels who descend from glory to the Savior to minister to Him and serve Him on earth, pray to Him that He may forgive our sins and send us His grace."

4. Next the *Gloria in excelsis Deo* is said. Then we must sweetly praise Our Lord: "Most gentle and glorious God, may You be honored, may You be praised, may You be blessed, may You be worshiped, etc."

5. Then, we say the orisons to the saints and to Our Lady. We must pray to the

---

1. These rubrics do not occur in the MSS in this article, but we have introduced them here to divide the subject matter for clarity.

most kind Mother of God and to the saints that they may intercede for us, saying: "Most glorious Mother of God, who are an intermediary between your gentle Son and the repentant sinners, pray for me to your Child. And you, blessed saints whom we remember, help me, and pray with the Lady of the angels that God, by His grace, will pardon my sins and light my heart with His blessing."

6. After this the Epistle is read to remind us that a messenger approaches, bringing letters announcing the imminent arrival of the Lord of the world.

7. Next we sing the Gradual or the Alleluia or, during Lent, the Tract, and then the Sequence. This demonstrates that the heralds of the Lord's appearance sound their horns to gladden the hearts of those who await with hope the coming of the Sovereign Lord.

8. Then the Gospel is read, the truest and nearest messenger, for it represents the banners, the pennants, and the standard that proclaim with certainty that now the Lord nears. Everybody must keep silent and stand erect, directing their attention to hearing and remembering what the Gospel says. For these are Our Lord's own words, spoken to teach us how to live if we wish to be counted among the household of our Sovereign Lord. Thus, each person must listen attentively to these words of the Gospel and recall them.

9. Next follows the Offertory, during which we must deliver some item into the priest's hand as a sign of offering our heart to God, saying while giving the contribution: "Holy Trinity, receive my heart that I present to You; enrich it with Your grace."

10. After this, the priest turns to the congregation and requests our prayers; and we must pray assiduously for him, because he assumes our burdens and prays for us.

11. The priest then says *Per omnia secula seculorum* and then *Sursum corda*; that is, "Lift up your hearts to God," and the acolyte[2] and others reply, "We lift them up to the Lord." We must then prepare ourselves and focus our gaze upon the priest.

12. At this point, we sing the praise of the angels, that is, *Sanctus, Sanctus, Sanctus*. The angels then hover to arrange, encircle, and protect the table on which God will descend and by His look alone nourish His faithful. We expectantly await His arrival and must prepare ourselves the way good, loving subjects make themselves ready when the king enters their city. We must gaze at Him and receive Him in love and joy, thanking Him for coming, praising and blessing Him, and in our thoughts petition for remission and pardon for our past sins. For He visits us for three reasons: one, to pardon all things, if we are worthy; the 2nd, to give us His grace, if we know how to ask Him for it; the 3rd, to remove us from the path to hell.

---

2. The altar boy or cleric who assists the primary celebrant of the Mass.

13. Afterward comes the *Pater Noster* that teaches us to call Him Father; and we implore Him to forgive our trespasses just as we forgive those who have sinned against us. Further, we petition that He not abandon us to sin or temptation but that He deliver us from evil, Amen.

14. Next the *Agnus Dei* is said three times and we beseech God for mercy, and that He give us peace, which can be understood as peace between the body and the soul—that the body may be obedient to the soul—or peace between us and our enemies. And for this we receive peace.

15. We sing the Postcommunion and enjoin and entreat our Lord please not to withdraw from us, leaving us as orphans without a father.

16. We say the last orisons and depart, recommending ourselves to the Blessed Virgin Mary, asking her please to beseech her blessed dear Child to remain with us. When all is completed and the priest has removed his vestments, then we thank Our Lord for the sense and understanding to have heard His blessed Mass and seen His blessed sacrament, which is a reminder to us of His blessed Nativity and of His holy Passion and Resurrection. We ask Him, in persevering to the end, to give us true and total absolution. And then, dear one, make yourself solitary, your eyes turned toward the ground, your soul in heaven. At this moment scrupulously consider all your sins with your whole heart, in order to purge yourself of them and deliver yourself from them.

Confession

17. But to let you know henceforth how this will be done, I will now tell you a bit, according to what I know and believe. My dear, be assured that whoever wishes to confess his sins properly for the salvation of the soul, whether man or woman,[3] must know that three things are necessary: contrition, confession, and reparation.

18. He or she must know that contrition requires suffering of the heart with great moaning and repentance, and it befits the sinner most humbly and contritely to request pardon and mercy, fervently beseeching our Creator and Sovereign Lord to forgive that which could have angered or offended Him. The sinner must understand that without contrition, his prayer is worthless, because his mind and heart are elsewhere. My dear, take example from the one who was promised a horse for saying a *Pater Noster* if he could keep his mind free from

---

3. Through the use of both masculine and feminine pronouns and varieties of nouns, the author generally demonstrates that a sinner may be male or female, except for those instances where we note he singles out the female sinner (see ¶ 88 on gluttony). The grammatical construction indicating that both genders are sinners has no graceful English equivalent; thus we have had to use the English masculine construction in some places where both sexes are indicated.

anything else. While saying the *Pater Noster* he wondered whether the one who would give him the horse would also leave him the saddle, and the wretched one thus lost everything! So it is for someone who prays to Our Lord without thinking about his prayer or to whom he is praying. Indeed, by chance he has already committed something for which he deserves to be hung on the gallows of hell, yet he sleeps in this sin and ignores it. If he were judged in this miserable world by a petty provost to be hung on gallows of wood or stone or to pay a large fine, which is an even lesser penalty, and he thought he could avoid it by weeping and entreating the provost or judge, how he would beg him in all sincerity, with great weeping, moaning, and heartfelt contrition—single-mindedly! Nevertheless, he fails to weep sincerely or to beg the great Lord his Sovereign and his Creator, Who from the lofty windows of His Providence in heaven sees all the disposition of the sinner's heart! And the sinner knows well that Our Lord is so compassionate and merciful that for the smallest prayer—provided that it be from a contrite and repentant heart—He would have forgiven all, even if the judgment against the sinner had already been pronounced and the sinner condemned to death. This Lord can rescind and exonerate all things, but on earth no provost or judge, whatever tears and entreaties the condemned might make, can annul the judgment made against him. Consider, then, dear, this comparison! Yet it is far worse when the Sovereign Judge condemns a man to death, because He does not recall his sentence—that is, the torment of death is perpetual and eternal. But when a provost condemns a man, the torment of his death lasts only a moment. Therefore, dear, there is no comparison between the power of the judges or the pain of their judgments. So it is better, my dear, to weep and receive punishment and address one's entreaties to the One with sovereign and absolute power, rather than to the one who has only designated power within a specific earthly scope which he cannot exceed.

19. Because this Sovereign Judge in the end will examine and judge us, therefore, dear girl, what account will we render to Him of the goods of fortune and of nature[4] that He has placed in our care and that we have wantonly spent for our own use and pleasure, without having delivered or donated any to Him or to the wretched and patient poor who for His love and in His name asked us for some? If in this instance He accuses us that we have stolen from Him, what will we answer? *Item*: concerning our soul, the daughter that He gave us healthy and pure, without stain or spot, which we poisoned with the drink of mortal sin. If He accuses us of murder, saying that we have killed His daughter whom He surrendered to our care, what defense will we make? *Item*: for our heart, of which our body is the castle, which He placed in our safekeeping, and that we handed over

---

4. See ¶ 34 for the definitions of these gifts of fortune and nature.

to His enemy, the devil of hell, what excuse will we have? Certainly, dear one, unless the Blessed Virgin Mary His Mother serves as our advocate, I fail to see how we will escape being punished and chained eternally to the gallows of hell like thieves, murderers, and traitors by the good judgment of this sovereign Lord, if hot tears of heartfelt contrition do not now chase the enemy from us! But this can be done as easily as hot water chases the dog out of the kitchen.

20. After contrition comes confession, which has six conditions or it is meaningless. The first condition of confession is to make it wisely. That is, wisely in two ways. Since he requires a model to emulate, the sinner—male or female—must choose a prudent and worthy confessor, just as any ill creature desires his or her health, and to recover this health wants to find and procure the best rather than an inferior physician. Further, this sinner must consider that since every creature must wish for health of the body, that fleshly and transient material, all the more reason should he be anxious about the noble soul which is ordained to receive either perpetual good or eternal evil. Thus, he ought to select a virtuous, wise, and most excellent physician to recoup immediately the health of the wounded or ill soul. For if he mistakenly recruits one unable to provide the remedy to cure him, he will perish. You may see it by this example: when one blind man leads another, it is no surprise if they both fall into a ditch. Therefore, a sinner must provision himself with a sage and perceptive counselor, able to cure him and advise him about all of his sins. Such a confessor needs to be able to discern between one sin and another so as to give the cure. This confessor must direct all of his thoughts and understanding to hearing and comprehending the sinner's confession, and he must also wield the power of absolution. Then this sinner is compelled to recognize all of his offenses and to have contemplated them long and attentively, as I have said, so as to be able to report and recount them all in order, setting them forth both by type and by particulars to his confessor and counselor. He needs contrition in his heart for having committed sin, dread of Our Lord's vengeance, remorse for these sins, and a firm purpose to amend himself, never to return to sin. Rather, the sinner should hate sin as venom. He should willingly desire to receive and then to perform joyfully the penance that the confessor mandates for his cure in order to recover his soul's health.

21. The second condition of confession obliges you to make haste to confess upon falling into sin. For you do not know when God will take away your speech and health, so it behooves you to confess frequently. Beggars prove it often, who from day to day and hour to hour show their afflictions to good folk in order to have new alms; the wounded show from day to day their injuries to doctors to have each day a swift and new remedy. The sinner must also show and reveal his sin without delay to have a new cure and more complete mercy.

22. The third condition of confession requires that one confess entirely and

disclose everything at the same time, for it is crucial to reveal to the doctor the entire wound. We must report everything in great humility and repentance and not forget or omit anything. However serious and mortal the sin may be, it must pass through your mouth and out your lips. If the proud heart of the sinner cannot endure this, he must make the sign of the cross at his lips so that the enemy who obstructs the passage of speech departs. Then the heinous sinner must force himself to tell the filthy sin that destroys his soul. For if he waits longer, the delay will make him forget everything. He will thus never confess it and thereby will remain in such peril that by reason of this sin—in which he will remain and of which he will have no memory—and lacking God's divine grace, the sinner can perform no worthy act that will not be canceled in God's eyes. Consider that he could never obtain forgiveness by fasting, almsgiving, or by the arduous toil of pilgrimages when he has not completely confessed! Imagine how someone who has not genuinely confessed would dare receive his Creator! And should he not receive Him, how he deludes himself and in what peril he places himself! Perchance this time he hides this sin, thinking he will soon confess, and failing to consider God's power to take away his speech or to cause him to perish suddenly. Now, if it happens that way, he will be damned for his negligence, and on the Day of Judgment he will not know how to answer for it.

23. The fourth condition of confession is disclosing our sins in the order they are ranked by theology. They must be placed one after the other without transforming or confusing them, or putting the last one first, without adorning or disguising them, without defending ourselves, and without accusing others. The sinner must tell the circumstances of the sin: how he thought of it, what was the motivation for his thought; what next he pursued, performed, said, or provoked; the time, the place; why and how he perpetrated it; if the sin he committed agrees with or violates nature; whether it was done knowingly or unwittingly. The sinner must recount all the circumstances and conditions that could cause harm to his soul.

24. The fifth condition requires us to confess all of our transgressions at the same occasion, and to one confessor, not to several. We must not divide them up into two parts and tell one to one confessor and the other part to another; for a confession made maliciously like that would be invalid. Indeed, it would be a more serious sin, since you undertake to deceive your confessor who represents the person of Our Lord Jesus Christ.

25. The sixth condition stipulates making a devout confession with great humility, our eyes downcast, manifesting our shame and disgrace, with our thoughts and our heart's attention on heaven. For you must remember that you are speaking to God and must address your spirit and words to Him and request pardon and mercy. For He alone sees into the desires of your heart, not the priest who has only the ear.

26. Now you have heard, my dear, how to confess. But five things prevent con-

fession: shame about confessing the sin, fear of performing serious penance, hope of a long life, despair that our delectation in sin prevents us from abandoning it or repenting; and the thought that it serves no purpose to confess, since we immediately afterward fall into sin again—and this leads to perdition.

27. After confession comes satisfaction, made according to the judgment and counsel of the wise confessor. Penance is performed in three ways: by fasting, alms, or prayer, as you will hear below.

Examination of Conscience: The Seven Deadly Sins

28. I spoke earlier about three things necessary in confession—contrition, confession, and satisfaction. Then I showed and taught you, as well as I could, what contrition is, and afterward the nature of confession and how it must be made, and I touched a little bit on the five things that deter it. Please pay attention and remember it all at the proper time and place. Finally, I explained about penance. Now, so that you can examine your conscience, I will teach you in what ways you may sin. We will first consider the names and conditions of the Seven Deadly Sins that are so evil that to some extent all sins derive from them. They are called "deadly" or "mortal" because of the death that overcomes the soul when the enemy can occupy the heart with this work. So that from now on you can protect yourself from these sins, I will instruct you in the names and powers of the 7 virtues that are the opposites of the seven sins mentioned above. They are the proper remedies against these sins and so contrary to these sins that the presence of the virtue drives away the sin.

29. Here follow the names of the vices, which you can confess if you have erred. The names of the virtues come afterward, for you to continue to practice.[5]

Pride	is the sin, the opposite virtue is Humility
Envy	is the sin, the opposite virtue is Friendship
Wrath	is the sin, the opposite virtue is Kindness
Sloth	is the sin, the opposite virtue is Diligence
Avarice	is the sin, the opposite virtue is Generosity
Gluttony	is the sin, the opposite virtue is Temperance
Lust	is the sin, the opposite virtue is Chastity

30. Thus you have heard the names of the Seven Deadly Sins and the seven virtues that remedy them. Now on to the characteristics, first, of the seven sins, and then of their opposing virtues.

---

5. The opposing virtues described in medieval manuals of confession are derived from the allegorical poem *Psychomachia* (Battle for the Soul) of Prudentius (c. 400). Practicing these virtues was protection against temptation to commit the Seven Deadly Sins.

31. Pride is the root and origin of all other sins. The sin of pride has 5 branches.[6] That is: disobedience, vainglory, hypocrisy, discord, and entitlement.

32. Through disobedience a person loses God and neglects the commandments. In disobeying God, he follows the will of the flesh and puts his selfish desires above God and against reason. All this results from pride.

33. The second branch of pride is vainglory, which arises when a person is elevated by pride in either the evil or the good that he has done, is doing, or could do. But good or evil, these two things do not come from us; for the good that a creature does comes from God's goodness and grace. The evil comes from the wicked condition and nature of the creature insofar as he is attracted to the condition of the enemy, who is evil. Certainly, a person's honorable acts spring from the Providence of God, Who is good. Therefore, He alone deserves the honor and the glory, and the person performing the estimable deeds deserves the profit. On account of the evil, we must despise the enemy who attracts us and leads us to it through pride.

34. Pride's third offshoot is hypocrisy, which causes one to pretend on the outside to be virtuous on the inside. The hypocrite seems more full of good works and pious words than he actually is. When he senses that others think highly of him, he preens in pleasure and vainglory. This conceit is the devil's currency with which he buys all the beautiful merchandise in this world's market. The merchandise is the bounty that God has given to man and woman, that is, the gifts of nature, the gifts of fortune, and the gifts of grace. The good things of nature derive from the body: beauty, merit, fine speech, intelligence, and memory. The gifts of fortune are wealth, eminence, honor, and prosperity. The gifts of grace are virtue and beneficial works. The proud man sells all of this abundance to the devil for the false currency of vainglory. The winds of vainglory fell all these goods. Know that in these gifts of God's grace—virtue and good deeds, as was said— man or woman is tempted by the devil in three ways: the first when the creature rejoices in the good acts he performs, the next when the creature loves to be applauded for such works, and the third when the creature performs such right acts with the intention of being praiseworthy. Such hypocritical people resemble a foul, ugly, and stinking dung heap covered with a cloth of gold and silk to make it seem more valuable. In this way hypocrites cloak themselves with fineness on the outside in order to acquire friends, to have greater rewards or a more important office than they hold—and of which they are not worthy—and to gain such

---

6. The likely source for this section, the *Somme le Roy* of Friar Laurent, contains an elaborate metaphor of trees, twigs, and branches for the relationships of sins to one another. The narrator in our text uses "branches" for new varieties of sin but does not carry out the metaphor systematically. Thus, we substitute synonyms for some of the many repetitions of "branch."

endowments as others possess who are more admirable than they. From this it often follows that they desire and pursue the death of the one who holds the office that they covet, thus becoming like evil murderers as they dwell in such a vile hope without satisfaction. They then die in such foolish yearning and fry and burn in envious hope. They fall straight down into the frying pan where the devil makes the fritters of hell! Any good deed they did is thus lost and worthless, because it was done with bad intention. Alas! The false coin of pride from which this 3rd branch, hypocrisy, comes!

35. The 4th branch of pride is discord or strife, such that a person disagrees with others and wants what he does or says to be held as sound and true—whether it really is true or a lie—and seeks to discount as valueless the words of those wiser than he.

36. The 5th offshoot of pride is a sense of entitlement. That is to say, when the person does or says what no other would say or do, and selfishly wants to surpass others and be thought excellent in all things, for which he makes himself hated. For this reason they say that the proud man will never be without litigation, and so it is. All this stems from pride: disobedience, vainglory, hypocrisy, discord, and entitlement.

37. Any sinner must begin a confession to the priest in this way: "Father, since you are the vicar and lieutenant of God, to God Almighty and to the Blessed Virgin Mary and to all the saints in heaven and to you I confess all the sins I have committed in so many ways.

38. "First, concerning pride. I have been proud and vainglorious of my beauty, my strength, my praise, my excellent attire, and my physical skill.[7] In my demeanor I have been an example of the sin of pride to those who see me, and when others were not watching me, my thoughts dwelt on the strength that my descendents would inherit and also on my power, my wealth, my status, my friends, and my lineage, since it seemed to me that no one could compare to me in these things. Through different manifestations of this sin of pride I have fallen.

39. "The first branch of pride is disobedience. For through pride I have disobeyed God, and I have not borne Him honor or reverence as befits the Creator who made me and furnished me with the gifts of grace, of nature, and of fortune that I have betrayed and misused in the vanity and honors of the world, without recognizing or thanking Him or giving anything to the poor on His behalf. Rather, I held them in disdain and contempt, and because they appeared disfigured and stinking, I did not allow them to approach me but shrank from them so as not to see them. I did not show honor and reverence to my flesh and blood,

---

7. Here the author uses both the masculine and the feminine forms for the proud, emphasizing again that the sinner may be male or female.

especially my father and mother, who gave me life, and their successors, my natural brothers and sisters; or to my husband[8] and my other benefactors and superiors, or to my fellow brethren and sisters through Adam and Eve. For I valued no one beside myself. When people tried to assist me in being good and correcting the evil I had committed, I would not stand for it; rather I was indignant and scornful to them. And what is worse, I acted more viciously and haughtily toward them than before, accusing them behind their backs of shameful deeds. The vileness I spoke about them originated in pride's spawn, disobedience.

40. "Through vainglory, the second branch of pride, I avidly listened to the evil said of others, believed it and willingly repeated it, or spread an even more vicious version. Sometimes, in vengeance or wickedness, I gossiped about others and invented cruel stories. I puffed myself up and boasted of the malice I had told and done, glorying in it. If anyone said something within earshot about the excellence of my intelligence, repute, or beauty, though it was invalid, I did not protest its overstatement; rather, I remained silent in agreement and took great pleasure in it. I bragged and was conceited about my extravagant expenditures on overblown and excessive dishes, throwing large parties, decorating luxurious chambers, inviting high society to gatherings, offering jewels to ladies and lords and to their officers and retinue to gain praise from them and to have it announced of me that I was noble, valiant, and generous. Certainly, of the poor I had no thought. Indeed, Lord, I affirmed some things to be true of which I was most uncertain, and I did so to cater to those conversing with me. And all of this I did on account of vainglory.

41. "Through hypocrisy I pretended to be a holy man or woman and went to great pains to acquire a reputation for piety in public, whereas I never restrained myself from sinning, even largely, when it was possible to do so clandestinely. And of course, before folks, I gave alms to the poor and did penance, more to be noticed and praised than for God's grace. Also, in order to gain admiration, several times I feigned wishing to do a certain good deed, while in my heart I really did not wish to do it, despite knowing that this displeased my Creator. I also offered help to many people when I had neither the inclination nor the disposition. Furthermore, I thought pretty highly of myself, which was unwarranted. And if any little speck of goodness were in me, I failed to acknowledge that it came from God, as I have already said, nor was I thankful for it. This I did through hypocrisy with inordinate pride.

42. "I was obstinate in discord and strife, which is the fourth kind of pride. For if I decided to support anything or anyone, in order to uphold that person or to

---

8. At this point, however, the author does not say "or wife," so this prideful sinner is specifically feminine.

destroy another, I would take great pains in defending that side or in confounding the other person, whether right or wrong. I have sometimes damaged people when telling lies that I affirmed as true to oblige and please others. Contemptuously I have incited others to wrath, anger, and discord, from which evil consequences ensued, and I caused others to swear, perjure, and lie. By the dissension that I provoked and the lies that I declared to be truth, and the oaths and affirmations I caused, I scandalized and angered many people by my unseemly behavior.

43. "Sometimes when I did confess, I began my confession by making excuses for myself and thus discounted the blame for my sin. Or I placed the blame on another person, complaining that he had committed the fault of which I was the most guilty, not excusing myself, but saying 'so-and-so made me do it, and I was not paying attention,' confessing in this manner to exempt myself from sins that seemed to me too horrible. Moreover, I overlooked and kept back the enormous and terrible sins, and even regarding the slight and venial sins that I did confess, I failed to provide the circumstances belonging to those sins, such as the people, the time, and the place, etc. I have dwelled in sin for a long time, and through that sustained contact have fallen prey to other deadly sins. To one of my confessors [I spoke of my minor faults],[9] while to another, whom by chance I liked better, I confessed the more serious sins, intending to receive a lesser penance because of the relationship that we had.

44. "I desired vainglory in seeking honors, in craving to be attired just as well as the foremost citizens in the finest of clothing, and in other ways. I had the triumph of being honored by the most eminent people, having their goodwill, being grandly saluted, and receiving honor and reverence for my beauty, wealth, nobility, lineage, my elegance, beautiful singing and dancing, graceful laughter, playing, and speech. I sought to be the most honored everywhere and was gratified to be so considered.

45. "I readily listened to different instruments and melodies, charms, and other games that are ribald, dissolute, and neither godly nor sensible; I laughed and carried myself most arrogantly and frivolously.

46. "I sought to have and wreak vengeance and to punish even those whom I merely suspected of wanting to damage me, and I haughtily and meanly wished to have my desire accomplished, wrong or right, without pity.

47. "These things, dear Father, I did through my pride, and I repent. I ask you for pardon and penance."

48. Next, the sin of envy, originating in pride and taking 5 forms: hatred, con-

---

9. Lacuna in the MSS after "confessors"; Pichon supplies "I spoke of my minor faults," and this seems a reasonable reading.

spiracy, griping, detraction, and rejoicing in another's misfortune or resenting his good fortune.

49. Envy is born of the sin of pride, for a proud person does not want anyone to be like him. A man envies if another is the most eminent, or equally eminent, in anything such as in possessions, in graces, or in knowledge, or if the other person has more merit than he. This inflames him with hatred, and he always endeavors to lay claim to others' praise and favors through his words and accusations. Thus, the first branch of envy.

50. The second type of envy is conspiracy, which can be identified as a person speaking ill of and plotting against another out of resentment, and gossiping spitefully about one person to another out of bad habit, diminishing the good reputation of others and increasing their evil fame.

51. The 3rd kind is griping, when the heart grumbles because someone more powerful orders him around, or because of what is said to him, or because he is not treated the same as the others, but he dares not speak openly about it.

52. The 4th branch of envy is detraction or backbiting, when a person says nasty things about another behind his back, blabbing what he knows and what he does not know about him, and fabricating and imagining what he could say to hurt and distress the other. Should he hear scandal about this person, he does everything he can to multiply and enhance it, and speaks about it most seriously whenever he has occasion, because he knows of no better way to spread harm. The envious one grasps that the good reputation that he ruins cannot be recovered and could result in the suicide of the man he maligns.

53. Delight in the misfortune or difficulties of others, and using one's power to destroy the good that should go to another, makes up the 5th category of envy. Another's success brings the sinner sadness and woe.

54. Of these offenses you must say in confession: "Father, in all these things I have named, I have sinned greatly, for in my heart I thought it, and through my evil actions I did it, and from my false mouth I spoke it and sowed it where I could. If I said anything good about anyone, I said it halfheartedly and in deceit and always praised myself for it. To those whose welfare and honor I should protect—and could have protected if I cared to—I caused evil. When I heard folks spreading scandal, I put myself in their camp, in accord with the evil, and I consented to speak ill and to hold to it, with the power of my heart, my mouth, and my body. And, dear Father, I did all through envy, and I repent and I beg your forgiveness."

55. After envy comes the sin of wrath, which originates in envy. The sin of wrath has 5 forms: hatred, contention, presumption, indignation, and swearing.

56. Hatred is when one person cannot subjugate another or command and cast down the one that he would like to be superior to, over whom he would like

to have dominion and domination. This failure swells his heart with sadness and anger. That is the first branch of wrath.

57. The second type of wrath occurs in discourse, when a person has a heart bursting to speak and commit evil, and when he utters harsh and immoderate words out of wrath against another.

58. The 3rd type involves the kind of angry speech that provokes disputes, battles, and dissention. The person must ask himself whether anyone from his side or the other has had either his property or his person damaged by his words, for in that case the hotheaded one would be the cause of all the ensuing misfortune.

59. The 4th sort of wrath is offending God by swearing.

60. The 5th sort of wrath is when your anger causes you to incite anger in others.

61. And for all this you must confess this way: "Father, I have taken the name of God in vain in my wrath, and spoken ill of God and the Blessed Virgin Mary His sweet Mother, and of all the saints in Paradise. Furious with others, in my wrath I recanted my promises to them. In wrath I have angered and spoken disdainfully to my lord father and my lady mother; and in wrath I have looked at them evilly and desired their death. I have spoken most contemptuously to the poor and in wrath called them 'rabble.' Father, my wrath has provoked several people to swear most villainously and to use vulgar oaths. I have moved my servants, as well as many others, to anger, causing them to do wrong. I have contemplated revenge on those whom I despise and, given the opportunity, willingly would have harmed them, if I could have. For an immensely long time I have dwelled in hatred, for which I repent. And for this, dear Father, I beg of you pardon and penance."

62. Next is the sin of sloth, the fourth deadly sin, from which springs idleness, a most foul condemnation and stain in a person who would like to be good. For the Gospel says that on the Day of Judgment each idle person will have to account for the time lost through his indolence. It makes one wonder what defense the idle will use when they are accused before God! Another place in the Gospel says that an idle body is the mortal enemy of the soul. My lord Saint Jerome made this authoritative statement: "Always be doing something so that the enemy does not find you idle; for he makes the idle do his business." And my lord Saint Augustine said in the book *Of the Works of Monks*: "No man able to work should be idle."[10] It would take too long to recite the sayings of all the wise men who have condemned idleness and sloth!

63. The sin of sloth has six varieties. The first is negligence, then holding grudges, carnality, vanity of the heart, despair, and presumption.

---

10. Augustine's book from c. 401 concerns what labors monks should perform and inspired a chapter in the *Rule* of Saint Benedict.

64. Negligence exists when one loves, fears, and recalls God so little, taking no account of Him, doing no good deeds for Him or for love of Him. This shows laziness and negligence, although such a man is not ordinarily a bit indolent in seeking his own pleasure and comfort. Certainly, it is a serious sin to be slothful about doing good deeds, for Scripture mentions that if a person had never sinned, nor would ever sin, yet did not perform any good acts, but simply allowed time to pass, he still might go to perdition. This first branch of negligence is born of the sin of sloth.

65. The second branch is when a person holds a grudge in his heart against another and, because of the rancor that he bears toward the other, applies himself to revenge. He goes to sleep with it and stagnates in it, and thanks to this grudge he neglects to do his penance, alms, and other good deeds. The person who holds a grudge focuses day and night on harming the one he hates and only that. Thus he neglects to do the good that he should. And that is the second branch of sloth.

66. The third branch of sloth is carnality. Carnality seeks pleasure of the flesh, such as having a good bed, sleeping a long time, and lying abed late into the morning. In the morning, lounging in bed, a person hears the bells ringing for Mass and pays no heed, turning over and going back to sleep. Such weak and vain people would rather miss 4 Masses and nap than expend any sweat. Hence, the 3rd branch of sloth.

67. Vanity, the fourth sort of sloth, arises when a person knows well that he lives in a state of sin and yet is so vain of heart that he cannot, will not, or does not deign to return to God through confession and devotion. On the contrary, each day he promises himself to mend his ways, and yet he never does. Lazy and negligent about rectifying his life, he furthermore makes no effort to perform any meritorious acts or to keep God's commandments, as a good person must. And such is the fourth branch of sloth.

68. God despises despair, the fifth type of sloth, and someone caught in this sin is damned like Judas, who hanged himself in despair, for he thought he had offended God so greatly that he would never obtain mercy. Whoever dies in this sin has no hope of God's mercy; he sins against the Holy Spirit and against the goodness of God. Thus, no one must in any way fall into or remain in this sin of despair. For if you err and commit a great sin such as burning the houses and the property of the Holy Church by violence, which is a sacrilege, you do worse than if you committed all the Seven Deadly Sins. Yet I repeat that God's mercy overcomes any sin. Always, if you consent to confess, do penance, and return to God, even if you had committed viler evil than the tongue could speak or imagine or the heart conceive, you would find mercy in Him. And that demonstrates the fifth kind of sloth.

69. The sixth branch of sloth is presumption, when a person becomes so

reckless and proud that he believes that he could never be damned for any sin of his. Such people opine that God did not make them in order to damn them. Yet they need to understand that God would not be just if He presented Paradise to those who have not deserved it as well as to those who have. No just judgment would dole out to each the same as the other, for if that were the case no one would ever do good, since one who did not serve God at all would have the same recompense as someone who served Him. Certainly those who believe that way sin against the good justice of God, against His mercy and gentleness. For although He may be full of mercy, as I have said above, He is a just judge and we are all made to serve the Creator and do His will. In so doing we can possess and deserve the kingdom of Paradise—which is not the case for those who, in sloth, neglect to serve Him.

70. Therefore you who are slothful must confess to the types of sloth, saying: "Father, I have also erred in all kinds of sloth through my negligence. I was slow in the service of God, indolent and negligent in faith, yet diligent enough about the comfort of my living flesh. Out of sloth, I did not recall or put into practice what I heard in Scripture. In addition, I failed to thank God as was fitting for the spiritual and temporal goods that He bestowed on me, nor did I serve Him as I should have, following the graces and virtues He gave me. I did not say or accomplish the good that I could have said or done, and I was slow and lazy in the service of Our Lord, although I was attentive in worldly service. In addition, I better served and catered more to my own flesh than to my sweet Creator. I was most idle for a long time, from which ensued many bad things, evil thoughts, and reflections."

71. Next you must confess that when Mass was being sung, or any of the hours, or when you were in devotion, or saying your hours, you indulged in frivolous reflection and evil thoughts, which were profitless and thus harmful to you and your salvation. For this you must say: "Father, when I realized these things, I did not return to God or make my peace with Him as I should have. Moreover, when the divine service was being prayed I joked and chatted pointlessly in church about inappropriate subjects. Father, I even slept in church while others prayed to God! Sometimes I did not confess when my conscience pricked me and I recalled my errors; and similarly when I had the appropriate time and space I did not employ it to go to confession, but said to myself out of sloth, 'another time, another week, or another day,' and through such delays and negligence I forgot many of my sins. Finally, by negligence and sloth I overlooked the imposed penances.

72. "I did not set a good example for my people, for by my improper behavior, which they of course attended to since I was their overlord, I modeled for them the path of sin. Father, when I heard my people swear villainously, I did not reproach or chastise them; instead, out of sloth, I let it pass.

73. "Afterward, Father, when I went to confession, I did not beforehand reflect on the sins that I should tell. Thus, when I left confession I was deeper in sin than before, and what is worse, I did not have the diligence to return to my confessor but let time slip away.

74. "Sloth did all of this to me, in which I dwelled and kept myself, and of which I repent. And for this, dear Father, I ask your pardon and penance."

75. After the sin of sloth is avarice. Avarice is tightness, stinginess, along with the immoderate desire and zeal to acquire the goods of this world, rightly or wrongly, regardless of how. Yet a person's reason knows whether something is right or wrong. Certainly, avarice has many pupils, such as the executors of wills who enrich themselves, retaining the goods of the dead who showed them such love near the time of their deaths that they chose them above all others to take responsibility for their salvation. Yet after the death the executors gnaw on the flesh like tyrants, fattening themselves from their blood and possessions. Such are the pupils of avarice! Likewise evil lords, who through hefty fines deprive their poor subjects of their belongings; innkeepers and merchants, who sell their goods beyond a just price and employ false weights and measures; deceitful lawyers who consume the substance of simple men in lawsuits and trickery, tormenting them in the courts of great lords so much and for so long that they secure what they want from them, whatever it is.

76. Avarice, as it is said, is born of sloth, since when a person is slothful and negligent in seeing to his own welfare, through avarice he abandons and forgoes providing for himself. So, to restore his resources, the desire to rob and the will to take unjustly and unreasonably from others overcome him. You sin in avarice if you are rich and powerful and have ample material goods with no worry that your property will be exhausted, and nevertheless you do not donate to the needy when it is urgent, or if you do not return what belongs to another, either loaned or otherwise wrongly acquired.

77. Avarice has seven divisions: the first is larceny, the second plunder, the 3rd fraud, the 4th deception, the 5th usury, the 6th gambling, and the 7th simony.

78. When a person unjustly and by night takes something unbeknownst to or against the will of its owner, he commits larceny, the first kind of avarice.

79. The second branch of avarice is plunder, which means that a person seizes something from another and, once in possession of it, will not restore it to its rightful owner but greedily keeps and hides it because he likes it. If by chance he hears it mentioned, he will not reveal anything but secretes it so that no one can discover it.

80. The third branch of avarice is fraud, when a person by deception, by trickery, or by dishonesty, in the purchase or sale of an item, misrepresents its value to the person with whom he makes the transaction.

81. The 4th branch of avarice is deception, which happens when a person displays an object that looks fine on the outside, with no apparent flaws, and he neglects to mention any problems. He says, affirms, and swears that the object is fit and true, yet he knows full well that such is not the case. So do false merchants who put the most beautiful and best on top and the worst underneath and swear to the fine quality of the lot. Tricking people and making false oaths like this is the essence of deception.

82. Usury, the fifth variety of avarice, involves lending money in order to receive a larger sum in the long term, or selling grain or wine more dearly because of long-term credit. And likewise for other merchandise—which I will pass over for the present because usury is a very long and wicked topic.

83. In gambling, the 6th branch of avarice, one plays at dice to win money from another, and gambling includes much trickery, covetousness, greed, and deception—such as counting falsely, lending money for gain, as one might lend 12 deniers for 13 deniers. Many wicked oaths are spoken in gaming, such as swearing by God, Our Lady, and all the saints in Paradise, with much evil said and done. Therefore, one should refrain from gambling.

84. The 7th sort of avarice, simony, concerns buying or selling the sacraments of the Holy Church or prebends of churches. This sin might be committed by clerks and monks, but also by anyone paying insufficient tithes, doing penance poorly, failing to keep the commandments of the Holy Church, and distributing God's largesse unfairly.

85. The devil gives the avaricious man six commandments: the first, to keep watch over his own capital; second, not to loan it without interest or perform any good deed with it before death; 3rd, to eat alone and avoid generous gestures or alms; fourth, to restrain his household from eating and drinking up his substance; fifth, not to leave crumbs or leftovers; sixth, to strive diligently to accumulate wealth for his heirs.

86. Confess all these things that your conscience accuses you of, everything related to the sin of avarice for which you feel guilty, and enumerate them one after the other in the above order. At the end you must say: "Father, dear Father, I repent very deeply for all the sins I have mentioned committed through avarice, and I beg for pardon and penance."

87. After the sin of avarice comes gluttony, divided into two varieties: eating too greedily, and speaking debauchedly and immoderately.

88. The sin of eating and drinking to excess is the sin of the devil. We read in the Gospel that God gave the devil the power to enter the bellies of swine because of their gluttony, and the devil went in and led them to the sea to drown. He also inhabits the bodies of gluttons who lead a dissolute life, driving them into the sea of hell. God orders fasting, and the glutton responds, "I will eat." God says to go

to church and get up in the morning, and the glutton says, "I need to sleep. I was drunk yesterday. The church is not a hare, it won't run away!" When a glutton has with some trouble roused herself from sleep, do you know how she says her hours? Her Matins are: "Ha! What will we drink? Is anything left from last night?" Next she says for her Lauds: "Ha! We drank good wine last night!" Then she says her prayers in this way: "My head aches. I won't feel comfortable until I have had a drink." Certainly, such gluttony shames a woman, for she becomes ribald, coarse, and rapacious. The tavern indeed is the devil's church, where his disciples go to serve him and where he performs miracles. For when people go there, they arrive straight and well spoken, wise and controlled and of sound mind. Yet when they leave, they cannot stand upright or speak coherently. They are intoxicated and belligerent and return swearing, hitting, and challenging each other.

89. The other part of the sin of the mouth consists of speaking wantonly in many ways: idle words, boasts, flattery, perjury, quarrels, grumbling, rebellion, and accusations. No word is so insignificant that you are not accountable for it before God. Alas! How much did you say at Prime that you have already forgotten by Terce! Idle words are like the sails of a mill that cannot be silenced. Boasters and mills speak only of themselves.

90. The sin of gluttony, divided into two parts as I noted, has 5 varieties. The first is when a person eats before he should—that is, too early in the morning, or before saying his hours, or before going to church and hearing God's word and commandments. For every creature should have the good sense and discretion not to eat before the hour of Terce, unless compelled by illness, weakness, or another condition.

91. In the second branch of gluttony a person eats more frequently than he should, without needing to; for as the Gospel says: "Eating once a day is angelic, twice a day is human, and three, 4, or more times is bestial and not human."[11]

92. The third branch of gluttony is manifest when a person eats and drinks so much in a day that he is the worse for it; he becomes drunk and sick and must retire to bed in great pain.

93. In the fourth branch of gluttony a person eats his food greedily without chewing and gulps it down in great chunks. Scripture says of Esau, the firstborn of all his brothers, that he ate so rapidly that he nearly choked.

94. In the fifth branch of gluttony a person craves ultraluxurious fare, no matter how expensive. But he could restrain himself and do very well with much less, the better to help one, two, or more paupers. We read of this sin in the Gospel,

---

11. This quotation also appears in chapter 89 of *Livre du Chevalier de la Tour,* another French fourteenth-century conduct book for women, and in its English adaptation, Caxton's *The Book of the Knight of the Tower,* ed. Offord, 120. It is not scriptural.

where the wicked rich man dressed in purple ate abundantly every day while never doing any kindness for the poor leper. And we learn that he was damned for his lavish living, for he contributed nothing in God's name as he should.

95. You must confess the above in this way: "Father, in all these things and in many others I have manifestly and many times sinned, and I have committed countless other sins and occasioned sin in others. I have often drunk when not thirsty, causing my body to be less controlled and ill disposed. I lost my reserve and spoke excessively and coarsely, and others, by following my example and being in my company, sinned more than they would if I were not present. I often consumed food when I was not hungry or in need, and when I could have managed with less. Sometimes I ate so heavily that my body suffered, and my nature was rendered groggy, weak, and too indolent to undertake good deeds. And all this came from the sin of gluttony, in which I offended as I have said. For this, dear Father, I repent and beseech your pardon and penance."

96. Then comes the sin of lust, born of gluttony. For when the wicked man has eaten and drunk well past satiety, the limbs adjacent to the belly heat up and provoke him to this sin. Immoderate thoughts and evil reflections proceed from this point, and then from the thought one moves to the deed.

97. Lust has 6 kinds: the first happens when a man thinks about a woman or the woman about a man, taking exceeding pleasure in the thought, delighting in it and dwelling on it. Because of this prolonged contemplation, the flesh arouses itself to delectation. However, if, when the first agitation came on unawares, he compelled his feelings to resist and oppose it, there would be no sin. But when the person does not resist or react against it as soon as he should and could, when he has neither the will nor the intention to turn his feelings elsewhere or resist, but persists and luxuriates, he sins mortally.

98. The second kind of lust is when the person consents to commit the sin and not only thinks of it but does everything in his power to find the time, the hour, and the place where he can act on it. Should he be unable to accomplish it, nonetheless he enjoys great pleasure in his heart, although carnally he has not committed the act. God says in Scripture: "What you want to do and cannot do is counted as done." And in another place in Scripture it says: "The intention counts as a completed act, whether good or bad." The first and 2nd branches are called lust of the heart. For there are two types of lust: lust of circumstance or lust of the heart, which are explained above, and lust of the body, which designates the accomplishment of the deed.

99. In the 3rd branch of lust unmarried persons—a man has no wife, a woman no husband—sin together, having relations with a man or woman to whom they are not bound. This is the sin of fornication.

100. The 4th sort of lust, adultery, occurs when a man has a wife and a woman

a husband, and they break the vow they owe to and promised to keep to their mates. They both sin and, even worse, could create false heirs who would succeed them.

101. The fifth sort of lust ensues when a man or woman has carnal relations with his cousin, or other relative close or far, or his mother, or a relative of his wife (or the wife has relations with someone from her husband's line), or with a nun, consecrated or not, or during the vigils of feasts, or in times of fast or feast days, or on the day when a husband must not go near his wife or any other woman (for that would be a more serious sin, which God defends in his law), or when a man lies with his wife or others in a way that is not permitted, shamefully and outside of what reason indicates in a marriage. For a man can sin greatly and in many ways with his own wife. Thus, Isaac says in Scripture that a man commits the sin of fornication through immoderation with his wife by having relations out of fleshly desire, for his sole delight, without the hope of procreation, or when he does it in a holy or sacred place. For this reason the devil strangled Sarah's 7 husbands.[12]

102. Sins against nature constitute the 6th kind of lust, such as defiling oneself in sodomy. For that sin, as we read in Scripture, God took such vengeance that five cities in Sodom and Gomorrah were destroyed and burned by rains of fire and stinking hell-flames. One should not discuss this sin at length because of its abomination. Even the devil himself, who pursues this sin, feels ashamed when people commit it. A person performs this sin also when he defiles himself all alone while awake, knowing well that it is against nature, or through improper and indecent touching that arouses the person, or in any other manner which is not fitting to speak of except in confession. Each soul knows this well and must know that it transgresses against God and nature, for when he commits such sins, his heart and mind clearly tell him.

103. Therefore the sinful creature must humbly enumerate to his confessor all of his sins in these matters, then ask pardon and say: "I offended in these sins, on great feast days, on vigils, and perhaps the vigils of Our Lady, on feasts or in Lent or in holy places such as in church." He should indicate whether it was one time, twice, or more, and which sins were more frequent than others. At the end he must say: "Dear Father, I erred and fell as I have said into the sin of lust. I truly repent and beg your pardon and penance."[13]

---

12. A confused reference to the *Somme* and *Genesis*. Asmodeus slew seven suitors of a woman named Sarah (Tobit 3: 7–8).

13. BF and BF/Ueltschi editions go directly to ¶ 104 but in the notes give the rubric that MSS B and C have here: "Afterward follow the names and conditions of the 7 virtues, virtues by which one can protect himself from mortal sin. First: . . ." MS A has a blank space here, the height of nine lines, obviously left for a rubric.

104. Humility is contrary to pride. For just as pride arises from a wicked, arrogant, and contemptuous heart causing the body and soul to be humiliated, lost, and suffer death, so also is humility born of a compassionate heart and gains the body honor in this world and eternal joy for the soul. Humility therefore is compared to the Virgin Mary. Pride is allied to folly, insolence, fury, short temper, disloyalty, reluctance to do good deeds, the arrogant intention to falsely judge another, and to several other wicked varieties of the sin of pride that you can have heard about above. But opposed to pride is the consideration to listen well, the strength of heart to bear burdens gracefully, and the justice to accomplish God's will without harming others or their works.

105. Here are 4 thoughts to encourage humility to join you and dwell within you, preventing pride from entering: first, you must consider the vileness and filth of sin in which you were begotten; second, your state of dismal privation without a soul, until God by His grace awoke you; third, how you exist in such distress and your death will come about unannounced; fourth, habitually recollect what joy and merit you will earn from doing good, and what pain and damage arise from doing wrong. Because decent acts gain you praise and honor in this world, after death you enter into eternal joy without sadness, riches without poverty, and well-being without illness. On the contrary, malicious acts that you commit with considerable effort and cost result in the contempt of this world, and in the next you will have sadness and perilous pain without joy, poverty without comfort, disease without remedy. Consider where your soul will travel on that unforeseen day of your death! Recognize that the passage of days and nights consumes your allotted time. So attend to how heedlessly you have spent your life, since from now until your death you are accountable for each hour. Recognize your time wasted in many contemptible sins. Note that you have done no beneficial works, and if by chance you have, they were enacted while in a state of mortal sin and so will not garner you a shred of profit.

106. Friendship remedies the sin of envy. For just as the sin poisons and burns the heart of the envious, as you have heard above, the holy virtue of friendship, the gift of the Holy Spirit, makes the heart humble and apprehensive; and therefore it is called the gift of dread.[14] The virtue of friendship is a sweetness, a drop

---

14. BF (290) note that the author telescopes Friar Laurent's *Somme le Roi* discussion of the preceding virtue of humility and transposes it into this section; the *Somme* has humility born of the virtue of holy dread and opposing pride. See the fourteenth-century English *Book of Vices and Virtues* which says "þe ȝifte of drede is þe first of alle þe ȝiftes þᵗ casteþ out al synne of a mannes herte or a wommanes, as we han seid tofore. But propreliche he destroieþ þe rote of pride, and sett in his stede þe vertue of humblenesse" (125–26). In the sections

of dew, and an antidote against envy. Just as the envious man feels always despondent and aggrieved about another's good fortune, so the fine heart filled with friendship rejoices in his neighbor's blessings and worries over and feels compassion for his adversaries. The virtue of friendship eliminates envy from the heart and makes man content with what he has. Affection drives out any resentment over a friend's riches and luck.

107. The virtue of friendship reveals itself in seven ways, just as the different parts of the body make their concern for the whole known in 7 ways. First, each limb is careful not to hurt another. This commandment is written: "Do not do unto others what you would not like done to you." Next, one limb tolerates the other tenderly, for if one hand hurts another, the other will not take revenge. Thereupon appears the great love and kindness that the parts of the body have for one another, since they are not upset about what one part does to another, nor do they desire or envy anything the others possess or do. They assist each other as needed, without being asked. All the limbs aid their lord, the heart. This is perfect charity without envy; it is complete obedience and brotherly love. Thus you must show this same pure friendship for your neighbor who is as your limb, for we are all limbs of God, and He is the body. In the Gospels, God provides heaven to the poor and earth to the kind and gentle. Consider then where the envious and vicious will be, if not in the torments of hell.

108. Kindness works against wrath. The holy virtue of kindness or moderation ever seeks peace, equity, and justice, without wronging anyone, without angering or hating anyone. Just as anger may compare to the fire that wastes all the goods in the house of the wicked heart, so also benevolence is the precious cure that brings peace everywhere and desires impartiality and fairness. Equity has eight steps that are important to note, by means of which the peaceful righteous man perceives the snares and tricks of the devil, who sees us although we do not see him, and who tests us fiercely in more than a thousand ways. The devil is a philosopher: he knows a man's state and character and temperament, and to which vice he is more prone either by nature or habit, and there he assails most vigorously. He fuels the choleric with anger and discord, the sanguine with debauchery and lechery, the phlegmatic with gluttony and sloth, the melancholic with envy and sadness. From such attacks each person must defend himself where his castle is weakest and fight against the vice most assailing him. The kind person spreads peace everywhere. Peace vanquishes all malice and ire. Without peace, no one can have victory. Saint Paul says that all the other virtues race with peace, but peace runs best, because it wins

---

that follow, the author has considerably abbreviated the *Somme,* resulting in some evident confusion.

the sword.[15] All the virtues compete, but peace has the victory, the honor, and the crown. All the virtues serve, but this one wins the prize. Justice is the armor of peace, which vanquishes all, as was said. Although the knight be armed with peace and justice, he needs a repentant heart, true confession from the mouth, and sufficient atonement. If one of these three is lacking, the armor is faulty, and he who wears it is defeated and vanquished and relinquishes the reward of Paradise.

109. Prowess, as worthy as diligence, is a holy virtue against the sin of accidie and sloth. For just as the bourgeois stays awake all night to acquire riches for himself and his children, the knight and the noble man are vigilant to acquire fame and glory in this world. Each one according to his estate pursues worldly goods. Alas! How few there are who seek to acquire spiritual goods! The virtuous folk without vainglory, who disown the world and desire to come before God, in their wisdom despise the world because of its host of perils and torments. It's a forest teeming with lions, a mountain overrun with serpents and bears, a battle full of treacherous enemies, a ghostly valley of tears, with no stability. No one trusting and delighting in the world has peace in his heart and conscience. The virtuous who are world-weary offer their hearts directly to God, their destination, and scorn earthly chattel. Few persevere in this immense and worthy undertaking.[16] Jesus Christ says: "All the other virtues compete: this one has earned the victory; they all toil, but this one carries away the prize in the evening."

110. Mercy or charity counteracts avarice. For the merciful have sorrow and compassion for another's misfortune, need, or poverty, and they help, counsel, and comfort him with all their might. In the way the devil proffers his commandments to the miser, as you have heard, so also the Holy Spirit has his own commandments to tender to the merciful and charitable folk, directing them to have contempt for temporal things, give alms, clothe the naked, give drink to the thirsty, food to the hungry, and visit the sick. Also, as the miser is the spawn of the devil and resembles him, so the charitable person has God as his father. Just as avarice schemes day and night about acquiring and amassing, whether rightly or wrongly, so charity and mercy attend to accomplishing the Seven Works of Mercy. Alas! How right it is to contemplate and then realize them in actions, or in intention and compassion, if one can. For our great Judge will sentence us on Judgment Day, the fear of which should inspire us to charity most forcefully.

---

15. A garbled version of the *Somme*'s notion of the necessity of perseverance (not peace), as BF (290 n. to p. 41) note, the confusion is amplified by employing the passage later (in ¶ 109) referring to prowess and conflating two scriptural allusions.

16. This abridgement of the *Somme* passage, rather than extolling the valor and values of the knightly class over those of the bourgeoisie, on the contrary equates the two groups in the false pursuit of worldly vanities (BF, 290 n. to p. 42).

Then God will say to misers: "Go hence with the devil your father!" and to the charitable: "My sons, reside with me." Alas! What great anguish to come when he dismisses the sinners from his company.

111. Mercy has seven branches: the first, to give sustenance to the poor; the second, to clothe the naked; the third, to lend to paupers in their need and to forgive the debt; the fourth, to visit the sick; the fifth, shelter the homeless; the 6th, visit those confined by illness;[17] and the 7th, bury the dead. Do these things out of charity and compassion, for the love of God alone and without conceit. Cheerfully, rapidly, discreetly, devoutly, and humbly give alms of your own lawful possessions, without contempt for the needy in thought or in deed. He does well who provides for them when requested, but he does even better who provides for them without needing to be asked.

112. Temperance remedies gluttony. For just as the holy virtue of temperance is the countermeasure against the mortal sin of gluttony, it is also the virtue that the gift of wisdom bestows and plants in the glutton's heart to protect against excess. Sobriety is a very precious tree, sheltering the life of the body and the soul. For one dies by eating and drinking too much; excessively wicked speech makes the head ache and slays the body and soul. Through temperance the body lives long and peacefully in this world, and the soul has eternal life.

113. This virtue must be maintained above all the others because of the good it works. First, temperance guards reason, understanding, and intelligence. Without his wits, the drunken man, so sodden with wine that he loses reason and understanding, becomes a beast. He thinks he drinks the wine, but the wine drinks him. Second, temperance delivers the gluttonous man from bondage to the belly. Saint Paul says that he who loses his freedom and becomes serf to a lord debases himself immensely. But the person enslaved to his belly, from which exits only filth, degrades himself far more. Temperance keeps a man under his own governance, for spirit and sense must rule the body, and the body must serve the spirit. Through drunkenness and gluttony the glutton abandons sense and spirit to the point that he cannot control his body. Third, temperance guards well the castle's entrance so that the devil does not enter man's body through mortal sin. The devil enters the castle through the mouth to battle the virtues, through the treachery of the false lords Gluttony and Evil Tongue, who leave the door of the mouth ajar for the devil.

114. This virtue has lordship over the body, for the body is mastered through temperance just as the horse is mastered by the bridle. Temperance commands

---

17. Theologically, this work of mercy should be to visit the incarcerated and help them to be delivered if you can. BF find the emendation "more relevant to his wife's circumstances" (291), but it may be a misreading or a scribal eye skip.

the first battalion of the army and guards over the other virtues. The devil tempts man through the mouth, just as he did Jesus Christ, when he told Him to make bread of stone, and Adam, when he compelled him to partake of the fruit. Compared with other creatures, man has a smaller mouth relative to his body. His other members are double—two ears, two nostrils, and two eyes—but he has only one mouth. That reveals to us that man must eat, drink, and speak soberly.

115. Temperance consists of nothing other than moderation, the median between too much and too little. Above all things, man must have measure in his heart and mind, just as the bird governs itself by means of sober eyes. He flies away but often falls into the fowler's, that is, the devil's, net, who hunts the bird constantly.[18]

116. Chastity operates against lust. The holy virtue of chastity keeps the conscience completely pure of evil thoughts and the body's members pure of all touch. Creatures filled with the vile sin of lust have consciences teeming with and bedeviled by evil thoughts. Their body parts are filthy and vile from evil touch, and God considers them, like the devil, ugly and dark. The chaste, on the other hand, have clear, clean, and shiny hearts and consciences and possess the brightness and light of God.

117. As you have heard, it is proper that the chaste have a spotless conscience. For such a clear conscience three things are required: the first is to listen willingly to the things of God; the second, to confess to Him often and fully; the third, to recollect the Passion of Jesus Christ and the reason He died, remembering that you cannot escape from death. That is the first degree of chastity. In the second degree of chastity you refrain from speaking coarsely, for such words corrupt good morals. The third degree is vigilance over the 5 bodily senses: keeping the eyes from wanton gaze, the ears from immodest listening, the nostrils from overmuch relishing of delectable odors, the hands from impure touching, and the feet from entering evil places.[19] These are the five doors and windows through which the devil comes to steal chastity from the castle of the soul and of the weak body. The fourth degree consists of fasting and keeping always before you the remembrance of death, which can so suddenly seize the unwary and drag them off forever. The fifth degree requires fleeing from wicked companions, as did Joseph who fled when the woman tempted him.[20] For the sixth degree, you need to busy

---

18. Neither BF nor Pichon provides a clear reading of this passage, but BF suggest that the eyes of temperance are the master's, as in hawking, where a bird is controlled and not free-flying.

19. Usually, the last of the five senses is taste, but including the feet here may be absentminded, as BF (291) note, or a recollection of the last rites, where the feet are anointed as well as the hands. See also the beginning of the Melibee story, 1.9.

20. Potiphar's wife in Genesis 39: 7.

yourself doing good works, because when the devil finds anyone idle, he is eager to lure him to his evil business. The 7th degree is true prayer. For prayer, three things are necessary: sincere faith, hope that the prayer will be answered, and single-minded devotion of the heart without wayward thoughts. Prayer without devotion is a messenger without letters. In prayer God looks for a humble and devout spirit and ignores the adornments or haughty bearing of those bold, frivolous women who go about impertinently, their necks stretched out like a stag in the woods, looking around recklessly, like a bolting horse.

118. And that, my dear, is enough on this subject. For anything more, the natural sense that God has furnished you, your desire to be devout and honorable toward God and the Church, the preachings and sermons given in your parish and elsewhere, the Bible, the *Golden Legend,* the Apocalypse, the *Life of the Fathers,* and various other good books in French that I possess, and that you are free to take at your pleasure, will help you and draw you profoundly to what remains, whenever God, who wishes to lead and inspire you to these things, decides.

¶ 1.4 *On Chastity*

1. The fourth article of the first section states that you must remain continent and live chastely. I am certain that you will do so. I have no doubts about it, but because I appreciate that after you and me this book will fall into the hands of our children or our friends, I choose to include all kinds of things that I know. Indeed you must instruct your friends, and especially your daughters, and tell them, lovely lady, that it is a certainty that all qualities are diminished in a maiden or woman who lacks virginity, continence, or chastity. Neither wealth, nor beauty, nor intelligence, nor noble lineage, nor any other excellence can ever erase a reputation for vice, particularly in a woman, if she has committed it once, or even been suspected of it. So for this reason many honorable women have kept themselves not only from the act but especially from suspicion, so that they might have the title of virgin.

2. Regarding this term, the holy writings of Church Fathers Saint Augustine, Saint Gregory, and many others state that all honorable women, past, present, and future, whatever is or was their condition, can be deemed and called virgins. Saint Paul confirms this in the 11th chapter of his second letter to the Corinthians: *Despondi enim vos,* etc. "I want you to know," he says, "that a woman married to a man, if she lives chastely, without thinking of having relations with another man, can be called a virgin and presented to Our Lord Jesus Christ." Jesus Christ also says about every virtuous and honorable woman, in a parable in the 13th chapter of the Gospel of Saint Matthew: *Simile est regnum celorum thesauro abscondito in agro,* etc.; "The kingdom of heaven is like the treasure that lies in a field, a treasure that a man, while working and digging in the field, discovers and then hides with great joy, then goes away and sells everything he has and buys the field." In this same chapter Our Lord recounts the parable: "The kingdom of heaven is like a merchant seeking precious gems who, when he finds a good and valuable one, goes out and sells everything he has and buys it." By the treasure found in the field and the gem we can understand every virtuous woman, because whatever her estate—maiden, married, or widowed— she can be compared to a treasure and a jewel, because she is so virtuous, so pure, so spotless that she pleases God, and he loves her like the Blessed Virgin, whether her estate be married, widowed, or maiden. And be assured, no man, no matter his rank, noble or not, can have a better treasure than a principled and modest wife. This we can know well and prove by examining the acts, seemly manners, and pious works of the glorious ladies who lived in the time of the Old

Law, such as Sarah, Rebecca, Leah, and Rachel, who were wives of holy patriarchs: of Abraham, Isaac, and Jacob, who is called Israel. They were all chaste and lived unsullied and virginally.

3. *Item,* on this matter we find written in the 13th chapter of the book of Daniel that after the Babylonian migration (that is, after Jechonias king of Jerusalem and the people of Israel had been led to prison and captivity in Babylon and the city of Jerusalem had been destroyed by King Nebuchadnezzar), there was in Babylonia a rich Jewish gentleman named Joachim. Joachim took as his wife the daughter of another Jew named Belchias. The maiden's name was Susanna. She was very beautiful and God-fearing, because her father and mother, who were just and decent people, had raised her well and instructed her in chastity according to the law of Moses.

4. This Joachim, husband of Susanna, was wealthy and had a lovely garden full of fruit trees. The Jews went there often to enjoy themselves because the place was more respectable than all others. Susanna herself went often to delight in that garden. It happened that two priests of the Old Law were made judges for one year by the people. These judges saw Susanna, so very comely that they were ignited by consuming passion for her. Together they conferred to devise a way to deceive her, and they agreed that they would follow her into the garden and speak to her if they found her alone.

5. One afternoon the judges were idling in a corner of the garden. Susanna came into the garden to wash herself, in accordance with their law, bringing two of her maidservants, whom she sent back into the house to get oil and ointments for anointing herself. When the two old men saw her alone, they hastened to her and whispered, "Suffer what we want to do with you. If you don't do it we will testify against you and say we discovered you in adultery." When Susanna saw and recognized the evil of the judges, she steeled herself and said, *Angustie michi sunt undique.* "My God," said she, "I am trapped, because if I do this, I will be dead to God, and if I don't do it, I won't be able to escape from their hands without being tortured and stoned. But better that I fall into their trap, without committing a wrong, than to sin before God." Then she screamed loudly. The two old men cried out also, so much that the servants ran out of the house. The judges said that they had found her in the very act of sin with a young man who was strong and vigorous and so had escaped. They didn't know him, nor could they recognize him. The servants were deeply troubled and astounded by this because they had never heard such accusations against their lady, nor had they ever seen any evil in her.

6. Nonetheless, she was imprisoned, and the next day the judges sat in judgment. All the people assembled before them to see the extraordinary event of Susanna brought to trial. Her family and friends, crying tenderheartedly, watched

her. Susanna had covered her head out of shame and humiliation. To her great mortification and despair, the judges made her uncover her face. Weeping, she lifted her eyes to heaven, for she had confidence in Our Lord and in the rightness of her own innocence. The two priests recounted before the people how, while enjoying themselves in the garden, they had seen Susanna arrive with the two maidservants, whom she sent away and then barred the door after them. They said that a young man then arrived, whom they saw lie with her carnally. That was why they rushed toward the pair and the young man fled through the door. They were able to stop and seize only Susanna, who refused to name the young man. "Of this misdeed we are both witnesses, and for this misdeed we condemn her to death." Susanna then cried out and said, "Eternal God, you know all secret things and all things as they occurred, and you know that they bear false witness against me. Remember this and have mercy on me!"

7. After this they led her off to her torment, and as they passed along a road Our Lord empowered the spirit of a small child named Daniel, who began to shout with a loud voice, "O people of Israel, this woman has been judged falsely! Return to judgment! Return! For the judgments are false!" Then the people clamored and had Susanna returned to the place where the judgment had been given, and they brought in the judges and the child named Daniel, who pronounced these words: "Separate these judges for me, and lead one here and the other there." When this was done he went to one and asked him under which tree he had seen the man and Susanna committing their sin, and this judge responded, "Under an oak." After this, Daniel went to the other judge and asked him beneath which tree he had seen Susanna lying under the young man, and he responded, "Under a tree called *lentiscus*." Lentiscus is a tree that gives oil; its root is the spice called mace. In that way their lie was discovered, and Susanna was set free as pure and clean without the stain of evil contact. It is well proven that she was full of the virtue of chastity when she said to the judges, "I prefer to fall into your hands, the hands of my enemies, and die without sin than sin before God Our Lord."

8. O woman full of faith and great loyalty, who so greatly feared God and the sin of violating marriage that she preferred to die rather than let her body be touched basely! Certainly it is true that the Jews, men and women, who currently live in this realm hold this sin in such horror that if a woman were found in adultery she would be stoned and tortured with stones until death, according to their law.[1] Since even the wicked keep this law, we must keep it also, for it is a good law.

---

1. The Jews were banned from France in 1394 by royal edict. Pichon and BF cite this passage as evidence that the *Le Ménagier* text was compiled before that date.

9. There is another example, which Cerxes the philosopher includes in his book *Of Chess* in the chapter about the queen.[2] He says that the queen must above all things protect her chastity and instruct her daughters likewise. For, he declares, we read about many girls who have been queens because they kept their virginity or maidenhood. Paul, historian of the Lombards,[3] recounts that in Italy there was a duchess named Raymonde who had a son and two daughters. It happened that Cantamus, the king of Hungary, quarreled with this Raymonde and came before one of her towns and laid siege to it. She and her children were in the castle, and at one moment she looked out and saw her enemies skirmishing with the people of her town, who were fiercely defending themselves, and among the enemies she saw an exceedingly handsome knight. She so burned with love for him that she sent word to him that she would deliver the town to him secretly, through her castle, if he would take her as his wife. The knight agreed, after which she opened the gates of the castle for him and he and his men entered.

10. Once they were within the castle, his soldiers marched through it into the town, taking men and women and pillaging all that they could. Her sons were so deeply shamed and pained by her treason that they abandoned her. Subsequently, they were so estimable that the youngest of these children, Grimault, became duke of Benevento and afterward king of Lombardy.

11. The daughters, who were unable to flee, were so afraid of being raped by the Hungarians that they killed pigeons and hid them beneath their breasts, so that from the warmth of their breasts the flesh of the pigeons stank. When the Hungarians attempted to get near them, they smelled the stench and their desire cooled and they let them be, saying to one another, "Fie, how these Lombards stink!" In the end, these maidens fled by sea to safeguard their virginity, and in later years, because of this good act and their other virtues, one became queen of France and the other queen of Germany.

12. As for the knight, he took the duchess and had his pleasure with her for

---

2. The name Cerxes comes from Jean Freron's 1347 translation of *Solacium ludi scacchorum* by Jacobus de Cessolis, called *Moralitez sur le jeu des eschés,* a collection of sermons on the duties of persons in various social ranks. Each rank is represented by a chess piece.

3. BF have "Pelistongraphe des Lombars" as in MS B. Here we follow the more likely reading, Pichon's "Pol istoriographe des Lombars," in MSS C and A. Paul the Deacon, Lombard historian and poet (Paulus Diaconus, 720–c. 799) from a noble Lombard family, was a monk in the monastery of Monte Cassino, became part of the entourage of Charlemagne (782), and later returned to Monte Cassino, where he may have died. The unfinished history of the Lombards, *Historia gentis Langobardorum,* is his most important work and was in use until well into the fifteenth century. See *History of the Langobards by Paul the Deacon,* trans. Wm. Dudley Foulke (Philadelphia: University of Pennsylvania Press, 1974), and the entry in the *Catholic Encyclopedia.*

one night to respect his oath, and the next day he gave her to all the Hungarians to share. The following day he had her impaled on a post from her groin to her throat, saying, "The wanton woman who for her lust betrayed her city and delivered her people into the hands of her enemies deserves such a husband." He also had these words written on her garments in several places. When she was completely dead, he tied her corpse to the outer bars of the city gate for all to gaze upon, and he left her there.

13. Cerxes provides in his book another example of how to protect marriage and chastity, referring to Saint Augustine who in the book of the *City of God* narrates (and I have also seen it in Livy) that there was in Rome a most good lady of great and virtuous temperament named Lucretia, whose husband, a Roman named Collatinus, once invited the emperor Tarquin the Proud and his son Sextus to dinner. They dined and were celebrated as guests of honor, and after dinner they relaxed. Sextus studied the countenance of all the ladies, and above all the others, he preferred Lucretia's bearing and beauty.

14. A short while afterward, the people of a castle four leagues from Rome rebelled against the emperor, who then traveled to besiege them, accompanied by his son Sextus and several of the young men of Rome, including Collatinus, Lucretia's husband. One beautiful, clear day during this long siege, the emperor's son Sextus together with several of the young Romans and Collatinus were assembled, drinking after their midday meal. They plotted among themselves to sup immediately and then hasten to Rome to each man's house, to discover the behavior, demeanor, and governance of each of their wives. The one whose wife was found in the most reputable and blameless circumstances would have the honor of lodging Sextus, the emperor's son, in his house.[4]

15. This scheme was agreed upon, and they went to Rome, finding there some ladies gossiping, some playing bric, others playing hot cockles, others "pinch me," others at cards and diverse pastimes with their neighbors. Some who had dined together were singing songs, telling fables and tales, and asking riddles. Others were in the road with their neighbors playing blind man's bluff, bric, and other similar games. Except for Lucretia who, within the innermost chambers of her house, in a large room far from the road, sat alone and apart, a short distance from her wool workers, holding her book devoutly and with bowed head saying her hours humbly and piously. Neither then nor any time when her husband Collatinus was away, in whatever company or celebration she was, had man or

---

4. This theme of the testing of wives appears in many instances in the rest of the text, with men vying with each other to shame their peers by finding whose wives were either of easy virtue, haughty, or defiant, thus showing that the husband could not control his household. See article 1.6 below.

woman seen her dance or sing, except on the day when she received letters from him or when he returned to see her. At those times she sang and danced with the others, if there were a feast.

16. Collatinus, therefore, had the honor of receiving and lodging in his home Sextus the emperor's son, who was served and treated like a relative by all the others and their wives. Early the next morning he was awakened by the ladies and dressed, heard Mass, and then the ladies watched the men mount their horses and ride off. On this journey Sextus was greatly smitten with love for Lucretia, so deeply that he planned to return to her accompanied by other people who were not friends of hers or her husband's.

17. He did just that, arriving one evening at Lucretia's house. She received him honorably, and when the moment came to retire, they prepared a bed for Sextus suitable for the emperor's son. But this evil emperor's son observed where Lucretia slept, and after everyone was in bed asleep, Sextus went in to her, placing one hand on her breast and the other on his sword, and said to her, "Lucretia, be silent! I am Sextus, son of the emperor Tarquin. If you speak one word, you are dead." She cried out in fear, and Sextus began to importune her, but all in vain. Then he offered and promised her gifts and services, but that too was of no use. He threatened to destroy her and all her line if she did not consent, yet to no avail. When he saw that she would not acquiesce to his advances, he said to her, "Lucretia, if you do not do my will, I will kill you and I will also slay one of your varlets, and then will I say that I found you both in bed together and killed you for your debauchery." So she, who feared more to be shamed before the world than to die, consented to lie with Sextus.

18. That same day, as soon as Sextus had gone away, the lady summoned by letter her husband, who was with the army, and also sent for her father, her brothers, all her friends, and a man named Brutus who was her husband Collatinus's nephew. When they arrived, she told them with great dread, "Sextus, the emperor's son, came yesterday as a guest unto this house, but he left not as a guest but as an enemy to you, Collatinus, for know that he has dishonored your bed. However, although my body is defiled, my heart is not; therefore I absolve myself of the sin but not of the punishment."

19. At that moment her husband Collatinus saw that she was completely pale and colorless, her face white and tearful, for traces of tears were on her face from her eyes all the way to her lips, with her eyes puffy and swollen, the lids lifeless and thick, and the insides reddened from the flow of her tears, and she looked and spoke agitatedly. He began to comfort her gently and to pardon her, pointing out many good reasons why her body had not sinned, since her heart had not consented or taken pleasure, and he began to invoke examples and authorities. But none of this placated her. She interrupted his speech, crying passionately, "Stop!

Stop! No, no, it is too late. It's useless, for I am no longer worthy to live. For he who has done this to me has done it to his own great misfortune, if you have any merit. So that no harlot may rule by the example of Lucretia, let him who would take example from the sin and the offense likewise take example from the atonement." She straightaway pierced herself through the body with a sword she had concealed beneath her robe, perishing before them all.

20. Then Brutus, the counselor, with Collatinus her husband and all her friends, weeping and lamenting, took the bloody sword and swore on and by Lucretia's blood that never would they cease until they had destroyed Tarquin and his son, and that they would pursue him with fire and blood, extinguishing all his race, so that none of them could ever achieve power.

21. And this was carried out immediately. Lucretia's body was carried through the city of Rome and so moved the people that each man swore to exterminate the emperor Tarquin and his son by fire and bloodshed. They then barred the gates, preventing anyone from exiting and warning the emperor of their attack. The men armed themselves and set out, heading like madmen toward the emperor's army. When they drew near to the emperor and he heard the noise and tumult and observed the people, all dusty, and the steam of the horses, and heard what was told him, he and his son fled into the desert, fearful and despairing.

22. About which the *Romance of the Rose* says: "Because of this rebellion, the Romans never again wished to establish a king in Rome."

23. You now have two exempla, one about honorably keeping widowhood or virginity or maidenhood, the other about protecting marriage or chastity. Remember that riches, beauty of form and face, lineage, and all other virtues are lost and ruined in a woman who has a stain or suspicion against one of these virtues. In those cases, all is certainly vanished and erased, for once a woman has raised suspicion or rumors, she has fallen and will never rise again. Even if the rumors are false, they can never be wiped away. See, therefore, in what endless peril a woman places her honor and that of her husband's lineage and her children, when she does not guard against blame, which is easy to do.

24. For on this topic it is worth noting, as I have heard tell, that after the queens of France are married, they never read sealed letters alone, unless the missives are written by their husband's own hand—or so they say—and those they read all alone. As for any other letters, the queens call for company and have them read by others in their presence, and they often report that they cannot read the letters or writing of anyone but their husband. They arrive at this custom through good upbringing and extremely great virtue in order to dispel talk and suspicion, for as for the deed, there is absolutely nothing to worry about. Since so great and honorable ladies act thus, lowly ones who need their husband's love and a good reputation just as much must do likewise.

25. I advise you to receive with great joy and reverence your husband's loving personal letters and secretly read them unaccompanied, in isolation, and write back to him when you are alone, with your own hand, if you know how, or by the hand of another very discreet person. Write to him sweet and loving words and tell him your joys and diversions, and do not receive or read any other letters, or write to any other person, except by another's hand and in another's presence, and have them read in public.

26. *Item,* they also say that after queens are married, they never kiss any man —not father, brother or kinsman—besides the king, as long as he lives. The reason they abstain, and whether it is true, I do not know.

27. These things, dear, are enough to impart to you for this article, and they are given to you more for the tale than for the teaching. There is no need to instruct you about this matter, for, thank God, you are and will be protected from such danger and suspicion.

¶ 1.5 *Devotion to Your Husband*

1. The 5th article of the first section enlightens you about your obligation to be especially loving and intimate with your husband above all other living creatures. Be moderately affectionate and close toward your and your husband's nearest blood relatives, but distant from all other men. Most of all, steer clear of swaggering and idle young men who live beyond their means and who, possessing no land or lineage, become dancers. Refrain also from consorting with courtiers of great lords, and don't mix with any men or women with reputations for leading trivial, amorous, and licentious lives.

2. Regarding what I said about acting lovingly toward your husband, it is of course true that every man must love and cherish his wife and that every woman must love and cherish her husband, for man is the origin of woman. And I can prove it: for in the second chapter of the first book of the Bible, called Genesis, after God created heaven and earth, sea and air, and all things and creatures for the adornment and perfection of nature, He brought before Adam every living creature, and Adam named each one as he pleased by the names they are still called. But no other being existed who was similar to Adam or suitable to be his partner and companion. Therefore, God said: *Non est bonum hominem esse solum; faciamus ei adiutorium simile ei.* "It is not good for man to be alone. I will make him a helpmeet who will be like him." Then God put Adam to sleep and removed one of his ribs, filling the space from which He had taken it with flesh, just as Moses says in the second chapter of Genesis. He who wrote *Ystoire sur Bible* says that God took flesh along with the rib, and Josephus says the same.[1] Our Lord fashioned the rib He had taken into a woman. Indeed, according to the *Istoire*, He fashioned flesh from the flesh He had taken with the rib, and the bones from the rib, and when He gave her life, He led her to Adam so that Adam might name her. When Adam looked at her he said: *Hoc nunc os ex ossibus meis, et caro de carne*

---

1. The reference is to Petrus Comestor's *Historia scholastica* (c. 1160), a kind of glossed Bible and biblical abridgement, characterized as "the primary text for biblical instruction in the late Middle Ages. . . . As a work of literature, the *Historia* made the Bible, which can be very strange and intractable, into a coherent, orthodox, and entertaining narrative." James H. Morey, "Peter Comestor, Biblical Paraphrase, and the Medieval Bible," *Speculum* 68, no. 1 (1993), 35. BF note that the text here has no identifiable source in Petrus or in the work of his fourteenth-century translator, Guyart des Moulins; it is spelled variously *Ystoire, Histoire, Istoire, Istoria.* Flavius Josephus was a first-century historian of the Jews.

mea. Hec vocabitur virago, quoniam de viro sumpta est. "This one is bone from my bone and flesh from my flesh. She will be called *virago,* that is, made from man." She had that name first, and after they had sinned she bore the name Eve, which means *vita,* for all human creatures who afterward had and will have life have come from her. Furthermore, Adam added: *Propter hoc relinquet homo,* etc. "Thus man will leave his father and mother and will cling to his wife, and the two will be one flesh." That is, from the blood of both (from the man and the woman) will be made one flesh in the children who will be born of them. God thus created her and, from the very first, established marriage, as the historian says. For He said to unite: *Crescite et multiplicamini,* etc. "Increase and multiply and fill the earth."

3. Hence, for the reasons stated from the Bible, I say that woman must love her husband deeply since she was made from man's rib.

4. *Item,* one reads in the eleventh chapter of Genesis that a patriarch named Abraham took as his wife in the city of Chaldea a virtuous and holy lady named Sarah. She was subsequently a sovereign princess and the first among the fine and valiant ladies mentioned by Moses in the first 5 books of the Bible. One reads there that Sarah lived a holy life and was most loyal and faithful to her husband Abraham and obedient to his commandments. One reads there too that when Abraham left Damascus because of the great famine in that land and journeyed to Egypt, he declared to his wife Sarah: "I know that the men of this land are lecherous and lustful, and you are an extremely desirable woman. So I fear greatly that if they discover you are my wife, they will kill me to possess you. Thus I beseech you to claim that you are my sister, not my wife, and I will say the same, enabling me to live peacefully amongst them with my people and my household." Sarah obeyed this counsel and commandment, not gladly, but to save her husband's life and that of his people. When the men and the prince of this country saw Sarah's great beauty, they took her and led her to the king Pharaoh who was delighted, and he had her confined. But not once, from that moment on, no matter what the hour, could the king Pharaoh go to her without finding her in tears pining for her husband. Consequently, when the king Pharaoh saw her in this state, his desire for her vanished and changed, and so he released her. Of this it may be said that because of the goodness and fidelity that God discerned in Sarah, such sadness and vexation that her husband had been separated from her, He protected and defended her so that Pharaoh could not lie with her, and he and his entire household were tormented because of Sarah, whom they had reft from Abraham. The author of the *Histoire* says of this that as long as Pharaoh kept Sarah he was unable to lie with a woman, nor could any of his men. They were also all unable to beget children. The priests of his law made sacrifices to their gods inquiring why this happened, and they were answered that it was due to Sarah, the wife of Abraham whom the king Pharaoh had seized. At the time the

king learned this, he called for Abraham who was living peacefully in his land, and queried him: "Why did you deceive me and do such an ill deed? You alleged that Sarah was your sister, but she is your wife. Take her, and lead her out of my land." Then he ordered his men to escort him out of the land of Egypt safely, without taking any of his goods.

5. It is written in Genesis 6 that when Abraham left Egypt he went to dwell in the land of Canaan, toward Bethel. Sarah considered herself barren and unable to bear a child, to her great grief. She pondered about presenting to her husband Abraham her maidservant Hagar, whom she had brought from Egypt, to see if he might beget a child with her, for Sarah feared greatly that he would die without an heir. She explained this plan to Abraham, who consented to her will. So she delivered to him her servant Hagar, who immediately conceived a son, to Sarah's joy. But when Hagar understood that she had conceived, she held her mistress in contempt, acting arrogantly toward her. Seeing this, Sarah said to Abraham, "You are behaving badly to me. I gave you my servant because I could not provide children for you, desiring that I might have a son from you and her, whom I could raise and foster so that you would not die without descendants. But because my servant Hagar realizes that she has conceived, she disdains me and does not esteem me. May God judge between me and you, for you are wrong to countenance this disrespect."

6. Now we see the great goodness and loyalty of this good and holy woman, Sarah. She loved her husband Abraham so faithfully and realized that he was such a holy and worthy patriarch that it seemed to be a tremendous misfortune and shame were he to die heirless, lacking a son of his own bloodline. Clearly perceiving that she was barren and unable to conceive, and because of her eagerness to have a son from her husband to raise, Sarah sent him her servant, letting her sleep in her own bed, consenting to remove herself. How many ladies or women could one find who would do such a thing? Very few, I think! For this reason Sarah is considered the most loyal wife to have lived from the time of Adam, the first man, until the law was given to Moses.

7. Her servant Hagar was erroneous to disdain her after she had conceived from Abraham. It is commonly said that "He who raises up his serf makes of him his enemy." But Abraham, the good patriarch, recognized that the maidservant Hagar was in the wrong. Accordingly, he said to Sarah, "Here is your servant Hagar. I place her in your hands to do with her as you wish." Sarah then approached Hagar and abused her until Hagar herself, by the order of the angel, humbled herself, importuning her lady's pardon. Sarah retained her until she had given birth to her son who was named Ishmael, for which Sarah was filled with happiness, and she nurtured him carefully.

8. After this, Our Lord visited Sarah, appearing also to Abraham in the Valley

of Mamre in front of his tent, announcing to him that he would have a son from Sarah his true wife, and he would be named Isaac; and this son would live and He would multiply his descendants as numerous as the stars of the sky and the sand of the sea or the dust of the earth. Furthermore, God said to Abraham, "All the descendants from your seed will be blessed." Sarah, who was behind the door of their tent, heard that she would conceive and she began to laugh, saying to herself, "I am aged, and so is Abraham. How could I have a child?" It was no wonder that she laughed and spoke that way; she was already over 80 years old and Abraham more than a hundred! God, who clearly saw her laugh, said to Abraham, "Why did your wife Sarah laugh?" And Sarah, who was afraid, answered that she had not laughed. God scolded her: "I certainly saw you laughing behind the door! Are not all things simple for God when He wants to do them?" Following this, Sarah conceived when God wished, and gave birth to a son whom Abraham named Isaac and circumcised on the 20th day after his birth. Then Sarah said joyfully, "God made me laugh, and all the men and women who hear that I have given birth will also laugh with me. Who would believe Abraham, when he said that Sarah would nurse a child that she had given birth to in her old age?" Assuredly, all the people who heard about this knew and believed that God loved Abraham and Sarah dearly when He granted them such a fine favor. Because Abraham was so holy and such a good patriarch, God spoke to him many times and promised him that He himself would enter into Abraham's line. He also loved Sarah greatly for her absolute loyalty and goodness.

9. Sarah raised her son Isaac admirably, and when he was ready to be weaned and eat at his father Abraham's table, she invited friends and made a lavish meal and feast for Abraham's son. When Sarah saw Ishmael, the son of Hagar the Egyptian, playing with her son Isaac, she said to Abraham, "Chase away the servant and her son. He will not be an heir with my son Isaac." It says in Genesis 21: These words were painful for Abraham, but God said to him, "Do not be upset about pushing out the servant and her son. Listen to Sarah and do all that she says, for it is through Isaac's line that your name will be carried on." (That is, the descendants that God had promised Abraham would come from Isaac.) "Because," continued God, "the son of the servant girl is from your seed, I will grant him many descendants." So Abraham arose the next morning and provided Hagar the servant with some bread and a skin of water and placed them on her shoulders. Then he bade her take her son Ishmael and depart to travel wherever she wished; and she did.

10. Now some people might perhaps consider that Sarah had chased away her servant Hagar and her son Ishmael out of evil or envy; but for those who will ascertain the cause, she did not act unjustly. The *Histoire sur Bible* explains: "Sarah saw distinctly that Ishmael acted cruelly toward her son Isaac while playing with

him. Indeed, through prophetic spirits, she perceived that Ishmael had made images of clay that he worshiped like God, and tried to compel Isaac to worship them also. On reflection, she fully realized that if Ishmael remained with them until Abraham died, he would try to disinherit Isaac and take his position by force. For these reasons she did the right thing to chase away the mother and her son."

11. Although I have furnished the whole story here—I did not wish to break it or chop it up because the content is beautiful and coheres—the only part that truly can be linked to my purpose is that Sarah was most loving, trusted, and obedient to her husband, insofar as she left her country, her parents, her family, and her land to go alone with her husband to a foreign place with a strange language. Furthermore, for love of her husband and at his request, she relinquished the name of spouse or wife—the closest relationship in kinship, affection, and love —and took the name of sister. Besides, as long as she was apart from her husband, she wept day and night for love of him. In addition, in order for her husband to beget descendants so that he would leave a lineage after his death, she relinquished her bed and the pleasure of her husband and gave to him Hagar her servant, thereby making of her a lady, and made herself servile and humble, not including those other generosities and modesty recounted above, which I omit because the repetition would be too lengthy.

12. *Item,* it is written in chapter 29 of Genesis, the first book of the Bible, that when Jacob left Isaac his father and Rebecca his mother and Beersheba their town, he traveled as far as Mesopotamia near the town of Harran where his uncle Laban dwelled. There he tarried next to a well where the local shepherds watered their flocks. This well was covered by a large flat stone. Jacob asked the shepherds gathered by the well if they knew Laban, son of Bethuel who was son of Nahor. The shepherds replied, "Yes, very well." He inquired of them if Laban were healthy and thriving, to which they responded, "Yes. Here comes his daughter Rachel to water the animals at this well." Jacob said to them, "Gentlemen, water your animals, then bring them back to pasture, for it is still broad daylight and too early to lead the animals back to the stables." While he spoke, Rachel came to the well. Jacob lifted the stone from the well so that she could water her flock. Then he addressed her and kissed her, telling her that he was her first cousin, the son of Isaac and Rebecca, the sister of Laban her father. When Rachel heard that, she hurried home to tell Laban her father that she had found his nephew Jacob. At this, Laban was joyful and asked Jacob the reason for his journey there. Jacob revealed that he feared his brother Esau, who desired to kill him because he had received their father's blessing, although it was their mother Rebecca who had made him do it. Laban responded, "You are bones of my bones and flesh of my flesh, and for this reason you can remain with me."

13. When Jacob had dwelled with his uncle Laban for a month, Laban told him,

"Even though you are my nephew, I don't want you to work for me for nothing. Tell me what compensation you would like to receive for your service." Now Laban had two daughters: the eldest, Leah, had watery eyes from an illness; the youngest, Rachel, was beautiful in face and figure, and Jacob was deeply in love with her. For that reason he spoke to Laban, "I will work for you for 7 years for Rachel, your youngest." Laban answered, "It is better that I bestow her on you than on another man. Therefore, stay with me." Jacob remained with Laban and labored for him for 7 years to gain his daughter Rachel, and the time passed quickly because of the great love he had for her.

14. On this topic the *Ystoire* says, "The seven years did not seem brief to him because of his great love, but extremely long, for when a person loves and desires something, the time appointed for him to possess it seems to arrive very slowly. But when the Bible says that the days seemed short to Jacob, we can understand this: he loved Rachel so much, and she seemed so beautiful to him, that if he had had to work twice as long as he did, it still would not have seemed to him that he had merited her."

15. At the end of 7 years he said to Laban, "Give me my wife. It is time for me to have her." So Laban invited all of his friends and neighbors and held a grand wedding. But as night fell, he led Leah, his eldest daughter, to Jacob and gave her a servant named Zilpah. The morning after Jacob had lain with Leah, discerning it was she, he said to Laban, "What have you done to me? Did I not serve you for 7 years for Rachel? Why did you give me Leah?" Laban answered, "It is not our custom in this land to give in marriage the younger daughter before the older. Wait until the wedding week has passed, and then I will give you the other, for which you will serve me for seven more years." Jacob accepted what Laban decreed. When that week had passed he took Rachel as his wife, to whom her father had given a servant named Bilhah.

16. Some say that since Jacob had taken Laban's eldest daughter, he then worked another 7 years before Rachel became his wife, but they are wrong. We find in the *Histoire* that Saint Jerome said, "Immediately after the week of festivities celebrating his marriage to Leah, Jacob took Rachel. Because of his great happiness at this, he worked willingly for the next 7 years."

17. In Genesis 29, it says that Jacob loved Rachel, who was beautiful and graceful, more than Leah, who was not as pleasing. But because God did not want him to have too much disdain for Leah, He made her conceive a son, to her great joy. She named him Reuben and said, "God has seen my humility. From now on my husband will love me for it." Again she conceived and gave birth to another son whom she called Simeon, saying, "Because God heard me, he gave me another son." She conceived a third time and gave birth to a son and said, "My husband will be pleased with me because I have given him three sons," and for this she

named the child Levi. She conceived and delivered a fourth son and said, "I will confess to Our Lord." And for this the child was named Judah, which means confession. Leah then ceased having children for a long time.

18. In Genesis 30 it is written that Rachel was pretty envious of her sister Leah because she had given birth, for she was barren and could not conceive. For this reason she said to Jacob her husband, "Give me children; if you don't I will die." Jacob responded angrily, "I am not God, I cannot cause you to conceive." Rachel responded, "I have a servant, Bilhah; sleep with her so that she will give birth and I can have a son from her and you." Jacob did as Rachel wished, and Bilhah conceived and bore a son. Then Rachel said, "God has pronounced judgment on my behalf. He has honored my plea and given me a son." She thus called the son Dan. Bilhah then had another son, causing Rachel to pronounce, "Our Lord has likened me to Leah." Because of this the son was named Naphtali.

19. Behold a wondrous thing and sign of great love! Rachel had such immense desire to have a son from Jacob that when she saw that she could not conceive, she gave him her servant. She loved those sons her maid bore as much as she would have loved her own. Now because Leah saw that she was no longer conceiving, she gave to Jacob her servant Zilpah. Leah received the first son Zilpah was delivered of with great joy and said, "Fortune has come to me!" For this the son had the name Gad. When Zilpah bore another son, Leah said, "It is for my good luck, and because of it all women will call me fortunate." This son was called Asher.

20. At harvest time Reuben brought his mother Leah some mandrakes he had found in their field. When Rachel saw them, she desired them greatly and said to her sister Leah, "Give me some of the mandrakes." Leah answered, "Is it not sufficient that you took my husband from me? Now you wish to take my mandrakes?" Rachel said, "I would be willing for him to lie with you tonight in exchange for the mandrakes your son has brought." Leah gave them to her, and that evening when Jacob returned from the fields she went to him and said, "You will come and sleep with me tonight, for I have purchased you with the mandrakes that your son gave me."

21. The *Istoire sur Bible* offers many opinions about these mandrakes. Some say that they are trees bearing delicious-smelling fruit, similar to apples; others say that they are roots in the earth with green leaves like grass and that these roots resemble the face and body of men and women, down to all of their limbs and hair. The *Catholicon* says,[2] it seems to me, that they can be grass and roots and that the fruit can help barren women conceive, unless they are too old.

---

2. The *Summa grammaticalis* or *Catholicon*, completed in 1286 by John Balbi of Genoa, a Dominican, was a religious Latin dictionary widely used throughout the late Middle Ages that aided

22. That night Jacob slept with Leah and she conceived a son. At the birth she said, "God has made me rich because I gave my servant to my husband." Thus she named her fifth son Issachar. Then she had a sixth son. After giving birth to him she exclaimed, "God has enriched me with a handsome gift this time, and my husband will come to me again." She thus called her son Zebulun. She then delivered a daughter whom she named Dinah. After this Our Lord remembered Rachel and answered her prayer. He made her conceive and bear a son which filled her with joy, "Our Lord has removed my shame." She called her son Joseph and said, "May God give me another one."

23. After all of these events, Jacob called his uncle Laban, insisting, "Give me my wives, for whom I have served you 14 years, and my children. I will return to the land of my birth." Laban answered, "Remain with me, I beg you, for through you God has blessed me and multiplied my possessions." Jacob responded, "I must see to my needs and those of my children, my wives, and my family."

24. I will not recount the rest of the story because it is unrelated to my subject: but from what is said above you can learn of the great goodness of Leah and Rachel, who simultaneously and in the same house served Jacob their husband in peace and love, without jealousy, tension, or envy. Furthermore, to serve their husband in a foreign land they had left their own country, their birthplace, their father, their mother, and their language. The deep love and passion that Rachel felt for having descendants and a lasting lineage for Jacob, to whom she had given her servant Bilhah, are estimable. How many women today would do that and would live so peaceably that when one would have the husband, the other would not pout or grouse? But even worse, for by God I think that today they would slap each other! O God! What good and holy women they were! It isn't for nothing that these words are recalled in the wedding blessing: *Sit amabilis ut Rachel viro, prudens ut Sarra, sapiens ut Rebecqua.*

25. *Item, notatur* Tobit 10. When Raguel and his wife Edna bid farewell to young Tobias and his wife Sarah their daughter, they kissed their daughter and admonished her to love her husband with all her heart and to honor his family. And so she did. On this same subject, you will find in Maccabees 11 that when Alexander learned that the king of Egypt who had married his sister was coming to see him, he proclaimed through all the local councils that his people were to leave their cities and welcome the king of Egypt with honor. He thereby showed respect to his relatives in honoring his sister's husband.

26. In order that I not be charged with failure to speak about husbands' duty

---

in interpreting the Bible and contained treatises on etymology and grammar. In it an educated citizen like the *Le Ménagier* narrator might find much of the knowledge of his time. See *Catholic Encyclopedia* online http://www.newadvent.org/cathen/08472b.htm.

as well as that of wives, I add that it is written in Ephesians 5 that a husband must love his wife as his own body. That is not to say with dissimulation or with well-chosen words, but faithfully from the heart.

27. To correspond to what is said above, and to demonstrate further my comments adjuring you to be intimate and loving with your husband, I include here a rustic example. Even wild birds and beasts, tame or wild, nay, even rapacious beasts have the sense and aptitude to follow this practice. Female birds stay close to their mate and no other, accompanying and flying after only him. If the male birds stop, so do the females, who settle near their mates. If the males fly away, the females fly after them, side by side. Wild birds—be they ravens, crows, jackdaws, indeed, even birds of prey such as sparrow hawks, falcons, blackbirds, and goshawks and the like—that are fed by strangers take to those people more than others after receiving food from them. It is the same with domestic and field animals as with wild beasts.

28. Regarding domestic animals, witness that a greyhound, mastiff, or small dog, whether it is walking on the road, at table, or in bed, always stays closest to the person from whom he takes his food and neglects and is distant and timid with all others. If the dog is far off, he always has his heart and eye on his master. Even if his master beats him and casts stones at him, the dog follows him, wagging his tail and fawning before his master to appease him. Over rivers, through woods, into thieves' dens, and through battles, the dog follows him.

29. Another example may be observed in the dog Macaire that saw his master murdered in the woods and after his slaying did not forsake him but rather lay down in the woods near the dead man. Though during the day he went afar to forage for food, bringing it back in his mouth, he returned without having eaten it and lay down and drank and fed next to his master's corpse, guarding the dead body in the wood. Afterward this dog several times attacked and fought the man who had killed his master, assailing him each time he came across him. In the end he vanquished the man in the field on the island of Notre Dame at Paris, and there still remain traces of the lists that were made by the dog for the field of battle.

30. By God, in Niort I saw an old dog who lay on the grave of his master who had been killed by the English. Monseigneur de Berry and a great many knights were taken there to witness the marvel of the loyalty and love of the dog who day and night did not abandon the grave of his master. Monseigneur de Berry had 10 francs given to a neighbor so that he could provide for the dog for the rest of its life.

31. The same holds for livestock. You may observe that sheep and lambs follow and are tame with only their masters and mistresses. Likewise with wild animals—such as boar, stag, or doe—who have a wild nature, yet follow and remain near their masters and mistresses and avoid others.

32. *Item,* carnivorous wild animals such as wolves, lions, leopards, and such-like may be savage, fierce, cruel, voracious, and rapacious, yet they follow, serve, and are docile with those who feed them and love them, but are otherwise aloof.

33. Now you have seen many diverse and odd examples, true enough to be noticed with your own eyes. By these examples you observe that birds of the sky and beasts, tame or wild, and even predatory beasts have the sagacity to love completely and be friendly with their owners and benefactors, keeping their distance from others. So much more should women, with God-given sense and reason, have perfect and solemn love for their husbands. Accordingly, I beseech you to be especially loving and intimate with your future husband.

❡ 1.6 *Obedience (including the Story of Griselda)*

1. The 6th article of the first section tells you to be humble and obedient to the one who will be your future husband. This article contains four parts.

2. The first part advises you to be obedient, by which is understood to your husband and to his commandments, whatever they be, whether they be made in earnest or in jest, or require you to do something strange, or whether they concern trivial or important matters; because all things must be considered important by you since it will be your husband who will have commanded them.

3. The 2nd part is relevant when you have any matter you have not talked over with the man who will be your husband, and which he has not considered, and thus has neither ordered nor forbidden; if the matter is urgent and it is prudent that you take care of it before your future husband knows it; or, if you wish to do it in one manner but feel that this future husband would prefer it done in a different way. Choose rather to please your husband than yourself, because his happiness must come before yours.

4. The 3rd section concerns your husband's prohibitions to you, whether such interdiction be made in jest or in earnest. Whether it concerns a trivial or a serious matter, see to it that you never do anything he forbids.

5. The 4th section charges that you not be arrogant or answer back to your future husband or to his words and do not contradict him, especially in front of others.

6. Returning to the first of the four sections, which says to be humble and obedient to your husband: the Scriptures command it, in chapter 5 of the Letter to the Ephesians, where it is said: *Mulieres viris suis subdite sint sicut domino; quoniam vir caput est mulieris, sicut Christus caput est ecclesie.* That is to say, "God commands women to be subject to their husbands as to lords, because the husband is the head of the wife just as Our Lord Jesus Christ is the head of the Church." It therefore follows that just as the Church is subject and obedient to the commandments, large and small, of Jesus Christ, its head, so must wives be subject to their husbands as to their leader and obey their orders large and small. Thus did Our Lord command it, as Saint Jerome says, and likewise the *Decretum*, 33, question five, chapter five: *Cum caput.*[1] That is why the Apostle says in chapter 13 of

---

1. "With the head . . ." Gratian's *Decretum* (1140) was the most important canon law source for the Middle Ages; it demonstrates, using an array of authorities, that the husband's rule over his wife was divinely sanctioned and part of the order of creation.

his letter to the Hebrews: *Obedite prepositis vestris et subiacete eis,* etc. That is, "Obey your sovereigns and be good subjects to them." Furthermore, it is sufficiently demonstrated that this is Our Lord's own pronouncement, because it was said previously that woman must be submissive to man. For it is written that when in the beginning Adam was made, Our Lord himself declared, "Let us provide him help," and then from Adam's rib He made woman as support and subject, and thus one makes use of her, and rightly so. Therefore, a woman ought to consider well the condition of the man she will take as a husband before she takes him. This sentiment resembles what a poor Roman said, who without his knowledge or desire was elected emperor by the Romans, when they brought him the throne and crown and he was completely astonished. One of the first things he declared to the people was, "Be careful all of you of what you do or have done. For if it is true that you have elected me and that I remain emperor, rest assured that from this moment on, my words will be as sharp as freshly whetted razors." He thus warned that, as soon as he had been made emperor, whoever did not obey his prohibitions or commands would do so at the risk of losing his head.

7. Similarly, let a woman take care how and to whom she will be married, for however poor or lowly his estate before the marriage, he nevertheless must be and is her sovereign lord for all time to come after the marriage, and he can increase or diminish everything. For this reason you must consider more the character than the wealth of your future husband, because you cannot change him afterward. When you have espoused him, hold him in affection and love and obey him humbly, as did Sarah of whom the preceding article speaks. For, through their obedience many women have gained and have come to great honor, while others by their disobedience have been humbled and have fallen from their rank.

8. Concerning this matter of disobedience and indeed how benefits come to a woman who is obedient to her husband, I can cite an example that some while ago was translated by Master Francis Petrarch who was crowned poet laureate in Rome. The story reads as follows:

The Story of Griselda

On the borders of Piedmont in Lombardy, at the foot of the mountain that divides France and Italy, called in that region Mount Viso, lies a long and broad region, full of castles and towns and ornamented with woods, meadows, rivers, vineyards, hayfields, and arable lands.[2] This land is called Saluzzo, which has since antiquity exercised dominion over the neighboring regions and from thence to

---

2. MS A supplemented by Pichon's edition is the source of our text for this section. Pichon's additions from the other MSS, where they provide a better reading, are included in brackets.

the present has been governed by noble and powerful princes called the marquises of Saluzzo. One of the noblest and most powerful among them, according
to the story, was called Walter, to whom all the others in this region—barons,
knights, squires, burgesses, merchants, and laborers—paid homage. This Walter, marquis of Saluzzo, was handsome, strong, and nimble, from noble blood,
rich in possessions and power, imbued with good morals, and endowed by nature
with a sterling character. But he had one failing: he greatly loved solitude and did
not consider the future, and by no means would he marry. All of his joy and pleasure was in rivers and woods, in dogs and birds, and he took few pains with the
government of his domains. For this reason his barons prodded and admonished
him to marry, and his people were in a good deal of distress, specifically because
he did not want to hear about marriage. One day they assembled in great numbers and the principal ones approached him. One man spoke for all, "Oh, marquis, our lord, the love that we feel for you gives us the courage to speak sincerely.
Whereas we are pleased and have always esteemed you and everything about you,
and we consider ourselves happy to have such a lord, there is one thing lacking
in you, which, if you were willing to grant it to us, we would deem ourselves to
be more fortunate than all our neighbors. It is, to wit, that you be willing to submit your heart to the bonds of marriage and that your past liberty be somewhat
restrained and brought within the laws of marriage. You know, sire, that the days
pass fleetingly without ever returning. Although you are now young, nonetheless
each day death menaces and approaches you; death spares no age and no one can
escape it. All must die, but no one knows when, nor how, nor the day, nor the
term. Thus, your men, who would never refuse your command, beg most respectfully that they may have the liberty to seek a lady of appropriate lineage, of
noble blood, beautiful and intelligent, whom you would be pleased to marry, and
through whom we hope to have your descendants and a lord of your lineage to
succeed you. My lord, do this grace to your loyal subjects, so that, if anything
were to happen to your high and noble person, and you were to depart from this
world, it would not be without providing an heir and successor so that your sad
and mournful subjects might not be bereft of a ruler."

The speech finished, the marquis, moved with pity and love for his subjects,
replied to them most gently, saying, "My friends, you compel me to that which
in my heart can never be; for I delight in liberty and in the freedom of will that
seldom exists in marriage—as those who have experienced it know well. However, for your love, I submit myself to your wish. Yet it is true that marriage is an
unreliable thing, for many times children do not resemble their fathers. Thus, if
ever any good comes to their father through them, he must not therefore say that
it is rightfully his, but that it comes from God above. To Him I commend the fate
of my heart and marriage, hoping that in His sweet goodness He may grant me a

wife with whom I can live in the peace and tranquility necessary to my salvation. I grant you, my friends, and promise you that I will take a wife. But I wish to select her myself. On your part, I desire that you promise and pay heed to only one thing. Assuredly it is this: that you must love completely and honor the one whom I shall marry by my own choice, be she the daughter of the prince of the Romans, or a serf, or anything else, and that none of you be unhappy with my choice or grouse or murmur against her."

At that all the barons and the marquis's subjects were delighted to be granted what they had requested, and about which they had so often despaired. With one voice they thanked their lord the marquis and promised willingly the reverence and obedience he had asked of them. Great joy prevailed in the palace of Saluzzo, and the marquis set a day for his wedding, when he would take a wife. He ordered extensive preparations for the festivities, more elaborate than had ever before been made by any other marquis, and directed that relatives and friends, neighbors and ladies of the land be summoned for the appointed day, which was solemnly carried out. While the arrangements were attended to, the marquis of Saluzzo, as was his custom, amused himself in hunting and hawking.

Not far from the castle of Saluzzo was a little village where a few laborers lived, through which the marquis often passed, and among these laborers there was an aged and infirm poor man named Janicula. This humble man had a daughter called Griselda, fair enough in body, but more fair still in her behavior and virtuous habits. She had been raised humbly by her father's labor. Never had she known delicious foods or refined things. A mature and virtuous heart dwelt sweetly in her virgin breast. Gently and in great humility she supported and sustained her elderly father and provided for him. She diligently tended his few sheep, spinning continually with her distaff in the fields. When Griselda returned in the evening and herded the beasts back to her father's house, she gave them fodder, and prepared for herself and her father the food that God furnished. In brief, all the kindness and service that she could do for her father, she did sweetly.

The marquis, made aware of the virtue and great goodness of this Griselda through her local reputation, would often gaze at her when passing through the village in his search for amusement. Her beautiful countenance and great worthiness penetrated and attached her to his heart. In the end, he determined that Griselda and none other would be raised up by him to be his wife, the lady of Saluzzo, and he instructed his barons to come to the wedding on the day that had been selected. That day approached, and the barons, not knowing which maid the marquis was intent on choosing, were much bewildered. However, they knew well that the marquis was having prepared rich robes, belts, clasps, rings, and jewels fitted on a maiden of Griselda's stature. Thus it happened that the wedding day arrived and the palace of Saluzzo was filled with barons and knights, with ladies and damsels, burgesses and other people, but there was no news of their lord's bride, a thing that greatly astonished them all. What is more, the hour of the feast drew near, with each official ready to perform his official duty. Then the marquis of Saluzzo, just as if he desired to journey to meet his bride, set out from his palace, followed by a large company of lords and ladies, minstrels and heralds.

But the maid Griselda knew nothing of all this. That same morning she prepared, cleaned, and straightened up her father's house before she could travel with the other maidens to see their lord's bride. When the marquis neared her abode, Griselda was carrying a jug full of water, and at this moment, with all his company, the marquis called to her by name and asked where her father was. Griselda set her jug down and, falling to her knees, with great reverence, answered, "My lord, he is in the house." "Go to him," said the marquis, "and tell him to come speak with me." She went, and then the poor man Janicula came out of the house. The marquis took him by the hand and led him aside, privately saying to him, "Janicula, I am well aware that you have always loved and still love me and that what pleases me must also please you. I want one thing from you: namely, that you give me your daughter in marriage." The poor man did not dare say a word, and after a short pause he answered humbly on his knees, "My lord, I must not want or refuse anything except what pleases you, for you are my lord." The marquis then said, "Then go into your house alone, just you and your daughter, for I want to ask her something." The marquis entered the house of the poor man Janicula, as it is said, and all the people remained outside, astounded. The maiden placed herself beside her father, fearful, bashful, and confused at the unexpected coming of her lord with his great and noble retinue, for she was unaccustomed to such guests.

The marquis addressed her saying, "Griselda, it pleases your father and me that you be my wife, and I think it likely that you will not refuse me. But I have one thing to ask you here before your father. Namely, that if I take you now as my wife, will you consent to submit yourself entirely to my will, in such a way that I may do with you and everything concerning you as I wish, without resistance or opposition from you, either in word or in deed, in sign or in thought?" Then Griselda, marveling and bewildered at such a weighty situation, answered, "Lord, I know well that I am not worthy to be called your wife, or even to be called your handmaid. But if it pleases you and fortune offers it to me, I will never be capable of doing or thinking anything against your will, and I will never dispute anything that you will ever do regarding me." "That's enough," said the marquis, taking the maiden by the hand and leading her out of the house into the midst of his lords and his people. He announced: "My friends, this is my wife, your lady. Revere, fear, and honor her, and if you love me, love her very dearly." In order that Griselda not bring with her any relic of the wretched misfortune of poverty, the marquis ordered that she be undressed by the ladies and matrons until naked from head to foot, and then clothed in rich robes and bridal garments.

The ladies became quite busy: some dressed her, others put on her shoes, others tied her belt, others fastened clasps and sewed pearls and precious stones on her garments. Others combed and arranged their lady's hair and placed a rich crown on her head, to which she was not accustomed; thus it was no wonder that she was overwhelmed. It might astonish anyone to see such a poor maiden, sun-browned and thin from poverty, now so nobly adorned, so richly crowned and suddenly transformed that people hardly recognized her. The lords took their lady then and joyfully led her to the church where the marquis placed the ring on her finger and espoused her according to the ordinance of Holy Church and the custom of the country. When the divine service was over, accompanied by the entire crowd, the lady Griselda was seated on a white charger and led to the palace, which resounded with instruments of all sorts. The wedding feast was celebrated, and the day was passed in great joy and gladness by the marquis and all his friends and subjects. The lady was naturally genteel with a gracious demeanor toward her lord and husband. This lowly lady Griselda shone with divine grace in such a manner that everyone remarked that she seemed not to have been brought up and nurtured in a shepherd's or laborer's hut but rather in a royal or imperial palace. She was so loved, cherished, and honored by all who had known her from her childhood that they could hardly believe that she was the poor man Janicula's daughter.

The fair lady led such a worthy life and spoke with such sweet words that she drew the hearts of all to love her, not only the marquis's subjects and neighbors, but also the people of the surrounding provinces. The lords and ladies came to visit her because of her good reputation, and all left her joyful and comforted. And thus the marquis and Griselda lived happily in the palace in peace and quiet, in the grace of God, and in good favor with all men. Still, many marveled that such great virtue had grown in a person nourished in such poverty. Furthermore, this lady occupied herself wisely and diligently with the oversight of all things suitable for a woman, and similarly with public affairs, at her lord's command and in his presence. When debate and discord arose among the nobles, she so appeased them by her discreet words, excellent judgment, and perfect fairness that with one voice all said that this lady had been sent to them by heaven for the salvation of the realm.

Not long afterward, the lady Griselda became pregnant and gave birth to a beautiful daughter. The marquis and the people of the land were joyful and cheered, though they would have preferred a boy child. Time passed and the day came when the marquis's daughter was weaned. Then the marquis, who so loved his wife for the great virtue that he saw increase in her daily, decided to test and tempt her greatly. He entered her chamber wearing a troubled expression and, speaking as if angry, said to her, "O Griselda, even though you are now elevated to this pleasant good fortune, I imagine that you have not forgotten your previous estate and in what manner you entered this palace. You have been honored here, and by me you are still cherished and loved. But contrary to what you may think, my vassals do not feel the same way, especially since you have borne a child. For they loathe being subject to a woman from such humble parents and low estate. Since I, as their lord, desire to have peace with them, it is suitable that I take them seriously and comply with their judgments—even if I do not share them— and do with your daughter a thing that could not be more sorrowful to my heart, something that I do not wish to carry out without your knowledge. So I desire your free assent to endure with patience what will be done, that patience that you promised me at the beginning of our marriage."

When the marquis finished his speech, [which naturally must have pierced the marquise's] heart, this lady, without changing color or showing any trace of sadness, answered her lord humbly, "You are my lord, and I and this little girl are yours. Do what you wish with your possessions. Anything that pleases you must also please me, and this have I so fixed within my heart that no length of time, or even death, can remove it, and nothing could make me change my mind." Then the marquis, hearing his wife's reply and seeing her steadfastness and humility, felt great joy in his heart, but he concealed it and left her, feigning a sad and miserable countenance.

Several days later, the marquis summoned one of his loyal and trusted subjects, charging him with all that he had arranged to be done to his daughter, and sent him to the marquise. This sergeant went before the lady and spoke deferentially, "Madam, I beg you to forgive me and not blame me for what I am bound to do. You are a wise lady and understand what it is to be subject to lords against whom you cannot resist, by either force or cleverness. Madam, I am compelled to seize this child and carry out my orders." Then the lady, remembering her lord's words in her heart, grasped the import of the sergeant's speech and suspected that her daughter must die. Within herself she found virtuous reserves of courage and, struggling against nature, consoled herself that she was fulfilling her promise of obedience to her lord. Without sighing or indicating any grief, she took her child, gazed at her for a long time, kissed her gently, and made the sign of the cross on her. Then she handed the babe over to the sergeant, saying, "Go and carry out fully all my lord's commands; but I beseech you, do not allow the tender body of this maid to be devoured by birds or wild beasts, unless those are your orders."

Carrying the child, the sergeant left the marquise and secretly went to the marquis and showed him his daughter, informing him that he had found the marquise to be a lady of outstanding courage and obedient to him without complaint. The marquis considered his wife's great virtue and while looking upon his daughter was overtaken with fatherly compassion. Yet he would not change the rigor of his purpose, and he ordered the sergeant, whom he trusted, to wrap up the child comfortably and place her in a basket on a mule with a gentle gait. Without delay she was to be secretly transported to Bologna la Grasse, to his sister, the wife of the count of Perugia. The sergeant was bade to inform his sister that, in the name of her love for her brother the marquis, she have the child raised and instructed in good morals and do it so secretly that neither her husband the count nor any living person could ever discover it. The sergeant swiftly departed by night and carried the maid to Bologna la Grasse, diligently delivering his message as he was ordered. The countess received her niece joyfully and did sensibly all that the marquis her brother had asked of her.

Griselda patiently endured this torment, which pierced her entrails. Deep in her heart she believed that her child was dead and slain. The marquis acted toward his wife as before, without uttering a word to her of her daughter, often studying her face, bearing, and comportment, to perceive any sign of grief in her. But he detected no change of disposition in her. On the contrary, the same cheerfulness, the same respect, the same love, the same character. The lady continued toward her lord as always, showing no sadness nor mentioning her daughter in her husband's presence or in his absence.

In this way the marquis and his wife spent four years together in great affection, leading a loving and peaceful life. At the end of four years the marquise Griselda bore a son of extraordinary beauty, which thrilled the marquis, his friends, his subjects, and all the country. When the child was weaned from his nurse and two years old, growing in good looks, the marquis was stirred again to use his dreadful and perilous test, and he went to the marquise saying, "You know and have heard before that my people were unhappy with our marriage, particularly when they saw that you are able to bear children. Never, however, were my barons and my people as discontented as they are now, especially because you have borne a male child. They often say in derision, and I have overheard this murmuring myself: 'Let's kill Walter, and then the good man Janicula will be our lord; what a lord for this noble land to be subject to!' Every day yields such statements of conspiracy, and because of these words and fears, I, who desire to live in peace with my subjects, and also because of great fear for my life, am forced and impelled to make plans for dealing with this child as I did with his sister, which I tell you so that a sudden sorrow does not break your heart."

Oh, what a mournful surprise this lady must have had in her heart, remembering the vile death of her daughter [and realizing that her only son], merely two years old, awaited the same fate! Who is there—not only among women, who are by nature tender and loving to their children, but among the strongest men of courage that could be found—who could conceal his thoughts about such a judgment enacted on his only son? Queens, princesses, marquises, and all other women, hear what the lady replied to her lord and take example: "My lord," she said, "I told you before and I repeat it, there is nothing that I wish or anything that I will refuse unless it pleases you. You are sovereign over me and our children. Exercise your rights with your possessions, without asking for my consent. When first I entered your palace, I divested myself of my threadbare clothes and my own will and affection and put on yours, and for that reason everything that you wish, I wish. Indeed, were it possible for me to know your thoughts and desires before you told them to me, whatever they were I would carry them out to the best of my ability. For nothing in the world, neither family, nor friends, nor mine own life can compare with your love."

The marquis of Saluzzo, hearing his wife's response and marveling in his heart at her great virtue, incomparable steadfastness, and her true love for him, did not reply but went forth with bowed head, as if troubled by what he must do to his son. Yet soon afterward, as he had before, he sent a loyal sergeant secretly to the marquise. After many excuses and gentle explanations that he must obey his lord, the sergeant humbly and piteously asked for his lady's pardon if in the past he had done anything to displease her and, if he must transgress again, that she forgive his great cruelty. He then asked for the child. The lady, without hesitation or any sign of grief, took her fair son in her arms and without a tear or sigh gave him a long look, and as she had done to his sister, she signed him with the sign of the cross and blessed him, tenderly kissing him, then handed him over to the sergeant, saying, "Take him, my friend, and do as you have been ordered. But like the last time, one thing I beg of you: if possible, save the tender limbs of this child from being disturbed or devoured by birds and wild beasts."

The sergeant conveyed the child secretly to his lord and recounted all that his lady had said, which caused the marquis to marvel at his wife's great and unwavering fortitude. Had he not known well the great love she had for her children, he might have thought that such courage came not of humanity but of bestial cruelty. Now he saw clearly that this wife loved nothing beneath heaven more than her husband.

The marquis sent his son secretly to Bologna to his sister, just as he had sent his daughter. His sister, the countess of Perugia, following her brother's wishes, raised his daughter and son so discreetly that no one could ever discern whose children they were, until the marquis arranged it, as will presently be told.

The marquis of Saluzzo, such a cruel and exacting husband, should truly have been satisfied by this trial of his wife, without testing or tormenting her any further. But there are some who, when they have become suspicious, do not know how to assuage their uncertainties. After all these events, often the marquis in conversing with his wife would scrutinize her to see whether she evinced any trace of what had happened. But he never detected in her any alteration of disposition. Day after day he found her joyous and loving and more obedient, to the point that no one could perceive that in these two people there was more than one mind, and that single mind and will was the husband's, for as was said above, his wife had no desire or inclination of her own but deferred all to her husband's will.

Living thus lovingly with his wife in great repose and joy, the marquis learned that a rumor was circulating about him that he was ashamed to have married the daughter of the poor man Janicula without considering his own distinguished lineage, and because he was disgraced to have had two children with her, he had ordered them slain and thrown into a place where no one could discover what had befallen them. So however much they had loved him before as their natural lord, for this reason his subjects had come to despise him, which he could well sense. Nonetheless, he would not bend or soften his inflexible purpose but conceived of an even more certain and painful manner to test and tempt his wife: by taking another woman.

Twelve years had passed since his daughter's birth. The marquis [sent] secretly to Rome to the Holy Father the Pope to request sacred bulls, which started a rumor among his people that he had permission from the Pope of Rome, for the peace and repose of himself and his subjects, to relinquish and cast aside his first marriage and take in lawful wedlock another woman. This news seemed credible enough to the unlettered people who were indignant with their lord. The harsh news of this bull, by which the marquis was to take another wife, reached the ears of Griselda, daughter of Janicula. Her heart was greatly troubled, as is not surprising. But she who had freely chosen, after careful consideration and reflection, to submit herself and all that was hers to her lord's will steeled herself and, fortified, decided that she would wait for any orders that her husband, to whom she had submitted herself, might issue.

The marquis then sent a letter to Bologna, to the count of Perugia and his sister, asking them to bring him his children without revealing their identity, and his sister responded that she would do so. As soon as their visit was announced, the rumor spread throughout all the land that a fair virgin of a great lineage was coming to wed the marquis of Saluzzo. The count of Perugia, accompanied by great lords and ladies, set forth from Bologna, bringing with him the marquis's son and daughter. The boy was eight years old, and the girl, twelve, was of a marriageable age. With a gracious figure and beautiful face, she was arrayed in fine fabrics, rich garments, and gems and was slated to reach Saluzzo on the day arranged.

While the count of Perugia and the children were on the road, the marquis of Saluzzo sent for his wife Griselda and in the presence of some of his barons said to her: "In the past, I enjoyed well enough your company in marriage, considering your good morals and not your lineage. But now, as I see it, great destiny falls upon me and I am at its mercy, and I cannot tolerate that a poor laborer—such as the one from whom you descend—should have such authority over my vassals. My people compel me, and the Pope allows me, to take another wife, and she is traveling here and will soon arrive. Be thus strong of heart, Griselda, and vacate your place for the newcomer. Take your dowry and pacify yourself. Return to your father's house; for nothing that man or woman has in this world lasts forever." Griselda then answered, "My lord, I believed, or at least I thought, that between your magnificence and my poverty there could never be any equality, nor did I ever deem myself worthy to be your wife or even your servant. And in this palace where you brought me and made me a lady, I take God as my witness that I always considered and conducted myself as your servant. For all the time that I have lived with you I give you thanks, and now I am ready to return to my father's house, where I will spend my old age and die like a happy and honorable widow, after having been married to such a lord. I leave my place to God, who so wills that a worthy virgin will come to occupy the position in which I have lived most happily. Because it is, of course, your wish, I depart without complaint or rancor. As for my dowry that you have ordered me to take with me, it is obvious. You know well that when you came to take me away, you first had me stripped naked at my father Janicula's door and clothed in your garments. This was the attire that I came to you in, and I never brought with me any other riches or dowry besides faith, loyalty, reverence, and poverty. Take then this robe that I remove, and also the ring with which you married me. The other rings, jewels, garments, and adornments with which I have been ornamented and enriched are in your chamber. I left my father's house naked, and I will return there naked. Excepting that, I think it would be disgraceful for this womb, in which your children were carried, to appear uncovered before the people. Therefore, only if it pleases you and not otherwise, in compensation for the virginity I brought to your palace and which I leave without, I beg that you arrange that a smock be supplied me, so I may cover the womb of your wife, formerly the marquise. Also, for the sake of your honor, I ask that I may depart in the evening."

The marquis could not hold back tears of pity for his loyal wife. He turned his face away and, weeping, ordered them to give her a single smock that evening. Thus it was done, and at nightfall she stripped off her clothes, took off her shoes, and removed the ornaments from her head, humbly content to dress herself in that one smock that her lord had allowed her. She left the palace barefoot and with no head covering, accompanied by tearful barons and knights, ladies and maidens, who pondered her great virtues and loyalty and remarkable goodness and patience. Though everyone else wept, she did not shed a tear. Rather, honorably and simply, with eyes downcast, she traveled to the house of her father Janicula, who heard the noise of this great company's arrival. Janicula, who was old and wise, deep in his heart had always harbored suspicions about his daughter's marriage, thinking that when his lord had had enough of such a lowly union to a poor creature, he, a great magnate, could send her away without consideration. Thus, Janicula was alarmed and hurried to the door. Finding his daughter there naked, quickly he snatched up the poor, tattered dress that she had long ago left behind and in tears ran to meet his daughter, kissing her while clothing and covering her with the shabby garment.

Once at the threshold of her father's house, displaying no sign of resentment or anger, Griselda turned toward the knights, ladies, and maidens who had accompanied her, sweetly and humbly thanking them for their escort and company. She explained to them with friendly, gentle words that for the love of God they should not say, or think, or believe that her lord the marquis had done her any wrong—it was not at all so—but he had good cause to do all that he wished with her, who was bound by duty to suffer and bear it. They could see that she was not distressed about it. She admonished them for the love of God to love their husbands loyally and wholeheartedly and to serve and honor them with all their might, since they could in the end achieve no greater good or higher renown than in that way.[3] Upon which she bade them farewell and entered her father's house. The lords and ladies who had accompanied her turned back, lamenting, moaning, and sighing so loudly that they were scarcely able to look at or speak to one another.

Yet Griselda was then entirely content. Disregarding and indifferent toward the abundant comfort and riches that once were hers and the grand service, reverence, and obedience that had been shown to her, she led a humble life with her father as before, sober and showing great humility toward her unfortunate friends and her father's neighbors. How easy to imagine poor Janicula's pain and distress in his old age, upon seeing his daughter in such a meager and lowly condition, after experiencing such magnificent and high honor and wealth. But it was marvelous to observe how graciously, humbly, and wisely she cared for him and how well she comforted and distracted him when she noticed he was melancholy.

Many days passed in this way. As the count of Perugia and his noble company drew near, all the people of the country murmured against the marquis's nuptials. The count of Perugia, the marquis's brother-in-law, sent several knights ahead to assure the marquis of Saluzzo of his arrival date and also to inform him that he

---

3. This speech does not appear in the source, *Le Livre de la vertu du sacrement de mariage* by Philippe de Mézières, and seems to be an authorial addition, reinforcing the leitmotif of the tyrannical husband who must be obeyed by a long-suffering wife.

brought with him the virgin that the marquis was to wed. For in truth he was not aware that the children raised by his wife the countess were the marquis's children, since the countess of Perugia had hidden this fact from her husband while raising her niece and nephew and had led him to believe that they were children from some foreign land, a belief that the children's refined ways seemed to confirm.[4] The count hoped that once the maid was married to the marquis and the news had spread through the world, the father's identity would be acknowledged.

At that point the marquis of Saluzzo sent for Griselda to be brought at once to his palace; she came without question. He said to her, "Griselda, the maiden whom I am to wed will be here tomorrow at dinner. For love of this virgin who is arriving, I want her and the count my brother and the other lords of their company to be received honorably, in such a way that each one is honored according to his rank. In my palace no woman or chambermaid knows as well as you do how to arrange matters as I wish, for you know my ways, how to receive such people properly, and all the rooms and quarters and the organization of my palace. I therefore desire that without regard for the past or embarrassment about your poor attire and despite your lowly position, you should take charge of all these affairs, and all the officers of my house will obey you." Griselda responded gladly, "My lord, I will do everything that I can for your pleasure, not only willingly but with all my heart, and I will never be tired or worn out, or pretend to be, as long as any breath remains in my body."

Then Griselda, like a poor servant girl, took the humble implements and gave them to the household, ordering some to clean the palace and others the stables, urging the officers and the chambermaids each to complete carefully his particular task, and she began to arrange and straighten the beds and bedrooms, spreading the fine tapestries and all the embroideries and blazons used to decorate the palace, making it fit to receive her lord's wife. And even though Griselda was in a lowly estate and dressed as a poor servant, to all who saw her she appeared as a woman of great honor and exceptional prudence. This virtue, goodness, and obedience were so wonderful that all the ladies marveled.

The next day at the hour of Terce, the count, along with the maiden and her brother, entered Saluzzo. Everyone exclaimed at the beauty and fine bearing of the maiden and her brother, and some who were there remarked, "The marquis Walter does well to change his wife, for this one is more tender and of nobler birth than Janicula's daughter." With great celebration, dismounting from their horses, they entered the palace. Griselda, who was present for all of this, appeared cheered to participate in such a great event and unashamed of her pitiful raiment. With

---

4. It is notable in a treatise about a good wife that the countess of Perugia's loyalty is to her brother, and she feels free to lie, or at least conceal information, from her husband.

a joyful face she came to meet the damsel, greeting her from a distance, falling to her knees and saying, "Welcome, madam," and saluting the son and the count, "You are welcome with my lady." She then led each to his richly decorated room. Having seen and considered Griselda's deeds and composure, all were astonished that such refined manners could be displayed in such humble attire.

Next Griselda went in to join the damsel and young boy and could not leave them. For an hour she gazed upon the maiden's beauty and then the young boy's gracious bearing, and she could not praise them enough. As the time approached for everyone to sit down to dine, the marquis summoned Griselda and in a loud voice, in front of everyone, asked, "What do you think of my new wife, Griselda? Isn't she quite beautiful and honorable?" Kneeling, Griselda answered wisely in a resonant, clear voice, "Lord, in my opinion, she is certainly the most beautiful and praiseworthy maiden that I have ever seen. With her you will be able to lead a happy and honorable life, which is what I in good faith desire. Yet, my lord, I do entreat and warn you not to torment this new wife with strange ordeals, but consider her youth, her nobility, and her genteel upbringing. She could not endure them, I think."

Hearing Griselda's wise and gentle words and weighing the good countenance and steadfastness that she showed and had always shown, the marquis was deeply moved to compassion and could no longer refrain from revealing his intentions. So in the presence of everyone he declared aloud, "O Griselda! Griselda! I see and am satisfied with your true faith and loyalty. I have tested and now know the depth of your love for me and your steadfast obedience and sincere humility, which compels me to admit that I do not believe there is a man on earth who has tested his wife as much as I have you." Griselda then blushed, bowing her head in virtuous modesty for the great praise that the marquis her lord gave to her before so many people. Weeping, the marquis then took her in his arms, kissed her, and said, "You alone are my wife, and I will never have another. This girl whom you thought was to be my wife is your daughter, and this child is your son. These two children were supposed by our subjects to be lost. Let it be known then, to all who thought otherwise, that it was not my wish to show my loyal wife contempt or scorn but to test her curiously and rigorously. I never had her children killed or slain but planned for them to be raised secretly by my sister."

Upon hearing Walter's words and from the joy of seeing her children, the marquise Griselda swooned at his feet. Immediately people gathered her up, and when she revived she gently embraced and kissed her two children, so much that they were covered with her tears, and no one could separate them from her arms—a moving sight! The ladies and the damsels, weeping in gladness, took their lady Griselda and led her to a chamber where they relieved her of her poor garments, dressed her anew, and honored her as befits a marquise. The whole palace solemnly and jubilantly celebrated the children's return, which brought im-measurable consolation to their mother, the marquis, and his friends and subjects. Great joy spread throughout the land, with many tears of pity shed that day in the palace of Saluzzo. No one tired of faithfully relating the great and unequaled vir-tues of Griselda, she who in her bearing resembled the daughter of an emperor, or in her prudence resembled a daughter of Solomon, more than she did the child of the impoverished Janicula. Following the celebration, which was grander and more joyous than their wedding feast, the marquis and the marquise lived to-gether in great love, peace, and harmony for twenty years. As for Griselda's father Janicula, to whom her husband had paid no heed in the past as part of the test-ing of his daughter, the marquis had him moved into the palace of Saluzzo where he was held in great honor all the days of his life. The marquis married his daugh-ter to a grand and powerful lord, and when his son was of age he was married likewise, and they both produced children whom the marquis lived to see. After his gracious end, the marquis left his son as his heir and successor in Saluzzo, to the great consolation of all his friends and subjects.

∗ ∗ ∗

9. My dear, this story was translated by Master Francis Petrarch, crowned poet in Rome, not to persuade good ladies purely for love of their husbands to be pa-tient in the tribulations that their husbands cause them. Rather, it was translated to show that since God, the Church, and reason require that they be obedient, and since their husbands will that they have so much to suffer, to avoid worse they must submit themselves in all things to the will of their husbands and endure pa-tiently all that their husbands require. Nonetheless, these good ladies should con-ceal their sufferings and be silent concerning them, yet despite it all appease and reconcile themselves to their husbands and always joyfully reclaim and cherish the affection and love of these husbands who are mortal. Thus, it is all the more rea-sonable that men and women suffer patiently the tribulations that God, immor-tal, eternal, and everlasting, sends them. Notwithstanding the death of friends, loss of children or kin, defeat by enemies, captures, slayings, losses, fire, tempests, storms, floods, or other sudden tribulations, one must always forbear and return to, accept, and recall ourselves lovingly and graciously to the love of the sovereign, immortal, eternal, and everlasting God, through the example of this poor woman, born in poverty, from a lowly family without distinction or learning, who suf-fered so much for her mortal friend.

10. I have placed the tale here as instruction, not to apply it to you, or because I expect the same obedience from you, since I am not worthy. I am no marquis, nor were you a shepherdess, and I am not so foolish, presumptuous, or immature as to fail to recognize the inappropriateness of my abusing or testing you in such

ways. God keep me from trying you in this or any other manner, under any false pretenses! Nor in any other way do I wish to assail you, for the proof already provided by your good reputation and that of your ancestors, together with what I sense and see with my own eyes and know from real experience, suffices for me. And I apologize if the story contains excessive accounts of cruelty, in my opinion more than is fitting, and I don't believe it was ever true. But the story is thus, and I must not amend or change it, for someone wiser than I compiled and recounted it. Since others are familiar with it, I very much wish that you also may be familiar with it and be able to converse about such things as everyone else does.

11. Thus, dear one, I repeat, you must be obedient to your future husband, for it is through good obeisance that a wise woman obtains her husband's love and, in the end, receives from him what she desires. Similarly, I can assert that if you act arrogantly or disobediently, you destroy yourself, your husband, and your household. I cite as an example the following story: It happened that a married couple were quarreling with each other—that is to say, the wife against the husband—because each of them claimed to be the wiser, the nobler in lineage, and the most worthy. Like fools they exchanged accusations, and the wife maintained such bitter acrimony against her husband—who, in the beginning, as it so happened, had not instructed her carefully—that friends had to intervene to avoid a scandal. There were many meetings of the friends, and many reproaches flung at each other. Out of pride, the wife would accept no alternative but, on the one hand, that all of her rights be written down, point by point, with all of the obligations she owed her husband, and, on the other hand, that her husband's rights and obligations to her also be clearly listed. With that they should be able to live together in love—or if not in love, at least in peace. Thus it was done, and they abided by the contract for some time. From then on the wife narrowly guarded her rights as listed in the document. It behooved the husband, in order to avoid worse, to have or to feign patience in spite of possessing none, for he had set about to correct her too late.

12. One day they were going on a pilgrimage and needed to cross over a ditch by means of a narrow plank. The husband crossed first, then turned and saw that his wife was frightened and did not dare follow him. He was worried that if she tried to cross, her fear itself would make her fall, so he kindly returned and took her by the hand, holding her and talking to her as he led her across the plank, reassuring her that she need not be afraid. All the while speaking to her, the good man walked backward and thus fell into the water, which was deep. He struggled hard to save himself from drowning, catching hold of an old plank that had fallen in long ago, and was afloat clinging to it. He asked his wife to use her staff to draw the plank toward the bank to save him. She responded, "No, no, indeed not! First I will look in my charter to see if it says that I must do so; if it does, I will do it,

but otherwise I will not." She looked, and since her document did not mention the current situation, she told her husband that she would do nothing, and she left him and went on her way. The husband remained in the water a long time, so long that he was in peril of death. The lord of the land traveled through the area with some of his people just at that time. They saw the husband and rescued him when he was nearly lifeless. Making him warm and comfortable, once he was able to speak they asked him what had happened. He told them everything. The lord had the wife pursued, then seized and burned. Now you see to what end pride brought this woman who, in great insubordination, tried to preserve so strictly her rights against her husband.[5]

13. Well, by God, it is not always advisable to say to one's lord, "I will not do it. It isn't right." More good comes from obeying, as in the example I take from the words of the Blessed Virgin Mary. When the angel Gabriel brought her the news that Our Lord would be conceived in her, she did not respond, "It isn't right. I am a maiden and a virgin; I will not tolerate it, for my reputation would be ruined." Rather, she obediently replied, *Fiat michi secundum verbum tuum*, which means, "Be it done according to His will." She was thus true, humble, and obedient, and through her humility and obedience great good has come to us.

14. On the other hand, through disobedience and pride occur great evil and bad outcomes, as in the case mentioned above of the woman who was burned, and as you can read in the Bible about Eve, by whose disobedience and pride she and all women who came and will come after her were and have been cursed by the mouth of God. For, as the author of the *Histoire* explains, because Eve sinned doubly, she had two curses. For having attempted, out of pride, to raise herself to be like God, she was cast down and humbled with the first curse, when God said, *Multiplicabo enumpnas tuas, et sub potestate viri eris et ipse dominabitur tui,* which means, "I will multiply your suffering. You will be subject to the power of man, and he will have dominion over you." The *Histoire* says that before she sinned she had been somewhat subject to man, since she had been made from his rib, but that subjection was most sweet and moderate and born of natural obedience and sincere willingness. But after this curse, she was obliged to be subject in all things, willingly or not, and all other women who were born and will be born of her had and will have to suffer and obey their husbands' wishes and will be forced to carry

---

5. The attempt to murder a husband was considered treasonable, rather than simply criminal, since the wife was legally her husband's subject. Thus, the punishment of death from the local justice was defensible. The English Statute of Treason (1352), for example, mandated such a crime as a violation of the peace of the king, and conviction resulted in burning at the stake, as happens in the narrator's anecdote. See Paul Strohm, "Treason in the Household," chapter 6 in *Hochon's Arrow* (Princeton: Princeton University Press, 1992), 121–44.

out completely their commands. The second curse was this: *Multiplicabo concep-tus tuos. In dolore paries filios tuos.* God said, "I will multiply your conceptions." That is to say, "You will conceive numerous children. You will give birth to your sons in pain and suffering." The *Histoire* says that the curse was not for the child but concerning the pain that women experience in childbirth.

15. Consider also the curse that Our Lord chose to give Lucifer for his disobe-dience. For Lucifer was once the most celebrated and beloved angel in Paradise and the closest to God. And for that he was called Lucifer by all—which is roughly *Lucem ferens,* which means "bearing light," since in the eyes of the others he brought light and joy wherever he went, because he represented and called to mind the sovereign Lord Who loved him so much and from Whom he came and to Whom he was so close. As soon as this Lucifer abandoned humility, his heart swelling with arrogance, Our Lord cast him farther away, causing him to plum-met lower than any other, that is, into the deepest depths of hell, where he is the basest, the worst, and the most wretched of the wretched.

16. Likewise, you should know that you will be so close to your husband that wherever he goes he will carry the memory, recollection, and reminder of you. You notice it in all married couples, for as soon as we see the husband, we ask him, "How is your wife?" and as soon as we see the wife, we ask her, "How is your hus-band?" for that's how closely the wife is connected to the husband.

17. Thus you behold, as much by the judgments of God himself as by the ex-amples invoked above, that if you are not obedient to your future husband in all things, large and small, you will be more blameworthy and punished by that hus-band than would be another person who might disobey him, in that you are closer to him. If you were less compliant and your chambermaid, whether willingly, out of obligation, or otherwise, showed such a degree of obedience that your hus-band abandoned you and committed with her the intimate relations that he should share with you, entrusting nothing to you and neglecting you, what would your friends say, what would your heart presume, when they noticed? And after he had switched his attention to that place, how would you be able to regain it af-terward? Certainly, it will not be the least bit in your power! For the love of God, beware so that this misfortune may not transpire, that he may not once take in-timate service other than yours! Thus let his orders, even the little ones that at first seem unimportant or odd, be so attached to your heart that you do not con-cern yourself with your own wishes, only his. Be careful that by you alone his contentment may be accomplished. With regard to him and his affairs that con-cern you, do not allow anyone near them; let no one touch them but yourself. Also let your dealings be commanded and committed by you to your children and your trusted servants who are under you, to each according to his place. If they do not do it, then punish them for it.

18. Because I have told you to be obedient to your future husband, that is to say, more than to any other and above all other living creatures, this word "obedience" can be understood and explained as: in any situation, under any terms, in any place or season, you must perform without objecting all his orders whatever they may be. For recognize that since he is a rational man and of natural good sense, he will not command anything without cause and will not let you do anything unreasonable.

19. However, there are some women who want to gloss and dissect their husband's reason and good sense, and what is worse, to look wise and masterful, they do it more in public than in private. For although I don't at all wish to say that they should not know their husbands' business and that their husbands should not tell them everything, nonetheless it should be said and done in private and must come from a husband's will and courtesy, not at all from the authority, mastery, and lordship of the woman who interrogates him in front of people. In public, to show her obedience and to maintain her honor, she should not speak a word, because it would seem to people who would hear it that the husband was accustomed to giving his wife an account of his reasons. Women should not wish others to perceive this, for in such cases they show themselves to be uppity and sovereign, and they bring blame to themselves and great villainy to their husbands.

20. There are yet others whom their husbands order to do some things that seem to them small and insignificant, and they are not concerned about crossing the one who gave the order or about the obedience that they owe him, but only about the significance of the thing. That significance they weigh in their own mind and not at all according to the truth, for they do not know it, since no one has told them.[6]

21. Here's an example of what can happen: A man named Robert, who owes me 200 francs, comes to bid me adieu and say that he is going overseas, and he tells me, "Sire, I owe you 200 francs that I have given to my wife, who does not know you. But I told her to hand them over to the one who brings to her her name written by my hand, and here it is." And with that he left, and as soon as he departed, and without explaining the circumstances, I ordered my own wife, whom I trust, to keep the paper. My wife had another person read it, and when she saw on it a woman's name, thinking the worst, she threw it in the fire. In a fury, she stormed in and scolded me, saying that she would not serve as my pimp. There is fine obedience for you!

---

6. Pichon and BF agree that this statement should be negated, as we have it here, even though MSS A, B, and C read "since someone has told them." But the sense could be: "since someone simply told them (what to do/ordered them around)." See BF 295 n. 77, 36.

22. *Item,* let us say I handed over to her a trifle, either an old nail or a pebble that had been delivered to me as a token of some great matter, or a thread or twig of wood to measure some important business, about which—out of forgetfulness or by other happenstance—I did not mention anything about either the situation or its nature, but I gave it to her to safeguard carefully. In defiance of me for not showing her the honor and reverence of informing her of the entire matter, she will only consider the value of the thread or the branch and will pay no attention to my order.

23. Such rebellious, haughty, and sly women, when they have spoilt everything in order to show their mastery, think to excuse themselves by convincing their husbands that they considered the matter trifling and for that reason did not carry out the order. But wise husbands well apprehend that it is from disdain and spite for not receiving the honor of being confided in about the situation at once, or perhaps their wives are indifferent to the order out of pride. They care not one bit about their husbands' displeasure, provided that they have the opportunity to excuse themselves and say, "It was nothing—although had it been something important, I would have done it." And for that, they think they will be excused. But they are mistaken, because although the husband keeps silent about it at the time, nonetheless they lose forever the recognition of having the virtue of obedience, and that stain of disobedience remains a long time afterward in the husband's heart, so embedded that at another time he will recall it when the wife thinks that peace has been made and that her husband has let it slide. Let women avoid this serious peril and pay heed to what the Apostle said in Hebrews 13: *Obedite,* etc.

24. This article also states that a wife must obey her husband and carry out his orders, whatever they may be, great or small or even really minor. Furthermore, it is not at all fitting that your husband tell you his reason or the motive behind his order, for that would seem to be a signal to you to do or not do his bidding based on whether or not you found the rationale to be valid. But such a decision should not fall to your judgment, for it rests on him alone to know all, and it is not your role to ask him, unless after the fact when you two are alone. With regard to his orders, you should never hesitate or refuse to carry out his instructions or in any way slow down or delay their execution. Also, never do anything that he has forbidden or in any way modify, exaggerate, diminish, broaden, or narrow his prohibitions. In and for all things—good or bad—that you have done, you are free and clear of blame when you say, "My husband ordered me to do it." Even if a wrong comes from your constancy to your husband's commands, it is said of a married woman, "She acted well, since her husband directed her; in so doing she performed her duty." Thus, at worst, you will not only be excused but also well praised.

25. On this subject, I will tell you a piteous and astonishing tale, which provokes

sympathy. I know a woman from a bourgeois family of distinction who is married to a good man, and they are both decent creatures, an irreproachable couple with two beautiful young children. The woman is blamed for having received the company of a great lord, but, by God, when people speak about it, the other women and men who know the story, and even those who hate the sin, say that the woman should not be held responsible because she was following her husband's orders. This is the situation: they live in one of the greatest cities of this kingdom. The king because of a rebellion of the city's inhabitants imprisoned her husband and several other compatriots. Each day, three or four of these prisoners were beheaded. The woman and the other wives of the prisoners went before the lords each day, in tears, on their knees and with clasped hands, imploring them to have pity and mercy and agree to set their husbands free. One of the lords who was close to the king, a cruel and treacherous tyrant fearing neither God nor His justice, sent a wicked message to the bourgeoise saying that if she agreed to satisfy his lustful desires, he would have her husband set free without fail. She answered nothing to this missive but begged the messenger that, for the love of God, he arrange with those who guarded her husband in prison that she might visit and speak with him. And thus it was done. In the prison cell with her husband, weeping, she reported to him what she saw or could perceive of the others in prison with him and also about the prospect of his deliverance because of the foul request made of her. Her husband bid her do what was necessary for him to escape with his life, whatever it took, and not to spare her body or her honor or any other thing to save him. On this they parted from each other tearfully. Several of the other prisoners were beheaded, but her husband was freed. She is excused for such a grave matter because, supposing that it is true, she has neither sin nor guilt, nor has she committed a crime or bad deed, since her husband had commanded it. On the contrary, she acted wisely to save her husband, as a good wife. At any rate, I now leave this matter that is unpleasant to tell and too serious (cursed be the tyrant who did it!), and I return to my topic, that one must obey one's husband, and I will leave such weighty matters for those of lesser magnitude.

26. In God's name, I believe that when two good, virtuous people are married, all other loves outside of each other are remote and forgotten. It seems to me that when they are in each other's presence, they look at each other more than at others, playfully tweak one another, press close, and do not willingly recognize or speak to anyone besides each other. And when they are separated, they think of each other, saying in their hearts, "When I see him, I will do this for him, say this to him, ask him about this." All their private pleasures, their dearest desires, and their perfect joys are satisfied in pleasing and obeying the other. But if they don't love each other, then they don't value obedience and reverence any more than does the average couple, which is, in most cases, not much.

27. On the topic of games and pleasures between husbands and wives, by God, I heard the bailiff of Tournai say that he had attended several gatherings and dinners with men who had been married a long time, making with them several bets and wagers to pay for the dinner they had just eaten. They also bet on future dinner bills, on the condition that together all the members of the party would go to each married man's house to ascertain who in the group had a wife so obedient that he could, without a warning and without her making any mistakes, order her to count to 4 without pause, contradiction, derision, or protest. Such a man would be free of his share of the bill, and the one or ones whose wives were rebellious and answered back, mocked, or refused would have to pay for the others' dinner. When it was thus agreed, they went simply for fun to Robin's house. He summoned his wife Marie, who was very full of herself. In front of all the husbands Robin asked her, "Marie, repeat after me what I say." "Willingly, sir." "Marie, say: 'One.'" "One." "And 'two.'" "And two." "And 'three.'" To which Marie, a bit peevishly, replied, "And one, and 12, and 13! Come now! Are you making fun of me?" In this way, Marie's husband lost. Next, the husbands all went to Jean's house, whose wife Agnes was one to put on airs. Jean told her, "Repeat after me what I say: 'One.'" Agnes answered disdainfully, "And two." And thus he lost. Tassin said to the lady Tassine, "One." With pride, Tassine responded aloud, "This is something new!" Or she said, "I am not a child learning how to count," or she said, "Come now, by God! Have you become a musician?" and the like. And so he too lost. But all who had married young, well-bred, and well-instructed women won and were happy.

28. Consider even what God, who is all-wise, did and how angry He became because Adam, disobeying and disregarding His commandment and prohibition, ate the apple—though an apple is a small enough thing. Yet God was not incensed about the apple itself but about the disobedience and the disregard Adam had for Him. Think about how much He loved the Virgin Mary for her obedience. Recall the obedience and deeds of Abraham, which are mentioned hardly two pages above,[7] who purely because of a command did such great and awful things without asking why. Consider Griselda, what things she bore and endured in her heart, without inquiring about the reason. One can perceive no cause or shadow of a cause, no future profit and no need to act as she did, only her husband's will, both dreadful and terrible. Nor did she ask him for any justification or, indeed, say a word about it. Consequently, she won such praise that now, 500 years after her death, we still read of her goodness!

29. This doctrine of obedience of women to their husbands does not begin in

---

7. The section discussing Abraham, 1.5.4 ff., concerns primarily Sarah and the engendering of Abraham's children.

our time but is found in Genesis 29, where Lot and his wife set forth from a city and Lot forbade his wife to look behind her.[8] She obeyed for a while, but then, scorning the commandment, she glanced backward. Immediately, God transformed her into a pillar of salt and she remained there; and thus she is still and will be always. This is the actual content of the Bible, and we must believe it or we would not be good Christians.

30. Hence, you see that God tested His friends and servants in small things, an apple for one, a look backward for another, etc. So it is not surprising that husbands, who out of their goodness have placed their whole heart, their joy, and their delight in their wives and put all other loves behind them, take pleasure in their obedience and test them in loving jests, without harming others. For this reason, going back to what I said earlier about how husbands try the obedience of their wives, although it is only in jest, all those men who were disobeyed and thus who lost the bet had heavy hearts because of the mockery and loss they suffered. Whatever face they put on about it, they were all ashamed and less in love with their wives who had not been humble, fearful, and dutiful to them, as they should have been for such a small thing—unless there had been a good reason, and the wife should have told him the reason in secret and in private.

31. Sometimes foolish young husbands are so malicious that without better reason than small and trivial motives, arising from sport and pettiness and incessant disobedience on the part of their spouses, they accumulate and amass a secret anger in their hearts, the result of which is a bad outcome afflicting both members of the couple. On occasion husbands frequent wretched and dishonest women who obey them in all things and honor them more than they are honored by their own wives. These husbands, like fools, console themselves with these miserable females who know how to assure them of a peaceful existence and who honor and obey them in all things and do their bidding. Do not doubt: there is no husband, no matter how miserable, who does not want to be obeyed and gladdened by his wife. Hence, when husbands find themselves better deferred to elsewhere than in their own homes, unwisely, they nonchalantly abandon their wives because of their haughtiness and disobedience, wives who then become angry. Later, these wives see that in society they are not as honored as those women with whom their husbands now consort, and the husbands imprudently have hearts already so strongly leashed elsewhere that one cannot untie them. You cannot recapture a bird escaped from the cage as easily as you can prevent him from flying away. Likewise wives cannot reclaim their husbands' hearts when these husbands have tried and found greater deference elsewhere. Moreover, these wives transfer to their husbands the guilt they should assume.

---

8. This refers to Genesis 19.

32. My dear, you see that what is said about men and women can be claimed also of wild animals, even of ferocious ones like bears, wolves, and lions that carry off and devour their prey. For these animals can be lured and tamed if you appease them. They follow those who nurture, accompany, and love them. For bears can be ridden like horses, and monkeys and other animals can be trained to jump, dance, somersault, and obey all their master's wishes. By this reasoning, I can show you that your husband will cherish, love, and protect you if you attend to his contentment. Whereas I said, and I spoke truly, that wild animals can be tamed, I declare on the contrary, and you will find it so, that not only your husband but also your father, mother, and sisters will become estranged from you if you are defiant toward them and not meek and obedient. You know well that your primary home, your principal labor and love, and your principal company is that of your husband, on account of whose affection and companionship you are rich and honored. If he flees, withdraws, or abandons you because of your disobedience or for any other reason, rightly or wrongly, you will be left alone and impoverished and you will be blamed for it and held in less esteem. If just once you displease him, you will have a difficult time ever appeasing him enough so that the stain of his anger does not remain engraved and written on his heart. Although he may not show it or mention it, your misdeed cannot soon be smoothed over and erased. Should a second act of disobedience occur, watch out for his vengeance, which will be discussed in this same chapter and article, in the paragraph beginning "But it is far worse."[9] Therefore please love, serve, and obey your husband even in minor, insignificant things because sometimes people test us in inconsequential and seemingly playful matters, since less harm comes from insubordination in such trivial things. In this way one knows what to expect about compliance or defiance in important matters. Indeed, you must speedily obey even strange and outrageous orders that your husband expresses to you, whether in play or in all seriousness.

33. On this subject I cite a tale of three abbots and three husbands who were gathered and one of them raised a question, asking who was more obedient, wives to their husbands or monks to their abbot? Much was debated on this topic, with arguments and examples offered on both sides. I don't know whether the examples were true, but in the end they remained in disagreement and decided that a test would be conducted, loyally and secretly sworn between them by faith and oath. That is, each abbot would order each of his monks without the others' knowledge to leave his room open and place a switch under his pillow and wait for the discipline that his abbot would come to give him. And each husband would secretly order his wife, as they were going to bed, and without anyone ex-

---

9. ¶ 48.

cept themselves in the household knowing about it, to place and leave all night a broom behind their bedroom door. Within a week the abbots and husbands were to reassemble in the same place. They all swore to carry out their trial by that time and to report faithfully and loyally, without deception, what had ensued. Whichever group—the abbots or the husbands—had been shown the least obedience would pay a sum of ten francs.

34. In this way it was agreed upon and carried out. The report of each abbot was that, upon their souls, each one had given the order to each of his monks. At midnight the abbot had visited every room and found his order executed.

35. The husbands gave their reports next, one after the other. The first said that before going to bed he had secretly given the order to his wife, who asked him persistently what the point of it was. But he would not say. She then refused to do it, and he feigned irritation. At this, she promised him that she would comply. They went to bed that evening and dismissed their servants, who carried away the candle. The husband then made his wife get up, and he listened carefully as she placed the broom where he had indicated. He was pleased with her and fell asleep for a bit but awakened soon after and sensed that his wife was sleeping. He got up quietly, went to the door, found no broom, then crept back into bed. Waking his wife, he asked her if the broom was behind the door. She answered yes. He replied that indeed it was not, since he had checked. She then replied, "By God, I would not have it remain there, even if it meant losing my best dress. Because when you were asleep my hair began to stand on end and I broke out in a sweat, and I could not have slept as long as it was in the room. So I threw it out the window into the street."[10]

36. Another of the husbands said that once they were in bed he had made his wife get up, and most grudgingly and irritably she had placed the broom behind the door. But she had immediately gotten dressed again and left the room, saying that she would never sleep in a room where a broom was and that truly the devils of hell might come. So she went, completely dressed, to sleep with her chambermaid.

37. The remaining husband stated that his wife retorted that she had not come from or been born of magicians or sorcerers and that she did not know how to play at conjuring and broomsticks in the night, and even on pain of death she would not do it or consent to it, nor would she ever remain in the house if that was the case.

38. Thus, the monks obeyed their abbot, with whom they have a more distant relationship than marriage, in a weighty matter. This is logical, since they are

---

10. Broomsticks, ancient symbols of power and sorcery, might drive out those spirits that protect house and home.

men. But in a minor matter, the wives were less compliant to their own husbands, with whom they should have a special relationship. Yet it is their nature; they are women. Because of them, their husbands lost 10 francs, and their outrageous boasts about their wives' obedience were deflated. I beseech you, my dear, don't be like them! Rather, be submissive to your husband-to-be, both in insignificant and in bizarre things, whether he asks in all seriousness, in jest, for amusement, or any other reason, because all that matters to him merits your attention.

39. By God, I beheld a very strange thing in Melun, during the time that the sire d'Andresel was captain of the town. The English were lodged in several places in the vicinity and the men of Navarre inside the castle. One day after dinner the said sire d'Andresel was at the door, bored, griping that he had no idea where to go to have a good time and pass the day. A squire said to him, "Lord, do you want to go see a damsel living in this town who does anything that her husband commands?" The sire d'Andresel replied, "Yes. Let's go!" They set off, and on the way a squire was pointed out to the sire d'Andresel as the husband of the young woman in question. The sire d'Andresel called to him and asked whether his wife did what he ordered. This squire responded, "By God, sire, yes, if there is no great villainy." The sire d'Andresel told him, "I will bet you a dinner that she will not do as you ask when you give her a command that I will provide you and that will contain no villainy." The squire answered, "Certainly, sire, she will do it, and I will win. Yet there are several other ways that I could win a bet with you more honorably. Since there is more honor for me in losing a bet and paying for the dinner, I beg that you wager that she will do it and allow me to wager that she will not." The sire d'Andresel said, "I order you to bet as I said." Then the squire obeyed and accepted the wager.

40. The sire d'Andresel wished to be present at the test, accompanied by his entire group. The squire agreed. Then the sire d'Andresel, who was holding a stick, told him, "I wish that, as soon as we arrive and without uttering anything else, in our presence you insist that your wife jump over this stick and do it without a frown, wink, or any other face." Thus it was concluded. They all entered the squire's house together, and the young woman came immediately to meet them. The squire set the stick on the ground and said, "Madam, jump over this." She jumped right away. He told her, "Jump again." She jumped again. "Again!" She jumped three times, without saying a single word besides "Willingly!"

41. The sire d'Andresel was thunderstruck and granted that he owed the squire a dinner and would repay it the next day in his house. Straightaway they all set out for the house, and as soon as he entered the door the lady d'Andresel met and greeted him with a bow. Once the sire d'Andresel dismounted, still holding the stick over which the young lady had jumped in Melun, he placed the stick on the ground and tried to make his wife jump over it, which she refused. This enraged

the sire d'Andresel, and I will keep silent about the rest, and for a good reason! But this much I can well say, and I know it truly, that if she had executed her husband's command, issued more as a joke and test than for profit, she would have retained more honor and been more esteemed by him. But to some women merit does not come, and to others it does.

42. Further on this topic, I can relate another story just as strange. One summer day, I was traveling from Chaumont in Bassigny to Paris and one hour before Vespers stopped for lodging in the town of Bar-sur-Aube. Several young men of the town who were married there and knew me somewhat came to entreat me to have supper with them, and they presented their situation as such: These men were married fairly recently to young wives, and there was not a sage amongst them. They had inquired of each other and realized from each man's answer that each of them believed he had the best and most obedient wife, compliant in all things—orders or interdictions, large or small. So they plotted, as they said, to go together to one another's homes, and there the husband would ask his wife for a needle, a pin, a pair of scissors, the key to their coffer, or something of the sort. Should the wife respond, "What for?" or "What are you going to do with it?" or "Is this in earnest?" or "Are you making fun of me?" or "I don't have any!" or if she made any other reply or hesitation, the husband would pay one franc for the supper. But if without argument or delay she immediately gave her husband what he requested, the husband would be considered fortunate to have such a humble and tractable wife and deemed wise to maintain and keep her in such submission. Consequently, he would be seated at the head of the table and would pay nothing.

43. Although some women cannot or deign not to yield to such minor and odd directives, but disdain and despise them, along with those who conduct such acts of deference, nonetheless, my dear, be assured that it is necessary that human nature take enjoyment in something. Even the poor, the powerless, the sick or languishing, or those on their deathbeds feel and seek pleasure and joy, as do, for even greater reason, those who are in good health. Some people find gladness only in hunting or hawking. Others enjoy playing instruments; yet others swimming, dancing, singing, or jousting, each finding delight according to his condition. Even you seek your entertainment in diverse ways. Therefore, if your husband imagines that he would find happiness in your service or obedience, as I described above, then serve and content him. Understand that God will give you a great grace because your husband finds more comfort in you than in anything else. While you are the key to his pleasure, he will show devotion to you, attend to, and love you. If he finds his happiness in something else, he will follow it and you will be forgotten. In this way I counsel and admonish you to do his will in all things, even the insignificant and eccentric ones. Carry this out and his chil-

dren and you yourself will be his music, his joys, his bliss; he won't seek gladness elsewhere. This will be a great gift and a great peace and honor for you.

44. Should it happen that upon departing from home, your husband forgets some business or other and for this reason fails to mention it to you or give any order or prohibition concerning it, you should nonetheless act according to his desire, despite your own inclination. Set your own opinion aside, and always place his pleasure first. But should the matter be a weighty one, and you have the time to let him know about it, write to him that you think it would be his will that you handle it in such a way, etc., and therefore that you wish to do his bidding. But because doing it that way could lead to inconveniences, losses, or damage, and it seems to you that it would be better and more honorable to do such and such, etc. —something you don't dare do without his authorization—would he please make known his wishes on this matter? You will carry out his orders most willingly and with all your power, etc.

45. All women do not proceed in this way, with the result that things go badly for them in the end. At that point, when they lose their husband's esteem, and when they see the good, obedient wives who are so fortunate, accompanied and loved by their husbands, these wicked ones who do not act prudently accuse Fortune of attacking them and their husbands of not trusting them. But they lie: Fortune is not responsible, but their own disobedience and irreverence toward their husbands. After these wives have disobeyed and lacked respect so often, husbands no longer dare trust them and so have sought and found obedience elsewhere, where they place their trust.

46. And, by God, I remember seeing one of your cousins who is fond of us both, as well as her husband. She came to me and said, "Cousin, we have such a matter to take care of, and it seems to me it would be well done thus-and-so. That would really please me. What do you think?" So I told her, "The first priority is to know your husband's opinions and wishes. Have you not spoken to him about this?" She responded, "By God, cousin, indeed not, because through various means and curious words I felt that he would like it done in a way different from what I just said. I myself would really like to do it as I explained. And as you know, cousin, it is less blameworthy to do something without one's lord's permission than after he forbids it, and I am certain that he would forbid me this. Surely he loves you and considers you a good person, and if I acted on the matter as I want to and tell him I proceeded that way through your advice, whatever came of it, I could explain that I followed your counsel. He would be easily appeased, for he loves you so much." "Well," I told her, "since he values me, I must value him and do his wishes. Therefore, I advise you to act according to his desire and not insist on your own way." She could procure no other opinion from me and departed quite irritated at my failure to help her have her own way, which was completely

contrary to her husband's. Her husband's anger did not matter to her, for she would have been able to respond as an excuse, "You did not order me to do otherwise, etc. Your cousin advised me to do it this way." Now consider her intention, and how much inclination this woman possesses to please her husband, and what kind of obedience she shows him!

47. My dear, there are other women who, when they fancy to do something one way but doubt that their husbands would want it done that way, neither respect his method nor venture to gainsay him, but squirm and seethe. When such a woman finds herself alone with her husband and they discuss their business matters and amusements, the woman by hinting around subtly investigates and realizes that her husband intends to handle this matter otherwise than she would prefer. The woman briskly changes the topic of their conversation, before he has the chance to say, "In this matter, do thus." Cunningly she maneuvers out of the touchy situation and turns her husband to another subject and concludes their conversation on a topic distant from the one on her mind. As soon as she sees the opportunity, she has the initial matter accomplished according to her own wishes and does not concern herself about her husband's viewpoint, which she ignores, and having a ready excuse will say, "You said nothing about it to me!" because she flouts the anger and displeasure of her husband, caring only that she has control. It strikes me that it is wrong to trick, deceive, and try one's husband like that. Nevertheless, there are many who make such attempts and more, which is acting in bad faith, because a woman must always aspire to gratify her husband, whenever he is wise and reasonable, that is. It is a bad business secretly and craftily to test a husband through malicious and extraordinary pretense, assuming it is a better method for achieving success. Because with one's beloved, one should not act with cunning or malice, but openly and completely, heart to heart.

48. But it is far worse when a woman has an honorable and genteel husband, and she neglects him because she expects to be pardoned or excused for acting wrongly. As it is written in the book of the *Seven Sages of Rome*,[11] there was in the city a wise widower, elderly and well endowed with land and good reputation, who had outlived two wives. His friends advised him to take another wife. He enjoined them to locate one for him, and he would gladly marry her. They procured

---

11. *The Seven Sages of Rome,* a popular medieval story collection, had versions in nearly every European language. The first surviving version of these stories dates from the 1150s in France, but their origin lies in *The Book of Sindbad* composed perhaps in the fifth century BC in Persia, the Holy Land, or India. The stories influenced Chaucer and Gower, and various printed versions have survived in English from the sixteenth century. See Jill Whitelock, ed., *The Seven Sages of Rome* (Midland Version), edited from Cambridge, University Library, MS Dd.1.17, Early English Text Society (Oxford: Oxford University Press, 2005).

for him one who was beautiful, young, and graceful of body, because of course you will scarcely see a man so old that he does not willingly take a young wife! He married the lady and was with her one year without doing you-know-what with her.

49. Now this lady had a mother, and one day she was at church with her mother and whispered to her that she had no pleasure from her husband and for this reason desired to take a lover. "Daughter," said the mother, "if you did it, your husband would treat you incredibly harshly. For certainly there is no greater vengeance than that of an old man. Therefore, if you believe me, you will not even attempt it, because you could never appease your husband." The daughter replied that she still wanted to do it. The mother then said, "Since it cannot be otherwise, I would like you first to put your husband to a test." "Willingly," said the daughter, "I will test him this way: he has in his orchard a beautiful grafted fruit tree that he loves more than all his other trees. I will cut it down, and then I will see whether I can placate him afterward." They agreed on this, left the church, and parted.

50. The young woman returned home and found that her lord was out walking in the fields. She took an axe, went to the grafted tree, and began striking it left and right until she felled it, then had it chopped up by a varlet and carried to the fireplace.

51. As the varlet was hauling it in, the lord entered his house and saw the man carrying the logs from his fruit tree, and also the lady who strode in front of him holding a log of the tree in her hand. The lord asked, "Where does this firewood come from?" The lady answered, "I just returned from the church and they told me you were in the fields, and since it had rained, I feared that you would return wet and be cold. So I went into the orchard and cut down this fruit tree, because there is no firewood in the house." "Lady," said the lord, "that's my good fruit tree." "Truly, lord," said the lady, "I didn't know."

52. The lord went off to his orchard and beheld the stump of the beloved tree. He was quite a bit angrier than he looked. He returned and found the lady making a fire with the fruit tree, and it seemed that she was doing so with good intention to warm him. When the lord arrived, he spoke these words, "In fact, lady, it certainly was my best fruit tree that you cut down." "Lord," said the lady, "I did not pay attention to that, for truthfully I did it because I knew that you would come in all wet and soaked with rain, and I feared that you would be cold and take sick." "Dame," said the lord, "I will let it go, since you say that you did it for me."

53. The next day, the lady returned to church and found her mother, to whom she said, "I tested my lord and cut down the fruit tree, but he showed no sign of rage. Therefore, mother, know that I will love." "No, you will not," said the mother. "Let it be." "Surely," said the daughter, "I will do it. I can contain myself

no longer." "Dear daughter," said the mother, "because it is such that you say you can no longer restrain yourself, put your husband to the test once again." The daughter said, "Willingly. I will test him in this way: he has a greyhound that he loves deeply. He would not take a cent for it, it is so good, nor would he allow any of his varlets to chase it away from the fire or anyone to feed it but himself. I will kill it in front of him." With that, they parted.

54. The daughter arrived home. It was late and chilly. The fire flamed beautiful and bright, and the beds were well adorned and covered with fine coverlets and rugs, and the lady was dressed in a new fur-lined tunic. The lord returned from the fields. The lady rose to meet him, took off his cloak, and then wanted to remove his spurs, but the lord would not allow her and had them removed by one of his varlets. The lady gave herself entirely to serving him. She ran and brought him a lined robe, draped it over his shoulders, arranged a chair, placed a cushion on it, made him sit by the fire, and said to him, "Lord, you are certainly pale with cold; warm yourself and relax." When she had spoken thus, she settled down close to him and lower than he, on a footstool, spreading the skirt of her tunic, gazing the whole time at her husband.

55. When the greyhound saw the welcoming fire, by misfortune it came and lay down on the edge of the lady's dress and tunic. The lady saw a varlet nearby with a large knife. She seized it and stabbed it through the greyhound's body, which began to shudder, and then it died right before the husband's eyes. "Dame," he said, "how were you so bold as to kill in my presence my beloved greyhound?" "Lord," said the lady, "don't you see how they muddy us every day? Two days never go by that we don't need to do a laundry here because of your dogs. And now look what has become of my tunic that I had never worn before! Did you think I would not be upset?" The old wise man replied, "By God, it was ill done, and I am displeased with you! But I won't speak any more about it." The lady said, "Sire, you can do with me as you will, because I am yours. Understand, though, that I am sorry for what I have done, because I know that you loved the dog dearly, and it distresses me that I have angered you." When she had said this, she made a great show of weeping. When the lord observed this, he let the deed pass.

56. The next day she went to the church, found her mother, and told her all that had happened, remarking that since it had turned out so well for her, she really would take a lover. "Ah! Dear daughter," said the mother, "you will not do so, you can control yourself!" "Certainly not, lady!" Then the mother said, "All my life I have remained faithful to your father; I have never committed such a folly, nor have I had the inclination." "Ah, lady," replied the daughter, "it is not the same for me as it is for you. You and my father were wed when you were both young, and you had your pleasures together, but I have no pleasure or delight

from my husband, so I need to seek it." "Well, dear daughter, if it is crucial that you love, who will you love?" "Mother," said the daughter, "I will love the chaplain of this town, because priests and monks fear shame and are more discreet. I would never want a knight as a lover, because he would soon boast and brag about me and ask for pledges of commitment." "Now, dear daughter, do as I advise once more, and try your husband again." The daughter said, "Putting him to the test so much, again and again, I will never be finished!" "By my head," said the mother, "you will test him one more time, if you ask me, for never will you see such fearsome and cruel revenge as that of an old man!" "Well, lady," said the daughter, "I will willingly follow your commandment and will test him this way: Thursday will be Christmas day, and my lord will hold a great feast for his kinsmen and other friends, for all the vavasors of our village will be there. I will be seated at the head of the table. As soon as the first course is served, I will entangle my keys in the fringe of the tablecloth, and doing this, I will stand up abruptly, pulling everything toward me and scattering and spilling everything on the table. And then I will calm him once more. Thus I will have put my lord to the test three times, with three great trials, and easily appeased him. So by this, know well that I will pacify him just as easily in situations more obscure and sly, so that he will be able only to suspect, but have no proof." "Well then, dear daughter," said the mother, "God grant that you do well." At this they parted.

57. Each went to her home. In all appearances, the daughter served her lord cordially, graciously, and pleasantly, until Christmas day came. The vavasors of Rome and the damsels had come; the tables were set, the tablecloths laid, and everyone seated. As lady of the house and hostess, the lady presided at the head of the table. The servants brought out the first course and broth and placed them on the table. At the moment when the varlets in charge of carving began to carve, the lady twisted her keys in the fringe at the end of the tablecloth. When she knew that they were well entwined, she stood up suddenly and took a large step backward, as though she had lost her balance while rising. She pulled on the tablecloth, and bowls full of broth and goblets full of wine and sauces spilled, and everything on the table was overturned.

58. When the lord saw this, he was ashamed and wrathful, and he remembered the earlier incidents. At once, the lady removed her keys that were entangled in the tablecloth. "Dame," said the lord, "you have behaved badly." "Lord," said the lady, "I could not help it. I was going to look for your carving knives that were not on the table, which troubled me." "Dame," said the lord, "now go get us other tablecloths." The lady had other cloths brought, and more food began to arrive. They ate happily, the lord displaying no evidence of rage. When the guests had eaten enough and the lord had shown them great honor, they departed.

59. The lord suffered all night until the next day. He then said, "Dame, you

have caused me three displeasures. If I can help it, you will not cause a fourth. I know well that it is bad blood that has made you do so. You need to be bled." He sent for the barber and had the fire prepared. The lady told him, "Sire, what do you want to do? I have never been bled!" "So much the worse," said the lord. "It is time you started. It's the bad blood that made you play the three ill tricks on me." Then he had her right arm warmed over the fire, and he had her bled until thick red blood came. Then the lord had her staunched and then had her other arm pulled out from her dress. The lady began to cry for mercy, but it did no good. He had her second arm warmed and bled, holding her until she fainted and lost speech and turned as pale as death. When the lord saw that, he had her staunched and carried to her bed in her room.

60. When she regained consciousness, she began to cry out and weep, and she sent for her mother who came immediately. When she was before her daughter, the others left the room, and the two remained alone together. When the lady saw her mother, she said, "Ah! Mother, I am dead! My lord had me bled so much that I think I shall never enjoy my body!" "Indeed, daughter, I do think that bad blood was consuming you. Tell me, now, my daughter, do you still desire to take a lover?" "Absolutely not, lady!" "Daughter, did I not tell you that you would never see vengeance as cruel as that of an old man?" "Lady, yes; but, for the love of God, help me to recover and restore my health, and by my soul, mother, I will never seek a lover." "Dear daughter," said the mother, "you will act sensibly. Your lord is a good, wise, and honorable man. Love him and serve him, and believe me, only good and honor will come to you." "Certainly, mother, I know well now that you have given and give me good advice, and I will believe it from now on and will honor my husband, and never will I neglect or anger him."

61. My dear, that will suffice concerning this matter for one who wishes to retain the lesson and obey. On obedience, to recapitulate: we have spoken above concerning what must be done when the husband makes a command, be it a trifle, in jest, in earnest, or otherwise. And then how to act when the husband has neither ordered nor forbidden, because he has not remembered whatever it is. And thirdly, of the exceptional things women do to assert their own willfulness, above and beyond the wishes of their husbands. Now at the last, let us say that they should not act contrary to their husband's bidding, whether in small or large things, because to do so is a serious wrong. I began with small matters, in which one must obey; I proved it through the judgments of God, because, as you know, my dear, owing to the disobedience of Adam, who despite the prohibition ate an apple, in itself a minor thing, everyone was placed in servitude. Accordingly I advise you that whatever petty things of little value—even a straw—that your husband who will come after me orders you to attend to, without inquiring as to the purpose or to what end, you keep it carefully and conscientiously, since the re-

quest will have come from your future husband's mouth. For you cannot know and therefore you must not ask what gives rise to or motivated him to this command—if he has a reason, or if he does it to test you—unless he explains it to you on his own initiative. For if he has a reason, you are wise to do whatever he has asked of you. If there is no motive except to test you, then you must wish him to find you tractable and diligent in following his orders. Keep in mind that since he found you obedient to his will concerning a trifle and you deemed it of great account, he will believe that in an important matter he will discover you one hundred times more obedient. Realize that Our Lord entrusted Adam to be mindful of a small thing, that is to say a single apple tree, and you can well imagine that Our Lord was not angry with Adam over an apple—because for such a great lord, an apple is such a small thing—but He was displeased by Adam's holding His orders in such little esteem and wronging Him for such a small profit. Understand and consider too that because Adam was closer to Our Lord, who had made him with His own hand and regarded him as a family member and guardian of His garden, all the more bitterly was Our Lord roused against him for such a little thing and afterward did not wish to sanctify the disobedience. Similarly, and all the more because you are akin and so near to your husband, he would more quickly and for a less significant thing be more sharply angry with you, as Our Lord was angry with Lucifer who was closer to Him.

62. But there are some women who think they can adroitly avoid their duty. When their husband has forbidden them to do something they really would like to do, they tarry and wait and let the time pass until their husband forgets his restrictions forbidding the matter, or until he goes on a journey, or he is preoccupied by business so weighty that he might not recollect this issue. Accordingly, the woman hastily carries out this matter as she wills and against the will and veto of the husband. Or she may have it accomplished by her people, saying, "Proceed boldly, my lord will never notice it. He will be ignorant of it." Now you perceive from this rebellion that this woman, in her innermost spirit, is disobedient, and her defiant spite and wickedness weaken her cause and clearly reveal her bad intentions. Rest assured that in the end nothing remains hidden. Consequently, when the husband perceives that she separates the union of their wills that should be one, as it is said above, this husband will perhaps keep silent as did that wise man of Rome earlier in this article. However, his heart will be so deeply wounded that it will never heal, but every time that he remembers it his pain is renewed. So I beseech you, my dear, be on your guard and protect yourself most especially from attempting to try another husband, if you have one. Rather, let your sympathies and his be one, as you and I are at present. And that suffices for this article.

¶ 1.7 *The Care of the Husband's Person*

1. This 7th article of the first section discloses that you should be attentive to and thoughtful of your husband's person. On this topic realize, my dear, that if you have another husband after me, you must consider his physical comfort, for after a woman has lost her first spouse and marriage, it is challenging to find another man in her social class that she might favor. For a long time, she remains distraught and forlorn—and all the more so if she also loses the second one. Therefore love your husband's person carefully. I entreat you to see that he has clean linen, for that is your domain, while the concerns and troubles of men are those outside affairs that they must handle, amidst coming and going, running here and there, in rain, wind, snow, and hail, sometimes drenched, sometimes dry, now sweating, now shivering, ill fed, ill lodged, ill shod, and poorly rested. Yet nothing represents a hardship for him, because the thought of his wife's good care for him upon his return comforts him immensely. The ease, joys, and pleasures he knows she will provide for him herself, or have done for him in her presence, cheer him: removing his shoes in front of a good fire, washing his feet, offering clean shoes and socks, serving plenteous food and drink, respectfully honoring him. After this, she puts him to sleep in white sheets and his nightcap, covered with good furs, and satisfies him with other joys and amusements, intimacies, loves, and secrets about which I remain silent. The next day, she has set out fresh shirts and garments for him.

2. Dear one, such services without doubt make a man cherish her! He will long to return to see his beloved wife and home and will keep his distance from other women. I therefore advise you to provide these comforts for your husband each time he arrives home. Keep it up, persevere! Also maintain peace with him and remember the peasant proverb that says: "There are three things that drive a good man from home: a roofless house, a smoky chimney, and a quarrelsome woman." Therefore, to continue in your husband's affection and good graces, I beg you, my dear, be gentle, lovable, and gracious toward him. Treat him the way the good simple women of our country claim their sons have been treated when they have fallen in love elsewhere and their mothers cannot put a stop to it. For certainly when a child loses his father and mother, his stepfather and stepmother torment, scold, and push him away, not caring about where he sleeps, what he eats and drinks, his hose, shirts, or any other necessities. If he finds outside the family a safe refuge and the help of a woman who welcomes him, taking care to warm him sitting with her by a little fire, to clean and mend his hose, breeches, shirts, and other

clothing, subsequently he will follow her and desire her company, wanting to sleep and warm himself between her breasts. Thus will the child cast off his stepmother and stepfather, who beforehand paid no attention to him and now want to take him back and have him again. But that will not happen, for such a child now values more the company of this stranger who considers and cares for him than that of his relatives who paid no heed to him but currently lament and cry. They wail that the woman has bewitched their child and that because of the spell he cannot leave her or be happy unless he stays with her. But whatever they say, it is not witchcraft; rather it is due to the love, the courtesies, the intimacies, joys, and pleasures that the woman has shared with him. On my soul, there is no other magic! Assuredly, if you show kindheartedness to a bear, a wolf, or a lion, that same bear, wolf, or lion will follow you. Other beasts, if they could speak, might make similar accusations, that those tamed in this way were bewitched. On my soul, I believe that there is no other witchcraft than doing good, and you cannot enthrall a man any better way than by pleasing him.

3. And that is why, my dear, I urge you to bewitch and bewitch again your future husband, and protect him from holes in the roof and smoky fires, and do not quarrel with him, but be sweet, pleasant, and peaceful with him. Make certain that in winter he has a good fire without smoke, and let him slumber, warmly wrapped, cozy between your breasts, and in this way bewitch him. In summer take care that there are no fleas in your bedroom or bed. This you can remedy in six ways, as I have heard tell. I have been informed that if you scatter alder leaves throughout the room, the fleas will get caught in them. *Item,* if you set in the room one or two slices of bread smeared with glue or turpentine, with a lighted candle in the middle of each slice, the fleas will come and get stuck and trapped. The other way, which I have tried and it works: take a rough cloth and spread it in your room and on your bed, and all the fleas that land there will get caught, and you will be able to carry them away with the cloth to wherever you wish. *Item,* it works the same with sheepskins. *Item,* I have seen white blankets placed on the straw mattresses and on the bed, and when the black fleas landed on them, they were quickly spotted on the white background and killed. But the most difficult part is to safeguard oneself from those within the coverlets, the furs, and the clothing that covers us. I have tried this: if the furs and robes that are infested with fleas are closed up and shut away, as inside a chest tightly strapped, or in a bag tied up securely and squeezed, or enclosed and pressed in some other way, depriving them of light and air and imprisoning them, the fleas will quickly perish.

4. *Item,* I have witnessed often in different places that once people go to bed, the rooms fill with mosquitoes, attracted by the breath of the sleepers. The insects land on their faces and sting them so hard that they have to get up to make a fire of hay in order to create enough smoke so that the creatures must fly away

or die. This remedy can also be used by day, one would imagine, and anyone who has a mosquito net can protect himself just as well by using it.

5. If you have a room or a floor in your dwelling infested with flies, take little sprigs of fern, tie them together with threads like tassels, hang them up, and all the flies will settle on them in the evening. Then take down the tassels and throw them outside. *Item,* close up your room firmly in the evening, leaving just one small opening in the eastern wall. At dawn, all the flies will exit through this opening, and then you seal it up. *Item,* take a bowl of milk and a hare's gall bladder, mix them together, and then set out two or three bowls of the mixture in places where the flies gather, and all that taste it will die. *Item,* otherwise, tie a linen stocking to the bottom of a pierced pot and set the pot in the place where the flies gather and smear the inside with honey, or apples, or pears. When it is full of flies, place a platter over the opening, then shake it. *Item,* alternatively, grind raw red onions, squeeze the juice into a bowl, and set it where the flies gather; all that taste it will die. *Item,* use little paddles with which to kill them by hand. *Item,* place twigs covered with glue over a basin of water. *Item,* cover your windows with oiled cloth, parchment, or something else, so firmly that no fly can enter. Kill the flies that are inside, using a swatter or other suggestion from above, and no others will come in. *Item,* hang a string that has been soaked in honey, and when in the evening the flies land on it, trap them in a bag. Finally, it seems to me that flies will not settle in a room in which there are no tables, benches, sideboards, or other things on which they can land and rest. For if there are only straight walls for them to cling to and rest on, they will not linger there, nor will they remain in a shady or damp place. Therefore it seems to me that if the room is kept moist and tightly closed and shut up, and if nothing is left lying on the floor, no fly will land there.

6. In this way, serve your husband and have him waited on in your house, protecting and keeping him from all irritations and providing him all the creature comforts that you can imagine. Rely on him for external matters, for if he is considerate, he will make even greater efforts and work harder than you could wish. If you do what is said here, he will always miss you and his heart will always be with you and your soothing ways, shunning all other houses, all other women, all other services and households. If you look after him in the way this treatise urges, in comparison with you, everything else will be dust. Your behavior should follow the example of those who traverse the world on horseback. As soon as they arrive home from a journey, they provide fresh litter for their horses up to their bellies. These horses are unharnessed and bedded down, given honey, choice hay, and ground oats, and are always better tended when they return to their own stables than anywhere else. If horses are made so comfortable, it makes good sense that a person should be treated similarly upon his return, particularly a lord at his own household. When dogs return from the woods after the hunt, a white litter

is prepared on the hearth in front of their lord—sometimes the lord himself prepares it—and there by the fire the dogs' feet are greased with lard. They are given sops and well provided for, in recognition of their labor. Likewise, if women look after their husbands as men treat their horses, dogs, asses, mules, and other beasts, certainly all other houses where they have been served will seem to them like dark prisons and inhospitable places, next to their own, which will be a paradise of relaxation for them. Thus, while on the road, husbands will reflect on their wives' fineness. No effort will seem like a burden to them because of the hope and love they will have for their wives, whom they yearn to see again as much as poor hermits, penitents, and ascetic men of God desire to see the face of Jesus Christ. These husbands, tended solicitously, will never prefer another abode or any other company. Rather, they will shun, withdraw, and abstain from them. Other havens will seem to them like a bed of stones compared with their home, provided there is constant and sincere comfort.

7. But some sly old dames pretend to be proper and feign devotion by declaring what an immense duty they perform with love, without actually doing anything. Know, my dear, that their husbands can't be too sharp if they are conned by this. Should the husbands notice, and if the husband and wife remain silent and conceal their thoughts from one another, the bad beginning will lead to a worse end.

8. Some women early in the marriage fawn on their husbands excessively. They imagine that their husbands, who appear so adoring and gracious toward them, would, over time, hardly dare to become vexed at somewhat less attention lavished on them. So they slacken up and little by little show less respect, attention, and obedience. What is more, they assume authority, command, and lordship, at first in a small thing, then in a larger, and then a little more every day. Thus they test and advance and gain ground, or so they think. They believe that their husbands, who keep silent—whether out of graciousness, chance, or because they are setting a trap—do not discern anything, since they accept this conduct. Certainly these women are imprudent! When the husbands perceive that the wives are becoming less solicitous and more domineering and that something awful could come of tolerating the situation, the wives are felled with one stroke, by their husbands' rightful will, just as was Lucifer, the leader of the angels of Paradise, whom Our Lord so loved that He allowed and tolerated him to do as he pleased, whereby Lucifer grew haughty with pride and presumptuousness. He overreached, undertaking so much that he went to excess and displeased Our Lord, who had long concealed His thoughts and suffered him without a word. Then in a flash He called it all to mind and cast the angel down into the deepest depths of hell, because he did not continue the service that he had been ordered to do, which had in the beginning greatly endeared him to Our Lord. For this reason, you should be obedient at the outset and always persevere according to this example.

¶ 1.8 *The Husband's Secrets*

1. The 8th article of the first section directs you to be silent or at least to speak sparingly and wisely so as to protect and conceal your husband's secrets. About which, dear, understand that anyone who speaks in excitement lacks moderation. Therefore knowing how to rein in one's tongue is a sovereign virtue. Many dangers have come from overmuch talk, especially when speaking with arrogant or strong-tempered people or persons of the court or lords. Above all, refrain from conversing with such folk, and if by chance they should speak to you, it will be wise of you, and indeed it is crucial, to avoid them, withdrawing sensibly and courteously. However much it pains you, you must nonetheless master the control of your speech, for a person who cannot do so is not wise. As the country proverb goes: "No one is worthy of mastery over another if he cannot master himself."

2. For this reason, in this matter and in all others, you must control your heart and tongue so that they may be subject to your reason. Consider always before whom and to whom you speak. I urge and advise you, whether in society or at table, to restrain yourself from too much conversation. For if one speaks freely, it is not possible to avoid some ill-chosen terms, and sometimes one speaks spirited words in jest, which afterward are taken and remembered out of context, to the derision and mockery of the speaker. So pay attention to who may overhear you, to the matter of your conversation, and to your intention, speaking what you have to say directly and simply. When you utter something, take care that nothing comes forth that should not and bridle your mouth to hold back the excess.

3. Be a trustworthy confidante, remembering always to keep your husband's secrets. First, regarding his misdeeds, vices, or sins, if you know of any: conceal and cover them up, even without his knowledge, so that he may not be disgraced. You will hardly ever find a person whose love for a friend does not diminish once that friend perceives his sin, for then the relationship is colored by shame and apprehension. Thus I counsel you never to reveal to anyone, no matter how close to you, what your husband confides to you in private. In so doing you will conquer your woman's nature that, so it is said, can hide nothing.

4. At least it is so for the evil and wicked females, about whom a philosopher named Macrobius relates in the book of *Scipio's Dream*.[1] There was in Rome a young boy named Papirius who, with his father, a senator of Rome, went into

---

1. Macrobius's commentary on Cicero's *Somnium Scipionis*. BF note that the *Le Ménagier* author knew the story of Papirus through Jean Freron, not Macrobius. See Georgine E. Brereton,

the hall where the senators held their assembly. There the senators swore that anyone who divulged their counsel did so threatened by the loss of his head. When they had finished their meeting and the child returned home, his mother asked him where he came from, and he replied that he had been at the senate assembly with his father. His mother asked him what the deliberations had been, and he answered that he dared not say on pain of death. Then the mother was even more curious to know, and she began first to flatter and then to threaten her son, to make him tell her. When the child perceived that he could not resist his mother, he made her first promise that she would not repeat it to anyone, and this she promised him. Then he told her a lie, that is, that the senators had debated whether a husband could have two wives or a wife two husbands. When the mother heard this, she forbade him to disclose it to anyone else. But she went straight to her women neighbors and passed on to them the counsel in private, and each told it to another, until at last everyone knew the deliberations, although told to each as a secret.

5. Soon afterward, it happened that all the women of Rome came to the senate house, where the senators were assembled. They cried out many times in loud voices that they would prefer that a woman have two husbands than a man two wives. The senators were thoroughly confused and did not know what all this meant. Silently, they looked at one another and wondered where this notion had come from, until the child Papirius unfolded to them the story. Hearing of it, the senators were vexed. They made him a senator but ruled that from then on no child could attend their assembly.

6. This example makes it clear that the male child knew how to keep a secret and remain silent and thus escaped. Yet the woman, who was old enough to have sense and discretion, did not know how to hold her tongue and keep a sworn secret she had promised on her oath, not even a secret that concerned her husband's and son's honor.

7. But the worst of it is that when women gossip to one another, the last one always adds a little more to the story, making it more her own, and then the next one embellishes even more, thus increasing the falsehood. On this matter there is a country tale about a housewife who was an early riser. One morning, when she did not get up at her usual time, her neighbor, worried that she was ill, went to her bedside and asked her repeatedly what ailed her. The good woman, who was ashamed that she had lain about so much, did not know how to reply other than that she was quite indisposed, so much so that she could not discuss it. The busybody begged and pressed her to divulge her reasons for love of her and swore,

"Deux sources du Ménagier de Paris: Le Roman des sept sages de Rome et Les Moralitez sur le jeu des eschés," Romania 74 (1953): 348.

promised, and bound herself never to reveal what she heard for anything in the world, to a living soul, father, mother, sister, brother, husband, confessor, or any other. After this promise and oath the good woman, who did not have a clue what to say, randomly told her that she had laid an egg. The busybody was completely astonished and pretended to be most distressed, swearing more loudly than before that not a word of it would ever be revealed.

8. Shortly afterward this gossip left and on the road home met a fellow gossiper who inquired whence she came. The first woman answered that she had been to see a good woman who was ill and had laid two eggs. She begged the other to keep this secret, and so it was vowed. The second gossip met another and in confidence told her that the good woman had laid four eggs. That third woman met another, disclosing to her that eight eggs were laid, and so the number multiplied more and more. The housewife rose and traveled about the town where people were saying that she had laid a whole basket full of eggs. Thus she realized how poor females are at keeping secrets, and even worse, each retelling further corrupts the truth.[2]

9. Therefore, my dear, know how to conceal your secrets from everyone, except for your husband. That will be quite sensible. Do not imagine that another person will hide for you what you yourself have been unable to hide. For this reason be private and discreet to everyone except your husband, for you should not dissemble with him but should unburden yourself when you and he are together. As it is said in Ephesians 5: *Sic viri debent diligere uxores: Scilicet ut corpora sua. Ideo ibidem dititur: Viri diligite uxores vestras, etc. Unusquisque uxorem suam diligat sicut seipsum.*[3] In other words, a man should love his wife as his own body, and therefore you two, that is, man and wife, should be as one and consult each other in all things and entirely. That is what good and wise people do and must do.

10. I also want husbands to know that they should likewise hide and cover up their wives' blunders and gently protect them from committing more. There was a good worthy man from Venice who did just so. In Venice there was a married couple with three children. As the wife lay upon her deathbed, she confessed among other things that one of the children was not her husband's. The confessor advised her that he would deliberate concerning what counsel to give her and would return. The confessor then went to the physician taking care of her and inquired about the state of her illness. The physician said that she would not recover. The confessor revisited her, declaring that he had considered her case and

---

2. The egg-laying anecdote also appears in the *Livre du Chevalier de la Tour* and Caxton's *Book of the Knight of the Tower*, chap. 74 (via the *Livre du Chevalier*), but in it the egg layer is a woman's husband who tests her by asking her to keep a secret.

3. This biblical verse is not exactly as in the Vulgate.

did not deem that God would grant her salvation unless she begged her husband's forgiveness for the wrong she had done him. Sending for her husband, she made everyone else leave the room, except for her mother and her confessor, who assisted her up onto her knees in the bed. With her hands clasped before her, she humbly beseeched her husband for his mercy for having sinned against the law of marriage, since one of her children was conceived with another man. She continued her admission, but her husband cried out and said, "Ho! ho! ho! say no more!" He then kissed her and pardoned her, chiding, "Never speak of this again, nor tell me or anyone else which of your children it may be, for I want to love them all equally, so that you will not be blamed either during your life or after your death. For I would be shamed by your guilt, as would your children, and others through them, such as our relatives, would receive vile and perpetual reproach. Be silent; I do not wish to know any more. So that no one will ever suggest that I am doing wrong by the other two, whichever he may be, I give him in direct gift already now during my life all that would come to him by the law of succession."

11. Dear one, thus you see how the prudent man subdued his own feelings to save his wife's honor, which touched his own and his children's honor. This clarifies what wise men and wise women must do for each other to safeguard their reputations.

12. Another example can be drawn concerning this matter. The wife of a great and wise man left him for a young man and went off to Avignon. When this young man had had his fill of her, he abandoned her, as such men frequently do. Poor and brokenhearted, she turned to prostitution because she couldn't support herself. Anguished when he learned of her life, her husband arranged the following remedy. He gave his wife's two brothers money and sent them on horseback to seek their sister, now a prostitute in Avignon. He told them to dress her in sackcloth, load her with cockle shells, as was the custom of pilgrims coming from Santiago de Compostela, provide for her a suitable mount, and when she was a day's journey from Paris, send for him. They set forth at once, and the sensible man spread the word and told everyone of his delight at his wife's return in good health, thanks be to God, from the place where he had sent her. When they inquired where that was, he answered that he had a long time ago sent her to Santiago de Compostela to make a pilgrimage on his behalf that his father had charged him with upon his deathbed. Everyone was perplexed by his statement, considering what had beforehand been insinuated about her. When his wife arrived within a day's journey of Paris, he had his house decorated with greenery and fresh herbs and assembled his friends to go forth and welcome his wife, with himself at the head of the group. The couple kissed at meeting; then both began to weep and then rejoice. He quietly warned his wife to speak gaily, clearly, and

strongly to all and likewise to their household and that, once in Paris, she should visit all her neighbors one after another and show them nothing but joy. Thus the good man saved his wife's honor.

13. In God's name, if a man protects his wife's honor and a wife criticizes her husband or permits him to be blamed, either secretly or openly, she herself shares the blame and with good reason. For he is either wrongly blamed or rightly blamed. If he is wrongly blamed, she should ardently avenge him; if he is rightly blamed, then she should graciously cover for and sweetly defend him. For it is evident that if such censure remains without being canceled, the worse her husband's reputation grows, and thus her own reputation will suffer equally with that of her husband. She would share his fault because she married one so wicked. For just as a chess player holds his piece in his hand a long time before setting it down, reflecting about putting it in a safe position, so must a woman take time to consider, choose, and set herself in a good place. For if she does not do so, she garners reproach and will share whatever is her husband's blame. If he becomes tainted in any way, she must exercise all her power to cover and conceal it, and the husband must do the same for his wife, as is said above and shall be said below.

14. I knew a well-respected lawyer in Parliament who had a daughter by a poor woman, who sent her out to a wet nurse. And for lack of payment, visits, or other courtesies that men do not know how to offer to nurses in such situations, rumors spread and were heard by the lawyer's wife. She also heard that I was aware of the situation and was paying for the child's care, to protect her lord's honor, since he is a man to whom I was and am much beholden, God protect him! For this reason the lawyer's wife came to me, advising me that I was committing a great offense, that her lord risked being slandered and defamed, and that she was in a better position to take charge of this care than I, and she asked me to lead her to the place where the child was. She put the child under the supervision of a seamstress, arranged for her to be taught her trade, and then married her off, without ever showing her husband ill temper or uttering a single angry or unpleasant word. That is how good wives act toward their husbands and good husbands toward their wives when they make a mistake.

Introductory Note to Article 1.9

The bulk of article 1.9 consists of the tale of the mollification of vengeful Melibee by his wife, Prudence, to which we have referred in the introduction. As he recounts the tale of this model wife, just as with the story of Griselda, the narrator provides the reader with the interpretation he wishes her to give the tale. The lesson here, he says, resides in learning the importance of selflessly and unobtrusively swaying a foolish and furious husband from his follies through "wisdom, discretion, caution, and gentleness," and not by attempts at mastery, scolding, complaining to the neighbors, or other actions taken in irritation. Husbands, he says, resent a woman's dominance and may be placated and corrected only through indirection. The wife, in this case the admirable Prudence, must not show her indignation or acknowledge her injuries, but only self-effacingly, gently, and persistently counsel the husband away from his misdeeds. As with Griselda and other wives he praises, the narrator upholds Prudence's concealment of her own private pain for the higher aim of bringing her husband around to goodness. Since every man wants to "rule as a lord" in his home, the narrator demonstrates that the prudent wife must subdue her anger or grief in order to reform her husband's foolish and dangerous impulses which would destroy the peace of that home. Here again, we have a tyrant presented as so unself-aware and egocentric as to need backstage manipulation and coddling by his wife.

The text of Prudence's advice subduing Melibee's rage at his enemies' attack upon his home, wife, and daughter is a tissue of proverbs, biblical quotations, and classical sententiae that she organizes as evidence in her campaign to pacify his vengeance. The biblical quotations are familiar, especially the words of Solomon and the Psalms, and accompany material from Cicero, Seneca, Ovid, Cato's *Distiches*, the Church Fathers, and other philosophers, legal experts, and theologians—all incorporated into the dialogue between Prudence and Melibee. Many of these sayings are misattributed in the Latin source, the *Liber consolationis et consilii* by Albertanus of Brescia (for example, material said to be from Seneca is often actually from Publius Syrias's work), and these misidentifications have been carried over to Renaud de Louens's French version and copied from that text into the *Le Ménagier* manual by the author-compiler. The point, of course, in this conduct manual is not for the young wife or any reader to have accurately identified quotations from the authorities named but rather to know that the sentiments Prudence espouses come with a lengthy pedigree of wisdom. Who said it is vastly less important than that it was uttered by a known wise (male) authority from the past, and that Prudence has this ammunition in her educational arsenal for her crusade against Melibee's anger. Because of this relative unimportance of accuracy in attribution for medieval readers, we have not sought to annotate each quoted source, but have along the way noted some significant ones. Citations in the *Riverside Chaucer*'s explanatory notes to Chaucer's version of the tale identify most of the quotations and sententiae.[1] Readings provided by Pichon, from either the other MSS or the sources that clarify the text, are in brackets.

1. See also Askins, "*Tale of Melibee,*" where he has provided further annotations for many of the quotations used by Prudence and Melibee. Askins used Paris BN MS fr. 578 as his base text and has also consulted Renaud de Louens's Latin source, Albertanus of Brescia's *Liber consolationis et consilii*, ed. Thor Sundby (London: N. Trübner and Co. for the Chaucer Society, 1873). MS 578 is not the source text for the story in *Le Ménagier*. Other explanatory notes on the French version are in J. Burke Severs's section on Chaucer's *Melibee* in *Sources and Analogues of Chaucer's Canterbury Tales*, ed. W. F. Bryan and Germaine Dempster (New York: Humanities Press, 1958), 560–614.

¶ 1.9 *Providing Your Husband with Good Counsel (including the Story of Melibee)*

1. The 9th article teaches you to be wise when your husband acts foolishly, as young or imprudent people often do, and to dissuade him gently and sensibly from his follies. See to it that you placate his proud cruelty with patience and gentle words. If you can do this, you will have vanquished him so that he will never be able to harm you, no more than if he were dead. Indeed, he will from then on recollect your goodness so well that though he may never mention it, you will find him your ally in all things. If you cannot prevent him from abusing you in anger, take care not to complain to your friends or anyone else, since should he discover your conversations, he would be bound to regard you unfavorably because of this disclosure, and he would not forget about it. Rather, go into your chamber and weep gently and quietly in a low voice and complain to God. That is what wise ladies do. Further, if he turns out to be more threatening, soothe him wisely. On this topic, there is a story or treatise that says:

The Story of Melibee

A powerful and rich young man named Melibee had a wife named Prudence, with whom he had a daughter. One day he went out to divert himself and indulge in pleasure, leaving his wife and daughter in the house with the doors shut. Three of his old enemies came up to the house, leaned ladders against the walls, and entered through the windows. They beat the wife and inflicted on the daughter five mortal wounds in five parts of her body—her feet,[1] ears, nose, mouth and hands —and leaving her near death, they departed.

When Melibee returned and saw this harm, he began to lament and cry out and strike himself like one berserk with grief and to tear his clothing. His wife Prudence then admonished him to compose himself, but he wailed the louder. Prudence then recalled Ovid's maxim, from the *Remedies for Love,* which says that he is foolish who tries to keep a mother from mourning the death of her child before she has emptied all of her tears and sated herself with crying. Afterward is the time to comfort her and ease her pain with gentle words.

Prudence therefore restrained herself for a while, then seized her moment, asking, "Lord, why are you behaving like a fool? It is unsuitable for a wise man to display such intense grief. Your daughter will recover, God willing. Even if she were

---

1. The Latin source says "eyes."

now dead, you should not destroy yourself on her account, for Seneca said that the wise man must not be disconsolate over his children but must endure their death as easily as he awaits his own death." Melibee responded, "Who could refrain from weeping with such great cause for anguish? Even Our Lord Jesus Christ wept about the death of his friend the leper." "Certainly," answered Prudence, "those who are sad or amongst the grieving are not forbidden to weep. They are permitted because, according to Saint Paul the Apostle in the letter to the Romans, we must be happy with those who are happy and weep with those who weep. But although moderate tears are allowed, weeping uncontrollably is not. Thus, we must respect the limit that Seneca sets. 'When you have lost your friend,' he states, 'your eye must be neither too dry nor too moist, for although tears fill the eyes, they must not spring forth. When you are bereft of a friend, try to find another, for it is better to make a new friend than to weep for the [lost] one.' If you wish to live wisely, dispel sadness from your heart, for Seneca[2] also said, 'A glad and joyful heart maintains you in the flower of your age, but a sad spirit dries out your bones,' and he remarked that grief kills many people. Solomon held that just as the clothes moth damages clothing and woodworms harm wood, so also does sadness aggrieve the heart. Thus we should endure the loss of our children and other worldly goods as did Job who, when his children and all of his possessions were wrested from him and he had suffered many physical tribulations, said, 'Our Lord gave it to me. Our Lord took it away. He did to me just as He wished. Blessed be the name of the Lord!'"

Melibee responded, "All that you utter is true and for my profit, but my spirit is so disturbed that I do not know how to proceed." Prudence answered, "Call all of your loyal friends, your kinsmen, and your relatives, ask their advice, then act according to what they advise, for Solomon pronounced, 'You will do everything with advice, and thus you will not regret it.'"

Melibee then summoned many people, that is, surgeons, physicians old and young, and some of his former enemies who were [seemingly] reconciled and returned to his grace and love, and some of his neighbors who paid honor to him more out of fear than love. And with these came several flatterers and many wise clerks and skilled lawyers. When they were all assembled, he informed them of what had occurred and [made manifest by his manner of speaking] his fury and his thirst for retaliation by waging war. Nonetheless, he sought their advice on the matter.

A surgeon, speaking for the other surgeons, arose and spoke, "Lord, it is the role of a surgeon to serve all men and not to harm them, and so it sometimes

---

2. The French source probably says "Jhesu Syrac." This epigram is from Proverbs 15: 13, and the last part on grief is from Seneca's *Ecclesiast* 30.25 (Pichon).

happens that when two men fight and wound each other in malice, the same surgeon will cure both of them. For this reason, it befits us not to incite or encourage a war or to support either side, but to heal your daughter. Although she has been seriously wounded, we will attend her day and night, and with the help of Our Lord we will return her to health." The physicians all agreed, with some of them adding that just as in the art of medicine sickness is healed through opposites, so should war be healed through vengeance. The envious neighbors, the uneasily reconciled foes, and the flatterers pretended to weep and began to aggravate the situation by praising Melibee's strength in possessions and friends, while scorning the strength of his enemies, charging that he absolutely must take immediate revenge by commencing war. At that point a wise lawyer, with the consent of the others, arose and declared, "Fair lords, the situation that assembles us here is grave and weighty, owing to the grievous affront and crime plus the myriad grim things that may proceed from it in the future and because of the great wealth and power of the parties involved. Therefore, it would be dangerous to err in this affair. Thus, Melibee, we advise you from this moment on to be diligent in protecting yourself. Surround yourself with spies and guards for safety. Equip your home with a strong garrison for your defense. But as for starting a war and avenging yourself without more ado, we cannot so rapidly judge what is best. We ask for some time to deliberate, for it is commonly said, 'He who judges quickly, repents quickly,' and it is also true that the good judge understands early and judges late. Adequate and reasonable delay, however irksome, keeps your judgment and vengeance from being overturned. Our Lord teaches this to us through example: when the woman who was caught in adultery was brought before Him to judge her fate, even though He knew very well what He should say, nonetheless He did not answer right away. Rather, He reflected a while and wrote twice on the ground. For these reasons, we request time for deliberation, after which we will advise you, with God's help, what path is to your advantage."

The young people and most of the others jeered at this sage man, making a huge racket, declaring that just as you must strike while the iron is hot, so must you avenge an insult while it is fresh. They shouted noisily, "War! War! War!"

One of the elders stood up and raised his hand demanding silence, saying, "Many cry 'War! War!' who do not know how war is mounted. In the beginning, warfare is so expansive and has such a large entrance that anyone may find it easily and can enter in, but only with great difficulty can he find his way out. When war begins, many are yet unborn who, because of war, will die young or in pain and misery and finish their life in wretchedness. For this reason, before initiating a war, one must employ eminent counsel and forethought."

While this elder man thought he bolstered his speech with arguments, almost all the others rose against him, interrupted him frequently, and told him to abbreviate his speech, for the narration of one who preaches to those who do not wish to hear it is irksome. That is, lecturing someone who finds it irritating is the same as singing to someone who is crying. When the wise old man realized that he would not be attended to, he abandoned his effort, uttering, "I perceive clearly that the proverb holds true: good counsel is lacking when the need is most dire." Having spoken, he seated himself, abashed.

Further along, Melibee received advice from many others who told him one thing privately and quite another in public. When Melibee attended to all the advice, he recognized that by far the largest number were in agreement and counseled war. He concurred with this judgment. When Lady Prudence saw that her husband was preparing for vengeance and war, she approached him speaking most sweetly,[3] "Lord, I beg you not to be hasty and as a boon to allow me a voice, for as Pierre Alphonse said, 'Whoever does good or evil to you, do not be in a hurry to return it in kind. Just as your friend will wait longer for you, your enemy will fear you longer.'"[4] Melibee answered his wife Prudence, "I do not aim to follow your counsel for several reasons. First, because everyone would take me for a fool if, on your advice and with your approval, I changed what has been agreed by many good people. Next, because all women are evil, not a single one is good, according to Solomon who declared, 'Among one thousand men, I found one honorable man, but among all women, I have not found a single good one.' The next reason is that if I followed your advice, it would appear that I was handing you authority over me, which should never be. For Jesus-Sirach[5] said, 'If the wife has mastery, she opposes her husband.' And Solomon, 'To your son, to your wife, to your brother, to your friend, do not give power over you or your life, for it is better for you that your children seek from you what they need rather than to see yourself in your children's hands.' Further, if I followed your recommendations, it would be necessary that the plan be kept secret until it was time to reveal it, and that could not be done, for it is written, 'The chatter of women cannot hide anything except what they do not know.' Finally, the philosopher said, 'Women vanquish men through bad advice.' All these reasons compel me to disregard your suggestion."

---

3. Prudence opens this speech with sentiments echoing Ovid's *Remedia amores* (Sundby, in Askins, "*Tale of Melibee*," 337).

4. *The Scholar's Guide: A Translation of the Twelfth-Century Disciplina Clericalis of Pedro Alfonso*, by Joseph Ramon Jones and John Esten Keller (Toronto: Pontifical Institute of Medieval Studies, 1969). Many quotations from this work appear in the narrative. Petrus Alfonsus lived c. 1062–1110.

5. MSS A, B, and C have "Jeremiah," but Pichon corrects it and references a passage in Ecclesiastics 25: 30, which he explains is a book of the Bible written by Jesus-Sirach. In a passage several paragraphs forward, Pichon also emends "Jeremiah" to Jesus-Sirach.

Lady Prudence, after listening graciously and patiently to what her husband claimed, asked permission [to speak] and said, "Lord, there is a simple response to the first argument you made. I pose that it is not foolish to change one's mind when the situation changes or when things appear different than before. I furthermore assert that had you promised and sworn to undertake an enterprise and then abandoned it for just cause, you should not be called a liar or perjurer, because it is written, 'The wise man does not lie when he changes his mind for the better.' Although your venture was settled and organized by a multitude of people, that is no reason to undertake it, for the truth and advantage of things are better perceived by a small number of wise men speaking with reason than by a throng of people with everyone screaming and shouting at once. Such a crowd is not reputable.

"As for your second argument, when you assert that all women are evil and none are virtuous, with your kind pardon, you disparage all women, for it is written, 'He who scorns everyone is disliked by everyone.' Seneca said that he who wished to acquire wisdom must not scorn anyone. Rather, what he knows he must teach without presumption, and what he doesn't know, he must not be ashamed to ask someone beneath him. That many women are moral is handily proven. First, because Jesus Christ would never have deigned to descend from a woman if they were all evil as you say. Next, because of the goodness of women, at our Lord Jesus Christ's Resurrection he appeared first to Mary Magdalene, not the apostles. When Solomon said that among all women he had not found a single good one, it does not follow that none are good. For even though he did not find one, many others do know good and loyal women; or, perhaps, when Solomon said that he has not found a good woman, he means the absolute goodness which no one except God possesses, as in the Gospel where it says that 'Compared to the perfection of his Creator, no creature is so excellent that he is not lacking something.'

"The third point you bring up, that if you governed yourself by means of my advice, it would seem that you were giving me authority over you. With your kind pardon, such is not the case. The result of this line of reasoning would be that people accepted advice only from those who held authority over them, and this is certainly untrue, for he who asks advice has the liberty and free will to follow the advice or ignore it.

"As for the fourth argument, where you think that women's chatter can only hide what they are ignorant of, that is applicable only to those babbling women about whom it is said, 'There are three things that chase a man out of his home: smoke, rainwater, and a bad woman.'[6] Solomon described such women when he

---

6. Cf. ¶ 1.7.2.

declared: 'It would be better to live in desert land than with a cantankerous and angry woman.' Yet you indeed recognize that I am not that sort. You have known my deep silence and patience and my ability to keep a secret when necessary.

"With regard to your fifth argument, when you insist that women vanquish men through bad advice, this argument is illogical. For you do not seek advice to do evil, and if you wished to follow bad advice and do evil and your wife could dissuade you and win you over, that would not deserve reprimand, but rather praise. In this way the philosopher must be understood: women defeat men in the matter of bad advice in that sometimes when men wish to act on bad counsel, women dissuade and prevail over them. Where you blame all women and their direction, on my side I can provide multiple arguments about good women giving beneficial advice. First, we are accustomed [to say], 'Women's advice is either very precious or despicable,' for although lots of women are evil and their advice is vile, one can still find enough good ones who give sound and valuable counsel. Jacob, with the guidance of his mother Rebecca, won his father Isaac's blessing and dominion over all his brothers. Through her prudence, Judith delivered the city of Bethulia, where she lived, from the hands of Holofernes who had besieged it and wished to destroy it. Abigail saved her husband Nabal from David who wanted to kill him and appeased the king with her good sense and guidance. Through her direction, Esther helped raise up her people in King Ahasuerus's kingdom. Of course, the same could be said of many others. Next, when Our Lord had created Adam, the first man, He said, 'It is not good [for man] to be alone. Let us make him a helpmeet in his likeness.' If then women were not honorable nor their counsel, Our Lord would not have called them men's helpers, for they would not aid men but rather do damage and harm. In addition, a master penned two lines in which he asks and answers the following: '[What is more valuable than gold? Jasper. What is worth more than jasper? Understanding.] What is worth more than understanding? Woman. What is worth more than woman? Nothing.' On these grounds and many others you learn that plenty of women are good, with useful and beneficial counsel. Should you now wish to trust my advice, I will return your daughter to you in good health and will do so in a way that brings you honor."[7]

When Melibee had heard Prudence, he responded, "I see clearly that Solomon was right when he said, 'Good words well ordered are honey, for they lend sweetness to the soul and health to the body.' Because of your extremely sweet words and also because I know firsthand your great wisdom and loyalty, I defer to you."

---

7. This is a confusing spot in the story, since the discussion appears to be primarily about the vendetta, not the daughter's health. Chaucer's version names the daughter Sophia, providing an allegorical dimension to the restoration of her health.

"Because," said Prudence, "you wish to follow my recommendations, I will tutor you about how to conduct yourself when considering advice. First, in all your acts and before any other advice, you must love and follow and seek God's guidance, putting yourself in such a place and state that He deigns to direct and comfort you. Hence Tobias said to his son, 'Bless God at all times and beseech Him to point to your path; may all your decisions be always through Him.'[8] Saint James wrote, 'If any of us has need of wisdom, let him ask God for it.' Next, you must consider and examine your thoughts, discovering what is best for you. Remove from yourself [three things that are opposed to reflection: anger, greed, and haste. First of all, he who consults with himself must be without ire for many reasons, primarily because the angry person always thinks he is more capable, and thus his plan will exceed his strength. Yet another reason is that a wrathful man, according to Seneca, speaks only of criminal things, and thus he incites others to anger and wrath. Furthermore, the enraged have skewed judgment and thus cannot think properly. Next, you must rid yourself of greed, for according to the Apostle, avarice is the root of all evil, and the greedy cannot judge carefully about anything unless it leads to the accomplishment of their desire, which is impossible, since greedy folk are never satisfied.

"Next you must not be] hasty in judgment, choosing as best that which first occurs to you. Finding the right path requires reflection, since as we have heard, they say, 'Who judges quickly, repents quickly.' You are not constantly of a good disposition. In fact, something that once seemed proper to do will seem ill-advised on another occasion. When you ponder the matter and decide what is fittest after considerable deliberation, hold it secret and refrain from revealing it, unless by the disclosure you may improve your condition and gain an advantage. For Jesus-Sirach said, 'Do not inform your friend or enemy about your secret or folly, for they may hear you, look at you, and support you in your presence, but behind your back they mock you.' Another man held, 'Only with difficulty will you encounter one single person who can conceal a secret.' Pierre Alphonse thought, 'As long as your secret is in your heart, you imprison it; when you reveal it to another, you place it into his prison.' So it is better to keep quiet and hide your secret than to beg anyone to whom you told it to suppress it, for as Seneca teaches, 'If you cannot keep your secret, how dare you ask another to keep it?'

"If you think revealing your private business to someone and hearing his opinion will improve your situation, then do so, behaving in this manner: first, do not reveal which side you are on or what outcome you want, for in general

---

8. Tobias 4:20. The Latin source has here a long disquisition on the nature of prudence and on the value of scholarship, which Renaud de Louens omits.

all counselors are flatterers, especially those who counsel powerful lords, because they strive more to say pleasant than profitable things. Consequently, a rich man will never have sound advice other than from himself. Consider then your friends and your enemies. Among your friends, seek opinions from the most loyal and wise, the eldest and the most experienced in advising. Call to your aid your close and faithful friends, since Solomon says, 'As the heart delights in perfumes, advice from devoted friends brings sweetness to the soul,' and also, 'Nothing compares to a loyal friend, for neither gold nor money is as worthy as the judgment of a reliable friend.' He said too, 'A dependable friend is a strong defense: he who finds one has found a wonderful treasure.' Then take care that the loyal friends you call upon are wise, for it is written, 'Always seek the guidance of a wise man.' For this same reason, call on the elders who have much experience, since it is written in Job: 'Knowledge and often prudence is found among the elders.' Cicero attests, 'Great works are not accomplished with force or agility of the body, but through good counsel, intelligence, and knowledge.' These three things do not weaken as one ages but strengthen and grow every day. In seeking assistance, keep this rule: at the beginning call upon only a few, from your most intimate circle. Solomon's opinion: 'Strive to have many friends, yet among a thousand, choose but one as your counselor.' When you have only a couple of advisers, you may reveal your business, if necessary, to a handful of others. However, the three conditions set above must always be followed by your counselors, and having but a single counselor is not sufficient, for you need several. Again, Solomon speaks: 'Numerous counselors make for healthy decision making.'[9]

"After having guided you about where to seek counsel, I will demonstrate what recommendations you must flee. Avoid the advice of fools, for Solomon says, 'I do not want to take the advice of a fool because he is able to advise only on his own likes and amusements.' It is written, 'A fool characteristically believes all wickedness belongs to others and all goodness to himself.' Next, you must eschew the counsel of hypocrites and sycophants who make more of an effort to praise your person and cater to your vanity than to speak the truth. Cicero shows, 'Among all the plagues of friendship, the worst is flattery.' Thus, you must fear and escape from the honeyed words of the one who [applauds more than the bitter words of the one who] tells the truth. As Solomon says, 'The man who speaks words of praise is a trap to catch the innocent.' Elsewhere he goes on, 'The man who speaks gentle and pleasing words to his friend places a net before his feet to ensnare him.' For this reason, according to Cicero, 'Watch that you not incline

---

9. These last two quotations from Solomon (Ecclus. 6:6 and Prov. 11:14) contradict each other as do many biblical sayings.

your ears toward flatterers and do not confuse flattery with advice.' Cato says, 'Avoid syrupy, agreeable words.'

"Next, shun the counsel of former enemies with whom you may now be reconciled, for it is said, 'No one returns safely into the good grace of his enemy.' Aesop writes, 'Fear to trust those with whom you were once at war or dispute, and obscure your plans or secrets from them.' Seneca expounds on this matter, 'Where there was fire for a long time, smoke will remain.' Hence Solomon advises, 'Distrust your former enemy, and even should you reunite and he seems contrite, bowing his head to you, do not believe him, since he does it more [for his own benefit] than for love of you, so that he can achieve victory over you by humbling himself and fleeing from you, a victory he could never have by pursuing you.' Pierre Alphonse notes, 'Do not surround yourself with former adversaries, for whatever good you do, they will pervert or lessen it.'

"You must also pass up the advice of those in your service who pay you reverence, since they perform out of fear more than love. A philosopher stresses this, 'No one is really loyal to him whom he fears greatly'; as does Cicero, 'No empire is stalwart enough to endure if it is feared rather than loved.' Keep away from asking drunks for their opinions since they cannot be discreet, and Solomon says, 'No secret is there where drunkenness reigns.' Next, be suspicious of those who counsel one thing in secret and then declare another in public. As Cassiodorus[10] says, 'One way to harm your friend is to state openly the opposite of what you really want.' After that, distrust the advice of unsavory men, because it is written, 'The advice of evil men is always full of fraud,' and David says, 'Happy is he who has never taken the counsel of evil men.'[11] Further, eschew the counsel of youths, for their reason is immature. Thus Solomon preaches, 'Woe to the land with a child as its lord!' The philosopher cautions us not to elect young men as princes because they are generally imprudent.[12] Solomon too suggests, 'Sorrowful is the realm where the prince does not rise early in the morning!'

"Because I have demonstrated from whom you should take advice and those you must avoid and flee, I want to teach you how to interrogate the advice. According to Cicero's teachings, you must consider several things. First, take care to preserve and speak the truth about that for which you seek counsel, since it is impossible to advise someone properly who is not forthright. Next, contemplate the things that support the plan you propose to implement through the advice: whether reason, your own power, and the majority of your best advisers concur

---

10. Flavius Maximus Cassiodorus Senator, c. 490–585. The *Variae* contain twelve books of his letters written c. 537.

11. The opening line of the Book of Psalms.

12. This sentence is not in the Albertanus or in the Renaud version.

or disagree. Ascertain the source of the counsel, whether it proceeds from hatred or love, peace or war, advantage or harm, or other possibilities. Among all these elements, always select the one most advantageous to you, refusing and rejecting all others. Afterward, examine the root of your decision, what advantage it can conceive and engender, and considering too all its causes.

"Once you have examined all of the advice in the manner stated and decided upon the best path, the most advantageous and most tested by wise and aged men, resolve whether you can accomplish it, for no one should begin something that he cannot complete or assume a burden that he cannot carry. As a proverb says, 'He who embraces too much grasps little.' Cato explains, 'Try to do what you have the power to do, so that the charge does not weigh so much on you that you must abandon what you have begun, and when in doubt, don't start what you can't complete.' Pierre Alphonse says, 'If you are able to do something about which you will repent, it is better to desist than to begin.' Those who forbid others to undertake [painful acts of dubious suitability] offer sound advice. In the end, when you have examined your decision in the above manner and feel certain about its completion, then solidify and confirm it.

"Now here's when, how, and why one may retract a decision without blame: one can change his mind and revamp his strategy when the need vanishes or a new reason arises. For the law states, 'New things that occur need new decisions.' Seneca says, 'If your plan becomes apparent to your enemy, then change your plan.' Next, one can alter his decision upon learning that, for whatever reason, harm could come of it. Or should the advice be dishonest or arise from shady motives—the laws say that all dishonest promises are worthless—when the plan is impossible or cannot be done well, and so on. Finally, keep as a general rule that a decision is faulty if it remains so fixed that one cannot alter it, no matter what."

When Melibee had heard these insights from Lady Prudence, he responded, "Prudence, until this moment you have instructed me about how to request or follow advice. Now can you turn to particulars and tell me your opinion of the deliberation on the critical situation at hand?"

Lady Prudence replied, "Lord, I beg you not to bear a grudge if what I say displeases you, for my intent upholds your honor and profit, and please take it in that vein. Sadly, I have to report that your decision isn't a decision but a foolish impulse, lacking discernment and error ridden. In the first place, you were mistaken in assembling your council. Early on [you should have summoned] just a few people, perhaps conferring with more later if the need arose. But right away you convened an unwieldy and disagreeable collection of people. Instead of soliciting the aid only of your devoted, wise, and longtime friends, you erred by calling also upon strangers, youths, fools, flatterers, former enemies, and people who bear you hatred without love. Then you blundered when arriving at a decision, for you were simultaneously angry, covetous, and hasty—three things that are detrimental to deliberation—and you did not squelch this temper in yourself or in your council as is proper. Displaying to your counselors your eagerness to conduct war and take immediate vengeance was not a sound scheme, since they naturally inclined toward what you wanted more than toward what was beneficial for you. Again you went wrong to be content with only a single deliberation, whereas in a matter so weighty and important several meetings were essential. You were remiss not to follow the guidance of your wise and aged loyal friends, but considered only the majority opinion. Yet surely you know that there are always more fools than wise men, and if one puts more credence in the number of voices than in the merits of the people, the advice of assemblies and crowds of people can go amiss, for in such deliberations the fools win by their numbers."

Melibee then responded, "I truly confess that I have lost my way, but because you just said that he who changes his mind in many situations is not to be upbraided, I am prepared to reconsider according to your precepts, for sinning is the work of man, but persevering in sin is the work of the devil; thus I no longer wish to persevere in this."[13]

Then Prudence said, "Let us examine all of the advice. To accomplish this in the optimal way, we begin with the surgeons and physicians who spoke initially. These surgeons and physicians spoke properly and wisely in council, for it is incumbent upon their profession that they serve everyone well and harm no one and care conscientiously for those they treat, just as they sagely answered. For this reason I advise that you recompense them handsomely, so much so that they apply themselves more gladly to your daughter's cure. For although they are your friends, you must nonetheless never accept their services gratis but rather pay and reward them most generously. But as for the proposition that the physicians offered, that in illness one disease is cured by its opposite, I would like to know how you understand it."

"Undoubtedly," offered Melibee, "here is how: as enemies caused me harm, I must in turn cause them harm, and since they took revenge on me and did me injury, I will in turn take revenge on them and do them injury, and thus I will rid one hurt by another."

"Well, see here," retorted Prudence, "how each one easily believes what he wants and desires! Certainly," she added, "the physicians' words must not be understood that way, for evil is not the opposite of evil, nor vengeance of vengeance, nor wrong of wrong; rather, they are the same. For this reason, vengeance is not

---

13. From the sermons of Saint Augustine 164.10.14, *Humanum est errare, diabolicum est in errore perseverare.* Cited in *Riverside Chaucer* for l. 1264.

cured through vengeance, or a wrong through another wrong; rather, they increase each other. The speech must rather be construed thus: just as good and
evil are opposites, so are peace and war, vengeance and tolerance, discord and
harmony, and many others. That is, evil must be healed through good, discord
through harmony, war through peace, and so on. Saint Paul agrees with this in
several places: 'Do not,' he says, 'return evil for evil or slander for slander, but be
kind toward the one who wrongs you and bless the one who slanders you.' In
many other passages in his letters he exhorts peace and harmony.

"Now it is appropriate to speak about the counsel from the lawyers, wise men,
and old men, who agreed that before all things you must be diligent in the protection of your person and home, adding that in this matter one must proceed
carefully and deliberately. As to the protection of your person, know that it is incumbent upon a man who is at war, as the first thing each day, humbly and de-
votedly to ask for God's grace and love. Thus the Prophet David says, 'If God is
not the guardian of the city, he who guards it keeps watch for naught.' Next, place
your home in the protection of your proven and recognized loyal friends, and
ask them for aid in shielding yourself, for according to Cato, 'If you need help,
find it in your friends, for there is no better physician than a steadfast friend.'
Also, you must keep away from foreigners and strangers and hold their company
suspect, since in the words of Pierre Alphonse, 'Do not travel with anyone with
whom you are not acquainted, and if anyone joins you against your will and in-
quires about your life and path, pretend that you wish to go farther than you intended. If he is carrying a lance, stay on his right side; if he carries a sword, stay
by his left side.'

"Guard yourself wisely then from those whom I have mentioned. Avoid and
flee their counsel. After that, protect yourself and don't overestimate your force
and thereby scorn your adversary and let your guard down, for a wise man must
always be suspicious, especially of his enemies. As Solomon says, 'Happy is he
who always doubts himself, for ill fortune will come to him whose hardness of
heart leads him to excessive presumption.' You must therefore expect snares and
spies. For, according to Seneca,[14] a distrustful man will not fall for any trap. Furthermore, 'One who is suspicious is wise and avoids misfortune.' Even though
you may think you are secure, nonetheless always be vigilant to protect yourself,
for Seneca remarked, 'He who keeps himself secure fears no danger.' Also defend
yourself not only from a powerful enemy but also from the smallest one, as Seneca
also said, 'The well-taught man ought to fear his least foe.' To quote Ovid's *Remedies for Love*, 'The small viper kills the large bull, and the puny dog restrains the

---

14. Here as in many other instances, the words of Publius Syrias's *Sententiae* are attributed to
Seneca.

boar.' Nonetheless, you must not be so fearful that you mistrust even when there is nothing to fear, for it is written, 'There are those who have a great desire to deceive, yet dread themselves to be victims of deception.' Next, you should veer away from the venomous company of jeerers, for it is written: 'Do not keep company with mockers; rather flee them and their words like poison.' About the second point, in which the wise men counsel the thorough fortification of your home, I would like to hear what you think."

Melibee answered, "The way I see it is that I must secure my house with towers, ramparts, turrets, and other edifices of self-defense, in order to intimidate enemies when they approach."

Prudence then rejoined, "The fortress of high towers and great edifices can be compared to pride. One builds towers and splendid edifices with tremendous effort and expense, yet when they are completed, they mean nothing if they are not defended by wise and trustworthy friends and at great cost. Thus, the largest and strongest citadel that a rich man can possess to protect his body and his chattel is the love of his subjects and his neighbors, for Cicero held that 'the love of citizens represents a fortress that cannot be vanquished or defeated.'

"With regard to the third point, where the wise men and elders urge you not to dive into this matter suddenly or hastily, but thoughtfully to plan and equip yourself, I believe they spoke wisely. Consequently, strategize with forethought before engaging in vengeance, war, melee, and defense, since Cicero also said, 'Long preparation for combat makes for a speedy victory,' and from Cassiodorus too, 'Long-term planning results in the strongest defenses.'

"We shall now consider what sort of counsel those neighbors provide who show you reverence without love, plus your former enemies, flatterers, those who advise one thing in private and another in the open, and young people—all of whom urge immediate vengeance by means of war. Certainly, as I have indicated earlier, you erred gravely in calling on those folks for advice, and their judgment is reproachable for all the reasons stated above. Nonetheless, since it was all discussed pretty generally, let us ponder the items individually. First, to examine the truth of this advice: according to Cicero, one does not need to hunt too far to establish the truth of your situation, for of course we know who committed this injustice against you and how many of them there are, what they did, and how and when they did it. Let us examine therefore the second condition Cicero sets out, which he calls 'consent.' That is, how many are there who approve this plan of action and your own wishes, and who are they? Then consider how many agree with your adversaries, and exactly who are they?

"On the first part of this condition, we know well who concurs with your wishes, for all of those that I named earlier recommend that you make war right away. Let's see then who you are and who are they whom you consider enemies.

For you, although you are rich and powerful, you are nonetheless all alone and without a male heir. All you have is a daughter. You lack brothers, first cousins, or any other near relatives for fear of whom your enemies would cease to pursue and destroy you. Once you are dead, your wealth will be divided into different portions, and once each has his part, they will not be obliged to avenge your death. On the other hand, you have three enemies, and they have many children, brothers, and other close friends and relatives, such that when you have killed two or three of them, there will still be enough left able to avenge their deaths and slay you. Though you may have more friends than your adversaries, their relationship to you is more distant, whereas their friends are much more devoted, so their situation is superior to yours.

"Next, does the advice to take immediate vengeance conform to reason? Surely you are aware that it does not. Legally, no one must take vengeance, nor is it permitted when it is not moderate, within the limits of the law. Still considering this word 'consent,' you must verify that you have the might to do what you want to do. And certainly you must say no, for to be exact, we can do nothing except what we can do duly and legally. Because according to the law you must not wreak vengeance through your own authority, it can be stated that your power does not agree with your will.

"Examining the third point which Cicero called 'consequence': be aware of the consequences of the reprisals you wish to enact, for more vengeance, dangers, wars, and other numberless evils as well as damages may result, which you can't now realize.

"With regard to Cicero's fourth point, 'origin,' recognize that hatred engenders injustice, vengeance inflames enemies, wars are born of hatred and contention, laying waste all goods.

"About the 'causes,' which is the last argument Cicero offers, know that there are two working and effective causes for the injury you suffered, a remote one and a near one. The remote cause is God who is the cause of all causes; the near one is your three enemies. The accidental cause was hatred. The material causes are your daughter's five wounds. The formal cause was the manner in which the offense was done—that is, that they leaned ladders against the walls and entered through the windows. The final cause was their desire to murder your daughter, which they did not complete. But the distant final cause, the end for which they undertook this business, we cannot really know except by conjecture and presumption, for we must presume that they will reach a bad end, since the logic of the *Decretum* states, 'Things begun wrongly are only with difficulty made to turn out well.' It is hard to respond with certainty to those who would ask why God wished and tolerated that such an offense be perpetrated against you. According to the Apostle, Our Lord's wisdom and judgment are so profound that no one can adequately understand or scrutinize them. Nonetheless, by some presumptions I find that God, who is just and righteous, allowed this to happen for a just and reasonable cause. For your name Melibee means 'he who drinks honey,' [and you so wished to drink honey] or the sweetness of temporal goods—wealth, the delights and honors of this world—that you were intoxicated with such material considerations and forgot God your creator. Nor did you bear Him the honor and reverence you should. You did not remember Ovid's words: 'Under the honey of the sweetness of the goods of the flesh is hidden the venom that kills the soul.' And the same for Solomon, 'If you have found the honey, eat of it moderately, for if you eat of it excessively, you will vomit.' Thus, perchance God, in contempt of you, turned away His face and the ears of His mercy and suffered that you sinned against Him. This sin against Our Lord was allowing the three enemies of the human race—the world, the flesh, and the devil—to enter your heart freely through the windows of the body, with inadequate defense against their assault and temptations, in such a way that they hurt your daughter, that is, your soul,[15] with five wounds that comprise the mortal sins that enter into the body through the five senses. Through this 'semblance' our Lord wished and allowed these three enemies to enter into your house through the windows and wound your daughter in the way previously described."

"Truly," considered Melibee, "you exert yourself a great deal to convince me through sweet words to refrain from revenge on my enemies, and you have shown me quite wisely the dangers and the misfortune that could result from such settling of scores. But he who takes the time to consider the perils that result from each act of reprisal would never exact vengeance. That would be a great shame, because through retribution the bad are removed from among the good, and those of evil intent refrain when they see that malevolence is punished."

To this Lady Prudence replied, "Surely, I grant that from retaliation comes much good, but taking vengeance belongs not to the individual but only to judges and those who have authority over felons, and I would go so far as to say that an individual would sin through revenge [just as the judge sins who tolerates vengeance], given that Seneca said, 'He who spares the bad harms the good.' Further, according to Cassiodorus, people are afraid to commit wrongs when they know that it would displease judges and kings. Yet another said, 'The judge who fears doing justice turns people to wrong,' and Saint Paul the Apostle wrote in his letter to the Romans that the judge does not carry a sword without cause but carries it to punish the wicked [and to defend] worthy men. Therefore if you wish

---

15. See 1.3.19. Daughter and soul are not equated in Renaud, but the narrator makes this connection earlier.

to punish your enemies, appeal to the judge who has jurisdiction over them, and he will chastise them according to the law and, should they merit it, even take their possessions, leaving them poor and ashamed."

"Oh!" said Melibee. "That type of retribution displeases me! I consider that Fortune has nourished me from my youth, aiding me through difficult situations. If I test her now, I believe that with God's help she will help me avenge [my shame]."

"Surely," admonished Prudence, "if you wish to employ my advice, don't test Fortune or depend on her, for according to Seneca, things done in the hope of Fortune are done foolishly! For Fortune resembles a glass pane: the more clear and translucent it is, the more easily it is broken. So do not depend upon Fortune and her instability. Just when you are most certain of her assistance, she will disappoint you. As for Fortune's having nourished you from childhood, rely on her and your own sense even less, for Seneca noticed that Fortune turns the one she has pampered into a fool. Because if you seek retaliation, and the vengeance made lawfully before a judge does not satisfy you, and revenge made relying on Fortune is bad, perilous, and uncertain, your only recourse for remedy is the sovereign and true Judge who avenges all wickedness and injury. He will avenge you, according to what He himself asserts, 'Vengeance is mine and I alone will administer it!'"

Melibee responded, "But if I do not avenge the wickedness committed against me, I would incite the perpetrators along with all other evildoers to add to their wrongs against me, since we read, 'Tolerate an injury without avenging it, and you encourage a new one.' Therefore, by my patience, so many offenses from all directions would be hurled at me that I could not suffer or bear it; rather I would be debased, since we see that 'by bearing much, dreadful things will happen to you until you are unable to bear them.'"

"Certainly," said Prudence, "I grant you that excessive fortitude benefits no one. Nonetheless, it does not follow that each person who suffers a wrong must take revenge, for that belongs only to judges, who must not tolerate wickedness and injury to remain unpunished. Accordingly, the two authorities you cited earlier apply only to magistrates who allow too much malice and injury to occur without penalty. Plus, not only do they encourage injustice, but they also command it, for a wise man said, 'The judge who does not reprimand the sinner commands him to sin.' Judges and sovereigns might well permit so many ills in their realm that the evildoers would evict them from their own land, and it is only fitting that they cede their authority in the end. But now supposing you have license to avenge yourself, I would argue that at present you do not have the strength. When you compare your power to that of your adversaries, as I have demonstrated already, you will find plenty of ways in which they have an advantage, and that is why I feel that it is wise, for the moment, to restrain yourself and be patient.

"Next, you know that it is ordinarily said that to quarrel with someone stronger shows madness; to fight against an equal is dangerous; to fight against a weaker foe is shameful. So one must avoid [contention], if at all possible, for Solomon finds it honorable for a man to recognize how to be on guard against squabbles and battles. Should someone stronger cause you harm, apply yourself more to appeasing him than to avenging yourself, for Seneca exhorts that a man places himself in great peril who becomes angry with someone mightier than he. Cato, too, cautions, 'If someone stronger harms you, hold back. He who has injured you once may help you another time.'

"Now let us suppose that you have license and strength to avenge yourself, I still say that many reasons require you to retreat and submit yourself to suffering patiently the injury that was done to you as well as the other tribulations of this world.

"First, [you need to consider your faults,] because of which God permitted such tribulation to befall you, according to our earlier discussion, for the poet[16] said that we must bear patiently the wrongs that happen to us when we deem that we have deserved them. Saint Gregory holds that when a person contemplates his own numerous faults and sins, the pain and trials that he endures seem lesser to him. The greater his sins, the lighter the pain feels to him. Next, you must incline yourself toward forbearance, the patience of Our Lord Jesus Christ, as described by Saint Peter in his epistles: 'Jesus Christ suffered and offered an example for each man to follow, for he never sinned or spoke any vile thing. When others defamed him, he did not respond in kind; when others beat him, he did not threaten them.' Next, emulate the patience of the saints in Paradise, who endured tribulations, though they were guiltless. Furthermore, find patience because the difficulties of this world are ephemeral, passing quickly, while the glory gained from enduring tribulation is eternal, according to Corinthians 2.

"Believe steadfastly that he who does not know patience is not well schooled, for Solomon finds that the quality of a man's instruction is reflected by his forbearance. Our Lord said that patience conquers, counseling also that through serenity we control our souls. Elsewhere Solomon noted that the man who is constant governs himself prudently, while the angry man creates disturbances that the patient man tempers. He tells us that it is better to be resigned than mighty and that one who controls his heart is more praiseworthy than he who conquers great cities by force. For this reason Saint James, in his epistles, says that forbearance is the work of perfection."

---

16. Unidentified, resembles Luke 23: 41.

"Undoubtedly," said Melibee. "Granted, Lady Prudence, patience is a supreme virtue, but not everyone can have the perfection that you seek. I do not number among the perfect, and for that reason my heart cannot be at peace until I am avenged. Although in this vengeance lies peril, I recognize that nonetheless my adversaries did not consider their risk but boldly accomplished their will. Really, it seems that no one should reproach me if I take on a bit of danger to avenge myself, or even if I act impetuously, for they say that only outrage corrects excess."

"Alas!" cried Lady Prudence. "You speak your will, but in no case should one ever commit an outrage or excess to avenge himself, or for any other reason, for Cassiodorus said that he who takes revenge with offensive action conducts himself as wickedly as he who committed the first outrage. Therefore, do not fail to adhere to the law of the land regarding retaliation: no excess or outrage. Just as your adversaries have sinned against you through their offense, if you failed to live by the law, you would sin too. For this reason Seneca argues that one must never retaliate for a wicked act. Should you say that the law grants that you may repel violence with violence and fraud with fraud, it is certainly true when the defense occurs right away, without an interval, and in self-defense, but not for deliberate vengeance. One must use care not to be accused of fanatical defense, since that would be against law and reason. Right now you are not mounting an immediate resistance or acting in self-defense, but rather retaliating, quite intemperately; thus restraint still seems to me essential, for Solomon said that the impatient man will suffer harm."

"Of course," said Melibee. "Naturally, when one is impatient and angry about what does not concern or belong to him, no wonder harm comes his way. The rule of law dictates that he who intervenes in something not his concern is guilty. As Solomon said in Proverbs, he who butts into the troubles of another resembles a person grabbing ahold of the ears of a dog he does not know. Just as the strange dog sometimes bites the one holding him, it follows that harm comes to one who, in irritation and fury, gets involved with another's trouble. But you must be aware that this situation touches me closely, and it is no surprise that I am angry and intolerant! Do not be upset, but I cannot comprehend at all how great harm can come to me by avenging myself, for I am richer and mightier than my adversaries. Surely you understand that money governs and accomplishes what happens in this world, for Solomon said that all things obey money."

Prudence, hearing her husband vaunt his wealth and power, rejoicing in them and scorning the poverty of his adversaries, responded: "I grant that you are rich and powerful and that wealth may be useful for those who acquire and employ it properly, for just as the body cannot live without [the soul, likewise it must have] temporal goods. Riches help one acquire a grand family and many friends. Pamphile[17] thus said, 'If the daughter of an ox driver is wealthy, she can select a husband from a thousand men, for none will refuse her.' He also warned, 'If you are fortunate—that is to say, rich—you will find a great many companions and friends. If your fortune changes and you become poor, you will remain alone.' Furthermore, Pamphile taught that riches transform the lowly to the noble class, although just as great goodness comes from great wealth, so does great misfortune come from great poverty. Penury often compels a person to commit evils, and thus Pierre Alphonse says, 'One of the great adversities of this world is when a man free by nature must [ask for] charity from his enemy,' and Innocent[18] presents the logic of this, explaining, 'The condition of beggars is woeful and miserable, for if they do not ask, they die of hunger, and if they do ask, they die of shame, and nonetheless necessity compels them to beg.' Thus, Solomon explains that death is better than dire poverty, for a bitter death is superior to such a life.

"For the reasons already mentioned and more, I allow that wealth benefits those who acquire and use it well. I wish, therefore, to illustrate the proper attitude to have when amassing and using riches. First, do not pursue gain ardently, but leisurely, moderately, and with restraint. A man who is too eager to acquire wealth abandons himself easily to other vices and evils. Thus Solomon said, 'The man overhasty to enrich himself will not remain innocent,' and elsewhere, 'Easy come, easy go,' but that which comes little by little multiplies. Acquire riches through your intelligence and work, for your profit, but without harming others, since the law declares that no one may enrich himself at the expense of another. Cicero, too, says that neither pain, suffering, death, nor anything else that can befall a man is more harmful and unnatural than increasing riches at the expense of another. Cassiodorus notes that from the little that the beggar possesses arises all cruelty. In order to acquire riches legitimately, do not be indolent or lazy in making your profit. Rather, flee idleness, which, Solomon asserts, teaches about many evil deeds. Elsewhere he predicts that a man who works and cultivates his land will eat bread, but he who is lazy will fall into poverty and die of hunger. According to the poet, a loafer doesn't find any time suitable to producing a profit, making excuses in winter because of the cold and in summer because of the heat. That is why Cato admonished, 'Keep watch, and do not abandon yourself to too much sleep, for too much rest is the nourishment of vices.' About this topic Saint Jerome said, 'Perform some good act so that the

---

17. Pamphilles, hero of a twelfth-century Latin poetic dialogue, *Pamphilus de Amore*.

18. Pope Innocent III's *De miseriis humane conditionis* (1195), 1.16, a work much admired in the Middle Ages.

devil does not find you idle, for he does not easily draw to his employment those who are busy with good works.' So, in the pursuit of riches, shun idleness.

"Next, employ those riches that you duly acquire through your wits and labor in such a way that you may be considered neither too miserly nor too foolishly liberal with money, for just as avarice is blameworthy, so is foolish prodigality reprimanded. Thus, Cato cautions, 'Use your possessions in such a way that you may not be called poor and wretched, for it is a great disgrace for a man to have a poor heart and a rich purse.' He also counsels, 'Use your possessions wisely, without abusing them, for those who foolishly consume what they have, when they find they have nothing, easily give themselves over to seizing from others.' Therefore avoid avarice and employ your riches in such a manner that no one says that your riches are buried, but rather that you have them under control. A wise man reproaches the miserly man in these verses: 'Why would a man who is ashes and destined to die bury his possessions in such great avarice? Why does he attach himself to his goods to the extent that he cannot be separated from them? For when he dies, he cannot take them with him.' Also, Saint Augustine writes, 'A greedy man resembles hell, for the more he devours, the more he wants to devour.' Just as you must take care to utilize your possessions so that you may not be called avaricious and miserable, so also must you avoid being taken for a generous fool. According to Cicero, 'The goods of your household should not be so locked up that neither pity nor goodness can release them, and likewise they must not be so open that they are surrendered to just anyone.'

"Additionally, in acquiring and using riches, remember three things in your heart of hearts: God, conscience, and reputation. You need God in your heart, doing nothing that displeases your Creator for any amount of riches, since according to Solomon, it is far better to possess little and fear God than to acquire a huge treasure and lose one's Lord. The philosopher said that it is better to be a worthy man owning only trifles than to be wicked and hold immense wealth. Accordingly, I exhort you always to protect your conscience when procuring and using riches. For the Apostle said that the thing for which we receive the most renown is the good testimony of our conscience. The sage says, 'Worthy is the material whose acquisition harms not the conscience.'

"As you acquire or employ riches, be diligent to maintain a fine reputation, for it is written, 'A gain that tarnishes a good reputation must be a loss.' According to Solomon, 'Good reputation is worth more than a fortune,' and elsewhere, 'Diligently tend your good name and character, for it remains with you longer than any grand and precious treasure.' Indeed he does not deserve to be called a gentleman who, after God and conscience, does not treasure his good standing. Because of this Cassiodorus said, 'It is a sign of a noble heart to love and desire an honorable name and reputation.' Saint Augustine also, 'You need two things, a

good conscience and a good reputation for your intimates.' He who is so confident in his clear conscience that he neglects his character and makes no effort to
protect it is cruel and base.

"Now I have disclosed how you must conduct yourself in procuring and using
riches. Even though you trust so much in your wealth that you wish to begin a
war, simply counting on your money is not sufficient to maintain a war. About
this, a philosopher said, 'A man who wishes to have war will never have sufficient
goods, for the richer a man is, the larger expenditures he must make if he wishes
to secure honor and victory,' and Solomon said, 'Where there is greater wealth,
there is greater spending.' Next, my dearest lord, although with your fortune you
may gain the support of many, nonetheless that does not justify opening hostili-
ties when you could otherwise have peace, which would be to your honor and
advantage. Victory in battles of this world lies not in the multitude of people or
the virtue of men but in the hands and will of God. That is why Judas Machabeus,
who was God's knight, when he had to combat an adversary with a larger force
than his, consoled his small band saying, 'God can give victory just as easily to a
few people as to many, for success in battle comes not from the great number of
men but from heaven.' And thus, my dearest lord, no one is certain that he deserves God's bestowing triumph on him, any more than he is sure whether or not
he deserves God's love. According to Solomon, each man must fear waging war
because of the many perils in battle, where it may happen that the nobles are slain
just as the churls are. For, according to the second book of Kings, the feats of battle are random and uncertain; thus at any moment one person or another can be
slain, and because of this peril, wise men must avoid war as much as possible, for
Solomon said, 'He who loves danger will fall into danger.'"

After Lady Prudence had spoken, Melibee responded, "I see clearly, Lady Prudence, from your beautiful words and the reasons you have put forward, that you
dislike contention exceedingly, but so far you have not addressed how I should act
here and now."

"Surely," she said, "I advise you to reconcile with your adversaries. Make peace
with them, for Seneca's writings show that through concord, small riches become
great, and through discord, large fortunes become small, ever declining and col-
lapsing. You know that one of the supreme goods of this world is peace. Jesus
Christ thus said to his apostles, 'Happy are the peacemakers, for they are called
the children of God.'"

"Ah!" said Melibee. "Now I perceive that you devalue my honor! You know
that my adversaries began the quarrel through injury and you see that they do
not sue for peace or ask for reconciliation. Do you desire that I humiliate myself
and beg for mercy? Surely that would not be honorable, for just as it is said that
too much familiarity breeds contempt, so it is with too much humility."

Lady Prudence fumed, saying, "Sire! Sire! With all due respect, I cherish your honor and profit like my own and always have! Neither you nor anyone else has witnessed the contrary! If I advise you to pursue peace and reconciliation, I am not as mistaken as you believe, for a wise man said, 'Dissension is always begun by someone else, and peace by you,' and the Prophet said, 'Flee evil and do good, seek peace and pursue it eagerly.' Nonetheless, I have not told you first to petition for peace from your adversaries, for I know well that you have such a hard heart that you would not readily do so much for me. Nevertheless, Solomon said that evil will come in the end to him who has too hard a heart."

When Melibee heard Lady Prudence's heated words, he said, "Lady, I beg that my speech may not displease you, for you know that I am angry—and it is no wonder—and those who are incensed do not discern clearly what they do or say. Thus, the philosopher said that the troubled see indistinctly. But say and advise what you wish, and I am ready to accomplish it, and if you reprimand my folly, I must love and esteem you more, for Solomon said that he who forcefully admonishes someone who commits a folly deserves greater thankfulness than one who deceives him with sweet words."

"My wrath erupts only for your benefit," retorted Prudence, "for to quote Solomon again, 'He who reprimands the fool and displays anger is more valuable than one who praises his errors and snickers at his greatest follies.' And later he said that a sad countenance can cause a fool to change his heart."

Then Melibee stated, "Lady, I cannot think how to respond to the many fine observations that you present. Tell me briefly your will and your counsel, and I am ready to undertake it."

Lady Prudence then revealed her wishes as follows: "I advise that before anything, you make peace with God and reconcile yourself to Him, for as I said before, He allowed this tribulation to happen to you because of your sinfulness. If you do this, I promise in His name that He will lead your adversaries [to your feet, ready to do your will], for Solomon said, 'When good men address themselves to God, He converts his enemies to him and constrains them to request peace.' Next, I beg that you allow me to consult in secret with your enemies and adversaries, without revealing that I do so with your consent. Then, when I know their desire, I will be able to advise you more securely."

"Do exactly as you wish," assented Melibee. "I place myself entirely in your hands."

When Lady Prudence saw her husband's good intentions, she reflected on how she might conclude this matter beneficially. Discerning the right moment, she called the adversaries to a discreet place and sagely expounded to them the prodigious advantages of peace and the awful perils of war, lessoning them gently about repenting for the offense they had committed against her lord Melibee, herself, and her daughter.

Heeding Lady Prudence's kind words, the enemies were more surprised and joyful than anyone could imagine. "Ha!" they said. "Lady, you have opened us up with blessed mildness, according to what David the Prophet said, to the reconciliation of which we are unworthy and which we, full of devotion and humility, should instead be seeking from you. Through your magnanimous indulgence you have offered us this peacemaking. We now mark clearly the truth of Solomon's maxim that sweet words multiply friends and mollify enemies." "Surely," they continued, "we place ourselves under your good counsel and are ready to obey entirely the words and commandments of lord Melibee. Thus, dearest gentle lady, we humbly beseech you that your sweet words turn into actions. However, most beloved lady, we understand that we have offended lord Melibee in far greater measure than we could amend. So we oblige ourselves and our friends to enact all that he wishes and commands. Given the depth of his wrath, he may deliver us such a punishment that we could not accomplish or bear. For that reason, please ensure that all of us are not disinherited and abandoned on account of our folly."

"Of course," replied Prudence, "it is difficult and dangerous for a man to entrust himself entirely to the judgment and power of his enemies, for Solomon said, 'Hear me, all peoples and all men and governors of the Church: in all of your life, do not give power over yourself to your son, your wife, your brother, or your friend.' If he thus forbade you to give power over yourself to your brother or friend, all the more reason for him to forbid you from turning yourself over to the control of your enemy. Nonetheless, I advise you not to mistrust my lord. Knowing him the way I do, I am certain of his goodness, generosity, and gentility. He does not crave material possessions; honor is all he desires. In addition, in this situation, I feel sure he will heed my counsel before acting. God willing, I will engineer this situation so that it comes to an auspicious conclusion and in such a way that you will be obliged to praise me."

"In that case," they solemnly vowed, "we place ourselves and our possessions utterly and completely at your command and discretion, and we will come on the day that you will designate and pledge sincerely to perform lord Melibee's will and yours."

Hearing this response, Lady Prudence directed them to return home secretly. For her part, she returned to her lord Melibee and reported that she had found his adversaries repentant, conscious of their sinful action, ready to suffer all punishment, and petitioning her pity and mercy.

Melibee then answered, "The man is worthy of pardon who does not excuse his sin but rather recognizes it, repents, and asks for indulgence, for Seneca said,

'Where there is confession, there is remission, for confession is almost innocence,' and elsewhere he wrote, 'He is nearly innocent who recognizes his sin and feels shame.' Thus I agree to the peace, but it is proper to conclude it with the advice and consent of our friends."

Prudence's countenance was then joyous. She exclaimed, "Certainly you have spoken well! Just as through the counsel and help of your friends you had planned to avenge yourself and make war, do not now make peace without also seeking their advice, for the law says that nothing is as natural as to loosen a thing by that with which it had been bound."

Lady Prudence immediately sent for their relatives and their old, loyal, and wise companions. In Melibee's presence she recounted the situation to them, the way that it is told above, and inquired of them what course of action they would counsel. The friends, having considered, examined, and deliberated about the entire matter quite carefully, recommended that he make an accord and receive the adversaries with compassion and mercy. When Lady Prudence heard her husband's consent and saw that her husband's and his friends' consent was congruent with her own judgment, she was most gratified. "A proverb," she remarked, "says: 'Do not wait until the evening or the next day to do the good that you can do in the morning.' Therefore, you should immediately send wise and well-briefed messengers to those people to tell them that if they wish to treat for peace and reconciliation as they proffered, they should come to us at once, with their loyal and appropriate guarantees."

It was accomplished just as Lady Prudence advised. When the three penitent evildoers heard the messengers, they were glad and joyful. Sending gratitude to lord Melibee and all his entourage, they responded that they were prepared to leave with the messengers instantly and to obey any orders completely. Forthwith, they set off for lord Melibee's court, together with their wives and some loyal friends.

Once Melibee beheld them before him, he said, "It is true that, without cause or reason, you harmed me, my wife Prudence, and my daughter by forcefully entering my home and committing the outrage everyone knows, for which you deserve death. For that reason I seek to hear from you if you wish to submit entirely to punishment and vengeance for this injury according to my will and that of my wife."

The oldest and wisest of the three responded for them all. "Lord," he said, "we are not worthy to come to such a noble court, before such a man as you, for we have done so great a wrong that in truth we deserve death, not life. However, we entrust ourselves to your kindness and goodness for which you are everywhere renowned, and thus we present ourselves as ready to obey whatever you order. We beg you, tearful and on our knees, to have pity and compassion for us." Then

Melibee benevolently accepted their pledges by their oaths and guarantees. He assigned them a day to return to his court to offer themselves to him to hear their sentence.

Once these matters were arranged, and each one had left in his own direction, Lady Prudence spoke to her husband Melibee, asking him what vengeance he intended to take on his adversaries. "Certainly," said Melibee, "I intend to disinherit them from all that they own and send them abroad, never to return to this land."

"Surely," said Prudence, "this sentence would be most unjust and unreasonable! You are wealthy and do not need the riches or money of another man. You could rightfully be charged with greed, a serious vice and the root of all evil. According to the Apostle, it would be better to lose with honor than to gain in shame. Elsewhere he says, 'A gain must be called a loss if it does not maintain a good reputation'; and furthermore, one must not only refrain from committing acts that threaten to tarnish a good name but always endeavor to enhance his renown, for it is written: 'An old reputation is soon gone when it is not renewed.' Next, with regard to your statement about banishing them overseas never to return, that seems to me an abuse of the power that they relinquished to show you honor and reverence. Justice says that he who misuses the sovereignty given to him deserves to lose his privilege. Moreover, I would extend that to declare that even if you could rightfully inflict this punishment on them, which I do not grant, you could not execute it. Rather, perchance it would be necessary to return to war just as before. That is why, if you want compliance, you must sentence them more courteously, for it is written, 'People obey him best who commands the most kindly.' Thus, I beg you, please get the better of your nature, for Seneca said, 'He who conquers his heart conquers two times'; and Cicero also said, 'Nothing is so praiseworthy in a great man as a generous and conciliatory nature.' Please conduct yourself in this vengeance so as to maintain your good reputation and cause yourself to be praised for compassion and humanity, in order that you need not repent of your actions. For Seneca said, 'He who must repent for his victory vanquishes badly.' With these reasons I urge you to add mercy to your judgment, so that God will have compassion for you in His Last Judgment, since Saint James wrote in his epistle, 'He who lacks compassion will himself be judged without pity, for justice without compassion is tyranny.'"

When Melibee had heard all of Lady Prudence's speech and wise instruction, he had great peace in his heart and praised God for giving him such a wise companion. On the day his adversaries appeared before him, he spoke to them benignly, saying, "While in your presumption you acted most arrogantly toward us, nonetheless the great humility you display compels me to forgive you, and thus we receive you in our friendship and good graces. We pardon all of your offenses and misdeeds against us, so that at the moment of death, God will pardon ours."

* * *

2. My dear, you can thus see how wisely this worthy Prudence quelled and hid the great sadness in her heart—dejection and sorrow about the outrage that she and her daughter had suffered to their bodies—of which she did not speak a single word because it truly seemed that Melibee would make himself more desperately upset than before. In this way she displayed that she loved him; she wisely mollified him. This good woman did not reveal herself to be angry, except at the anger that her husband showed. She concealed her own indignation and locked it in her heart, betraying no outward trace of it. You can also find in this story how wisely, subtly, and with what self-possession she exhorted her husband to tolerate and overlook the offense and how she preached patience to him in such a grave affair. Consider her serious and heartfelt reflection, day and night, resulting in such powerful arguments and sharp reasoning that she convinced her husband to let go of the plan he so strongly intended. Through this care for his vengeful nature, she showed clearly that she loved him and was impelled to dissuade him from his foolish will. You can see how in the end she wisely appeased his humor. This good lady persevered without pause in different stages and accomplished so much that she pacified him completely. That is why I state to you that good ladies must use this same wisdom, discretion, caution, and gentleness to advise and dissuade their husbands from the follies and stupidities that inflame and infect them, rather than think they can sway their men through mastery, or by lofty speech, by shouting to their neighbors or in the street, or by scolding them, by complaining to their friends and relatives, or by other power plays. For all that is useless and serves only to exacerbate the problem, since a man's heart amends itself but grudgingly through the domination and authority of a woman. Keep in mind that there is no man so poor or of such humble station who, once married, does not want to rule as a lord.

3. Furthermore, I must not fail to mention another example of dissuading a husband through kindness, a tale I heard told a long time ago by my late father, God rest his soul. He told me that there was a bourgeoise in Paris named Dame Jehanne la Quentine, the wife of Thomas Quentin.[19] She learned that her husband

---

19. Marguerite de Navarre recasts this tale in the *Heptameron* (day 4, story 8); it is known that she possessed a manuscript of *Le Ménagier*, which possibly served as her source. Georgine Brereton, "*Le Ménagier de Paris,* source de la xxxviiie nouvelle de l'Heptaméron?" *Bibliothèque d'Humanisme et de Renaissance* 16 (1954): 207.

frolicked foolishly and carelessly and frequented and sometimes lay with a poor girl who was a wool spinner. For a long time, without revealing that she was aware of it or uttering a single word, Jehanne tolerated the situation and concealed it.

4. Dame Jehanne suffered patiently. At last, she inquired about where this wretched girl lived, until she discovered the address. She went to the house and found the poor young woman, without provisions of any kind: no wood, tallow, candle, oil, coal, or anything, excepting only a bed with coverlet, her spinning wheel, and a few other household items. She spoke to her: "My friend, I am bound to protect my husband from scandal, and because I know that he takes pleasure in you and loves you and that he visits here, I request that for your part you keep quiet about your relationship and speak of him as little as possible in public, to spare him, myself, and our children from reproach. As for me, I swear to you that you two shall be well concealed by me. Since he loves you, my intention is to care for, help, and aid you in all that you have to do, and you will have sufficient evidence of this. But I pray you with all my heart that his indiscretion not be revealed or gossiped about. Since he comes from a fine family and was raised with tenderness and was then fed, nurtured, warmed, put to bed, and tucked in as well as I was able, and since apparently you have little means to provide him with such comforts, I prefer that you and I together maintain him in health, rather than for me alone to tend him in sickness. I pray you to love, care for, and serve him so that by you he will be dissuaded and protected from loitering elsewhere in diverse dangers. Without his knowledge I will send you a great basin so that you can wash his feet often, and provisions of wood to warm him, a good bed, an eiderdown, sheets and coverlets appropriate to his status, nightcaps, pillows, and clean hose and shirts. When I send you clean clothes, send me the dirty things, and let all of this remain between you and me, so that he knows nothing of it, so that he may not feel shamed. For God's sake, behave so wisely and discreetly with him that he does not learn our secret." In this way the matter was concluded.

5. Jehanne la Quentine left and carefully sent all that she had promised. When Thomas arrived in the evening at the girl's house, his feet were washed and he was laid in a down bed, on fine large sheets that hung over on each side, covered far better than he had been accustomed. The next day he had a white shirt, clean hose, and beautiful new slippers. He marveled greatly at these new things and became pensive. He went to hear Mass as was his custom, returned to the girl, and sharply accused her of crime, that these things were ill-gotten, so that she in self-defense might tell him whence they came. He knew full well that he had left her impoverished two or three days before and that in so little time she could not have grown rich.

6. When she saw herself thus charged, and that she must defend herself, she knew enough of Thomas's conscience to know that he would believe what she

told him. Not in the habit of lying, she bared to him the truth concerning all that is said above. Then this Thomas went all shamefaced to his house, more thoughtful than ever, but he did not speak a word to Jehanne his wife, nor she to him. Rather, she served him most joyously and tenderly, and he and his wife slept together that night without speaking of the matter.

7. The next day Thomas heard Mass on his own initiative and confessed his sins. Soon afterward he returned to the girl and made a present to her of what she had of his. He vowed abstinence from all women except his wife as long as he lived. In this way his wife reclaimed him by subtlety, afterward loving him most humbly and sincerely.

8. Thus, good ladies must advise and persuade their husbands, not by mastery and haughtiness, but through wisdom and humility. Bad women do not comprehend this, nor can their hearts endure it. Therefore, their affairs often deteriorate. Although many other examples could be set down, making quite a long list, what's here nonetheless should suffice for this article, for this last matter does not concern you, since you know well how to avoid this danger.

Introductory Note to Article 2.1

An allegorical dream-vision poem of 2,626 verses in French octosyllabic couplets constitutes nearly all of article 2.1. *Le Chemin de povreté et de richesse,* called in some MSS *La Voie de povreté ou de richesse,* or *Le Livre du chastel de labour,* possibly composed by Jacques Bruyant in 1342, depicts a newlywed man—he calls himself a "nouvel mesnagier"—experiencing the first trials of marriage.[1] In the dream, various allegorical figures such

---

1. Fifteen MSS contain the poem, including the MSS of *Le Ménagier.* See "Archives de littérature du Moyen Age" entry (online) on Bruyant. The most lavishly illustrated version of the poem (with forty-six miniatures) is by the Fastolf Master or the workshop of the Bedford Master (Paris or Rouen, c. 1430–40), MS Widener I, now in the Free Library of Philadelphia, Rare Book Department. The manuscript was likely made for an aristocratic family of Normandy, the Belvilles. Two leaves of this sumptuous manuscript are reproduced in *Leaves of Gold: Manuscript Illuminations from Philadelphia Collections,* ed. James R. Tanis, with the assistance of Jennifer A. Thompson (Philadelphia: Philadelphia Museum of Art, 2001), 203–4. The Bedford workshop in Paris, named after the workshop's key patron, the duke of Bedford (John of Lancaster, 1389–1435), was the foremost producer of illuminated manuscripts and books of hours in Paris between c. 1400 and 1450. It is apparent from the care with which the manuscript was prepared and the obvious cost of the bookmaking that the poem was admired and valued by whoever commissioned the manuscript. Its survival in so many manuscript versions attests to its popularity. A deluxe facsimile edition, with commentary volume containing modern German and French translations, is *Jacques Bruyant:* *Le Livre du Chastel de Labour,* commentary by Eberhard König and William Lang (Lucerne: Faksimile-Verlag, 2005). See also *Le livre de Chastel de Labour, par Jean Bruyant. A description of an Illuminated Manuscript of the fifteenth century, belonging to George C. Thomas, Philadelphia, with a short account and synopsis of the Poem,* author unknown ([Philadelphia ?]: privately published, 1909). An adapted and abridged version of the poem, Pierre Gringore's *Chasteau de Labour,* was printed in France in 1499, and shortly after that Alexander Barclay translated this version into English and Wynkyn de Worde printed his poem in England in 1506 as *The Castell of Labour.* See the Roxburghe Club facsimile, *The Castell of Labour, Translated from the French of Pierre Gringore by Alexander Barclay, Reprinted in facsimile from Wynkyn de Worde's edition of 1506 with the French text of 31 March 1501 and an introduction by A. W. Pollard* (Edinburgh: Constable, 1905). Barclay's translation of Gringore's poem is often quite sprightly. The 1909 anonymously authored book on the Widener I manuscript of the *Chastel de Labour* contains eighty lines of the poem translated into English couplets (and quite well, too). While we have not been able to locate any more of this translation, Jim DeWalt, head of the Rare Book Department of the Free Library of

as Want, Necessity, Penury, and Scarcity appear and physically assail him. Reason then intervenes to instruct him how to drive these troubles away through morality, and educates him about the vices and virtues. The dreamer finally gets directions to the Castle of Riches, via Diligence and Perseverance, and avoids Sloth. On his way, he finds the Castle of Labor where he joins the workers there for a long day of toil. Upon his return home—without having reached the Castle of Riches—his down-to-earth wife disbelieves his outlandish story of these travels, charging him with madness. Later, before going to bed again, he prays that if he is not to be allowed to attain riches, he may at least have sufficient for his needs.

One can certainly appreciate the similarities between the instructional materials that have gone before, such as in article 1.3 on the Seven Deadly Sins and the Virtues, and this poetic sermon on the merits of hard work for a wedded man and how to avoid vice. Still, this poem is ostensibly about a man's virtue rather than a woman's—which is the focus of much of the other parts of the volume—so it may act as a kind of bookend or diptych with its counterpart in section 1.3 to show the young wife that a virtuous man is a hard worker, and that seeking riches can be morally acceptable, as long as one does it through diligent labor. The vices and virtues, described in lengthy sermonizing detail in section 1, are here dramatically marshaled for further heuristic aims, so that the reader will visualize them as attacking the soul, with life lived as a struggle against these daily assaults. And perhaps too this poem is included to demonstrate to that *next* husband what is expected of him. In fact, this poem represents a version of a conduct book for secular working men within the larger context of this woman's manual. We find also in the *Chemin* poem allegorical figures lecturing on deliberation before acting and using reason and moderation as a guide for living, such as appear in the story of Melibee in article 1.9. A portion of the poem dramatizes Lady Reason's advice to servants to be faithful, willing, obliging, and

Philadelphia, noted that in the library's curatorial files "one photocopied fragment" mentions that the translator was F. W. Bourdillon (email to C. Rose, August 16, 2007). Francis William Bourdillon (1852–1921) was an Oxford-educated poet (his *Times* obituary says "minor") and author of thirteen volumes of poetry, as well as a scholarly editor of Old French verse (*Aucassin et Nicolette* [1887]) and author (*Early Editions of the Romance of the Rose* [1906]). He clearly is a contender for authorship of this 1909 book on the Widener MS, and perhaps too the translator of those eighty lines. See also A. Langfors, "Jacques Bryant et son poème: *La Voie de Povreté et de Richesse*," *Romania* 45 (1918): 49–83; and Paul Meyer, review of the anonymous 1909 book (above) on the *Chastel* in *Romania* 39 (1910): 419–20.

never insolent, and she advocates the service of Love over the service of Fear for both masters and retainers, as is reiterated in article 2.3. In this way the themes of the rest of the book are carried out poetically and recapitulated in this article before the narrator turns to his more practical advice on horses, hawking, gardening, and cooking.

Toward its conclusion, this poem offers an antifeminist diatribe about the impossibility of pleasing wives, a kind of corrective to or gloss on the earlier treatises in section 1 concerning the outrageous demands of husbands for wifely obedience, although this speech is couched in somewhat sheepish language by the "nouvel mesnagier," who seems grudgingly to enjoy his married state. All in all, this poem significantly and charmingly adds to the discussion in the book regarding the moral life and touches on the complex negotiation that was the medieval marriage, or any marriage for that matter. The man in the poem never reaches the Castle of Riches, but the *Ménagier* narrator may have other plans for his own life. Earlier, in his prologue, the narrator counsels his wife to act prudently so that they will reach such a castle: "The first article instructs that you take care of your household, with diligence, perseverance, and regard for your work. Take pains to find pleasure in your duties, and I will do the same so that we will reach the castle that is spoken of." It hardly seems

that he could be referring to the Castle of Labor that the man in the poem has arrived at (and must settle for), since the pains he undergoes in the Castle of Labor are ostensibly a prelude to being welcomed to the Castle of Riches.

In his introductory remarks to this article and the *Chemin* poem, the narrator worries aloud about boring his wife-pupil with his advice and verbose instructions, but he concludes he has not burdened her too badly after all and resolves to include this lengthy poem in his book for her. He informs his wife how much he admires this poem and how he is loath to change, excerpt, or abbreviate it in any way, so he incorporates it wholesale into his compendium for her education and, one hopes, for her entertainment. It is significant for the understanding of the taste of such medieval bourgeois householders— what they read and considered important to preserve—that, indeed, the wife was expected to read and understand poetry.

The Brereton and Ferrier edition omits this poem entirely and Ueltschi relegates the work to an appendix. Brereton-Ferrier find it "odd" that the author chose to include the poem in his compendium, and Ueltschi says that unlike the stories of Griselda or Melibee, the poem constitutes "an abrupt departure" from the body of the book.[2] But we disagree with these

2. BF/Ueltschi, 17.

assessments and find it eminently pertinent and consistent with the matter of the rest of the book, as we note above. As was our practice with the Melibee section, we followed MS A unless Pichon's reading substituted from another MS was superior. Such readings are bracketed in the text.

¶ 2.1 *Le Chemin de povreté et de richesse*

Here begins section 2, article 1: "Recapitulation."

1. My dear, I must say that I am filled with distress over whether to end my book here or to continue, because I fear that I may bore you. It is worrisome that I may be taxing you with so much that you might consider me unreasonable. I would be most ashamed if you were afraid that you could not accomplish what my instructions demand and were in despair of ever being able to bear the heavy burden of all my advice. For that reason, here I wish to mull things over a bit, in the hope that I will not instruct you excessively and that I will direct you to undertake only the most necessary and honorable duties—and even at that, as few as I can manage—insofar as you may better understand and accomplish these essential things and thus be more honored through your words and deeds. For neither you nor any other woman could retain it all. So first I wish to consider the amount of instruction I have given you, and what part of it is indispensable, and whether I should entrust you with additional material, and how much, or if there really already is more to do than you are capable of, in which case I will help you. These are my concerns as I begin this article.

2. At the beginning, I admonished you to praise God upon awakening and rising, and to attend church and behave yourself there, to hear Mass, to make your confession, and to wrap yourself in God's love and grace. Upon my soul, no one else can accomplish these obligations for you! After that, I advised you to remain continent and chaste, to love your husband, obey him, keep his secrets, and figure out how to dissuade him if he acts dissolutely or wishes to go astray. Indeed, these expectations are all fundamental and bring you honor. They are incumbent on you alone and not overly burdensome. By means of the teachings presented above, you should be able to perform all this well. This book will provide you with a great advantage, since other women never had such a guide.

3. Certainly, in the sections above you learned that you must be in charge of yourself, your children, and your belongings. But in each of these things you can certainly have assistance. You must see how best to apply yourself to the household tasks, what help and what people you will employ, and how you will occupy them. In these matters, you need take on only the command, the supervision, and the conscientiousness to have things done right, but have the work performed by others, at your husband's expense.

4. Well, you can see from what has gone before, my dear, that, really, you must not complain. You are hardly overburdened, and have only the obligations rightly

Chemin *poem illustration (c. 1430–1440) from* Chastel de labour *manuscript, Philadelphia Free Library, Widener I, fol. 1. Want, Necessity, Penury, and Scarcity harass the poem's newly married narrator.*

belonging to you, which should be pleasant, such as serving God and taking care of your husband's person, and in a nutshell, that is all.

5. Let us then continue our subject in this first article. I announce to all that this article does not spring from my own wit, nor did I render it in its present form, nor do I deserve any praise for it. As I have set here nothing of my own, the honor cannot be mine. Rather, it belongs to an admirable, skilled, and worthy man, the late Jean Bruyant,[1] once the king's notary at the Châtelet de Paris, who wrote the following treatise. I incorporate it chiefly to avail myself of the teachings within it about the diligence and perseverance a new husband must have. Because I have no wish to mutilate his book, or extract a fragment or excerpt it from the rest, and likewise, because it is all of a piece, I help myself to the whole to reach the only point that I desire. So for the first article I include the entire book that, in verse, relates the following:

Le Chemin de povreté et de richesse par Jaques Bruyant MCCCXLII

Though folks may often speak it in reproach, there is a proverb I like a lot that says: "Leave a fool by himself, and he will figure out how to get by."[2] For myself, I can promise the truth of this saying, since even if I have only the bare necessities, as Scripture instructs us, in this world sufficiency is perfect riches. As for gold, on that I will remain silent. Hereafter I will recount a vision that came to me nineteen or twenty days after I was married. The festivities of my wedding and the feasting were past, and it was time for troubles to begin. One evening I was lying in my bed, where I had little enough delight, and my wife was sleeping soundly by my side.

While I was lying there wide awake, a vision appeared to me that made me marvel, of a man and three women together, all seeming quite vexed, dejected, melancholy, and anxious. Disconsolate, sad, and wretched, they evinced no joy or comfort in their demeanors. Nor did they appear interested in amusing themselves, but all four were of the same countenance, looking as if they were more about to fracas than to feast. The man was named Want, and he was full of sadness and concern. The eldest woman was called Necessity, the second woman Penury, and the third, Scarcity. They were siblings, for Poverty was their mother, and Misfortune engendered them in great sadness and dread.

---

1. Scholars agree his name was Jacques Bruyant, but little is known of him besides his name and this poem. See Langfors, "Jacques Bryant et son poème." Note the author's expansion of his audience to "all."

2. "Set by himself a fool, and he / To his own comfort soon will see." From the anonymously authored 1909 synopsis of the poem. Barclay's 1506 translation says: "A natural fool in a house alone / Wyll make for hymself shyft or cheuysaunce."

Rushing toward me heatedly, they seized me, handling me roughly, not only threatening or mocking but acting as if they really were about to strangle me. Want assailed me first, clenching me so tightly in his arms that he nearly squeezed the life out of me. Necessity then joined in, most distressed and wrathful. Silently grabbing me by the neck and striving to grip tightly, she throttled me. Penury and Scarcity were on either side of me, one pulling and the other knocking me about, each scolding me loudly. In this way these [four] clutched me, beat and pummeled me, putting me in such distress that I lost all cheer.

A large gray-haired old beldame then raced toward me, hideous, witchlike, and withered, with wickedness on her mind: she was called Disquiet. This old woman caused me more misfortune than the others, for this vile stinking hag set herself upon my chest, tormenting my entire body. May her soul be the devil's! For she weighed so heavily on me that she put my heart in jeopardy of great suffering and misery, hurting me exceedingly. I began then to crawl on my belly and entered into such profound musing that no one can conceive of it, nor any mouth recount or tell it. Just as I was in the agony that Disquiet had given me, I glimpsed a gauchely built, ugly, wrinkled, hideous and hunchbacked, snarling, greasy, and hairy churl with rheumy eyes full of filth. This abominable creature, all scabby and shaggy, was called Worry. This one mistreated me so much worse! Alas! I did not need that! He gave me plenty of his brand of service and damaged me so much that there is neither limb nor extremity that I would not have agreed to relinquish. He made me tremble and wince, lose color, and stirred up my blood; I sweated profusely from misery, and he agitated me so, causing me to lament, grieve, and groan, toss and turn. In short, thus did Worry proceed to treat me. He was so villainous and violent to me that I became weak and [haggard] from his treatment and as dry as a log. When I recall it, I take no pleasure in it; rather I am so feeble and faint that it seems as if I have been ill. Alas! Surely, I was sick, with a much worse disease than tertian fever or quartan fever. For he who has affliction from Worry has ill health and healthy illness. It's devilry from Worry! When I remember it, I am very worried, for in him there is such great ferocity that it is a wonder that he whom Worry holds in his domain doesn't go mad, for he becomes just like the grease in the frying pan, which sputters from the force of the fire and then dries up and fries. In that same way Worry makes people burn with agitation and holds them so tightly in his clutches that he makes them often say, "alas!" Plus, he makes them live in such pain that they lose their robustness and become pallid. Worry is so unpleasant, so hideous, so terrifying, and so abominable to the heart that anyone who samples him would not want another taste. Worry has dismayed many souls and still does so every day. No one who has not experienced him realizes, as I have, despite myself, the pain, hardship, and terror.

When I saw this group with me—Want, Penury, Necessity, with Scarcity, Disquiet the old woman, and Worry—I raised my head and coughed. At once hurtled toward me an enormous churl blacker than mulberries who was named Distress. He too began to manhandle me, doubling my misery. Then my mind became cloudy, for I had suffered so greatly that I nearly lost my senses. I began loudly to lament and to torture myself by saying, "Wretch! What will you do? How will you pay your debts? You have nothing, yet you owe much. If only you were dead! You are a newly made head of household[3] without any collateral, unless you sell your robes. Alas, poor devil, what recourse can you have? You have nowhere to turn!"

Just as I spoke these words, a woman, looking quite mad and erratic, careered toward me. This gloomy and unkempt female was Despair, the daughter of Distress the hideous. Great pain and trouble came to me from those two! Through them I lost discretion, reason, memory, and thought. Turning ashen, with clenched jaw I cried, "Alas! What will I do? Here I am, landed in the grip of Despair, and now I will be wicked wherever I am. It doesn't matter to me now what happens! Whether in rain or in the north wind, he who cannot bend, breaks! He withers who cannot blossom! I have but one death to die, and a long time ago I heard it said that he who is determined to go to the devil does not care how long it takes. At this point, he cannot drown who is destined to hang, and he is disgraced who ever wishes to do anything except the worst of which he is capable! As for me, the castle of Riches cannot be reached, for she resides so far away that the extreme effort that one must undertake prior to getting there drains the life's blood. Even before they reach her, Riches turns many handsome faces pale, never to recover their health. For if a person waits until he is old and powerless to transgress, he could come to grief and lose his moment. Insofar as I cannot have property or possessions rightly, I thus would like to have them wrongly. For it is better to be fat and comfortable while in the wrong than miserable and distressed but in the right!"

Here I was, oblivious to having gone over to the side of badness, caring for nothing but accomplishing my own selfish will, for Despair stirred in me the desire to do wrong and through her evil nature caused me nearly to lose body and soul. But at that moment materialized a most noble lady, gracious, upright, pleasant, and fair. She did not seem obstinate but rather gentle and humble toward all. Her body, comely and elegant, bore such noble adornments that surely marked her as the daughter of a king. In truth, she was indeed the child of that King incomparable in majesty. She was called Reason and showed herself to be extremely wise and well instructed. As she sat down beside me, the dreadful Despair perceived this and fled in terror, as fast as her feet could carry her; for she could not tarry anywhere that Reason guarded. Reason hates her infinitely more than poison hates an antidote.

---

3. Middle French: "nouvel mesnagier."

Reason was thus overjoyed when her adversary Despair abandoned me. She leaned toward me and said, "Friend, may God protect you! You had a wicked concern, a wicked thought, and a wicked intention, because you were briefly of the opinion that for you all good has ceased. But no one ever fails in good who is intent upon the good and lives according to my nature and teaching, which gives salvation to souls. If you wish to pay heed, I can instruct you. First, you must love my Father sincerely, without bitterness, and esteem the sweet Virgin without conceit or hypocrisy, and praise all the saints [whether you are sick or hale,][4] both in prosperity and in adversity, in abundance and in wretchedness. For meekness in sad times and disdain in joy, or sweetness in happy times and fury in sorrow, come from bad habits acquired in youth. One who learns to act in a certain way renounces it only with great difficulty. Thus, it is important to cultivate practices that lead to honor and reward. If you aspire to nurture the habits of virtue, do not abandon your heart to any of the Seven Deadly Sins, and take care that you remain untainted by any occasions of sin, for much damage would thereby ensue. Rather, behave so that your heart is in accord with the Seven Works of Mercy, which are opposite to the Seven Vices. These are most necessary in order to acquire the love of my Father and of His glorious Mother.

"Concerning these Seven Vices, I will elucidate them and their various offshoots, all of which are intent on deceiving you while you make your way. If you willingly heed them, they become your masters and you are their serf. Night and day you serve them readily, while meriting the kind of recompense no one would consent to. Thus you will live in subjugation—to your damnation—if you do not learn to resist them and wrestle to escape from their clutches. I will teach you how to repudiate them when they assail you and assert their strength over you, so that you may have absolute power against the hazards of fortune that might flow from them. If you choose to trust in my wisdom, you will be so immune to them that they will not dare gaze at you through fear of the Seven Virtues, those good shields for you against the seven enemies who commit themselves to sending you to perdition. All you need do is enjoin the Vices to leave you. Should you wish this with all of your heart, the Virtues will bring your war to an end without taking any payment for it except your prayer. Not such an exorbitant price, and it is easy to pay! Therefore, no one can excuse himself from it without being dishonest.

"When you see Pride coming at you with his banner unfurled, gaping in all directions, and with him Derision, Disdain, Contempt, Presumption, Disregard, Audacity, Conceit, Scorn, and Bravado, plus all of his other companions who have hearts worse than curs, hastily muster to your assistance Humility, Devoutness, Magnanimity, Contemplation, Fear of the Lord, Gentleness, Pity, Justice,

---

4. Scratched out in MS A and rewritten in another hand.

Modesty, Equity, and numerous others with them who will dash to your aid. Each one will expend all that he has, provided that you wish them to stay the course. If you fight against Pride they will vanquish him, giving him no refuge, and will force him and all his entourage to flee. Upon your defeat of Pride and his army through Humility, protect yourself thenceforward, so that if he returns to confront you and bring you again to his camp, Humility and the others of her party will still be there to shield you when you need them.

"You must defend yourself to prevent another type of perilous assault by the captain Envy, who comes from a despicable assembly. With him forever are Hatred, Falsehood, Murder and Betrayal, False-Seeming and Detraction, Enmity and Evil-Tongue, who likes malicious blame. If they wish to assault you, you will be able to liberate yourself immediately, provided that you not allow them to approach near enough that they can pierce you with their spears. To withstand their threat, flee without delay! Entreat Faith and Loyalty to rescue you, so that without further ado, they will come to your aid with their corps; that is, Peace and Concord, True-Friendship, Mercy, Benevolence, Truth, Conscience with Unity, and all the rest of their congregation. They will cause Envy to retreat so that you cannot be harmed.

"Another fearful onslaught against which you must guard yourself steadfastly arises from Wrath the tyrant, who always makes things worse. Abounding in wickedness, he is the most pitiless wretch in the world. An attack from him calls for a strong defense because this one knows how to go so far that no one can stand firm against him. All those of his ilk have an equally wicked manner: Cruelty carries his standard, Perversity, Frenzy, Treachery and Fury, Fiendishness and other villains always tag along at his heels. When you see these folks coming, beware that none of them seizes you. Draw yourself nearer to Kindness, who will offer you good counsel in a trice to aid you against Wrath, accompanied by those of his lineage with mild dispositions: that is, Gentleness, Tolerance, Constancy and Temperance, Patience, Discernment, Restraint with Correction. Those under his command will persuade Wrath and all of his crazed minions to withdraw. Thus will you be delivered from Wrath if you follow Kindness, who is noble, courteous, and sweet. She never grouses about anything that happens. Good-Fortune makes her remain by his side and flee Wrath the evil tyrant, who with very little provocation becomes incensed. One must be wary of Wrath. Push him away and consider him an enemy, without making his acquaintance even for a day, nay, a half day! Wrath is a foul adversary, since as soon as a heart becomes enraged, it becomes so inflamed with treachery that it may lose its body and soul. When one forgoes self-control in anger and eschews temperance, my sister Moderation places herself in him and takes pains to harass him. With her sort, if one does not correct himself moderately, she will— with such force that she brings disgrace all in one blow. Truly she despises people on whom she performs this correction, and thus she throws them all into a stew without providing any terminus or respite, as soon as one defies her. Beware of her anger! Keep a gentle, courteous manner, like that of a man descended from a genteel lineage. No one should become angry or grumble about anything he sees, but always display a peaceful countenance, with ire put behind you. Abandon vice and take up virtue in order to save yourself. Avoid anger and sadness and seize joy and happiness truly, through good intentions, not dissolute living, for debauched enjoyment is valueless to the soul.

"Against yet another perilous assault you must be very watchful in order that you may not be surprised at home or on the road, for it is a most fearsome assault, damaging and deceptive. Most people are misled by it before they have been apprised of it. Sloth is the leader of this assault, who, without threatening, strikes and wounds furtively and cravenly. Indolence carries his standard; Deceit, Idleness, Cowardice, Negligence with Foolishness, Nonchalance with Faint-Heart follow. He whom they can trap is in a pretty bad way indeed. They are all timid rather than brave and, further, stupid, with sorrowful countenances. But Sloth is cowardly in such a way that when he realizes he has the upper hand, thereupon he is excessively wicked. He has a heart as proud as a lion and as harsh as a champion. When his prey does not rise against him in revenge, he strikes and hits, beats and kills. Thus it is proper to distance oneself from Sloth and his family, who are skilled only when they have dominance over you. But one must get the jump on them so that they cannot get back on their feet. If you want to obtain this advantage, take with you in your battle Diligence and Sincerity, Good-Heart and Good-Desire, Intent-to-Do-Well with Mindfulness, and Attention-to-Duty, who willingly procures victory against Sloth, if one consents to believe in him. If you retain this alliance close to you, enclosing it in your heart with love, you need never be apprehensive about Sloth or any of those under his banner. Rather they will withdraw, for they dare to assault only those who will capitulate forthwith.

"Next, guard yourself against the fifth attack because he who is its rightful captain leads such a skilled foray that he causes great affliction for those in his service. This deceptive captain Avarice lets Covetousness carry his standard. Rapine, Usury, False-Dealings are in step with him always; likewise follow Malice with Trickery, Murder, Larceny, Robbery, Cunning, Deception, Fraud with Guile, and the others of their horde. When you see this haughty group who wish to assault you, liberate yourself from them instantly! Make Charity your constable with all his retinue, so compassionate and affable, who all, according to God, prize Riches. That is, Sufficiency with Largesse—almsgiving done with a devout heart—being what God most desires among His followers. With this constable on your side, you will have conquered Avarice and his might. Avarice is a vile character, scheming evil deeds with his sidekick Covetousness who incites theft. Therefore, take nothing from anyone, if you do not intend to return it. The daily deception of folk by Covetousness causes some to die in torment through their own folly. For this Nature is often blamed—and reviled without cause, as she is not guilty. He sins who accuses her, and her grief increases the more she endures torment. Therefore he who scoffs at being moral is not naturally immoral; rather it comes to him by accident, apparently. Usually, one who has within himself a damaging vice accuses Nature of forming him that way. But don't believe it; it's a fabrication. The vice originates from the evil doctrine that has been taught to him.

"Protect yourself well from the sixth kind of damage, done by Gluttony, the waster of all good things. He prefers delectations and engenders all the wicked vices because he can never be satisfied and is always ravenous, even more than it appears. He never loses his desire, a terrible thing, for there was never gratification without excess. As befits a crafty warrior, Gluttony attacks from both the front and the rear, always dividing his battalion before his offensive. Gourmandise leads one half, which includes Appetite, Greediness, Drunkenness, Excess, Voluptuousness, and suchlike characters whom Gluttony recruits to follow him. The troops thus divided, he storms the victim from one side, and with this action diverts the unwary. The other battalion has Evil-Tongue, caring only for reproach, Calumny, Slander, Blasphemy, Rashness, Depravity, and a host of others who share the same nastiness. In a surprise attack, this battalion assaults the undefended side with great force. Gluttony charges and rouses both armies, enjoining them to stand unflaggingly firm to ensure their victory. Thus, to ward off such a strike, consider well and circumspectly how to oppose them. Get to a safe place along with Abstinence and Sobriety and others of their flock, since if you have these two and their followers, they will protect you without fail against that gormandizing riffraff. Above all, shun Drunkenness, so that he does not address his battalion against you. The life of one who relinquishes himself to Drunkenness is short, and hardship dogs what life he does have. The drunkard aches from head to toe. His hands tremble, and old age, illness, or feebleness comes early. He becomes emaciated as his entire liver decays. Such suicidal behavior causes grief and repugnance.

"Take care to guard against the seventh assault, led by Lasciviousness. Do not let her and her companions come across you in their path and trample you underfoot. If the skilled archer Foolish-Look tries to wound you, be wise and withdraw, hustling yourself out of range. When you are beyond their scopes, pay attention not to situate yourself in the path of Remembrance. For if he approached you and led you along, he would lead you right back within the bows' range, so that the arrow of Disquiet would quickly pierce your body, as well as that of Foolish-Pleasure, who would strive only for deceit. He would place you entirely at his beck and call and within range of Desire's crossbow. Desire would strike your heart so keenly that no physician would ever heal the wound. Your pain's intensity would preclude anything except persevering in the foolish business that arises from irrational love—which everyone eventually regrets. Through your frailty, Foolish-Love will ride roughshod over you, and you will have to capitulate. But if you wish to safeguard yourself from the amorous archers, they will never catch you unawares. Take the shield of Chastity and the lance of Resolution. Place the shield before your eyes—there is no better defense! She protects you mightily against the arrows of Gaze. Be mindful of this remedy against Foolish-Gaze, and Foolish-Thought will never hold you in subjugation. When these two will not attack you, neither will the others. Just as these two can do all things, they can also undo all things. Gaze is such a piercing thing; all pleasure is contained in it, as is all the opposite. His archery is first-rate. Those whom Gaze wounds, whether for the good or for the bad, in joy or in pain, become pallid. Thus what they say is true: 'What the eye does not see, the heart does not grieve.' Some try to excuse themselves by objecting that they were unable to protect themselves from Gaze's powerful arrows that compelled them to ogle one another when they were together. All this Holy Church unites in the holy design of matrimony. I will respond to those who excuse themselves.

"Briefly, I do not intend to forbid Fair-Gaze to anyone, but ask them only not to engage with Foolish-Gaze, who causes nitwits to imagine and through Foolish-Belief to fantasize. From this arises Foolish-Pleasure, who covets gratification of the body, and from him comes Ardent-Desire, who enflames all, if he does not satisfy his lust. He works on it until his lasciviousness is consummated. Such comes from Foolish-Gaze—a look not fitting for God, but rather for the devil. This look made for carnal delight pleases the devil and equally displeases God, unless done at the appropriate time and place. People who are married and yet whose hearts continually dwell on the acts of carnal pleasure night and morning sin together, without doubt, by means of the stratagem of Foolish-Pleasure, who often holds them in a net. But these wretched ones do not believe it, thinking this vice to be a virtue, so they behave imprudently and heedlessly. Spouses should never seek carnal intercourse unless with the intention of multiplying their descendants. For this I have united them in marriage so that, according to Nature's plan, they engender offspring together at the right time and place, just as God ordained. They should not delight in copulating with one another for its own sake. They are wanton who mate without the right intention. For when Nature takes its course in such partners, without calling on me or on Moderation, and hides her deed from us so that Temperance cannot arrive to manage her, this gratuitous intercourse, performed through frailty and not for procreation, inevitably leads to mortal sin. Foolish-Desire has encouraged them to give in to their lustful temptation, to which Nature is always inclined. Frail, wanton, and eager, Nature at no time refuses such urgings but always impetuously follows them. Nor does she know how to rein herself in from misfortune and torment, so that she ruins herself and empties her granary. Thus, without the steadiness and order of my sister Moderation, Nature runs amok. Moderation never acts disorderly; on the contrary, she performs so appropriately that wherever she is, there is no excess. Therefore, trust Moderation in all things and you will never be dishonored, I assure you, because whoever trusts her lives confidently.

"Here I will leave the assault by Lasciviousness and return to my earlier subject. Be at all times true in your faith. Love your neighbor as yourself. God my Father wants it that way. And do unto others just as you would like them to do to you. When you journey, be disposed to greet people. Never spit from your mouth evil words; a wise man speaks few words. A lover of peace listens well, observes, and remains silent. In company, whether the conversation is sense or folly, wait as long as you can before contributing. Listen carefully, so that you know what to say when the time comes, and say it well. Hence, you will be considered sagacious. Don't be in the thick of parrying for the group's attention, but take your time, since it is folly to hasten to have your say. Reflect a good while before opining on your topic, deliberating about what you want to say, to what end, and what may come of it. This way no harm ensues. Be courteous, humble, and friendly toward everyone, and cherish both the great and the lowly. Follow good and flee evil; love gentleness and peace. Keep out of quarrels, for no benefit comes of liking to argue. Friend, if you wish to reach Riches' castle, about which I have heard you complain so strongly that no man can get there without pain and suffering, let go of such mistakes and such thoughts and embrace Discernment. Select the better of the two roads, leaving the bran and taking the finest flour. Not to do so is madness. Always pick the superior choice of two options. Since you do not know the way to the castle, and you would like to go there, I will teach you the address [as well as the pitfalls of the journey, so that no bad results from it]. Because the way is confusing, just as you mention, one can fret about which path to take to the fair castle of Riches [and wonder who will be able to escort you so that you do not falter or get lost]. Take the straight path on your right and forsake that one on the left, for the right leads all people directly to the domain of Riches, but only if one does not stray from the path. This way no one wanders, and everything goes as one wishes. Now it is proper that I mention to you the path's name. It is so beautiful and renowned, and those who follow enjoy themselves.

"The path called Diligence is paved with Perseverance. If you have the will to remain on this byway, Riches lies ahead. After you finish the journey with ease, you will dwell with Riches in her most gracious castle. He who does not take that way has only himself to blame. He courts misery at his life's end by having thoughts so agitated that he scorns the beautiful right path and inclines to the foul left way. No escape or extrication is possible at that point, but the misled traveler must twist in that noose in pain, distress, and anguish. This left path op-presses many people, causing them lives of misery. Lay people call it Sloth; clerks call it *Accidia*. One finds there no comfort, no help, no counsel, no hope, and no livelihood other than pain, hardship, and tribulation. The traveler on this dam-aged road, full of potholes, will never enjoy fine weather and easy travel. Great puddles of Indolence, Ignorance, and Foolishness detain him there in cowardice. It is also the lane of Poverty, a woman who surely garners neither esteem nor re-spect in this world, any more than an old dog. Down this road comes all adver-sity: misfortune, pain, hardship and hostility. He does himself good who veers from this road to pace on the pleasant path of Diligence. Each one can decide on a road for himself; he has no obligation to take the worse. Should he take it and then wish to stop, if he cannot recover it again then it is too great a folly. Aban-doning the good and knowingly going astray will turn out badly, for once the heart wanders, reclaiming it is difficult. A man on the road of Sloth turns his backside to Riches and heads directly for Poverty who, as I earlier said, recruits people to evil. When the wanderer realizes his folly and decides to turn back, he becomes afflicted with the torment and pain of melancholy and preoccupied with thoughts of despair. From this he possibly becomes a thief and steals possessions from people, and in the end he dies in sorrow.

"Now, there are some who insist that Destiny led them to travel down this road. Such foolishness! They talk nonsense! Unfortunately, some wretches give credence to those who account for their misfortunes by blaming fate. They, of course, think what they say is true and in their hateful way glory in such talk. Ex-cusing themselves for their wrong, they proclaim that it would never have hap-pened of their own free will; rather, it took place through the destiny bestowed on them at their birth. They deceive themselves, for they have the wrong concept! No one is destined to be hanged or drawn or to die a vulgar death—unless he trou-bles himself to deserve it. Anyone can resist mischief who wishes to act morally, nor is it necessary that adversity befall anyone. Rather, it occurs by chance when one ventures imprudently. Destiny cannot compel anyone to the point that he cannot resist, provided that he has good will. Should he eventually be tempted to any offense, if I accompany him, I warn him and banish this thought from his mind and give him advice and wisdom to resist the temptation, if he chooses to trust me. This way he will reach salvation.

"Thus, you clearly perceive that Destiny in no way may wreak something that I cannot completely undo, unless it is concealed from me, which precludes my as-sisting in the matter. No act performed without me can end well but leads in-evitably to grief. Through misfortune it befalls that Destiny assumes the name of virtue and great renown, because many maintain that good and evil originate from her, and that no one can resist Destiny. But those who suppose this are misguided. Had it been God's will to ordain Destiny with the kind of authority over people they say she has, of what use, then, would be good deeds or good words or good intentions? No one would feel called upon to act morally when doing so would not be to his advantage! He may as well die shamefully. The logic would follow, although no one brings it up, that if a man endeavors to do evil, and steals, kills, assaults, and disputes, compelled by Destiny to do so, he should not be singled out, since he only did what he was forced to do. [Even God Himself, Who knows everything, should not harbor any anger toward him,] since Destiny was responsible, not the individual. Surely, however, it is otherwise, and whoever considers Destiny a virtue, he lies, and if he believes this, he deludes himself. Do then what I have taught you about achieving reward: leave the bad and take the good. And it can be easy, for it is a hundred times less wearying traveling the beautiful road named Diligence, which leads all people to honor, and a hundred times less travail than on that awful road of Sloth, so full of torment and sadness and lacking in comfort, pleasant diversions, good health, or nourishing food. That road is so decayed that one sinks waist-deep into it. Unfortunate is the one who travels it! No one runs on this road; it is foul and derelict, although it is short enough and you get where you are going before long, without seeking another way. The way heads straight for the manor, Poverty's home, where one arrives utterly defeated, naked, barefoot, and trembling with cold, appearing in extreme sorrow, the body bent, cringing so that one must take pity on such a creature. But actually, one should have little pity for such people in this low condition because they place themselves there willingly; therefore they deserve to be wretched.

"If you believe this counsel, offered for your profit, then despise this foul road. Remember the poor souls whom you see each day who become so miserable by following this route. They provide noteworthy models for a lesson. Whether he seeks it or falls into it unawares, as occurs often enough, when a man involves himself in a bad situation and from it comes to grief, no one watching him follows his actions; rather, to avoid injury, others seek a better direction to the destination. Entirely and at all times you must avoid that avenue which you recognize will lead to misery, anguish, and poverty. One observes constantly that along this road no one ever had good fortune. Therefore step aside forthwith, tuck in your shirt, and run hastily to the path on the right, the fair road leading all those who travel on it to honor: that is Diligence, the lovely road of nobility. Nothing but happiness results from the abundant gifts it bestows. All those who stick to this road find it marvelously long but not at all irksome to those whose object is the castle of Riches, and who journey day and night without a bother. What a desirable track! Right in the midst of the way lie two paths; one forks to the right and the other to the left. Let me tell you about the one on the right. This is the best one, for it has the power to lead to perfect Riches. It is Sufficiency, the dependable path who safeguards those who travel there, causing them to live hopefully, without despair, since what they have suffices for their needs. In loss or in profit, they tirelessly praise God for a little or for a generous amount. They are the truly rich. No one becomes rich unless he follows the way of Sufficiency, even were he in fact king of France. Here's the truth about the other path, I will not lie: it goes to the left, but indeed it leads to the reverse of the one that goes to the right, because there no one achieves satisfaction. This path, called Covetousness, enflames and excites hearts to crave possessions. The more one has, the more he yearns for, always coveting day after day, so compellingly! Hence, even when they arrive before the gorgeous castle of Riches, they are discontent and must push on for as long as this path stretches, notwithstanding the hardship. But certainly the path deludes them. They see adversity right from the beginning since, once on that trail, possessions don't suffice and these travelers yearn to devour everything. Of course, they do not cease but keep going, unrestrainedly, in search of bread better than wheat bread. Sad to say, this causes regrets, for just when they are poised at the top, they crash to the ground with one single blow from blind Fortune who has knocked them off her wheel into the mud. This happens all the time! When they see themselves deluded and downfallen, their hearts are so humbled and so weak that they collapse and wander, ashamed and stunned, considering themselves simpletons. Miserable, tired, bowed down, joyless, once entered into the road of Sloth, they go directly to Poverty, vanquished and never again to know ease. Thus they will languish and die in wretchedness. By chance they may commit some villainous crime for which they will be brought to justice.[5] Obviously that perilous path of Covetousness represents an extremely bad undertaking, so misleading and so precarious. Everyone who has invested his efforts there repents in the end. Avoid, therefore, this path and take the one of Sufficiency in order always to have adequate livelihood as long as you live. You have enough when you have what is needed to live decently among men and have suitable garments and other necessities. It is crazy to ask for more, for if you took the straight path, you have received what you possess through loyalty; thus, you have more than royalty!

"Should it happen that you must be a servant, I forbid you to be insolent, proud, disloyal, or unreasonable toward your master. Always be obedient and submit to his pleasure in all situations, without obstinacy. Never get involved in arguing or contradicting something you heard him say. When he speaks to you, respond without criticizing or grumbling. Fear angering him and do nothing that is sure to displease him. There is a lesson here, unless you can improve upon it. Respect your master sin-

5. The English summary of the Philadelphia Widener I manuscript says that the printed edition (Pichon) is missing two lines here that appear in the Widener I version: "And even worse, to their damnation, where they will live forever in torment."

cerely, using no falsity with him on any account. Esteem for him obliges you to do his bidding always and to fear him. For Love is so sovereign that all forces bow down before her, and such a powerful virtue that you must take her into your heart without delay, for he who loves with the heart, fears. Right love, which requires obedience through its might, compels a man to awe and holds him in submission with no deception. But if someone fears, it does not follow that he has in him one bit of love. Love does not obey fear, nor does anyone love through compulsion. For certainly everyone knows that one truly fears that which one hates. Nonetheless, he who loves well fears and dreads—of this there should be no doubt.

"Therefore, revere your master and serve him loyally, thus meriting his care in return, because when he notices your integrity, he will behave properly toward you. He will be unable to be hostile. Yet if you serve him in a kind of offhand manner, without devotion, no good will ensue, and you have thus wasted your time with him. Should you quarrel with him, he will dismiss you immediately. Indeed, he could defame you here and there, so that no one will hire you. You would thus be lost in all sorts of ways for serving him without devotion.

"Whoever serves his master sincerely, without rancor, and with such a loyal heart that he earns love in return must possess three qualities whose symbolic interpretations I will note here briefly and then explain them. First, he must have the back of an ass if he wishes to perform his work well. Secondly, he must have the ears of a cow, and thirdly a pig's snout. Don't disdain and cast off with scorn these strange symbols, but take pains to cultivate them, especially when you hear of their significance, which I will tell you now. The back of an ass means you must undertake the burden and the responsibility that your master entrusts to you, and you must remember and cater to all his requirements. You carry burdens in order to spare your master. To do your duty well, you must frequently apprise him of the condition of his affairs and, above all things, hold his welfare as dear as your own. Next, the ears of a cow mean that you must fear your master. Should he upbraid you, listen without ire, with ears wide open. Meanwhile, pretend that you hear nothing and see nothing. When you see him in heated argument, remain silent, tranquil, and cool. Whether right or wrong, do not respond while he is upset, for he could fly into a great passion. And another thing: a servant cannot prevail who talks insubordinately to his master. Whether he works for knight, bourgeois, or priest, he who holds his tongue without insolence possesses a wonderful virtue, believe me, and keep this in mind. By a pig's snout, likewise, I mean do not complain about the food or drink. Whether you are fed a large or small meal, accept it with eagerness and gratitude, if you are wise. Show no contempt or arrogance, pride, impertinence, or disdain, and eat it up just as the snout of a pig nudges everywhere. Receive everything gladly, spurning nothing. In this way, one is not choosy and lives happily on what he is given without grumbling and finds everything decent and delicious. Behave this way in your master's household, as if every-thing pleased and satisfied you, without refusing or scorning anything."

With that, Reason the wise became silent. As I turned to reflect, a renowned sage named Understanding drew up beside me. "Fair friend," said he, "now listen here! If you wish to use your time as Reason said, I think it rational. She has here preached at length and provided many good exempla. If you can retain it all, it will be to your great benefit with God and the world. Have faith in her and remember what she said. I would agree to be tonsured if you have any regrets for doing so! But of course you will see it with your own eyes. For now, I will hush since one can give his consent in one word as well as in a hundred." When I afterward contemplated what Reason taught me and recalled word for word the advice of Understanding, trying anxiously to retain everything in my mind, there appeared a man who seemed to be a lawyer, knowing how to speak in all situations and sounding conversant with logic and reason. Wearing a fur hood and cloak, he comported himself nobly. Without question, he must have been a gentleman. He had a clerk and varlet with him. This barrister was aptly named Fraud. His clerk was Trickery, and his varlet, Swindle.

Fraud sat down beside me, addressing me soberly with reassuring words, as if giving a lesson. "Have you thought enough for today? Well, wretch, what have you decided? Do you choose to believe Reason the fool who drives mad those who believe her? If you are her devotee, you will be desolate as long as you practice her creed. No one can attain any stature who chooses to depend on Reason. Rather, he endures great hardship and lives forever in suffering, lacking even the necessities. Only a madman feels satisfied when he has so much heartache! I would consider a person reckless who would work according to Reason. Never would he thrive but would remain stuck forever [and not the slightest bit rich]. He would always be impoverished, miserly, and grieving—subject and serf to the wealthy, because of which he would often hear himself scorned. Thus, he would subsist in privation. Someone with a pure, clean, and unsullied heart stays poor and obtains no justice in the world, nor can he ever rise in rank. Put Reason thus aside, my man, and trust me, if you are wise. For if you adhere to my practice, you can look forward to being promptly elevated to wealth, power, and honor. People will serve and revere you, and you may do as you please. One order from you and everyone will answer your summons. Follow my instruction and your lifestyle will be that of a duke or king, with every comfort. Here I will teach you by my own example that first you must be a flatterer. That's the right start toward making good and rising to a great estate. If you wish to arrive there, without fail, you must chant the *Placebo*.[6] Be deceitful

---

6. *Placebo Domine,* the opening of Vespers in the Office of the Dead; to chant the *Placebo* "I will please" is to use flattery, to be a sycophant.

in all situations, wherever you are, and smile to everyone's face. You will thus worm your way into their heart. Feign loyalty, sincerity, and intimacy. Acquire things from friends, but hold on tightly to what is yours. Be stingy, not generous; in that way you will be rich forthwith. Whatever crowd you find yourself in, avoid spending money on them. Have a shameless heart, and have a good laugh over it, and ridicule and jest when you see that it is the moment, and take care to do it sharply so that others will find you entertaining.

"Next, have no remorse for deliberately tricking all sorts of people out of their money, rightly or wrongly, either by force or by agreement. Should you wish truly to gratify me, borrow everywhere without repaying anything, and willingly mishandle all your accounts—don't worry whether it is sinful! Have those who owe you squeezed, and do not hesitate to devour them, and impoverish them pitilessly. Who cares if they lose their shirts, provided that you garner their goods! Always be at the ready to take, but refrain from returning anything. Since I forbid you to repay your debts to a soul, should a creditor summon you, my clerk, my varlet, and I will all go together to assist you, willy-nilly, in the event that you need to plead your case. With us on your side, you will trounce all those with whom you strive, without fail. Despite Reason, at any time, we will always succor you and stick by you, right or wrong! With our help you can conclude all your lawsuits and enhance your status and power to the utmost.

"Now I wish to teach you three things fairly important to undertake if you wish to rise in worth. The first is to dress in fine robes and decent furs. Indeed, you will be more elegant, more respected, better esteemed, and authoritative, and thought astute by everyone, even if you were idiotic and deranged. The second point is to lie skillfully and fluently, ooze fine and polished speech, be full of mendacity—most suitable with the fine clothing! Through your skill you can make lies accepted as truth and truth as lies, and blur the distinction. The third thing is boldness in whatever you set out to do in deeds, words, and thoughts. You must exert yourself audaciously if you wish to procure grand possessions, for he who does not dare garners disgrace and procures nothing; rather, he remains poor and miserable in this world. The confident always have power because they have subtle language to hand. Everywhere, night and morning, retain these last three points and retain them well, and you will perpetually have substance, though it may all be fraudulent. For no one can have assets unless he plots to deceive. He needs to be malicious, vicious, cunning, and clever, appearing gentle and courteous toward all, yet deep down false, coarse, and audacious, and ever a laugh on his lips, however deeply a point might touch his heart. Although he displays a friendly mien, the smile must not on any account pass beyond the Adam's apple. He should laugh from the teeth and not from the heart. He must always fawn; in all acts and speech he must toady to the powerful through clever words and jollity while displaying great reverence. One can acquire a lot in that way. He must not care a jot about the poor, for they cannot be worth anything. He does well to give them a kick unbeknownst to them. Turn your back on them utterly, since you can't get a penny from them.

"At this point you have heard me tell how one elevates oneself in society. Believe in my teaching and you will be perfectly rich, with all your desires fulfilled, as much as you could ever want. But if you are on Reason's side, in every season you will be dejected, begging, in penury, and played out. In her clutches, you will never attain status in the world. But do what you wish. Give yourself time to think about it. Being free to choose, you can decide to be a poor man. If so, abandon me and stick with Reason. But if you wish to be a rich man, then consider me your lord and master as long as you shall live. Believe me, and renounce Reason!"

With these words, Fraud became silent, for he had revealed enough of his business and doctrine and had taught all his methods. At that point, he went off. I pondered the alternatives that Fraud and Reason had presented and disclosed, but I had so posed the dilemma to myself that I did not know which to believe, Reason or the eloquent Fraud. Yet probably I would have placed my faith in the latter, Fraud, if I had not had other advice, for he had so well enthralled me that I was utterly duped.

Fortunately, after this Understanding turned up to instruct me about which of the two I should join forces with. "Fool," said he, "Are you so senile that you wish to leave behind Reason's teachings to trust in a false and wicked knave, a deceiver, Fraud the con man, who is worse than a robber? You are totally foolish and cocksure and without any native intelligence! You miss the point if you think to partner with Fraud and abandon wise Reason. For no one has ever forsworn her and gone over to Fraud who did not sooner or later definitely come to misfortune. In your time you must have seen many eminent masters gulled by him and put to shame because they did not pay attention to Reason or imitate her actions. Rather, they took pains to flee her and annihilate righteousness, turning against God, Reason, and Moderation. Although I was with them, they never gave me a hearing to oppose their desire, because they were so inflamed and tempted by the untrustworthy Foolish-Belief that they felt secure. These folks exalted Fraud since through him they rose in society and amassed vile and filthy treasures. Whatever comes from Fraud leads to no good. He is not a polished logician; he has a beautiful opening and fine middle but always makes his conclusion in shame and confusion. Everything that Fraud amasses in twenty years, Fortune annihilates in a single hour of one day—no one can put a halt to it. Thus Fraud cannot prevail because Right, who directs and sets all to justice, and who does nothing inexact, cannot endure Fraud but is disposed to everything that Reason wishes. Therefore, believe and serve Reason, for truly you will be serf to a miserable servitude if you attach yourself to Fraud. Several people far wiser than you have left Reason's society, to whom harm has come—it happens every day. Wiser than you? I lie, for they do not have half a brain, although they have the name and guise of intelligence. One sees all around us that some are considered wise in this world who are fools, I dare say, just as some are thought fools who are truly wise. According to the notions of this world, the man who abounds with riches and has plenty of gold and silver is deemed smart by the people and is valued in all lands, though he be a foolish simpleton. Thus he is both wise and foolish, it seems to me: truly wise for his possessions; a simpleton for his lack of knowledge. In contrast to that model, the poor man, however sagacious and intelligent he may be, gains no love, honor, or respect. Rather, the world considers him stupid and dull and his intelligence a vice. If he speaks rationally, people take him for a madman, so he cannot win praise for anything. Thus he is wise and yet foolish: foolish because he is a poor man; wise because he has reason. Now you have seen the proof of the pure truth of this contradiction that I expound. No one will be able to support the contrary if he wishes to follow logic. Be smart, therefore, and believe me. You never made such good sense! Believe Reason and stay true, [and recall Reason's instructions]. It is bound to lead to good for you within fifteen years. You cannot falter in any way if you divest yourself of Fraud."

At that, Understanding was silent. I began to reflect profoundly about his speech, concluding that it felt true, without deception. The sage Understanding demonstrated the wisdom of trusting Reason and not Fraud, and so I agreed, for no one ever repents of it.

Reason returned at once, white, red, colorful, welcoming and greeting me with joy and cheer as one who cherishes a person who gives himself freely to her. "Friend, God keep you," said Reason. "It is the moment for you to oblige me, now that I see you so disposed. Swear right here that you will not fail and that you will serve me willingly and obey me always, no matter what Fraud or any of his entourage says to you, however captivating their fine speech may be. Have a heart steadfast in promoting my works, and do not change your inclination in thought, in deed, or in speech. I cautioned you about this once before, but as soon as I turned my back, you were immediately spun by Fraud and the force of his wind, just as one often sees the weathervane spin in whichever direction the wind blows. Therefore fortify yourself with certainty, strength, force, and constancy to keep well the covenants that I require you to swear to me. I need assurance of your loyalty and your pledge to keep my commandments wherever you go. Keep in mind that my service is the legitimate freedom in this world. He who serves me can go anywhere and speak before all people boldly, without bowing his head and tucking his tail under. He need not have fear or shame before the pope, king, duke, or count, or before any magistrate of justice, or indeed before any man alive. A soldier of mine disputes with no one, wishing to fix his thought on maintaining right and truth and sustaining it day and night. For this reason, I desire you to become my cohort and in your heart to stand by me forever. I will reside within you, nor will I leave until death, fear not, unless against my will you force me away. If you love me, good will follow you; if not, it will desert you. If your understanding is not clouded, you surely see that any reward from me is double. I shall prove the truth of this statement beyond a doubt.

"By serving me, first, you can live in security, dreading nothing except God my Father. He who fails to believe this pays for it. When you leave this life, you join my Father in His glory, and there you will live fully with no death. For you must have firm belief that at the moment of death in the world, a man starts to flourish and begins life anew as he departs from this one, leaving the ephemeral life for life eternal. Thus, if you have any cleverness, it must be apparent that the recompense I reward is a double one, since a double good ensues from it. That is to say, perfect honor in the world by works and deeds and finally Paradise forever. And *that* is the supreme good, without fail. Therefore take care not to forgo my rewards, and keep watch that you studiously observe my works and comply with them so well that they become freely yours. Shrink from Fraud and all his business, since remaining in his service will cost you the greater for the lesser. You abandon those two beautiful and celebrated gifts of mine through service to Fraud, and your body consequently will be hanged in great anguish and ignominy. With him you will thus lose, I dare say, body, soul, and reputation, the three supreme goods. In addition, he can give you nothing but the pleasure of acquiring goods without conscience. His service always incites one to covet from another, and when his servant has amassed enough possessions and treasures, thinking he lives secure, some misfortune befalls him that turns it all upside down. No one can restore it again, and no one will weep over his hardship. Rather, everyone, in fact, attacks him. This fallen soul perhaps never sees the one who calumniates him and rejoices in his pains. The malicious one does nothing but sing and laugh and may in impertinence taunt: "You had become too rich! All of it came from the devil, and back it goes!" Thus people will ridicule and have no pity. Both God and the world will vilely scorn him together. You can certainly see how bad serving Fraud is—no merit ensues, only shame, anguish, and suffering. Following him is committing folly. Spurn him and love me, who can guarantee you esteem in every situation, toward God and the world. Keep your heart clean and pure. Be filled with humility, loyalty, faith, and truth. If you display humility, take care not to do it falsely, but be truly humble in heart and deed, not just before people whom you try to convince from your demeanor that you are a gentleman. Thus their hearts go ambling, beguiled by this hypocrisy, which is full of cunning and falsehood. Concealing himself under the shadow of naïveté, this kind of man deludes those who observe him, who may not be on guard against false bearing. He has without a doubt so blinded the unsuspecting that each person would swear firmly that he is a perfect gentleman, although he abounds in falsehood. Just like that he tricks the world! But he cannot deceive God, Who knows all about him, seeing into the wickedness hidden in his heart. This fraudulent person will have no answer for it all on Judgment Day. At that time sentences will be rendered rigorously on everyone according to his sins in this world. God will be enthroned, displaying His wounds to all—the nails, the crown, and the lance. Everyone will then be weighed on the scale. There will be no king or emperor who does not quake with terror. Cobblers and counts are scrutinized the same. Those who clothe royalty are judged by the same standards as are prelates and kings, provided that they were loyal, willingly accepted their poverty and the security of sufficiency, and had faith in God. At that Judgment, no one on account of his possessions will be at peace with my Father unless he merits it by his service. All those born of Adam shall fear damnation, be they ever so righteous. But God will send to His right hand my disciples whom He will recognize well, those who strove only to do good and lived according to me. There I will be a superb shield for them, and God will bless them all. My followers will doubtless part from Fraud's minions, who will be lamenting on the left side. Things will be divided in two: my followers on the right, rejoicing together in perfect happiness, exempt from sorrow and sadness; Fraud's followers on the left hand, whom my Father will have segregated from mine, because of their folly. Those lost souls will all commence awful weeping, howling, and woe when they see themselves condemned and turned toward perdition without hope of redemption.

"Now do not look as if I am dragging you along and forcing you to abandon Fraud, but surrender yourself to me freely and completely at this moment, without need for reprieve or delay. Give me homage immediately, hands joined, and direct yourself to following my dictates, just as I have earlier explained them. Persevere without lagging behind, for doing good today yet not sticking to it tomorrow is not worth a jot."

Reason then scolded me, "What are you doing? You seem not to be listening to me!" "Lady," said I, "I do hear you, and your discourse gives me so much pleasure that I delight in the virtuousness that you teach me. Ergo, you admonish me wrongly, because you have instructed me that to attain value, one must listen and consider and then respond. In addition, you insisted that one should speak appropriately based on cogitation so as not to err. Rushing to speak before thinking about it at least three times is imprudent, you say. So, my lady, I was only enacting your instructions by allowing you to speak and making no impetuous reply."

"That's true, you have retained the material well," said Reason, "and set it in your heart. Honor will be yours if you continue faithfully in this style. Since you wish to join my companions, be careful to follow without hesitation those commandments I have described."

I responded, "With pleasure, my lady, I am entirely yours, body and soul. I have placed all of my heart with you. Take me as yours and accept my homage, hands joined, on my knees! Indeed, I promise faithfully to observe my covenant wherever I am, nor may I ever behave to displease you."

Reason leaned to kiss me and she faded away, not to be seen or heard from again. But I felt her deep inside me, and never did I assent to commit any wrong against anyone or any other unreasonable act, insofar as I was able. While I sensed within me Reason the wise who is so dear to my heart, a most simple man and his wife drew near. Indeed, they appeared to be guileless and innocent of evil and acted in a most refined manner. Good-Heart and Good-Desire were their names —such names are not necessary to conceal. Good-Desire led a beautiful, gentle, and kind child, always gracious, named Intent-to-Do-Well. The gentleman Good-Heart was his father and Good-Desire his mother. All three came near to me, looking kindly upon me. Good-Heart most graciously addressed me, greeting me with mild words, like an ordinary man: "Friend," said he, "since you have Reason with you, you will always have me too. Never shall I abandon you, nor will my wife and son here before you. If you see fit, we three will conduct you to the road about which Reason told you, and by following it you may obtain great reward. Should you decide to rely on and heed us, we are all ready to vouch for what Reason expounded to you, because without the three of us you can do nothing that could please Reason, given that you will not have directions to the path you must take to the noble castle of Riches, seemingly so full of magnificence. Whoever wishes to go there without us would only wander further away until he landed on the road of Poverty, so muddy and filthy." Then I said, "Sire, I am in accord with all of you and indeed request that you please escort me to the byway that I so yearn for. It is the road of Diligence, and I have no idea where it begins or how to enter it, because I was never there, which causes me grief and resentment." "All in good time," replied Good-Heart. "Now quickly get up and get dressed. You will have to rouse yourself early, at such a time as you are usually asleep, if you wish to come to any good. On this road you must work hard, sleep little, and stay awake. Through sleeping too much, there is a lot to lose. No one should attach himself to sleep. It is like hanging onto old rags—clearly not anything you want to value if you fear shame. For this reason, a wise man compels himself to suffer from lack of sleep, an abstinence that assists one in reaching such excellence that one gains plenty of possessions."

Then Good-Desire spoke: "Fair son," said she, "listen to me! Employ your time in a vastly different fashion from how you have lived until now, and persevere so well in deeds that you can acquire goods without taking anything from another. Believe me and my lord, and honor will come to you." "So true, friend," added Intent-to-Do-Well. "Trust my mother who speaks here, and my father Good-Heart also. Place confidence in their counsel and cherish them; thus will you act sensibly. Get up straightaway and we will lead you directly toward the wonderful road of Diligence. Don't dispute this, for only by taking this road can you achieve great honor, as Reason has taught you."

To this speech I responded at once, "Sire, gladly, without delay! Never will I question, but rather strive to succeed." I dressed cheerfully and put on my shoes, saying, "Done! Let's go; I am ready!" Then Good-Desire lit a candle, for her heart was cheered that I had entered into Diligence, that fair road so full of excellence. She spoke softly, to her son Intent-to-Do-Well: "Here, sweet child, carry this candle before us, to light our way more clearly as long as we remain in Diligence." He sprang into action. "Lady, I am all set!" replied Intent-to-Do-Well then, for he never disobeyed. He went on ahead and we followed behind him in step.

Together we four journeyed until we came to Diligence, where I had never before traveled because I was unacquainted with the route. We had not traveled long on this expansive and paved road when we spied a castle such that no one has ever found—unless of course it was the very same one. As we came to the door and considered entering, the porter who guarded the entrance came to greet us, scrutinizing us harshly, and acted most surly as if he were too busy to be bothered with us. Rudely, he shouldered me aside to query: "What do you want, fair lord? Do you wish to waltz in without permission any time you feel like it? No one enters into this castle unless approved by me and my wife, whom you see here." "Oh, sire, for God's sake!" interjected Intent-to-Do-Well. "He does not wish to displease you two! Of course, he would not invade the castle against your will!" Good-Heart joined in: "Sire," said he, "this man is most worthy to proceed to enter without delay, and I can vouch for him." "Assuredly," said Good-Desire, "have no doubt about it, sire, for I am well aware of his aspirations, good intentions, and longing to accomplish all your pleasure and that of Lady Riches; otherwise, he would be worthless. Tell him what you wish of him, and he will oblige you without faltering."

Then the porter said mildly: "Because you have led him thus far with his consent, he must indeed have been very well guided." He then took me by the right hand and began to lecture me, saying: "My dear, dear friend, because you have entered here, you will from henceforth be obliged to obey me and my wife, if you care to visit Riches, who dwells nearby in a magnificent noble residence. No one can be received by her without first answering to those of us here and following our orders, persevering without hesitation. First, he must confer with me, the porter of this castle, called the Castle of Labor, where one works night and day. I am called Attention-to-Duty, who leads people by the wrist, between me and my wife Mindfulness, to the lord and lady in possession of this demesne,[7] named Toil and Pain. Fair friend, if you wish, we will take you straight to them. But there you will have to endure trials and you may be unable to last, since they will expel you instantly, without warning, if you do not accomplish your chores there. I do not wish to delude you. Stay, or turn back. It is often said that bakers make horn-bread as they put it into the oven."[8] "Sire," said I, "do not suggest my quitting, since I have no intention to, despite any hardship that I may endure here. My behavior will never alter on account of cold, heat, or sweat, as Good-Heart, Good-Desire, and Intent-to-Do-Well who led me here have already guaranteed you. Should you ever see me falter, then do not trust me."

Attention-to-Duty and Mindfulness led me swiftly to the Castle of Labor, where more than a hundred thousand workers toiled throughout the city, each one exerting himself at his designated task. No one was idle. This castle was so noisy with pounding and hammering that one would be hard pressed to hear God's thunder. Even a man who had not slept for three days would remain wide awake in that place! Seeing and hearing the workers gladdened my heart. I was impatient to involve myself there and to do as they did. Attention-to-Duty and Mindfulness observed me keenly and inquired of me if I wished to dwell in Labor and toil there. "Yes," said I, "for mercy's sake! I am most happy to abide here. Indeed, I will talk to the castellan and his wife later, toward evening." Attention-to-Duty and Mindfulness said, "You speak well. It is time to start, in God's name." I thus hastened to take my place in the party of laborers. I set my candle in its candlestick on the table in front of me, the better to see my work, and I prepared myself, eager to commence. I saw the chatelaine Pain briskly inspecting the multitude of workers. Her skirts were tucked up in her belt, and she went about rapidly, moving with so much industry that one worried that she might sweat blood! She dressed without a surcoat; rather she wore her shabby tunic and sometimes only her shift, when it was freshly washed.

In passing, Pain noticed me, and because she did not recognize me, she asked Attention-to-Duty the porter: "Who is that worker sitting all alone? I have not yet made his acquaintance! He arrived just today, and I want to inquire of him if he will agree to rely on me and strive as I desire." "Lady," said Attention-to-Duty, "please know that he longs to see you. Good-Heart, Good-Desire, and Intent-to-Do-Well attest to his fine character and industriousness." Then Mindfulness spoke up loudly and said: "Truly, indeed, therefore we love him sincerely. Between myself and my husband Attention-to-Duty, we will accompany him near

---

7. Feudal term for the ultimate holder of the land who can do with it as he pleases.

8. A form of "Well begun is half done." Here the baker shapes his bread as he is about to bake it.

and far; we are ready to pledge this to you and to commit ourselves to it entirely." Then the chatelaine Pain responded, "Since it is so, I shall test whether he can satisfy my standards as well as you insist he can. Now let him come forward, and if his work is up to the mark, for love of me he will acquire great possessions that one cannot have otherwise." Pain then approached me. "Friend, do not fret about this," she cautioned, "but perform your assignment gladly and skillfully, and concentrate on what is at hand without daydreaming. And no cheating! Rather, toil so that you sweat profusely by virtue of your exertion. No one should dare relax himself or take it easy here, or he would immediately be tossed out." I humbly responded, "Lady, I really desire to fulfill your dictates. As Attention-to-Duty and Mindfulness are my witnesses, never will you be able to criticize me for indolence or disloyalty to you." "Friend," said Pain, "well said. Ensure that the deeds are in accord with the words, or none of that is worth a clove of garlic! This evening, when my husband Toil arrives, he should notice that you have accomplished your duty fittingly. I inspect our people in the morning, and he inspects them in the evening. Work now in such a way as not to anger him, since he disagrees, quarrels, and complains about even minor things."

With that the chatelaine, full of anguish, became silent. I dove into my work, applying all my effort—mind and body. I labored like that without respite until bright daylight shone through the window, and then I blew out my candle. I continued to apply myself to my task, without seeking either quitting time or a break, until the breakfast hour—breakfast and dinner being one and the same according to the habit of laborers. For the first time I noticed the manners and the countenance of the laborers there, who lived in abstinence. All of them, large or small, took great delight in dry bread, garlic, and salt. They ate no mutton, beef, goose, or fowl.[9] After eating, they took the basin full of water with both hands and gulped it down, as much as they could. As I watched this, I craved to do likewise, although it was not my custom. But I took example from the workers who were eating, and indeed hunger overtook me. So I got some bread, some salt, and garlic. I even took some horse's wine[10] and ate with a greater savor and keener hunger than I had ever felt. This arrangement suited me splendidly. Whoever saw me bite into my bread would have his own appetite whetted by my enthusiasm. While working, I went on eating my bread and gulping down water with deep draughts —I did not care a twig about wine. After eating and drinking, I felt just as well as if I had been at a feast where I dined on delicacies in abundance: mutton, beef,

---

9. The medieval doctrine of social inequality of diets held that laborers needed to eat coarse heavy food that was hard to digest, in order to keep up their strength for manual labor. Leisured classes were provided with more delicate fare. See Redon, Sabban, and Serventi, *Medieval Kitchen*, 9.

10. I.e., water.

chicken, peacocks, pasties, tarts and flans, dainty rolls, and rare wines of Burgundy, Anjou, Beaune, Rochelle, and Saint-Pourçain, which one drinks for health. This all compelled me back to the job. I did not care to delay it, for Good-Heart, Good-Desire and Intent-to-Do-Well were at my side examining my deportment. Attention-to-Duty and Mindfulness were also there, encouraging me to exert myself at breakneck speed, so that I would receive good wages in exchange. Thus I toiled without dawdling until darkest night. Then Attention-to-Duty and Mindfulness went to prepare the candle so as to keep awake until the curfew, for in winter one customarily does not eat supper until the curfew rings.

I abandoned myself to my tasks, from top to bottom. All in all, I never acted ineptly, and I worked so strenuously that when I heard the curfew, I rejoiced, because of weariness and weakness from the exertion, and certainly I felt that appetite called hunger. At this point, in came the castellan Toil, who said, "Fair friend, truly you must love the one who brought you here, for I am convinced that you have executed your duty marvelously. Indeed it is clear that today you have set your nose to the grindstone with enthusiasm. Therefore, I shall arrange for you to join Repose, who offers comfort and the pleasure of drink, food, sleep, and rest to those who travail here doggedly and consoles them for the tribulation they endure from my wife when they choose to serve her. Because you have dedicated yourself to her and today suffer great fatigue, as a reward I give you permission to retreat to Repose, the gentleman who will ease your body and relax your flesh and blood that you have so greatly exerted with the chores of the day."

"Lord," said I, "I agree, since it comes from your order. Off I go to Repose!" Straightaway, I trod down the path to the gate, where I entreated Attention-to-Duty the porter and Mindfulness that out of love they let me out without delay. The porter responded, "Fair friend, willingly, for you are worn out and sleepy." Attention-to-Duty and Mindfulness then ushered me out, since it was time, but they both gravely warned me to arise at Matins, to complete the task that I had begun so that I might more quickly attain my goal of traveling to the castle of Riches, which one never reaches through laziness. One cannot even get there with diligence if there is no perseverance. Reason had said to me, I remember well, that determination is necessary in doing right and results in a worker's being rewarded for his good deed.

"Friend," said Attention-to-Duty, "Go to Repose, although you will not find anyone more deceitful! Repose has led many people to the hideous road of Sloth that turns its backside toward Riches. Repose has deceived all of those who took his side against Reason, and indeed he makes ready to deceive every day those who choose to accept what he has to offer. He will surrender all his goods to those who have a mind to take them. But, truly, in the end they all lament it, who contrary to

Reason take his things inappropriately, without urgent necessity. Indeed, in justice and truth, no one can live without Repose, whatever estate, great or lowly. But those who lean too much on Repose become in the end poor like Job. Do not trust him! Rather, remember what I instruct you here, and recollect it by this token."

As that token, Attention-to-Duty tugged my ear. Mindfulness, for her part, joined in to educate me in what Repose offers when he decides to be generous. "Friend," said Mindfulness, "do not rely on Repose except as a transient thing when you have urgent need of him. Even though, as Attention-to-Duty has explained, no one can live without Repose unless he is either out of his mind or drunk, nonetheless, he who trusts Repose excessively squanders all the good intentions that he had prior to working and cannot recover them as he desires, which, of course, ends in regret. Protect yourself well, therefore, so that he does not grab hold of you other than in measure, and remember me by this token." Then she also tugged my ear as Attention-to-Duty had done before as a reminder to me to act for my advantage.

Finally, I took leave of the porter and his wife and traveled from that place as fast as I could directly to Repose, who awaited me at my house, for it was truly the right moment. When I entered, I found my wife, heedless of any disgrace, busily and cheerfully preparing my meal. I washed my hands, and we two sat down to our tranquil supper of bread and cheese and what God gave us. When we had supped without squabbling and the tablecloth had been removed, my wife drew near and I recounted to her my adventure from beginning to end. "Lady," said I, "You cannot imagine what a difficult night I had while you slept! You did not notice during the night those wicked people hurting me and making such a ruckus—Want with Necessity, Penury, likewise Scarcity, the old hag Disquiet and Worry, Distress and Despair! They gave me so much misfortune, tugging, pushing, and tormenting me, that they nearly destroyed me! Luckily Reason, the good and wise, gave me directions to protect myself from adversity and live in prosperity. Understanding, like a good friend, also set me on the right way, making me withdraw from Fraud, who with his clerk Trickery and his varlet Swindle strove to attract me so that I would take the side of wickedness and cause myself shame and disgrace. Yet Understanding and Reason gave me such fine instruction that I am now the sworn vassal of Reason, that benevolent and prudent force who will always dwell within me. She has promised never to abandon me, and I have pledged my homage to her. Good-Heart and Good-Desire and their son Intent-to-Do-Well [have been splendid aids]. When I met them, I did as they ordered me and went where they led me. We traveled to the Castle of Labor, where we found Attention-to-Duty and Mindfulness, the gatekeepers of the castle. They received me gladly and led me directly to Pain, the chatelaine of Labor. She too welcomed me forthwith and accompanied me throughout the day. After nightfall, Toil found me, not to dispute with me, but to commend me for fulfilling my tasks and to recommend for me some comfort and sustenance for my body. But Attention-to-Duty and Mindfulness, who are against prolonged ease, urged me mightily to arise as early as Matins and buckle down to complete my task quickly. Honestly, that was my vision, and it was not a dream!"

My wife responded thus: "What are you talking about? Are you out of your mind? You are not making any sense rambling on to me about your night—it is a fantasy invented out of some kind of lunacy!"

I remained silent during these taunts, uttering not a word, for becoming vexed with her would gain me nothing. Plus, I recently learned from a wise man that no one should value anything that a woman says, whether good or bad, quarrel or slander. A woman always wants to be praised and acknowledged for her words. She does not want to be reproved; rather, she wants to be commended and esteemed as highly for the bad as for the good. This habit I know well, and so I ignored the derision. Yes, one must hold one's tongue before a woman and do what she wants.

I thus advise all those who have wives: however lunatic it may seem to let them have their way, it is even greater madness, in my opinion, to displease them. For a woman will never be satisfied if her husband defies her until, sooner or later, she has gotten the better of him twice over. Otherwise she betrays her woman's nature. Thus if he must choose the lesser of two evils, he does right to draw himself near one danger in order to withdraw from a greater danger.

Readying myself for sleep, I placed the tinderbox beside me under the stool, so I might light my candle without getting up. I recalled Attention-to-Duty and Mindfulness, who care so little for laziness, because I was quite inspired to follow their lead and will do so henceforth. And God, by his grace, sets me aright to live so well in Diligence and Perseverance, to the satisfaction of Toil and Pain, that I can envision myself in the demesne of the grand lady Riches, to the salvation of my body and soul. Yet should I, God's least creature, not meet the noble Riches and arrive at her castle, I pray with a pious heart to the Virgin who bore the blessed Son of God, her comfort to sinners, that I can reach Sufficiency. It is my firm conviction that he who directs himself toward Sufficiency within himself has true riches, nor will I ever believe the contrary.

Here I wish to draw to a close my book called *The Way and Direction of Poverty and Riches*.

✳ ✳ ✳

6. My dear, by what has been said, you can see what diligence and perseverance are. And thus, my dear, the substance of the first article has been demonstrated.

¶ 2.2 *Horticulture*

The second article of the second part discusses gardening:

1. *Primo,* take note that whatever you sow, plant, or graft, do so in damp weather, either in the evening or the early morning, before the heat of the sun, and when the moon is waning. Water the base of the plant and the soil, but not the leaves. *Item,* in the heat of the sun you should not water or cut cabbage, parsley, or other such green plants that give off shoots. Do these tasks in the evening or in the morning. For the heat of the sun will scorch and burn the cut, such that the plant will never regrow from that place. *Nota,* rainy weather is good for planting but not sowing, because the seeds stick to the rake.

2. From All Saints' Day[1] bog beans[2] can be grown, but to insure they don't freeze, plant them around Christmas and in January and February and at the beginning of March. Planting them at different times means that if some are lost to frost, others are not. When they come up, as soon as they sprout, you should till them and break the first shoot; and when they have six leaves, cover them with soil. Of them all, the first to come are the most precious and must be eaten the day they are shelled; otherwise they become black and bitter.

3. *Nota* that if you want to protect violets and marjoram against the winter cold, you must not move them suddenly from cold to heat, or from damp to cold, since keeping them a long time through the winter in a damp cellar and suddenly putting them in a dry place will cause them to perish; *et sic de contrariis similibus.*[3]

4. In winter you need to prune the dead branches from sage plants.

5. In January, again in February, and through June, plant sage, lavender, *coq,*[4] mint, and clary sage.[5] Poppies must be spaced widely when sown. Sorrel needs to be sown during a waning moon and through March or later.

6. *Nota* that the winter weather of December and January kills green vegetables,[6] that is, the part of the plant that is above ground. But in February—or as

---

1. November 1.

2. Fava beans.

3. Latin: "and vice versa."

4. Other names for this herb are costmary, alecost, mint geranium, and bible-leaf.

5. Clary or clary sage was used as a vegetable and to flavor beer (before hops were used) and wine.

6. Any green vegetable may be designated in Middle French as *la porée*; this loose term can stand generally for "greens," leeks and other garden produce, or for pureed or mashed vegetables.

soon as the frost is over—the roots send off new and tender shoots, and two weeks later you can have spinach.

7. February: Savory and marjoram—they taste much the same—are sown during a waning moon and take only eight days to sprout. *Item,* savory lasts only until St. John's Day.[7]

8. *Item,* trees and vines must be planted and white cabbage heads sown during a waning moon. *Nota* that runners take root well in the same year they are planted, if they are planted with some roots.[8]

9. Spinach comes in February and has a long scalloped leaf like an oak leaf and grows in tufts like greens. It must be blanched and then cooked well afterward. Chard appears later on.

10. *Nota* that March is a fine time to plant raspberry bushes; grafting should be done during a waning moon; house leeks are planted from March until St. John's Day.

11. Violets and clove pinks[9] are sown in March or planted on St. Remy's Day.[10] *Item,* in either case, when the frosts threaten, you need to replant them in pots when the moon is waning so that you can move them into the cellar to protect them. During the day you can place them in the open air or in the sun, and water them early enough so that the water is absorbed and the soil dry before you take them in, for you should never put them away damp in the evening.

12. Plant broad beans and break the first shoot by raking them, as said above.

13. *Nota* that parsley sown on the Eve of the Feast of the Annunciation[11] sprouts in nine days.

14. Plant fennel and marjoram in March or April during a waning moon. *Nota* that marjoram requires richer soil than violets, and if it has too much shade it turns yellow. *Item,* when it has taken hold, uproot it in clumps and replant in pots with plenty of room. *Item,* if cut branches are placed in soil and watered, they take root and grow. *Item,* cow and sheep dung fertilize the land better than horse dung.

15. Sweet and Parma violets[12] do not require either cover or shelter. And *nota*

---

7. June 24.

8. This probably refers to offshoots of plants (suckers) that may be fastened down into the earth alongside the mother plant; they then form roots and later may be cut free, dug up, and planted elsewhere. Middle French has *marquetz,* "layers." Layer is the botanical term for a stem covered with soil for rooting; "layering" is propagating plants in this manner.

9. Dianthus.

10. October 1.

11. March 24.

12. Middle French: "Violecte de Karesme ne violecte d'Armenie" (Lenten violets and Armenian violets). Sweet violets flower in March. Pichon identifies Armenian violets as Parma violets.

that Parma violets do not flower until the 2nd year, but gardeners sell them after growing them for a year, and when replanted elsewhere, they flower.

16. Sorrel and basil are sown in January and February and as late as March during a waning moon. If you want to transplant sorrel that is more than a year old, you need to transplant it retaining all the soil from around its roots. *Item,* there is an art to gathering it, for you should always pick the big leaves and let the little leaves underneath them grow. If by accident all leaves have been picked off, cut the stem down to the ground to encourage new growth.

17. Sow parsley, weed it, and remove the pebbles. Parsley sown in August is the best, for it does not go to seed and retains its vigor all year long.

18. Lettuces need to be sown. *Nota* that they do not linger long in the ground before sprouting and sprout up very thickly. To avoid overcrowding, thin them here and there, to give space to the others to grow larger. And *nota* that French lettuce[13] has black seeds, while the seeds of Avignon lettuce are whiter. Introduced here by monseigneur de La Rivière, Avignon lettuce is tastier and more tender than that of France. The seeds are gathered from one seed head at a time, when each head is about to disperse its seeds. *Nota* that lettuces do not proliferate themselves. When you want to eat it, pull it up by the root.

19. Squash: The pips, which are the seed, must be soaked for two days before being sown. Do not water them until they have germinated, and then only moisten the earth around the plant, without wetting the leaves. In April water them carefully and transplant them from a hand's breadth to a half a foot deep, with a half a foot between each plant. Keep the plant's base continuously moist by hanging a pierced pot from a pole, a straw and some water, etc., or a strip of new cloth from the pot.[14]

20. Sow chard in March, and when they are ripe, cut them down close to the root, for they always send out new shoots and will grow and remain green.

21. Borage and orache as above.

22. White cabbage and headed cabbage are the same thing; and they are sown during the waning moon of March. When they have 5 leaves, pull them up gently and plant them a half a foot from each other, placing them in the soil up to the eye with their roots watered. These cabbages are ready to be eaten in June and July.

Parma violets are fragrant but not winter hardy, as seen in ¶ 3, yet here it seems they do not require shelter, although the narrator may mean not in March and April. See the online garden plant encyclopedia (British examples) *http://www.plantpress.com/plant-encyclopedia/plantdb search.php?name=violet*

13. Lettuce from the region around Paris.

14. The straw or strips of cloth slowly draw the water out of the pot onto the plants below.

23. Cabbage heads are sown in March and transplanted in May.

24. Roman cabbages are of the same family as round cabbages and have the same sort of seed. Both seeds grow on a central stalk; the seeds on top grow into round cabbages and the seeds from the bottom grow into Roman cabbages.

25. The second growth of cabbage is called Lenten sprouts, and they last until March. The March sprouts have a stronger flavor; therefore they need to be boiled longer. This is the time to pull the stalks up from the ground.

26. *Nota* that cabbages should be planted in July when it is raining.

27. *Nota* that if ants infest the garden, throw oak sawdust on the anthills, and the ants will die or leave with the first rainfall because sawdust retains moisture.

28. April: *Nota* that throughout the months of April and May you sow the green vegetables that are eaten in June and July.

29. Summer vegetables must be topped and their roots left in the ground. After winter the roots put out shoots. Then you should cover them with earth, cultivate the soil around them, and there sow the plants to come and gather whatever growth is put out by the old.

30. *Nota* that you need to sow green vegetables from April to St. Mary Magdalene's Day,[15] and Lenten greens, which are called chard, in July through St. Mary Magdalene's Day, but no later. *Item,* spinach. *Item,* as for the chard, when they sprout above the ground, they must be transplanted in rows.

31. *Item,* April and May is the time to transplant white cabbages and round cabbages that were sown in February and March. In May you find early beans, turnips, and radishes.

32. *Nota* that in June, on St. John's Eve and again on the eve of mid-August, you must sow parsley.

33. August and mid-August: Sow hyssop. Easter cabbages are sown during a waning moon, parsley also, so that it doesn't grow too high.

34. *Nota* that greens in the ground like parsley put forth new leaf growth five or six times, and you can cut them down to the lower stem up to mid-September, but from then on do not cut them, for the stump would rot. Rather, strip off the outer leaves with your hands but leave the middle ones. At this season you need to cut down vegetables that have gone to seed, because the seeds cannot ripen in cold weather. But if the seeds are cut off and thrown away, the stump sends out new greens. *Item,* remember, at this time do not cut the parsley, but pluck its leaves off.

35. After the Feast of the Nativity of Our Lady[16] plant peonies, serpentine, lily bulbs, rosebushes, and currant bushes.

---

15. July 22.

16. September 8.

36. October: Plant peas and broad beans a finger deep in the soil and four inches apart. Use the largest possible beans, for when they are new they look larger than the little ones. You must only plant a few, and after each waning of the moon plant a few more so that if some freeze, others will survive. If you want to plant pierced peas, sow them in fine weather and not in rain, for if the rainwater enters the crack in the pea, it splits in half and does not germinate.

37. Cabbages can be transplanted until All Saints' Day. When caterpillars have chewed them so much that no leaves are left, only the veins, if they are then transplanted they will put out new shoots. Remove the lower leaves and replant them up to the highest eye. The stalks that have been stripped of their entire leaves are not suitable for transplanting but if left in place, they will sprout again. *Nota* that if you replant in summer in dry weather, water them, but not in damp weather.

38. *Nota* that if caterpillars eat your cabbages, spread ashes over the cabbages when it rains, and the caterpillars will die. *Item*, if you look under the leaves of the cabbages and find a large pile of white grubs, know that they will become caterpillars, and therefore you must cut off the leaves where these grubs lie and throw them far away.

39. Leeks are sown in this season and then transplanted in October and November.

40. If you want to have seedless grapes, at the waxing of the moon when the vines are being planted, that is, in February, take a vine with its root, and split the vine stock right through the middle all the way to the root, and remove the pith from each side. Then trim the vine stock, wrap it the whole length with black thread, then replant it, fertilizing it with good manure and filling the hole with earth up to the joint of the stock.

41. If you wish to graft a cherry or a plum tree on a vine stock, prune the vine, then in March cut it four fingers from the end, remove the pith from each side, and there make a hole of a size to fit the kernel of a cherry stone. Put the kernel in the opening, enclose it there, and bind up the vine stock with thread as described above.[17]

42. If you want to graft a vine stock on a cherry tree, prune the vine stock, which has been planted and has been rooting a long time next to the cherry tree. In March, around the Feast of the Annunciation,[18] pierce the cherry tree with an auger the size of the stock and push the stock through the hole so that it sticks out at least one foot. Then plug up the hole on both sides of the cherry tree with clay and moss, and wrap it with rags so that no rain can reach the opening. *Item*, the bark must be stripped off the vine stock, peeled all the way down to the green, so

---

17. See ¶ 40.

18. Our Lady's Day, March 25.

that this layer touches the inside of the cherry tree. For if it is done this way and the bark is peeled and removed, the pith of the stock will join the pith of the cherry, and they will knit together, which would be prevented by the bark of the stock if it remained. Having done this, leave them together for two years, and afterward cut the stock behind and below the union with the cherry.

43. *Item,* to graft 10 or 12 trees on the trunk or stump of an oak tree: In the month of March, around the Annunciation, prepare as many grafts from as diverse fruits as you wish to graft; have the oak or other tree on which you wish to make the grafts sawed down. Sharpen your grafts into a point on one side only, at an angle like this ◣, in such a way that the bark of the graft is intact on one side, without a scratch or cut. Then stick your grafts into the bark of the oak, with the flesh or pith of the graft toward the wood or pith of the oak. Then plug it up and cover it with clay, moss, and rags, so that neither rain, snow, nor frost can touch it.

44. If you want to keep roses in winter, take little unopened buds from the rose bush, leaving the stems long. Place them inside a small wooden cask like a compote cask, without water. Fit the lid on well, closing the cask tightly so that nothing can go in or out. At the two ends of the cask tie two large heavy stones and place the cask in a running stream.

45. Rosemary: Gardeners say that rosemary seeds do not ever grow in French soil, but if you pluck little branches from a rosemary plant, strip them from the top downward, take them by the ends, and plant them; they will grow. If you want to send them far away, you must wrap the branches in waxed cloth, sew them up, and then smear the outside with honey; then powder with wheat flour, and you may send them wherever you wish.

46. I have heard it said to monseigneur de Berry that the cherries are much larger in Auvergne than in France, because they graft their cherry trees.

¶ 2.3 *Choosing and Caring for Servants and Horses*

This third article of the second part treats choosing varlets, helpers, and chambermaids, etc.

1. Concerning which, my dear, in case you wish to become manageress of the household or instruct a friend in this matter, you should know that there are three kinds of servants: some are hired as help for a specific amount of time to perform a distinct job—such as porters equipped with padding who carry things on their backs, carters with wheelbarrows, packers of wares, and the like. Additionally, laborers may be hired on for a day or two, a week, or a season for a job that is urgent, difficult, or for strenuous fieldwork—such as reapers, mowers, threshers, grape harvesters, carriers of large baskets, fullers, coopers, and the like. The second type of workers are hired for a fixed period because of their specific skills (such as tailors, furriers, bakers, butchers, shoemakers, and those who do piecework). Still others are engaged as domestic servants to serve by the year and live in the home. Of all these, there is not one who does not willingly seek work and a master.

2. Regarding the first type of day laborers mentioned above: they are needed to unload and carry burdens, and to perform heavy and tough tasks. As a rule, these workers are troublesome, crude, and full of insolence, arrogant and impertinent—except about taking payment—always ready to insult and reproach if you fail to compensate them to their liking when the work is finished. I beg you, my dear, when you have to deal with these people, tell Master Jehan the steward, or another of your household men, to seek out and choose—or have chosen and engaged—only the peaceable ones. Always bargain with them before they even begin the work, so there will be no dispute afterward. Although, most of the time they do not want to bargain but rather wish to delve into the task without negotiating. They say, so agreeably: "Sire, it is nothing; it is pointless. You will pay me well, and I will be satisfied with whatever you decide." Yet, if Master Jehan hires them in this way, when the work is done they will gripe: "Sire, there was more to do than I thought. There was this and that to do, here and there." They decline the payment proffered and shout odious and vulgar words. So instruct Master Jehan not to hire or allow others to hire such men without first making a deal with them. For those who want to earn money are tractable before they begin working. Since they need the wages, they fear that someone else will grab the job before them and they will lose the contract and the profits, and so they are more reasonable beforehand. If Master Jehan were so credulous toward them and trusted their sweet words, and allowed them to begin work without haggling, they

know very well that after they have begun the job, no one else would touch it for fear of shame. Thus you would be at their mercy and they would demand more money. If they are not paid what they want, they will shout and howl nasty and disrespectful reproaches. Such churls are not ashamed of anything, and the worst of it is, they will give you a bad reputation. So it is better to wrangle with them openly and sharply beforehand to avoid any dispute. And most particularly I beg you that if the situation or task calls for it, make inquiries about the behavior of those you wish to hire, and do not have anything to do with impertinent people who are arrogant, haughty, disdainful, or offensive—despite whatever benefit or advantage you may see in them or how cheaply they offer their services. Rather, dismiss such folks from you and your business graciously and calmly, for if they elbow themselves in, you will not escape without slander or quarrel. Therefore, have your people take on tractable and gentle servants and helpers, and even pay them extra, for it gives you peace of mind to deal with worthy people. For it is said: "He who has to deal with good people has peace." Likewise, one could say: "He who has to deal with bad-tempered people has only increased his suffering."

3. *Item,* concerning those other workers, such as wine growers, threshers, field hands, and the like, or tailors, cloth makers, shoemakers, bakers, farriers, candle makers (and *nota* that for making tallow candles it is necessary to dry the wick well by the fire), spicers, blacksmiths, cartwrights, and such, my dear, I advise and pray that you always remember to tell your people that they must employ amiable help, always reaching an agreement before the job. Reckon up and pay often, without waiting to have long credit by tally or on paper, although tally or written accounts are still better than keeping everything by memory, for the creditors always imagine the total is more and the debtors less, and from this are born disputes, hatred, and foul reproaches. Have your honest creditors paid willingly and often what you owe them, and be kind to them so they do not leave you for another. It is not always easy to find truly peaceable people.

4. *Item,* concerning chambermaids and house varlets, who are called domestics, understand, my dear, that I leave you the power and authority to have them chosen by Dame Agnes the Beguine[1] (or another woman you choose to have in our service), to hire, pay, retain, or dismiss them from service as you wish, in order that they may obey you better and fear to anger you. Nevertheless, you should consult me privately about this and act according to my advice, because you are too young and could easily be deceived by even your own people.

---

1. A beguine was a member of a female religious order who, because of the nature of the order's constitution, lived her religious life in the world, sometimes as a nurse or weaver, or in another occupation in which she served society and the Church. Dame Agnes seems to reside in the household as a chaperone, companion, and overseer of the housekeeping.

5. Know that among those chambermaids without a position seeking masters and mistresses, many offer and present themselves out of great necessity. Do not take any of these without first discovering where they dwelled before, and send someone there to inquire about their behavior: whether they talk or drink too much, how long they were employed there, what services they performed and are skilled in, whether they have a room or acquaintances in the town, from what country and people they originated, how long they lived there, and why they left. Through familiarity with their past service, ascertain what confidence or trust you can have in their future service. Keep in mind that often such women from foreign parts have been accused of some vice in their country, leading them to seek work far from their own region. For if they were without stain, they would be mistresses and not servants; and I say the same of men. If reports from former master, mistress, neighbors, or others show that she suits your needs, ask the prospective servant directly—and in her presence have Master Jehan the steward write it down in his account book the day you retain her—her name and that of her father, mother, and any other relatives, where they reside, where she was born, and her references. For they will be more fearful of doing wrong since they recollect that you have recorded these things. Should they flee from you without permission, or commit any offense, they worry you will write and make a complaint to the justice of their land or to their friends. Despite everything, recall the words of the philosopher Bertrand the Elder,[2] who said: "If you take on a chambermaid (or manservant) who answers haughtily and proudly, know that when she leaves she will do you injury if she can. If instead she is a flatterer and cajoler, do not trust her at all, for she strives to trick you in some other way. But if she blushes and remains quiet and shamefaced when you correct her, love her as your daughter."

6. Next, my dear, know that after your husband, you must be mistress of the house, giver of orders, inspector, ruler, and sovereign administrator over the servants. It is incumbent upon you to require submission and obedience to you and to teach, reprove, and punish the staff. Thus, forbid them from such excess or gluttony of life that would ruin them. Also, do not allow them to quarrel with each other and your neighbors. Forbid them to speak ill of others, unless in private to you, and only insofar as the misdeed touches upon your welfare to avoid harm to you, and not otherwise. Prohibit them from chattering falsehoods, from unlawful gaming, swearing crudely, and using vulgar, lewd, or ribald words, like some miserable people who curse with "bloody bad fevers," "bloody bad week," "bloody bad day." They seem to know well what a bloody day, a bloody week, etc., is, but in fact, they don't; they certainly should *not* know what a bloody

---

2. Unidentified; perhaps Pierre Bertrand, a cardinal and theologian from Avignon, 1280–c. 1348.

thing is! Nay, worthy women do not know about such things; they are completely disgusted at the mere sight of the blood of a lamb or pigeon slain before them. Assuredly, women should not speak of anything filthy, especially about cunt, ass, or other private parts, for it is an indecent topic for women to discuss. I once heard of a young gentlewoman who was seated in a crowd of friends, men and women. By chance she said just in fun to the others: "You are pressing me so hard that my cunt is squashed." Although she said it in jest and among friends, thinking herself to be acting merry, nevertheless, in private the other wise gentlewomen, her relatives, rebuked her for it. *Item,* such ribald women sometimes say of a woman that she is a wanton slut, and it seems that they know what "slut" or "wanton" means; but honorable women should *not* know what it means! Therefore, forbid servants from using such language, for they do not know what it means. Prohibit revenge, and teach them with great patience through the example of Melibee, as recounted above.[3] As for you yourself, my dear, conduct yourself always so that by your actions you provide our servants with an example of goodness.

7. Now we must speak about putting your people and servants to work, occupying them at the proper times, and about letting them rest at the appropriate times. Concerning this, my dear, know that according to the tasks you need accomplished and the fitness of your people for your various needs, you and Dame Agnes the Beguine (who is with you to teach you wise and mature conduct, and to serve and instruct you, and whom I particularly charge with this matter) must divide up the work and allocate the different tasks according to what needs doing and the suitability of each servant to those tasks. If you order them to do a chore right now and your servants reply, "There is enough time; it will surely be done," or "It will get done early tomorrow morning," consider it forgotten. You'll need to begin again, since the effort was for naught. Also, concerning tasks you may order everyone in general to do, realize that each servant waits for the other to do the job, so it remains undone. Be thus forewarned. Tell Dame Agnes the Beguine with her own eyes to witness them starting the work that you want completed in short order. First, she must assign the chambermaids early in the morning to sweep and keep clean the entrances to your house (namely, the hall and other places where people enter and linger to talk), and to dust and to shake out the foot rests, bench covers, and cushions. Next, every day the other rooms should be similarly cleaned and tidied for the day, as befits our social position.

8. *Item,* see to it that Dame Agnes tends your house pets carefully and diligently, particularly the lapdogs and little birds. Also, you and the Beguine must care for the other household birds, for they cannot talk, and therefore you must

---

3. See article 1.9.

speak and think for them. When you go to the town house,[4] I charge Dame Agnes the Beguine to supervise those who are responsible for looking after the other animals: for example, Robin, the shepherd, cares for the sheep, ewes, and lambs; Josson, the oxherd, the oxen and bulls; Arnold, the cowherd, and Jehanneton, the dairymaid, the cows, heifers, calves, sows, pigs, and piglets; Endeline, the farmer's wife, the geese, goslings, roosters, hens, chicks, doves, and pigeons; and the carter or farmer, our horses, mares, and the like. The Beguine, and you too, must display to your people that you oversee it all, are quite familiar with their work, and deem it important, for then they will be more diligent. If you remember, have your people watchful about feeding these animals and birds; Dame Agnes should assign the task to the most appropriate people. On this topic, note that it is your responsibility to have Dame Agnes the Beguine keep a count of your sheep, ewes, and lambs, to have them regularly inspected, and to inquire about the increase and decrease of the flock and how and by whom they are tended. She must report all this to you, and the two of you should see that it is recorded in writing.

9. If you are in a region where there are wolves' dens, I will instruct Master Jehan your steward, or your shepherds and servants, on your behalf how to kill wolves without striking a blow, by the following recipe. For a powder to kill wolves and foxes: Take the root of black hellebore (the hellebore that has a white flower)[5] and dry the root well, but not in the sun. Remove the earth from it and then make the root into a powder in a mortar. Mix one fifth part of well-ground glass and a 4th part of lily leaf into the powder. Pulverize all this so finely that it can pass through a sieve. *Item,* Combine equal amounts of honey and fresh blood with this powder and make a stiff paste. Form large round pieces the size of a hen's egg and cover these pieces with fresh blood. Put them on stones or small tiles in places where wolves and foxes are known to dwell. If he wants to use an animal carcass as bait, he can prepare it two or three days beforehand. *Item,* without making the balls, he can throw the powder on the carrion.

10. In this way you and the Beguine assign some of your people to the affairs and tasks that are appropriate for them. Tell Master Jehan the steward to send, or arrange to send, men to inspect your granaries, to turn and air your grains and other stores. Should your household servants report that rats are spoiling your grain, bacon, cheese, and other provisions, tell Master Jehan that he can kill rats in six ways: *primo,* by having a good supply of cats; 2nd, by rat traps and mousetraps; *tercio,* by the device made of small boards propped up on sticks, which

---

4. It seems here that when the wife leaves the country house for the town house, Dame Agnes must oversee the servants who tend the farm animals.

5. Hellebore is a poisonous purgative.

clever servants make; 4th, by making fried cheese pastry tarts with powdered aconite and putting these in the rats' nests where they have nothing to drink; *quinto,* if you cannot prevent them from finding something to drink, put cut-up little pieces of sponge into the bait so that, if they swallow them, as soon as they drink, they will right away swell up and die; *sexto,* take 1 ounce of aconite, two ounces of good arsenic, a quarter of a pound of pork fat, a pound of wheat flour, and 4 eggs; from this make bread, cook it in the oven, cut it in strips, and nail them down with a nail.

11. Now I return to my topic of how to assign your people to work. You and the Beguine, at the proper season, have your women air out, shake out, and in-spect your sheets, coverlets, clothing, furs, skins, and suchlike. Be aware and in-form your women that to protect your furs and garments, one should air them often in order to avoid moth damage. Since such vermin breed in the humidity of the fall and winter and the larvae hatch in the summer, air out the furs and other garments in the sun on fair, dry days. If a dark, damp cloud comes and de-scends on your garments and you fold them in that condition, this air enveloped and folded into your garments will engender worse vermin than before. For this reason, choose continuous dry weather. As soon as you see stormy conditions coming, before it reaches you, have your garments brought inside, shaken out to remove most of the dust and then cleaned and beaten using dry sticks.

12. The Beguine knows well and will tell you that if there is any oil or other grease stain, here is the remedy: Take urine and heat it until it is warm, and soak the spot in it for two days. Then without wringing it, compress the part of the cloth with the spot. If the stain is not removed yet, have Dame Agnes the Beguine put it in more urine with ox gall beaten into it, and do as before. Or you can choose this: Have fuller's earth soaked in lye and then put on the stain. Let it dry, and then rub. If the earth does not come off easily, have it moistened in lye, let it dry again, and rub until it comes off. Or, if you do not have fuller's earth, prepare ashes soaked in lye, and put these well-moistened ashes on the spot. Or have very clean chick feathers soaked in really hot water to remove any grease they have clinging to them. Soak them again in clean water, rub the spot well with them, and everything should go away. If there is a stain or fading on a garment of blue cloth, take a sponge, moisten it in clear, clean lye, press and stroke it over the garment, rubbing the stain, and the color will come back. If there are faded spots on cloth of any other color, put very clean lye—which has not been poured on any other cloth—mixed with ashes on the spot, and allow it to dry. With rubbing, the orig-inal color will be restored. To remove stains from garments of silk, satin, camlet, damask, or other material: Soak and wash the stain in verjuice and it will go away. And even if the garment is faded, the color will return, although I am not sure I believe this. Verjuice: *Nota* that at the season when fresh verjuice is made, one

must take a flask of it, without salt, and store it, for it is useful for removing spots from dresses and bringing back their color. Fresh or old, it is always reliable.

13. *Item,* if any of your furs or fur skins have gotten damp and have stiffened, remove the fur piece from the garment, and sprinkle the stiffened skin with wine; it should be sprayed by mouth just as a tailor sprays water on the section of a garment that he wants to hem. Toss flour on the dampened part and let it dry for a day, then rub the skin well and it will return to its original state.

14. Now I revert to my earlier subject to note that your steward must be aware that each week he should have your wines, verjuice, and vinegars inspected and tasted and your grains, oils, nuts, peas, beans, and other supplies checked.

15. As for wines, recognize that if they become sick, the maladies must be cured in the following manner:

i. First, if the wine is moldy, in the winter he must place the cask in the midst of a courtyard on two trestles so that the frost strikes it, and this cures it.

ii. *Item,* if the wine is too green,[6] he must take a basketful of really ripe black grapes and throw them whole into the cask through the bunghole, and it will improve.

iii. *Item,* if the wine smells musty, take 1 ounce of powdered *seurmontain*[7] and an equal amount of powdered grains of paradise,[8] and put each powder into a little bag that has been pierced with an awl. Hang both bags inside the cask on cords, then plug up the bunghole well.

iv. *Item,* if the wine is ropy,[9] take 12 eggs and hardboil them in water. Throw away the yolks, leaving the whites and the shells together, and fry them in an iron skillet. Put all this, still hot, into a small bag pierced as above, and hang it within the cask on a cord.

v. *Item,* take a large new pot and set it on an empty tripod. When it is well cooked, break it up into pieces, and throw them into the cask. The wine will be cured of thickness.

vi. *Item,* to remove the redness from white wine, take a basketful of holly leaves and toss them into the cask through the bunghole.

vii. *Item,* if the wine is bitter, take a jug of water and pour it in to separate the wine from the dregs. Take a dishful of wheat, soak it in water, and throw away the

---

6. I.e., unripe.

7. Power gives "elderwood" for this; BF/Ueltschi give "surmountain" with a note saying *siler montanum* and referring to the sixteenth-century herbal reference book *Le Grand Herbier en François* (Paris, 1500); Lewis and Short's Latin dictionary gives "hartwort" for *siler montanum*; BF explain *seurmontain* in a note as a liquid made from a base of dried figs used to cure shortness of breath.

8. A spice related to cardamom, used as a substitute for pepper.

9. I.e., thick, viscous.

water. Boil it in fresh water until it is just about to burst, and remove it from the fire. Cast out any burst grains and toss all the rest, still hot, into the wine cask. If the wine still does not become clear, take a basketful of sand, well washed in the Seine, pour it into the cask through the bunghole, and this should clear it.[10]

viii. *Item,* to make a strong wine with the grape harvest, do not fill the cask, but leave room for two septiers more of wine, and rub all around the bunghole; then it cannot spill out, and it will be stronger.

ix. *Item,* to draw from a cask without letting air in, drill a small hole near the bunghole, and cover with a small plug of oakum the size of a coin. Then take two little sticks, put them crosswise on the plug, and put another plug on top of these twigs.

x. To clear clouded wine, if it is in a cask, remove two quarts, then stir in the cask with a stick or otherwise until the dregs are well mixed with it all. Then take a quartern[11] of eggs and beat the yolks and the whites for a long time until pure and clear as water. Immediately add a quartern of beaten alum and then right away a quart of clear water; then stop it up or otherwise it will run out the bunghole.

16. After all that's been said, my dear, have Master Jehan the steward direct Richard of the kitchen to scour, wash, clean, and do all the kitchen duties. Observe how Dame Agnes the Beguine, regarding the women, and Master Jehan the steward, regarding the men, assign the servants to work everywhere: one upstairs, another downstairs, one in the fields, another in the village, one in the chambers, another in the attic or the kitchen. They will send one here and the other there, each according to his position and skill, so that each retainer earns his or her wages doing what he or she knows best and is paid to do. In so doing, they will do well; for understand that laziness and idleness are the root of all evil.

17. Nevertheless, my dear, at the appropriate times have them seated at table and have them eat amply of only one kind of dish, rather than several kinds that are fancy or dainty.[12] Order them one nourishing beverage that is not inebriating, whether wine or something else. Encourage them to eat heartily and drink well and abundantly, yet it is proper that they finish it all promptly, without sitting too long dallying over their food or lingering at or leaning on the table. As soon as they begin to tell stories or exchange words or lean on their elbows, order the Beguine to have them rise and remove their table. For common people say:

---

10. This sentence perhaps logically belongs to item x.

11. Quarter measure.

12. One can see from the menus article (2.4) that the aristocratic household meals for guests, and probably those for the master and mistress of the house on ordinary days, often consisted of many dishes of a variety of meats. The servants are fed plainer meals, of course.

"When a varlet preaches at table and a horse grazes in the ford, it is time to take them away, for they have been there long enough." Forbid them to get drunk, and let no one drunk serve or come near you—this is dangerous. After their midday meal, when it is time, have your staff put to work again. After their second period of work and on feast days, let them have another meal, and after that, namely, in the evening, let them be well fed as before. If the season requires it, see to it that they are warm and comfortable.

18. Later in the evening, your house should be closed and shut up, either by Master Jehan the steward or the Beguine. Let one of them keep the keys so that no one may enter or leave without permission. Every evening before you go to bed have Dame Agnes the Beguine or Master Jehan the steward check by candlelight your stores of wine, verjuice, and vinegar to see that none disappears. Have your overseer or farmer find out from his assistants whether your animals have enough fodder for the night. When Dame Agnes the Beguine or Master Jehan the steward assures you that all the hearth fires have been covered, give your people time and place to rest their limbs. Make sure beforehand that each one has, distant from his bed, a candle and candlestick with a metal saucer, and that each has been wisely instructed to extinguish it by mouth or hand, and never with the shirt, just before getting into bed. Remember that each servant needs to know precisely what task he must begin the next morning when he rises and starts afresh his particular work. Nevertheless, I advise you of two things: first, if you have girls or chambermaids from 15 to 20 years old, who at that age are so foolish and have seen so little of the world, make them sleep near you in a dressing room or chamber, *scilicet*[13] where there is, of course, no dormer or low window onto the street. Make sure that they retire and arise when you do. You yourself, who will be wise by this time, God willing, watch over them closely. The other thing is that should one of your servants fall sick, putting all else aside, you should consider him most kindly and charitably, and check on him often, caring for him or her attentively while furthering the recovery. In so doing you will have accomplished the work of this article.

19. Now, at this moment I want to allow you to rest or be merry and will address you no more while you amuse yourself elsewhere. I will turn to Master Jehan the steward, who oversees our property, so that if any of our horses, whether cart horses or riding horses, are in pain or if it becomes necessary to buy or trade a horse, he will be acquainted with the subject.

20. Know, Master Jehan, that a horse should have 16 characteristics.[14] That is, three qualities of a fox: short, upright ears; a good stiff coat; and a straight bushy

---

13. Latin: "that is to say."

14. Actually, he provides eighteen characteristics.

tail; 4 of a hare: that is, a narrow head, great attentiveness, nimbleness, and speed; four of an ox: that is, wide, large, and broad *herpe*,[15] a great belly; large protruding eyes; and low joints; three of an ass: good feet, a strong backbone, and gentleness; 4 of a maiden: a handsome mane, a beautiful chest, fine-looking loins, and large buttocks.

21. Master Jehan my friend, one who wants to purchase a horse must first inspect it at the stable, for there one notices whether or not it is in the hands of a trainer, if it is well or badly kept up, if it has a good coat, and how the dung looks. After this, once outside the stable, note whether it has short upright ears, a thin or thick head, sound vision, and healthy large eyes protruding from its head. Feel under the gums whether there are large spaces between the teeth and ample, wide openings, and that the nasal passages are not inflamed, no abscesses or canker, and that the gorge is not in any way damaged.

22. Then, my friend Master Jehan, you must decipher how old it is. When a horse is two, it has baby teeth that are white, slender, and even. In the 3rd year, the three front teeth[16] change and become larger and stronger than the others. In the 4th year, the two teeth on both sides of the middle three[17] are replaced and become similar to the three already described. In the fifth year, the others change. In the 6th year those incisors come in that have a hollow base, which is the *feve*[18] or bottom of the hollow. In the 7th year the edges of the hollows of the incisors become worn and the feve disappears and the teeth become flat and even. From then on, one cannot figure out the age.

23. After this, Master Jehan, you must notice if the horse has good conformation and a good, open herpe, that it has neither curb nor bony spurs; if it has calluses, that is a good sign. Peer through the two front legs to the two hind legs to see that there is no spavin[19] or curb.[20] Spavin afflicts the hock and can be ob-

---

15. For the adjective *herpé*, Cotgrave gives 'out-breasted, and well voided or lanke in the Groine,' similarly, the *Littré* dictionary cites the adjective used to describe the shape of a greyhound—harp-shaped with a projecting chest and high, tight belly. In modern French, the BF/Ueltschi translation offers "hips/haunch" in ¶ 20 and "chest" in ¶ 23.

16. I.e., incisors. An informative webpage on equine dentistry is by Hanne E. Lynne DVM, MRCVS, MDNV at http://www.hanne.com/teeth-anatomy.html. The three front teeth here are on each side of the mouth, a total of six.

17. I.e., molars or cheek teeth.

18. Checking the condition of the dark spot or "dental star"—here *feve* (bean)—in the pulp cavity and the pattern of wear on the incisors is a traditional method of determining age in horses. As the teeth wear down throughout the horse's life, the pattern seen on the surface of the incisors gradually changes, providing a fairly accurate idea of the horse's age.

19. Arthritic swelling.

20. Ligament damage.

served best through the two front legs. Curb is in the same area but more to the rear: it occurs below the hock, at the point where the tail comes down. At first it is a small bump, which then swells, becomes elongated, and grows down along the bend of the hock. When one wishes to speak politely in front of a merchant, one says, "Here is a good horse; it is long and has large hocks"—by that one means that it has curb.

24. At this point, Master Jehan my friend, go to the side and look to see whether there are sores where the saddle rests, for do not trust in a horse with a tender back. Be careful also that it is not wounded in the withers, *Item,* that it has a good belly, that it has not been jabbed by riders' spurs, that the testicles are not too big, that the body is long. For a horse is said to be flat when it is not round or well quartered. Check also the impression given by the appearance of its ears and eyes and by the movement of its head and the spiritedness of its feet, and be careful that it does not have mallenders,[21] wind galls,[22] shin splints, greasy heel,[23] or nicks from the interference of one leg with another; for from that place one can see all of this. Next, make sure that the horse has large, flat, thin legs and that its knees are not scraped and that the pasterns above the coronet do not thrust forward. Note whether it has large and swollen or cracked hooves, permanent hoof damage, droopy heel, greasy heel, or *fourme.*[24] Fourme on the coronet is a swelling throughout the foot, which in a week affects the front and rear. While it is intact, it is called fourme and it causes droopy heels. When it has split, it is called greasy heel and cannot heal. It is found on the tip of the coronet of the hoof.

25. Afterward, as it has been said,[25] you must examine the animal on all sides to see that it is not wounded beneath the saddle or at the withers, whether it has a sound belly, if it has been pricked by spurs, that it does not have overlarge testicles, that it has a long body, the overall effect of the appearance of its ears and eyes and gait, and be careful that it does not have mallenders—mallenders are in the inside of the hind hock. Watch too that it does not have wind galls, shin splints, greasy heel, or those cuts one leg inflicts on another; for from that viewpoint one can see all of this.

---

21. Scaling skin down the front side of the cannons (shins).

22. Wind puffs or wind galls are soft spongy swellings around the back, front, and/or side of the fetlock joint. The inflamed joint capsule distends with additional synovial fluid in an effort to protect against injury. They are caused by joint concussion, excessive work while the horse is young and the joints are still developing, or stress and fatigue due to intense workload on the joints. (http://www.horsemanshop.com/legwraps.html).

23. Also called mud fever or cracked heels.

24. Callous tumor on the pastern.

25. This paragraph repeats what is in ¶ 24. Even ¶ 26 repeats quite a bit, but it is clear that one needs to check for all these flaws from every side of the animal.

26. Go behind it to see that it has well separated and turned-up buttocks, a beautiful, thick hairy tail so tight to the buttocks that one cannot raise it; for it is a good sign when the horse has good, strong hindquarters and healthy testicles. Once more, from this perspective be certain that it does not have any stumbling cuts from its own hooves, does not have cracked heels or scabs, does not have quittor[26] or mange, and the hind legs are not bowed, and low down there is no spavin, wind galls, no splints in the inside or outside of the legs, or mallenders, that it does not scrape its own legs or have dry scabby skin or cracked skin, either in front or behind.

27. Next, as you watch it trot awhile in its straight usual gait, establish that it raises its feet uniformly, to the same height and without effort, and that its forelegs bend easily without stiffness, whether it tosses its head, if it breathes through the nose and flares its nostrils, and if it can maintain the pace for a long while, for all of these things are good signs. Then have it trot faster, and consider whether it trots handsomely and that its legs do not interfere with one another; then have it run and gallop, and look carefully whether or not it takes large breaths, if it breathes deeply, if it takes large breaths from the mouth, and whether it pants or is winded. This can also be seen below the tail. Try to observe it the next day at rest and inspect its manure in the stable. Then trot and gallop and check its wind once more, which you can see under the tail. Watch it in the fields and elsewhere to see if it responds well to spurs. *Nota,* Master Jehan, if at the fair in Flanders you have bargained and found out the price of a horse and you ask to see it run, *eo ipso*[27] you disregard all other defects. So if it responds well to spurs and it runs, you have bought it, whatever other flaws it has.

28. Master Jehan, if there is a horse that is mature and has no shin splints, mallenders, curb, cuts on the leg, wind galls, *et similia,* that means that it is healthy. Since it has passed its youth without a mark, it will doubtless never have one.

29. *Item,* the shorter a horse is, Master Jehan, the stronger is its backbone. *Item,* the harder it trots, the stronger it is. *Item,* Master Jehan, if it is delicate on its lower parts, it is a bad sign.

30. Master Jehan, should you wish to fatten one of our horses for sale, *primo* it must be curried, washed, and bedded down cleanly with fresh straw. *Item,* if it has not recently been bled, have it bled on the side, that is, the belly, for a bleeding on the sides aids in a good bowel. Next, fill its hayrack with first-rate hay on one side and oat fodder on the other. Then take 4 bushels of clean wheat straw, two bushels of bran, one bushel of small beans, and a bushel of oats; mix them all together and feed it this mix 4 times a day, before it drinks. *Item,* afterward it is

---

26. Quittor is a serious infection of the cartilage of the foot, causing lameness.
27. Latin: "by that very act."

to drink some river water heated in the sun or on the manure pile, or in the winter heat it on the fire. Feed it bran in a nosebag, for without the cloth nosebag the horse would cough as if it had eaten feathers. Then give it hay. If it is a horse of little value, for its feed let it have boiled barley three times before drinking and beans and bran and a little oats after drinking.

31. Ointment for horses' hooves. Take a quartern of he-goat suet, a quartern of wax, a quartern of turpentine, a quartern of resin pitch and boil it all together, and rub it on the horse's hooves. *Item,* take a cloth dampened with old ointment and wrap it on the hoof with manure.

32. To heal rape,[28] scaly skin, mange, and quittor, wash the affected area with hempseed oil beaten together with water, and if it does not heal, you must bleed the animal from the tops of the hooves.

33. *Item,* note that when a horse is bled from the neck, you must keep its head tied up high and provide it with small amounts of food, also up high, for the movement of the jaw and the neck could make the wound burst open. *Item,* you must wait to give it drink as long as possible after the bleeding, and tie its head up high because lowering its head could cause the wound to burst. *Item,* if the horse is very valuable, it must be tended through the night.

34. Mallenders need to be washed twice a day with hot urine or hot water. *Item, idem* for swollen hind legs. If that does not heal it, make a poultice with dragon's blood,[29] egg whites, or well-sifted lime and egg white, and bind it around the leg, then dry it from behind with a burning firebrand.

35. When a horse loses its vision, have vitriol ground up and squirt some into its eye with a reed.

36. When a horse has colic, get it to lie down, and then with a small horn have a quartern of any oil placed into its anus, and then have someone ride it until it sweats, and then it will get well.

37. When a horse has strangles,[30] you must say these three words to it, with three *Pater Nosters*: + *abgla* + *abgli* + *alphara* + *asy* + *pater noster,* etc.

38. Against *farcin*[31] you must bandage the wound for 9 days, and each day, fasting, while touching the wound, say three times, each time with three *Pater Nosters*: + *In nomine Patris* + *et Filii* + *et Spiritus Sancti* + *Amen.* + "I invoke you, evil one, in the name of God the omnipotent, and in the name of the Father, the Son, and the Holy Spirit, and all of the saints and angels of Our Lord Jesus Christ, and all of the might God has invested in words and voice, the power with which

---

28. Cracked skin behind the knees.
29. Dragonwort sap.
30. Swollen glands, abscesses.
31. Skin lesions from worm larvae on the horse's skin, also called "summer sores."

God healed the leper of his illness, that you not spread and that you not double in size or swell, not open up or form fistulas, not more than did the five wounds of Jesus Christ; He saved the world and in doing so He earned the five wounds of Christ." *In nomine Patris + et Filii + et Spiritus Sancti + Amen.*

39. If a horse contracts glanders,[32] immediately have its forelegs bled at the very bottom and at the stifle, and collect the blood, using it to anoint the feet. Then wipe them with damp hay, and walk him without feeding or watering him. Within 4 hours or so, place a poultice on the coronets, so that the wound will not become infected, and you must walk it without stopping for 36 hours, giving it hay by hand if it wishes to eat, and then it must not drink for an entire day. 24 hours after the bleeding, have it drink hot water with bran. For this period of time, beginning when it is bled, have it covered with three damp sheets, all at the same time. After 36 hours or more, that is, when it will take bran to eat, has a good countenance, and has made manure, bed it in clean white litter and have it rest, and then walk it. Once it walks willingly, remove the first sheet, the next day another, and the third the last. Give the horse nothing to eat or drink except thin gruel made from bran until it looks healthy. Some give them an apple drink in a horn. For everything, the person in charge of doctoring the horses can receive one and a half francs.

---

32. Serious, highly contagious bacterial infection of mucous membranes and soft tissue. Chronic glanders affects the joints and muscles, forming ulcerated and purulent lesions.

Introductory Note to Article 3.2

In his prologue, the author indicates that he had planned a third section for his book, with three chapters: the first on parlor games, the second on the sport of hawking, and the third a collection of amusing calculations and number riddles. Of those three chapters, only the hawking tract occurs in the three MSS, inserted within section 2, between articles 2.3 (servants and horses) and 2.4 (menus). Brereton-Ferrier includes the materials on hawking within section 2, as in the MSS, which seems the best choice for our project as well. The older edition, Pichon, places it at the end, as announced by the prologue, but contrary to the MSS.

The vocabulary of the sport of hawking and falconry is a specific one, and our translation has been aided by the recent work of Robin S. Oggins, *The Kings and Their Hawks.*[1] We also consulted two seventeenth-century French dictionaries, since the first French dictionaries, which promoted courtly usage, paid particular attention to the terminology of hawking, falconry, and other aristocratic pursuits.[2] Several English incunable falconry texts very much resemble the *Le Ménagier* treatise and clarified some of the taxonomy and characteristics of the birds and the sports in our text, especially Latham's *New and Second Booke of Faulconry* (1633) and Turberville's *The Booke of Falconrie or Hawking* (1611).[3] Falconry or hawking

1. Robin S. Oggins, *The Kings and Their Hawks* (New Haven: Yale University Press, 2004). Oggins, whose book contains several references to the hawking treatise in *Le Ménagier,* does not locate a direct medieval source for the treatise. See Oggins, chap. 1, "The Sources," for background on medieval hawking literature and its antecedents (1–9). BF/Ueltschi note that probably three sources may have been consulted in the compiling of the treatise: *Livre des déduis, Livres du Roi Modus et de la Royne Ratio,* and Gaston Phebus's *Livre de chasse.* See BF introduction (xlvi–l), where they find that the author gives the impression in this section that he is speaking from his own experience. The website of the Richard III Society, American Branch, has an informative entry on falconry terms by Shawn E. Carroll (*http://www.r3.org/ life/articles/falconry.html*).

2. Jean Nicot, *Thresor de la langue françoyse, tant ancienne que moderne* (1606); *Dictionnaire de L'Académie française,* 1st ed. (1694). Both dictionaries available online through the Project for American and French Research on the Treasury of the French Language (ARTFL): http://www.lib.uchicago .edu/efts/ARTFL/projects/dicos.

3. Simon Latham, *Lathams New and Second Booke of Faulconry: concerning the ordering and training vp of all such hawkes as was omitted or left vnmentioned in his printed booke of the haggard faulcon and gerfaulcon, namely, the goshawke and tassell, with the sperhawke, and lanner and lanneret, as they*

is an ancient sport, and there were many treatises on the matter available for the *Le Ménagier* author to consult as he compiled his work. It may be that the author availed himself of some manual and added his own personal experience, or used a work that no longer survives.

The birds whose nurture and training the author describes here are hawks, rather than falcons, which he mentions only at the end of the treatise. The physical differences between each species' wings and tails give them dissimilar hunting styles and make the birds suitable for the pursuit of game in different terrain. The falcon's narrow wings and tail and style of swooping down upon prey from a great height at high velocity, killing the prey almost immediately from the force of the blow and the slash of the talons, suit it for hunting in open country. Hawks (goshawks or sparrow hawks), on the other hand, with shorter, rounder wings and longer tail, were flown in more wooded countryside, since they can cruise at lower altitudes and maneuver in tighter quarters. While the falcon's feet deliver a blow with great force to kill its prey, the hawk's feet are best at holding and killing its quarry by piercing it with its enormous and sharp talons. Strictly speaking, *falconer* is the term for one who flies falcons, while an *austringer* flies hawks, and in this book the Middle French *espreveterie* is not the general noun "falconry" but refers specifically to training sparrow hawks and goshawks. We have used *austringer* here, since our narrator discusses hawks only.

Originally the purview of the nobility, but by the late Middle Ages a sport of the upper classes as well, falconry or hawking signals to others the wealth and status of its participants because of the requirements of leisure time and significant expenditures. The raising and flying of hawks would have indicated to the *Le Ménagier* audience the elevated social status, the conspicuous consumption, and the life of ease of the narrator and his wife. It is unlikely that the medieval audience of the book, or indeed the young wife, would have needed to feed a household on the game the hawks killed. Oggins points out: "One can view medieval falconry as an as-

are diuided in their generation, the hobby and marlyn in their kindes: teaching approued medicines for all such infirmities and diseases as are incident to them: published for the delight of noble minds, and instruction of yong faulconers in all things pertaining to this art (London: Thos. Harper for John Harrison, 1633); George Turberville, *The Booke of Falconrie or Hawking: for the onely delight and pleasure of* all noblemen and gentlemen: collected out of the best authors, aswell Italians as Frenchmen, and some English practices withall concerning falconrie (London: Thomas Purfoot, 1611). See also Juliana Berners's fourteenth-century text, *Boke of Saint Albans. Selections: The boke of hauking huntyng and fysshyng, with all the properties and medecynes that are necessary to be kept* (London: Robert Toye, 1566).

pect of the eternal war between the haves and the would-bes—as one of the many ways in which people have sought to maintain or to achieve social distinction."[4] Medieval women both flew and cared for sporting birds of prey, and our narrator suggests that his wife should possess this skill in order to fit into her social milieu as a chatelaine of a great house and as a mark of distinction for the family. Some Churchmen espoused the attitude that hawking was immoral because it gave rise to vanity and because it had almost slothful aspects —the pleasures of the flesh[5]—but apparently the *Le Ménagier* narrator's strict moral code does not deem his wife's pursuing this sport as anything but admirable, socially sanctioned, and useful.

Symbolically, aside from its indicating wealth and worldly sophistication, flying birds of prey was also an activity connoting youth, and therefore well in keeping with the wife's rank and age. In fact, as Oggins notes, hawking was the occupation often depicted in books of hours—books often owned and commissioned by women—for the month of May. This allusion will not be lost upon readers who see in the marriage of the aged narrator and the teenager the symbols of January and May. To be able to recall a wild predator to the glove was a talent to be admired and cultivated,

again perhaps symbolizing the older man's desire to tame his fresh and frisky young wife. There are repeated injunctions in the hawking treatise to avoid allowing the hawk to become haughty or disdainful of its master's dominance. If that occurs, the bird won't return to the master, and poor training of the hawk puts the master at risk for social ridicule. The analogy to training a wife seems clear. From another angle, the language also evokes that relationship the moral treatise suggests, especially in article 1.6, between an abusive husband and his humble wife, when it says that the austringer must endure the hawk's talons, "no matter what pain it inflicts on you, for if you vex it one single time, it will never again love you" (¶ 11).

In this treatise the book's preoccupation with dominance and obedience is extended to include training dogs and birds of prey for hunting. The dogs used in the sport of hawking to flush and recover the prey are discussed first, then the birds themselves and their raising and schooling, including the diseases they are prone to and the remedies the wife must know to care for these high-strung creatures. Expensive and apparently difficult to raise, hawks are depicted in this article as delicate in health and sensitive in spirit. The labor and attention their nurture entails, including putting them in bed with someone to keep them warm, seems extraordinary: to oversee each aspect

4. Oggins, *Kings and Their Hawks*, 117.
5. Ibid., 130.

of the hawk's comfort and health day and night, as well as to train them to hunt and reliably return to the gauntlet. The treatise itself gets muddled here and there, especially toward the end, and Brereton-Ferrier conclude that its condition shows "a deterioration in the author's mental powers, or a diminution of interest and an anxiety to have done with his task."[6] At the least, some incoherence and repetition of phrasing indicate that the author may have left it in an unrevised state. Since this was the only article of the planned third section to have been written, it may be that the whole work was abandoned unfinished and that what had been composed on hawking was inserted by someone into an early manuscript in a logical place—after the treatise on horses and before the copious material on cuisine.

6. BF, introduction (1).

❡ 3.2 *Hawking Treatise*

1. To complete what I earlier promised you, my dear, I place hereafter what I know about being an austringer and the art of hawking, so that in the hunting season you can divert yourself with this pursuit if you so choose. To begin with, you must know that, for the season, a good austringer readies 9 dogs and three horses for hawking, if he wishes to continue and perform well the duties of the occupation. Additionally, one observes that the heart of the good season for hawking lasts only about six weeks, after which it becomes possible to hunt only quails, that is, from the month of July, when groups of young partridges leave their nests and take their first flights, until August when they become strong and then one must turn to flying the hawks at quail. The pleasure is then diminished, for once the young partridges are out of season and one finds only the adult partridges who are strong, one cannot capture them except in flight, that is, by stooping, and this I will treat later when I speak of hunting with hawks. But here in the beginning, I will first deal with dogs and then horses, as well as the rearing and training of sparrow hawks taken from the nest. Furthermore, I will speak of young sparrow hawks taken when they first begin to fly from branch to branch and about those captured after their first molting.

2. First, he who wants to have delight in hawking must soon after Easter equip himself with spaniels and bring them often to the fields to seek quail and partridge, and train and tame them expeditiously and so thoroughly that by June at the latest he possesses three well-trained dogs who know birds. At that point he should put them on leashes and guard them well, for in this season those who lack skilled hunting dogs will deliberately steal them. One must fasten the dogs to the perch on which the sparrow hawk will sit and make their beds underneath or next to the perch, once the bird has been captured, so that from that first moment the sparrow hawk sees the dogs continually, and they are familiar to each other. It is important to be aware that spaniels good at hunting hare are not suitable for the sport of hawking, because those that do well hunting hare pursue and chase after it and when they reach it they bite, stop, and kill it, so if they are trained this way, they could do the same to the hawk. Thus, use those dogs that know well how to flush partridges and quail and who do not pursue the sparrow hawk while it hunts the birds—unless, that is, they are trained to go to the hawk once they see that it has homed in on and struck down the partridge or other bird and holds it beneath it. At this point they stop and do not approach the hawk and its prey. These spaniels are proper for hawking, but the others are not.

3. *Item,* those dogs that are young, headstrong, and too flighty, who wander widely, are not satisfactory, because they course too far ahead and distant from the hawk. When they find the partridge or other bird and flush it, the hawk is at a distance and unable to arrive in time, tires from chasing it, and in the end cannot reach the prey. The hawk finishes weary and blamed for the loss of the game, and yet it is not its fault—for it flew well—but the fault of the trainer who did not previously school his dogs well enough in obedience training that they will halt at his call. What is worse, if the hawk is twice misled in that way, it will no longer rush to prey, for the sparrow hawk is excited and emboldened when it has power over its prey and frightens everything that it pursues. On the contrary, it loses heart and becomes hesitant when it is eluded or if the birds injure it. For this reason it seems to me that it behooves the austringer to be wise enough to have trained his dogs to hunt by his side and to set them to the chase at just the right moment. That is why I think that older spaniels who run two or three toises ahead of the sparrow hawk are what one needs. Since you do not know in the beginning which dogs they will be, he who intends to hunt with them in the hawking season must train them early, keep them tied up, and chastise them with switches or whips, so that they fear their master. Then, when he takes them into the fields and cries out "Back! Back!" they stop and wait for him or return to him if they see him take a different path. If they are thus trained, they will not harm the bird when recalled, and they will be obedient.

4. *Item,* know that it is in the nature of young dogs that the more often you lead them to the fields, day after day and hour after hour, and the harder you work them running in the fields from dawn to night, beginning again the next day and every day, and the more you chastise them, since they are well bred and always together, the more they will fear and love you and willingly follow you and obey. But as soon as you arrive home, be diligent that you yourself or your men ahead of you feed the dogs well, then give them fresh clean water in a basin to drink. Next have them put to bed on nice straw in a warm place, in front of the fire if they are wet or muddy, and let them always be held subject to the whip. If you act this way, they will not pester people at the table or sideboard and they will not get into the beds. If you do not care for their needs well, know that when they have worked hard and are hungry, they will scrounge under the table or seize a piece of meat from the sideboard or the kitchen, and they will snap at each other and cause upsets to provide for their needs. In so doing they tire themselves and do not rest at all, and thus remain beggars and badly behaved, and this is your fault, not theirs. So if you wish to be considered a good austringer, think first of your sparrow hawk and your dogs and only after them of yourself. *Item,* some say that dogs that bark should be given the lung of rams or sheep to stop the barking. Whether it is true, I do not know.

5. *Item,* you must be equipped with a small horse, easy to mount and dismount frequently, calm to ride, and not too lively, does not squirm, or buck, or bolt, or do anything to hamper the sparrow hawk's return to the gauntlet. The horse must remain quiet and immobile when waiting for its master to mount or dismount.

6. Because I already mentioned that it is necessary to have the first sparrow hawks of the season, know that they begin to brood—that is, the first ones—on the feast of Saint George which is the 23rd of April, and they brood for six weeks. For this reason, from Saint George's Day until the beginning of June, you must keep close watch on the hawks' aeries, which can sometimes be identified by their meat storehouse. Usually they keep dead prey they have caught on a tree facing their aerie, a bow's length away. On this tall tree the hawks strip the flesh from the woodpigeons and other birds that they have taken, allowing the bones to fall to the ground, and tear and cut the flesh with their beaks, then carry it back to the aerie to their young, whose beaks are then too tender. From the evidence of the castoff small bones one can find their food storage, and from the food one can find the aerie. It is worth noting that at the end of May or the beginning of June, the first sparrow hawks of the season hatch. One must try to procure for oneself some of these first birds, for the first are the most advanced and quickest to fly. Because everyone wants to have one of these first sparrow hawks, in order to get them, good hawkers are ever traitors and scoundrels to one another. For this reason, he who wants to have such a hawk must search until he knows an aerie's location and snatch the young birds from that nest before anyone else. Know that the best and strongest sparrow hawks are those that feed on woodpigeons or other large birds, and they make their aeries in low trees because they cannot carry such large birds very high.

7. Now you must know how they are fed if they are caught so young that they are only two days old. First, it is a good idea to raise several sparrow hawks together, or a sparrow hawk eyass[1] with muskets[2] or other fledglings, so that they may nestle together and maintain each other's natural heat. This natural heat is their sovereign requirement, for if they suffer however slightly from the rain or cold, they are at risk of perishing. Therefore, enclose several of them together to keep them all warm. They should be housed in the hollow of a snug small bundle serving as a nest, made of delicate well-beaten hay, feathers, cotton, oakum or other such soft things, and placed in a chicken cage, a tub or a washtub, or in another wooden vessel long and large enough that they can make their bird droppings far from themselves. If this nest is not soft enough, a piece of fine linen cloth can be placed underneath them to protect their claws. They may be kept

---

1. Chick.

2. Male sparrow hawks, a year or older.

warm by setting their cage on two high trestles and making a coal fire around them or placing them in the sun. If it is cold at night, have them protected with a large cover and a net for the cats. Be sure that they have enough air; check frequently that they are neither too cold nor too hot. You must shelter them that way during the night.

8. They must be fed as many times a day as they digest, beginning at sunrise and on through the day, for sparrow hawks that are well nourished when young do not cry out when they are on the fist, and the others do. They must be fed still-warm meat that has been stripped off a freshly killed small bird—the meat, without any fat, must be cut up small until they have a strong enough beak to tear the heart from fowl—or hearts of lamb that you procure from the butcher or, if you cannot do better, of pigeons (although this meat is too fatty and too rich, if you can procure another meat). *Item*, pork meat from the inner leg is even better than heart of lamb. But the sparrow hawk that hunts must not be given two mouthfuls one after the other, because it is too delicate, too purgative, and too runny and slippery. That is, never feed it a second time until it has digested the first helping. Also, it must be fed so that it is never hungry, for otherwise, if it is not well nourished when young, it will never hunt well or be strong in the hawking season. If your sparrow hawk was ever hungry, a good austringer can tell by the end of the feathers where there are stripes crossways. From the number of lines he can judge how many times the bird was hungry, and you will be mocked for failing to take good care of your hawk.

9. And *nota* that by three things one distinguishes a young sparrow hawk from a musket: that is, the musket's head and beak are rounded and the young bird's more elongated; *item*, the musket has thinner and shorter legs than the fledgling; *item*, one can differentiate them by their cries. *Item*, in their earliest youth, they must be kept very clean and fed often, and kept dry with white cloth and hay placed under their feet and often changed. Wash and dry the cloth. They should be tended in a basket covered with white cloths and kept warm by a fire or in the sun. At night, the young bird should be put between two sheets in bed with someone to retain its natural warmth and the next day again placed near a fire or in the sun. And continue thus until it is time to put them in the cage.

10. *Item*, if you can, have the sides of the birdcage in which your sparrow hawk will be kept enclosed not with solid wood but with a lattice or made of wire, so that the droppings fall out; for when the droppings remain in the cage, it stinks. *Item*, as the sparrow hawk grows stronger, it will raise itself on its legs, and then when it stands up one can put it in the cage, which should be made 5 feet long by three feet wide and three feet tall. In the cage put some vat or a tub covered with a net, and it is important to clean it frequently. Set hay at the bottom of this tub and an old piece of linen cloth over the hay to keep the bird's talons healthy, as

stated above. There it will grow stronger and more stable on its feet. The more it grows, the less frequently it will require feeding—only four times a day. Later, when it is sturdier and flutters its wings trying to fly, you must place in the cage or the vat a small block three fingers high, covered to protect its nails as already said. Once it begins to perch on this block, make two perches for inside the cage, stretched across the cage half a foot high. Instinctively, it will fly from one perch to the other and pass underneath them, and this instinct will teach it to direct its wings and its flight. At that point it will need feeding just three times a day. From then on it is proper that its cage be placed on the ground once a day in a place where the dogs dwell about it, so that they see and know it, and it them, and it eats in their presence so that when it hunts and catches its prey in the field and grasps it and the dogs then arrive, the hawk will not be frightened by them, nor will they fail to recognize it.

11. From then on you will have to pay attention to when it develops two clear black marks on its feathers, for then it will be necessary to put jesses[3] on it and feed it on the fist, and then perch it and maintain it peacefully there until it has swallowed and digested its mouthful. At first, attach it so closely that when it tries to pull away from the attachment, it does not damage its tail feathers. From the moment your sparrow hawk is first placed on the fist, be careful that it not be upset by you or anyone else. Understand, my dear, that anything that happens unexpectedly, suddenly, and tempestuously—whether person, animal, rock, stool, stick, or anything else—disturbs and agitates it strongly. *Item,* my dear, if your hawk holds and clasps you tightly, be aware that it is a sign that it is hungry, and if it does not do this, it is not hungry. For when it is hungry, it squeezes, and when it swallows, it does not. Any time that it holds or grips you, do not upset yourself or it. Rather, detach it gently, without agitating yourself or it, no matter what pain it inflicts on you, for if you vex it one single time, it will never again love you.

12. *Item,* you must continue holding it frequently on your fist amidst people as much and as long as you can. Should you leave your sparrow hawk to eat, sleep, or other reason, let it be perched in the open air, protected from the dampness of the rain and the heat of the sun, where it does not spy any chicks, pigeons, or other fowl, and where it is not in danger from cats, and make sure that nothing could surprise it suddenly. And, my dear, know that if it is perched right after it has been fed, it will stay peaceful until it has digested. But after, if it strikes at the perch, that is a sign of hunger and that it wants to be on the fist. For this reason it is good that there always be someone near it, so that if it hangs itself or thrashes about, it may be immediately rescued and taken up.

---

3. Leather tethers attached to the legs.

13. Know also that when the bird has been training on the fist for a while and has all 7 of the dark markings—although I have indeed seen some that had 8—and also when the 3rd black mark of the tail feathers grows past the tip of the wings, it is then considered fully developed. You must take care to bathe it, which leads it more quickly to preen, clean, and arrange its feathers and thus to fly better. Bathing it will now be explained. *Item,* at the end of its longes[4] there must be attached a little stick so that if the sparrow hawk ruffles its feathers, with the end of the stick you can put its feathers in order without using your hand. Otherwise, you must turn your fist about so that the bird thrashes anew, since by shaking, the feathers return to their spot. And always, as soon as it is fed, keep it so calm, in so fitting and peaceful a position that it has no reason to struggle at its neck (for if it pulls at its neck when it has eaten, it would be at risk to vomit); and whoever is unable to keep it calm, he must then perch it. About this, good austringers repeat this proverb: "When attaching and detaching / Keep firm possession of the hawk."

14. At this point you can perhaps ascertain whether your sparrow hawk will be worth anything on the fist and on the perch. First, some of them perch perfectly straight and are very attentive and gaze fiercely and piercingly when they are awake. When they are asleep they hold themselves very straight on one foot and have the other up in their plumage, and thus they sleep. This proves it is a good and healthy bird. Other sparrow hawks lie down on the stomach across the perch just like a capon and rest in that way asleep and awake; and that is neither a very good nor a very bad sign, for it is in their nature. And other birds are always full and sleepy, with one foot in their feathers, and this is a sign of laziness or illness.

15. *Item,* as regards recognizing the sparrow hawk by his plumage, you should note that some have white and delicate plumage[5] . . . across small . . . soft or russet positioned on their chest in a straight line, and they are mottled or speckled on the underbelly—that is, between the thighs and the tail feathers—and have good thick feathers on the flanks of the thighs. They say of these sparrow hawks that they are good for ladies, for they are quickly called back to the gauntlet and promptly give over their prey, also coming willingly to the whistle. They love their masters and are calm and not overly bold. Other birds have coarser, harder, and rougher plumage and larger speckles, and the spines of their feathers are harder, just as the feathers of an old hen or old cock are rougher and harder than those of a young capon, or as a field laborer has rougher skin than the son of a king. They have heart-shaped marks irregularly placed here and there, not aligned or in order, and they have small heads and large gleaming eyes like a serpent, and they are very lively. These are

---

4. Tether attached to the jesses.

5. Lacunae here in manuscripts in two places. The birds have barred breasts—males barred white with reddish brown, females barred white with gray.

rough, fierce, and bold and are more difficult to recall to the gauntlet, more voracious and overbearing at feeding, and more aloof in all things. This sort of bird puts its prey between its wings and defends it with claws and beak. Even when one feeds them, they clasp and jump at the face and bite (and one must wear a glove on the right hand from which the fingers have been cut off, in order to avoid scratches). These birds deliberately carry off the prey to eat it in secret. But if they are well nourished and responsive on the gauntlet, a good austringer avails himself of them rather than those spoken of earlier, for they are more daring, wiser, and stronger. *Item,* some birds have red legs and feet, and such are from the aerie of a young musket; others, who have yellow legs and feet, are said to come from the aerie of an old musket; some have round legs and others flat, *scilicet,* half rounded, I do not know what that means. But, in short, the choice sparrow hawk is one that has great courage, a serpent's head—that is, small and dry—is mantled, with bulging and attentive eyes, large in the shoulders, hard and straight plumage marked with large, rough, clear speckles, has good *cerceaux,*[6] good knives,[7] good long feathers, good wing feathers, good . . . without, a healthy tail, a large opening at the place of the bowels, short fat legs, unbroken talons—that is, the *pessouer,*[8] the *charnier,*[9] the large and small *sangle*[10]—and the rest of his body and feet must also be unbroken, and it must be attentive and sit well on its perch. However, of whatever kind it may be, since you wish to raise it for yourself, when it is first put on the fist, put beautiful jesses on the longes that are called small longes, touret,[11] and large longes and accustom the bird little by little, and increasingly farther, to fly to you on your fist to seek its prey and to be fed.

16. Now it is time, my dear, that I speak to you about recognizing the droppings. Keep in mind, my dear, that when the bird has let fall droppings, from the droppings you can judge whether or not it is healthy. If it drops far off and the droppings are completely white, compact, and well ground, it is good; but if the droppings are blue, green, or red like soapy wash water or clear like water, or if there is a black spot in the droppings, one can see from this that the sparrow hawk is unhealthy; and then you must clean it out by giving it feathers[12] in the way that is described later when calling the hawk back to the gauntlet and

---

6. Wing tip feathers.

7. Master penna, the large feathers of the wing.

8. BF/Ueltschi in modern French gives "paissoir," glossing it "pouce" (thumb). This seems to be the talon equivalent to a hawk's thumb.

9. The rearmost talon.

10. The middle claw and farthest left or right (pinkie) claws.

11. The touret is the cleat on the perch that secures the jesses.

12. The feathers act as a kind of emetic or purge for the hawk. See what follows for the way to perform this cure, called throughout the "feather." The early English texts call it "casting."

affeting[13] it to hunt are spoken of. For until one calls it back to the gauntlet with-out the *commande*,[14] it is not really necessary to give it feathers and cleanse it out often, not more than once a week.

17. But at this point in the training of the hawk, it is more crucial than before to hold it on the fist and carry it to court and among people, to churches and other assembly places and through the street, and hold it on the fist continuously, day and night, as long as possible. Sometimes perch it in the street so that it sees people, horses, carts, dogs, and becomes familiar with all things. Keep it in the shade and where it will not see any pigeons, chicks, or other poultry, as already said. And sometimes, at home, perch it over the dogs, so that the dogs see it and it the dogs. That done, you must practice calling it back to the gauntlet in a se-cluded place, gradually from farther and farther away, so much that it returns from afar, attached to its longes. Next you must call it back to the gauntlet using the commande or the creance, and then in different places and especially in the fields and meadows, first with the creance and then without, on foot several times and in the presence of the dogs, and then it is fitting to call it back to the gaunt-let while on horseback, and from up in the trees, until it is familiar with the horse.

18. At this point you must watch very carefully, as explained above, that its droppings are clean. As said previously, black indicates that it is impure inside. If the color is too black, in the evening give it chicken flesh or a lamb's heart that has been soaked and well washed in lukewarm water and pressed. Should you have no warm water, but only cold, soak your meat in it, then press it hard and warm it by the force of pressing it between two boards. Then feed your sparrow hawk with it as described above, for washed meat makes it become thinner. And when giving this, you must not call or exercise your bird, but keep the bird on the perch without whistling or calling it to the gauntlet and feed it without saying a word. For the meat is not at all tasty to it, and therefore he who would call it while giv-ing it this, when he would call it to the gauntlet later and from then on, the hawk would think that it is for this unpleasant meat, and thus it would be slower and later to come. *Item,* moreover, when it is sufficiently fed, you must give it, in place of a feather cure, some cotton the size of a fava bean, wrapped twice in flesh, or have the feathers of a partridge's pinion plucked for it. If it swallows some of the partridge pinion or the moistened cotton, it is a good cleansing. They say that

---

13. Training and gentling.

14. The commande is a creance, i.e., a long string (c. 30+ feet) attached to the longe—the leather strap that in turn was attached to the jesses. The commande was used when training the hawk to hunt. The word "creance" is used in English for this type of long tether that allows the hawk to fly out while still under the control of the austringer, who then backs up with food for the hawk, in order that it fly to the gauntlet and eat.

small feathers are the best, and one should not give it any meat after the feather, for whatever you give it next could not pass the ring of the stomach because of the feather that would be in the way. Know that when the sparrow hawk hunts and feeds itself from the hunt, it is not necessary to give it more feathers, for it takes enough of them from the birds it eats. Feather from the pinion of the wing is a good cleanser. The evening that one has given it the feather, clean up the area underneath the perch in order to be able to find the feather the next day. That next day, when you get up, look at its droppings to see if they are cleaner than before, and if the sparrow hawk has dropped far off, it is a sign that it is strong. If it has dropped nearby, it is the opposite. If its droppings are very white, pasty, and well ground, it is a sign that it is healthy. If the droppings are green, or if there is too much black, it is a sign that it is not healthy. And also look to see if it has expelled its feather dirty or clean. If you notice two or three times that the sparrow hawk is slow to pass the feather, dose it with the cotton and one or two grains of wheat, for this will quicken the expelling. When in the morning it has expelled it, feed it with good warm food. In the evening give it the feather again as before, and continue every evening until it is cleansed and its droppings are normal.

19. Be warned that from the moment when your sparrow hawk begins to fly, as explained above, *item,* it is necessary to cleanse it in this way twice a week, and also bathe it two times a week, on fixed days, between Tierce and noon in a garden or meadow in the sun and in a large enough basin that its wings do not hit the sides. Hold it on the commande or creance so that it does not fly off to dry itself without permission. In the beginning you must splash the water on its head and neck with a little stick to wet it, and as soon as it is bathed you must dry it in the noon sun. However, some people give the feather every night and bathe it every day that it has digested, and call it to the gauntlet while it is bathing or afterward. If during the time that you are bathing your sparrow hawk the sunshine turns to rain, or if while traveling it rains on your bird, you must dry it before a fine fire or in the sun on a stand. But be careful not to place it on a wet perch, for as soon as it has damp feet it gets a cold and becomes sick. Thus, always take care that its feet are dry and warm. When dry, it will fly strongly.

20. At this point in hawk training you must indeed be able to recognize whether it is too skinny or too plump; for if it is too skinny, it is weak, and if it is too fat it is slow and wearied. When it holds itself crouched or humpbacked, and the area around the eyes is green and yellow, and it presents a heavy head and does not hold itself straight and lively on the fist or the perch, the bird is sick. Probably because it is too lean. So you need to feed it pork numbles for one or two days to restore its health. If it holds itself straight and lively and its eyes bulge, it is healthy; but do not let it get too fat. If you see that it has gained too much weight, as a correction you must feed it washed meat or beef.

21. When it can be called with a commande to the gauntlet while you are on your feet, and it already knows the dogs and is of an optimal weight, having been cleansed and bathed, you should then train it by giving it small chicks to hunt in the fields, first while you are on foot and then on horseback. Once it has flown, stooped,[15] and felled them, dismount from the horse and approach it cautiously. Kneel down at a distance, then delicately draw near to it little by little, on all fours. Place your hand toward your sparrow hawk's feet, take the prey by raising the sparrow hawk's feet, and feed it from the prey. If you wish to prepare it to hunt magpies, make it fly in the fields for chicks and pigeons speckled white with black spots like the magpie. Sometimes have it fly in the fields after young magpies, when you can procure them. The hawk is equipped with small talons appropriate for this, and as soon as it has pounced on the magpie, it rips its legs and beak, so that the sparrow hawk, always attacking from the top, has the advantage over the magpie, without getting wounded. If you cannot obtain young magpies, but only strong adult ones, you must remove and tear off the beak and claws and two or three of the major feathers from each wing. The hawk thus trained will fly at magpies in the season. Nevertheless, its instinct will teach it more than this unnatural instruction from its master.

22. *Item,* it is ordinarily said that the person, dogs, and horse that the hawk is familiar with and accustomed to seeing must not be switched on it. If the bird had been cared for by a monk in white riding a black horse, and it was then put in the hands of a black monk riding a white horse, or a squire, knight, or bourgeois, or a woman or another person dressed differently, or in any other hands than those that had trained it, since it would not recognize this new master, the sparrow hawk would not as obligingly be called back to him as to the master whom it knew and who had fed it. That is why a hawk's master should not allow anyone beside himself to hold or feed the bird.

23. My dear, before you begin flying hawks in earnest, you need to inquire about the flights and habits of partridges from the inhabitants of the land. In a strange place or at home, the supreme pursuit that a good austringer can make is to solicit information from shepherds and cowherds and other people from down in the fields about partridge sightings and where their nests are, and then go in that direction. But above all, pay attention that the shepherds' dogs, or any other dogs unknown to you and your birds, especially mastiffs, do not follow you. This could cause your sparrow hawk to hunt less willingly and confidently. Plus, if it felled a game bird, it would be at risk of being attacked by the strange dogs, as has frequently happened.

24. *Item,* my dear, in this sport of hawking, on days that you do not wish to hunt, you must accustom your hawk to eating very early in the morning, so that

---

15. I.e., homed in on.

when you do hunt at that hour it will always be hungry and thus will fly better. For good austringers rise at dawn and hunt at that hour, but only when their sparrow hawk has passed its feather and it is not raining or too windy. For if you hunt in the wind, the gale will carry off your bird and it will be powerless to do anything about it, and people will mock you for it. *Item,* do not hunt near the woods, hedges, or vineyards, or ditches or other water obstacles. *Item,* do not have your hawks fly at small birds, for they are too swift and know the turns of the bushes where they are used to hiding. Thus the sparrow hawk fails to take them, even if it works hard, for these little birds are strong, and they do not bring nearly the honor to the trainer or to the hawk as partridges that fly weaker and are more quickly captured. Furthermore, when the small birds dive into the thickets, the sparrow hawk that follows them gets tired and discouraged despite boldly doing its duty. It might even break its tail and wings in this chase, so in the end it remains shamed because of it but cannot mend the situation.

25. Nevertheless, if your sparrow hawk flies there and you see that in doing so it has broken the tips of some of its plumes, moisten them immediately with your saliva in the area of the break, and when you return to the house, wet the spot with water not hot but less than tepid, and it will close up.[16] Otherwise it will break off. If it has broken its tail, it will not be less valuable for flying at quail, partridges, and large birds that fly close to the ground, but it will be uglier. It will do less well following small birds that fly with swift acrobatic turns, such as the lark, which wheels itself around at sharp angles, and so the sparrow hawk cannot rise to chase after it. *Item,* if your hawk ever breaks part of its tail, you must trim off the other part so that it can fly properly. And even though the bird is unattractive with a broken tail, it nonetheless manages well when flying at large birds. But it is the case that it does poorly in hunting the small ones.

26. The lark hunted for game is the lark born this year with a short tail minus any white, all ashen ginger-brown. This bird does not sing when it rises up in flight, then flies straight ahead and returns to rest again. Older larks have a long tail that has some plumes that are completely white and, when flying off, twitter and say, "Andrieu!" The older lark flies in an undulating pattern and bends, hooking turns first to the right and then to the left, then lands and perches rather far away. This one is not a game bird. Do not do any kind of hunting for larks in the months of August and September, but in September after they molt, the tail falls off, and because that weakens them, they become game again.

---

16. The instructions for mending feathers in the early English texts (and hence the continental texts they derive from) remind the austringer to set or mend the pinion as well as he can. Some treatises suggest using a splint made with a plant stalk, or even sewing the feather spine back together (see Turberville, *Booke of Falconrie or Hawking,* 97).

27. *Item,* it is said above quite truly that every good austringer must keep his hawk from diving at small quick birds, like the old lark, old sparrows, and others that dwell near bushes, because as soon as they see the sparrow hawk, they plunge in, and the hawk fails to capture them, and yet it rips its tail and tears its wings in the bush and because of this becomes weary of hunting. But the worst is that sometimes the sparrow hawk tired out like this does not return to its master but rather flies away and rests in a large tree. Hawks that are exhausted in that way are definitely slower to be recalled from up in a large tree, housetop, or other high place than from a low place, unless a great hunger stirs them. In a situation like this, you must have either chicks or other live birds that—without showing your face—you can make flutter their wings where it can see them to lure it back to the gauntlet.

28. Having attended to all these things, you are ready to hunt. On the first day of hunting, be sure to have a supply of chicks or other live birds to make your sparrow hawk fly in case you don't find any game birds. When your hawk takes its first bird in the field, as soon as it has felled it and holds it between its claws, dismount and advance unhurriedly, trying not to spook your bird. Kneel gently, at some distance, and in a casual manner extend your arm and carefully take and lift its prey with the bird on top if it. Next, break the prey's neck and feed the sparrow hawk with the brain. If your bird grips you tightly with its talons, free yourself claw by claw, very gently, without pulling or upsetting it. *Item,* when your bird has swallowed its meal you can hold it on your bare fist, without a gauntlet, for then it will not grip you. But if it is hungry, don't trust it at all; for then it grips forcefully, in fact so much that it draws blood. By this some judge the sparrow hawk's strength; for when they feel through the gauntlet the powerful clenching of the hawk's talons, they estimate that it is strong, and if not, then that's not the case. *Item,* at this time hold it in place on the fist so tranquilly that it has no need to thrash about after its mouthful, for it risks vomiting. If you are not able to keep the bird on the fist, carefully perch it in a peaceful vantage point for observing people, dogs, and horses, etc., but where it cannot spot pigeons or other fowl.

29. The 2nd time that you go hunting, let your sparrow hawk fly 2 or 3 times a day and not more, and feed it as described above; and the 3rd time, 2 or 3 flights and not more; and then the next days let it fly as much as it can, at as many birds as you find. *Item,* if you notice that it snatches and hides its prey, fasten the hawk to the bush where it went for cover and let it hang 2 or 3 times and no longer release it to go to a tree at feeding time. Your bird will thus decide not to repeat hiding the prey in the future. *Item,* begin to have it fly each day in the early morning until Terce. Then put your sparrow hawk in a meadow or field—or in a bush or tree if it does not hoard the prey—and recall it to the glove from there and feed and perch it. Take a rest yourself in the heat of the day, and afterward hunt with it in the evening. For whoever in the month of July and through mid-August flies the sparrow hawk in intense

heat will find that the bird makes an effort to cool itself by flying higher and farther, and at the first river or water that it comes to, it will descend from above to bathe in it. After bathing it will fly off to dry itself in a tree, and there will leisurely preen its feathers with its beak, one after the other, so much and so enthusiastically that not a single feather will remain ungroomed, and your hawk will not be located without extreme effort. If you do find it, there will be a long wait before it returns to the gauntlet. But after mid-August, it will not be so obstinate.

30. Nevertheless, just as it is explained above, always be equipped with fresh red chicks that look like partridges, so that if you do not find other weak birds, you can fly in the fields for this chick that you brought, and then feed the hawk the brain and more than his usual ration. Then remove the neck and the innards from the chick —it will keep longer—and then you can feed the hawk one time with the wings, another with the leg quarters, and then lastly with the carcass. If you did not find a chick to bring, have a pigeon, although it is warming food and too bitter for a sparrow hawk that hunts. For the flavor lingers and it stays full longer than with any other meat, and unfortunately will refuse the fist and remain aloof. *Item,* take care that from the moment you begin hunting with your hawk you allow nothing to startle it or approach it suddenly, shrilly, or wildly—be it person, dog, horse, or other distraction. Likewise, let nothing come up to it from the rear, for it is most agitated and frightened by what surprises it from behind.

31. *Item,* when you are in the pursuit, train your eye on your sparrow hawk and on your spaniels, and when the dogs wave their tails to flush game from an area, immediately spur on your horse straight toward them so that when the partridge flies up, your hawk will be near. If several partridges burst out, one of which your bird follows, homes in on, and fells, always remain intent on your bird and call out to your companions so that they spot the other birds. When your hawk has had its portion of brain, return to the area of the hunt where the birds were spotted, so that you take all the game birds, one after the other. *Item,* you can seek partridges in tall stubble fields, dwarf elders, heather, and around the sheaves left in the fields. Partridges and young partridges feed from the grains around these bundles, and they prefer to be under cover and not in fallow fields or other open areas, as much out of dislike of the heat as fear that a hawk or other birds of prey may spot them. When the heat lifts, these partridges and also quails are found in tall broom and in the vineyards as well as in fields of vetch, peas, and grain with stalks to provide cooling shade. *Item,* in this season you cannot hunt in the vineyards, for it would cause too much damage to the owners of the vineyards, and furthermore the sparrow hawk would be encumbered by the leaves and vine props, giving the partridges too great an advantage. Good austringers spot the game birds and set off after them through the fields or thickets, so the sparrow hawk can seize them in one swoop.

32. If the sparrow hawk carries off its prey to cover and its master recalls it to the gauntlet and whistles, the master must not show his face.[17] *Item*, know that from the time the sparrow hawk begins to hunt, it must not live off any butchered meat, or anything else except prey. In addition, it must fly day after day with no rest break, for the one that rests for one day regresses three days.

33. *Item*, the partridge as quarry lasts until mid-August, and then the quail season begins, because the partridges have become strong and remain willingly near the woods and hedges. In August one finds late-hatched partridges, which mate after the others, since they were not old enough during the treading season. They have not yet mated in the month of August, and they still have blood in their feathers (and the spine knotted); they are not as strong as their fathers and mothers who have molted, nor are the feathers on their wings as straight, and for this reason they are easier prey for the hawk than the older birds, unless it is in the period immediately after these fathers and mothers have hatched their eggs and they are feeding them and still keeping the partridge chicks warm under them. At that point the parent birds are stripped of their feathers and are thin and weak and can easily be caught by a sparrow hawk. But when they are revested in their plumes and have recovered their strength, they can be hunted only at the moment they are flushed and take flight, as was said earlier, or after their first flight when they have been spotted and relinquish their hiding place. On this second flight they are more tired than they were on the first. But on their first flight, you set your sparrow hawk on them in open fields at your peril, for if the hawk gets tired from swooping after them, or if it snatches the partridge yet she is strong enough to prevail, or if it is gotten the better of in any other way, either by this bird or another, it will never again hunt willingly.

34. In August you can hawk for pheasant, bustard, young rabbits, hare, field rail —which are red—and also quail, at least until mid-August. In September you must hunt them all day long, without returning home, because it is neither too hot nor too rainy nor too windy, and you must realize that in September the sparrow hawk does not fly high up into the air as readily as in the August heat.

35. *Item*, since the nights in September are longer, toward the end of the month give the hawk a larger meal in the evening than in the morning; but always remember that quail and pigeon are an unwholesome food, because their meat is difficult to digest and sits a long while in the stomach. And so the sparrow hawk becomes proud and refuses the fist as explained above.

36. *Item*, toward the end of September and afterward, when hawking quails and partridges is over, and even in winter, you can hawk—as is said—magpies,

---

17. This probably refers to the practice of calling the bird back using a lure baited with prey or meat.

jackdaws, teals from the river, or the other spotted ones with long legs that live in the fields and run on foot along the sandy riverbanks, along with blackbirds, thrush, jays, and snipes. This hunting can be done on foot with a bow and arrow. If the blackbird disappears into a shrub and dares not leave it because of the sparrow hawk who spies it from above, the lady or maiden who knows how to shoot can kill it with an arrow. In that way, from season to season you can have amusement from your sparrow hawk. When you want to keep your bird through its molting and you do not find anything to feed it from the hunt, give it a rest. Realize, though, that as soon as the hawk remains outside one night, it will revert to the wild and will feed itself on its own. For this reason you must call it in at dawn.

37. And, my dear, if you wish to keep the hawk through its molting, since it costs as much to molt a bad sparrow hawk as a good one, first consider whether your bird has been pleasing, good, and peaceful, for that's the one you should keep. But if it has given you any trouble, get rid of it, for it will be even worse after molting. Nonetheless, if you wish to molt it, you must feed it warm meat like hen, mouse, rat, and birds caught in nets or by crossbow. There is no denying the importance of the sparrow hawk hunting as often as you discover prey, and especially throughout Lent, for thus its feathers rapidly drop and it molts naturally. One must always, as said before, purge it and give it the feather. As for the sparrow hawks that one wishes to keep through the molt, some give them minced oakum, and also some say that hare and rabbit feet, deboned and then beaten with a hammer on an anvil, are a good purge. Bathe your hawk often and keep it on a perch, and feed it good warm and live meat, if you can, very diligently, and watch it more carefully than before. Be sure to feed it at least three times a day until mid-May. At that juncture you must pluck out all the tail feathers. Some say that the best moment is during the crescent moon of May, or otherwise the tail does not come back, that is, if it is plucked in the month of June. Here is the way to pluck the bird: someone holds the sparrow hawk in his hands, and another presses the end of the tail where the stems of the tail feathers attach. When the pelt is held that way to protect the bird, you must pluck the feathers one after the other all in one day. They say that as many days before Saint John's that the tail is plucked, that many days before mid-August is it ready. Although some say that you must bathe the sparrow hawk's . . . during Lent, I don't take this into account.

38. Once the aforesaid tail is denuded, put the bird in a mew[18] that is four feet long and 4 feet wide and three feet high, covered with a good cloth against the wind, and that has an opening for air. In this mew there must be a perch, about a half foot high. One half of it will be covered with felt, and along the other half there will be a sliding lath through which it will be given food, without being

---

18. Cage for molting birds.

touched. During this time protect it assiduously from heat and chill and place it in the sun during the day. Keep it from upset, fright, or bother of any kind, and nourish it with fine and warm food, minced until it is entirely softened. Sometimes you must feed it a bird. Rats and mice too are good, as are freshly slaughtered mutton heart and warm pork numbles. It takes a good seven weeks to two months before it will have its new feathers. What most speeds up a sparrow hawk's molting is feeding it every two days the glands of a sheep's neck during molting season. Nonetheless, they say that when the plumes of the tail and wings have come back, it is enough, and one need not worry about the back plumage and the other feathers. It would be such a shame to lose the bird after taking so much trouble, so it is best and safest to test shrewdly and cautiously if it will stay peacefully on the fist and eat there. If not, rectify this behavior adeptly by keeping it awake and making it weak with little food. *Item,* the surest way to call it to the gauntlet is by using the commande. Of course, all creatures desire their freedom and easily return to their wild state, so guard against this! The more pains you take in raising your sparrow hawk, the more valuable it is, for these are trained and know their prey, the dogs, and the horses, and they are stronger.

39. Since I have spoken to you of the nature of sparrow hawks that are called *niais*[19] because they were taken from the nest, presently I wish to speak of those called *branchiers, ramages,* or *rameges,* which are all the same. Afterward I will describe the *muiers,* who have undergone one or several moltings. A sparrow hawk is called branchier or ramage because, when it is captured, it is able to flutter around the small branches or on the branches. It is certainly necessary that the ramage sparrow hawk be trained, and hopefully it will descend toward the decoy where it may be captured. Nevertheless, before it can be trained, prepare a suitable place in front of the sparrow hawks' aerie, spread out the nets, and place in the snare a chick or a pigeon or another prey bird that will attract it. Near the trap you should place other sparrow hawks and muskets that cry out and flap about. This encourages the branchier sparrow hawk to drop more quickly to the snare. Once it is in the net, however, you can take it very gently, with one person holding it by the wings on both sides while the other takes it by the beak and seels[20] its eyelids. Right away put on the jesses and little bells, and set the bird on the fist, moving about and checking that it does not fall asleep. When evening is at hand, offer it flesh washed in tepid water. If it eats on the fist, that's the first good sign. If it doesn't eat, keep it awake and watch over it all night. If you cannot keep watch through the night, perch the bird on a swinging perch with each end attached to a cord, and from time to time pull on the perch to make it rock

---

19. Not yet able to fly.
20. Sews up a hawk's eyelids.

so that the sparrow hawk does not sleep. After it has remained awake for one or two nights and seems comfortable and secure on the fist and has eaten there willingly, the 2nd time it eats you must unseel its eyelids and carry it among people, again keeping it awake for the most part. If it seems quite secure, you must make it confident with everything else, then call it back to the gauntlet with a signal.

40. If the sparrow hawk captured thus in the nets has molted out in the wild, tame it by keeping it awake and hungry in the way described above. Although less docile and less likely to return as well as the tawny sparrow hawk—that is, one who is a year old—there are nonetheless some sparrow hawks from the last to be hatched of the previous year that hatched so late that they were barely mature when the first group had already finished their season. These have molted out in the hedge in freedom; however, because they are so young, they have neither laid nor hatched eggs this year. This type of hawk may also be caught after molting. One recognizes them from the tawny plumage they have retained from the previous year. You can have greater expectations for these than for those older hawks who have hunted more or have had several moltings. Some austringers recognize these well and will reject the older ones for this reason. *Item,* a molted sparrow hawk keeps its tail better because it does not enter the thickets after its prey; rather, it flies above. Yet the niais sparrow hawk does enter there. *Item,* the sparrow hawk that has molted in the wild has red eyes and yellow feet. Sometimes, by accident, sparrow hawks get caught in birdlime, and then you must free them from the birdlime, feather by feather, by hand, with fingers moistened with milk.

41. Now let us turn to the molting, which is of two types: that is, some molt in the cage and others molt in the hedge. Those that molt in the cage are good for hunting, and these are the most valuable. Those that molt out in the hedges can be recognized by their redder eyes and their feet that are more yellow. You should know that these molted in the hedge are less tame and certain in hunting, even though they have been seeled, kept from sleeping, and perform very well when called back to the gauntlet on a commande or creance, which is the same thing. Even so, when you set them to hunt and they all rise into the air vigorously, if a gust of wind carries them all away despite themselves, once they have lost contact with their master and have to fend for themselves and eat on their own, they revert to their wild state and will never again wish to return to the gauntlet.

42. An untamed sparrow hawk is one that has molted in the wild. At one year old it looks somewhat like a russet or tawny sparrow hawk. A bird without this tawny color has assuredly molted twice. *Item,* the molted sparrow hawk has very red eyes and yellow feet and stronger, straighter feathers of different colors. You can pick out the tawny feathers from among the others, for they are black on top and the others have more color.

43. *Item,* the male sparrow hawk is the musket, and the lanneret is the male

of the lanners,[21] and of others such as the goshawk, falcon, etc., the male is called the tercelet. My dear, as for other birds of prey, the male is called the goshawk tercelet, and he is smaller; the goshawk is the female and is larger. *Item,* the falcon tercelet is the male, and is smaller; and he is not a good bird for a poor man because he cannot be stopped. Falcon is the term for the female, and she is commonly called the falcon-gentle.[22] *Item,* the merlin tercelet is the male, and the merlin called formel is female. They hunt together and are called back to the fist with a lure. *Item,* the hobby tercelet is male;[23] the formel is its female.[24] *Item,* the lanneret—the male—is stronger and more valuable. The lanner is the female of that species.

44. If a sparrow hawk has jaundice, how do you heal it? Response: Where there is no illness, no cure is called for. Clearly they get the jaundice from comfort and health and because of the warm meats that they eat. For this reason, they are not actually ill.

45. If a sparrow hawk has a cold, show it some rue leaves. *Item,* have it warmed by the fire in the evening for a long time. *Item,* have it tear at a pig or piglet's tail that has no meat. *Item,* have a box or other vessel in which there is incense and a flame, and have the smoke reach its beak; it will thus cough and sneeze and shake its head and will rid itself of the cold. Let its perch be covered with felt and keep it warm. *Item,* have it tear at a chick's pinion, and in the hand with which you hold the pinion, hold also a branch of rue, so that it smells it while pulling. Whether on the fist or on the perch, be attentive that it has a completely dry and warm piece of animal pelt or felt underneath the talons. Night and day keep it in front of or near the fire or in a warm place. Have always in your belt a piece of fur, felt, or other warm thing; change it often and keep the bird warm.

46. If a sparrow hawk is so ill that it rejects food, open its beak with two hands and push down its throat some fresh butter the size of a fava bean. One or two hours later, feed it some fresh meat, still warm.

47. *Item,* you can tell if a sparrow hawk is too fat by feeling it under the wing as for a hen. Also it is overweight when it has a rounded breast with an indentation down the center, and it yawns. You must then give the bird cool water to drink to cool down the inside of its body and feed it sparely so that it becomes more slender.

---

21. The lanner is a species of European falcon smaller than the peregrine. In falconry, the lanner is the female and the male is called a lanneret. The male and female terms are reversed in this line, most likely in error, calling the male the "lanner," which we have emended to "lanneret." The author or scribe corrects it a few lines below.

22. A falcon-gentle is technically a female peregrine falcon.

23. The hobby is a small species of falcon flown at small birds (*OED*).

24. Formel is the female of either the eagle or hawk (*OED*).

48. The sparrow hawk with white eyebrows is arguably the best of them. *Item,* niais and ramage sparrow hawks are not as good as those taken by the net or lured with a kestrel.

49. For other sparrow hawk illnesses, look at the remedies for falcons on the next page, and proceed according to those instructions.

50. Of the birds of prey that can be trained, the eagle, griffon vulture, and goshawk fly at wild goat, hare, and bustards, provided that you have a greyhound trained for them. The goshawk tercelet flies at hare, partridge, rabbit, and plover. In the winter, you feed the goshawk only once a day, and twice in the summer. A sheep's heart is enough to feed it at one time and keeps it in good shape. *Item,* for a slice of sheep, a pigeon, a partridge, etc. A pork heart is fattening, as they say *hausse;*[25] a goat or billy-goat heart lowers, *id est* makes it lose weight. Use a sheep's foot for your bird to pull at to exercise. When you bathe it, remove the longes. Then it can bathe at the river-bank, preen its feathers, and return. For feeding a goshawk, a chicken lasts three days: one day you feed it the liver, gizzard, the neck with all its feathers, the head and brain; the next day one wing and thigh, and the next day the other. *Item,* during Lent it molts, and for three or four months needs hay, leafy branches, and three perches to perch on. Feed it then with fresh meat like turtledoves, doves, partridges, and live chicks. *Item,* once it has molted, you must keep it awake 4, 6, or 8 nights, then call it back to the fist little by little, using the commande, as in the beginning. *Nota* that the lanner falcon must be perched at one and a half feet in order to be trained to hunt partridge, and the falcon-gentle perches higher.

51. *Item, nota* that although the sparrow hawk and the goshawk are fed between the thumb and the pointer finger, nonetheless the other birds are fed with a handful. Flesh washed in tepid water is given to lower the weight and make the hawk thinner. When the droppings are white and clear and a little black is on the end that first comes out of the gut, it is a good sign, otherwise not. But if the droppings contain something reddish and large, it means that the bird must be trimmed down in weight.

52. The lanner falcon is called common because it feeds on all meats, such as beef, mutton, and goat. *Nota* that goat meat causes weight loss. Droppings excreted far from the perch are a healthy sign. The lanner has large speckles and is larger than the lanneret that has finer speckles and flies higher and with falcon-gentles, which the lanneret does not do. Other falcons, from Flanders, called saker falcons,[26] which have slightly coarser spots and have yellow feet, are someplace between gentle and common falcons. They are commonly called "good" when they

---

25. Raises.

26. A large lanner falcon (*falco sacer*) used in falconry, especially the female, which is larger than the male, the latter being distinguished as sakeret (*OED*).

are called back with a lure and "manly" when they respond well to the lure. The falcon-gentle is more finely speckled than any other and has yellow feet and is fed less with sheep's heart and more often with pigeons or poultry. Some other falcons are called Barbary falcons. These petite birds come from Granada and are useful in hunting heron, crane, and bustard. Barbary falcons are similar to the tercelets, the male falcons mentioned earlier. Peregrine falcons caught in the net, who feed themselves and have flown in the fields, are called "gentles."

53. *Item*, the lanner hunts only partridges, and sometimes rabbit and hare, but nothing else. The others hunt river fowl, heron, crane, bustard, etc. The goshawk hunts everything, but not the goshawk tercelet. The female common falcon is called lanner or formel, and the male is called tercelet. The falcon-gentle is black, and the lanner falcon has the softest color. The peregrine falcon is the best of all; it is the largest, with the best-developed muscles of them all. He who wishes to command them should not eat garlic, onions, or leeks.[27]

54. *Item*, when any bird of prey yawns three times in a row and does not look well, it is a sign that it is sick with an illness the falconers call *fils*,[28] which is a worm that pricks them. To cure the bird, feed it meat in which saffron has been wrapped, and the worms will die.

55. If a falcon has *pépie*,[29] take a thorn from a white hawthorn and scrape it around inside the nostril three times a day for three days, and for three days place on its tongue green figs, right from the tree. *Item*, you will know that it has pépie when it looks ill, does not want food or cannot eat, and sometimes snites.

56. If your bird has mites, you will see them in the sunlight moving over its whole head. For this affliction, get the best orpiment,[30] in the form of foil, and grind it finely and sift it most delicately. You will need three people: one to hold the bird, another to hold the orpiment, and the third to apply the orpiment powder. Then you must spew water over it from the mouth, as do needlewomen. Feed it warm hen, then perch it, and remove the glove that is covered with orpiment —for the orpiment is very strong—and the next day have it fly.

57. *Nota* that in May falcons begin to molt and need to be fed warm meat. Rats are an appropriate food. *Item*, you can molt it while holding it on the fist.

---

27. Turberville (*Booke of Falconrie or Hawking*, 141) notes that hawks do not like the smell of garlic.

28. Filanders. Turberville has various remedies for their cure (ibid., 252).

29. A hardening of the mucous membranes of the tongue, called "pippe" by Turberville (ibid., 306). He says the bird often wipes his beak (snites) when he has this ailment.

30. Arsenic trisulfide; lemon yellow, it is also used as a pigment.

¶ 2.4 *Menus*

The fourth article of the second section teaches you, as sovereign mistress of your household, how to order and plan dinners and suppers with Master Jehan and how to arrange the sequence of dishes and courses.[1]

1. I begin by giving you some terms as a bit of an introduction or at least as an amusement for you.

2. *Primo,* since you must send Master Jehan to the butcher's shop, a list follows of the names of all the butchers' shops in Paris and the meats that they supply:[2]

At the Porte-de-Paris there are 19 butchers who by common estimate sell weekly, if you average the busy season with the slow season: 1,900 sheep, 400 beef cattle, 400 pigs, and 200 calves.

Sainte-Geneviève: 500 sheep, 16 beef cattle, 16 pigs, and 6 calves.

Le Parvis: 80 sheep, 10 beef cattle, 10 calves, and 8 pigs.

At Saint-Germain, with thirteen butchers: 200 sheep, 30 beef cattle, 30 calves, and 50 pigs.

The Temple, two butchers; 200 sheep, 24 beef cattle, 32 calves, 32 pigs.

Saint-Martin: 200 sheep, 32 beef cattle, 32 pigs, 32 calves.

The weekly total for all the butchers' shops in Paris, without counting the households of the king and the queen and other lords of France, 3,080 sheep, 514 beef cattle, 306 calves, and 600 pigs. And on Good Friday from 2,000 to 3,000 salted pork sections are sold.

3. In addition to the amount of butchers' meat and poultry listed above, the king's household's weekly total of meat reaches at least 120 sheep, 16 beef cattle,

---

1. The glossary explains some of the culinary terms. If the recipe for a particular dish appears in the recipe section, the number is in brackets. An ellipsis indicates a lacuna in the MS. The first use of specialized terms is italicized.

2. Pichon has an informative footnote about the history and locations of Parisian butchers. The main meat market was at the Porte-de-Paris; Ste. Geneviève market served the university; Parvis was in the precincts of Notre Dame; St. Germain and St. Martin markets were named for their district and street; the Templars owned a meat market on their land. The Middle French *beufz* (modern French *boeufs*), which we have generally translated as "beef cattle," included oxen as well as cattle. An English cookery book of the time lists some of the meat as "oxen"; provisions for a large feast in 1387 include "Xiiij. oxen lying in salte. II. oxen ffreyssh." See *Two Fifteenth-Century Cookery-Books,* ed. Thomas Austin, Early English Text Society 91 (London: N. Trübner, 1888).

16 calves,[3] and 12 pigs; and 200 pieces of salted pork in a year. The daily sum of poultry: 600 chickens, 200 pairs of pigeons, 50 kid goats, and 50 goslings.

The queen and the children—weekly butchery: 80 sheep, 12 calves, 12 beef cattle, 12 pigs; and 120 pieces of salted pork a year. In poultry daily, 300 chickens, 36 kids, 150 pairs of pigeons, and 36 goslings.

The duke of Orleans, likewise.

The duke of Berry, also the same.

Monseigneur de Berry's people say that on Sundays and great feasts they need 3 beef cattle, 30 sheep, 160 dozen partridges, and as many rabbits as is necessary, but I doubt it. (This has since been verified. It is certainly so on great feasts and Sundays and Thursdays, but usually the other days it is 2 beef cattle and 20 sheep.) *Nota* again that at the court of Monseigneur de Berry the valets and pages receive the ox cheeks as their allowance. The muzzle of the ox is carved sideways and the mandibles left for the allowance, as was said. *Item,* the neck of the ox is also given as allowance to the varlets. (*Item,* and the part just below the neck is the best part of the beef, for that which is between the front legs is the breast and that which is above is the *noyau.*)[4]

The duke of Burgundy's expenses compared with the king's equals the ratio of Parisian money to the money minted in Tours.[5]

The duke of Bourbon's household uses half as much as the queen's.

4. *Item,* without spending or giving away your money every day you can send Master Jehan to the butcher and order meat by tally,[6] keeping in mind the following:

Half a beef breast has 4 pieces, the first of which is called *grumel;* this half costs between 10 blancs and 3 sols.

The loin has 6 pieces and costs between 6 sols and 6 sols and 8 deniers; the sirloin, 3 sols.[7]

The *giste* has 8 pieces and is the fattiest meat, but except for the cheeks it makes the best bouillon; it costs 8 sols.

---

3. See BF on MSS A and C. The folios are transposed here in MS A; that is, the folios 124 and 125 and the folios 126 and 127 have been switched, and so part of the hawking treatise appears where the menu information should be, after "calves," and vice versa. MS C reproduces the incorrect order of the text. Pichon uses this as evidence that C is a close copy of A.

4. Noyau cut is described in ¶ 2.5.25.

5. BF/Ueltschi (543 n. 2) give this ratio at 4:5.

6. On credit.

7. Pichon says, and other authorities agree, that it is difficult to determine exactly how the medieval cuts of meat were apportioned and to what parts of the cow the names of the various cuts refer. The sirloin mentioned here is not the modern cut of that name but likely the end of the loin, part of the rump. Even modern butchers in different countries use different cuts.

A quarter of a sheep contains 4 pieces, or 3 pieces plus the shoulder, and costs between 8 blancs and 3 sols; a quarter calf costs 8 sols.

Pork . . .

And *nota* that you say breast of beef but brisket of mutton. When referring to venison, the breast is called *hampe*.

As for the breast of beef, the piece closest to the neck is called the *grumel,* and it is the best. In mutton, the *flanchet* is what remains of the front quarter once the shoulder has been removed. *Item,* for venison we say *couart. Item,* the *deitez* are the testicles.

The sirloin costs 3 sols.

The loin, 6 sols.

The flesh of a sheep, 10 sols.

After these things, it is important next to speak of certain general cookery terms and then to explain how to know and choose foods, which must be prepared as follows.

5. *Primo,* for all sauces and thick pottages that call for ground spices and bread, first grind the spices and remove them from the mortar, then grind the bread, because it collects the spices that remain. Thus nothing is lost.

6. *Item,* do not strain the spices and thickeners used in pottages; however, do so for sauces, to make them clearer and thus more pleasing.

7. *Item,* know that pea or bean or other pottages hardly ever burn if when you are cooking you prevent the burning firewood from touching the bottom of the pot.

8. *Item,* before your pottage burns and to avert scorching, stir the bottom of the pot often, scraping your spoon on the bottom so that the pottage does not stick. And *nota* that when you notice your pottage beginning to burn, do not stir it, but remove it immediately from the fire and transfer it to another pot.

9. *Item, nota* that pottages on the fire commonly boil over and onto the fire until salt and fat are put into the pot, after which they do not.

10. *Item, nota* that the best caudle[8] is made with beef's cheek washed 2 or 3 times in water, then boiled and well skimmed.

11. *Item,* you know if a rabbit is fat by feeling the tendon or neck between the two shoulders. If the tendon is large, it is fat. You can tell if it is tender by breaking one of its hind legs.

12. *Item, nota* that cooks make a distinction between "sticking" and "larding," for sticking is done with cloves and larding with bacon fat.

13. *Item,* the soft roe of pike are better than the hard, except when you want to make rissoles, because rissoles are made from hard roe, *ut patet in tabula.*[9]

---

8. Stock.

9. Latin: "Whence it is made clear from writings."

14. People call pike: *lancerel, brochet, quarrel, luce,* and *luceau.*

15. *Item,* the season for fresh shad begins in March.

16. *Item,* carp must be cooked very well, or otherwise it is dangerous to eat it.

17. *Item,* unlike dab, plaice are soft to the touch.

18. *Item,* at Paris the goosemongers fatten their geese with flour, neither fine flour nor bran flour, but the coarse one that is between the two which is called *gruyaulx* or *recoppes;* and they take equal amounts of this coarse flour and oatmeal and mix them with a little water, until it becomes thick like dough. They place this food in a four-footed dish, with water on the side and fresh litter every day, and in 15 days the geese are fatted. *Nota* that their litter allows them to keep their feathers clean.

19. *Item,* when hanging capons and hens to cure, you must cut their throats and immediately place them in a bucket of very cold water to die, and they will be as well aged on that same day as though killed two days earlier.

20. *Item,* you can tell young mallards from old ones, when they are the same size, from the quills of the feathers, which are more tender in young birds than in old. *Item,* you can recognize wild river ducks by their completely black nails and red feet; domestic ducks have yellow feet. *Item,* the crest or upper part of the beak is all green, and sometimes the males have a white mark across the nape of the neck and iridescent plumage.

21. *Item,* wood pigeons are good eating in winter. You can distinguish the old ones because their flight feathers are all black, while the young ones, a year old, have ash-colored flight feathers, with the rest of their plumage black.

22. *Item,* you can tell the age of a hare from the number of holes under its tail. There are as many holes as its age in years.

23. *Item,* partridges whose feathers are tight and closely affixed to the flesh, and well ordered and placed, like the feathers of a sparrow hawk, have been freshly killed; and those whose feathers are ruffled the wrong way and falling away from the flesh, wildly out of place, have been long dead. *Item,* this you can feel by tugging on the feathers of the belly.

24. *Item,* a carp with white—not yellow or red—scales is from good water. If a carp has big eyes bulging from its head and a soft, smooth palate and tongue, it is fat. And *nota,* if you want to carry a live carp a whole day, wrap it in damp hay, put it in a pouch or sack, and carry it belly up without giving it air.

25. The trout season begins in . . . and lasts until September. White trout are good in winter, red in summer. The best part of the trout is the tail, while of the carp it is the head.

26. *Item,* an eel with a small head, fine, shiny, iridescent, and glistening skin, large body, and white belly is fresh. Otherwise it will have a big head, yellow belly, and thick brown skin.

Hereafter follow dinners and suppers for great lords and others:

27. From these you can choose, assemble, and learn to prepare whatever dishes you wish, according to the season and the foods that are available in whatever place you may be when you have to give a dinner or a supper.

28. Dinner for a meat day served in 31 dishes and 6 courses:

First course. Grenache wine with sops of toasted bread, veal pasties [166], pimpernel pasties, *boudin* [6], and sausages [353].

Second course. Hare stew [116] and cutlets, pea *coulis,* salt meat and joints of boiled meat, and eel and fish *soringue* [127].

Third course. Roasted rabbits, partridges, capons, etc., luce, sea bass, carp, and a quartered pottage.[10]

Fourth course. River birds *à la dodine, riz engoulé* [243], *bourrey* with hot sauce, and reversed eels [180].

Fifth course. Lark pasties [370], rissoles [261], larded milk [259], sugared flans.

Sixth course. Pears and comfits, medlars and peeled nuts, hippocras [317] and wafers.

29. Another meat dinner of 24 dishes in six courses:

First course. Pasties of veal minced well with beef fat and marrow, pimpernel pasties, boudin, sausages, *pipefarces* [264], and small Norse pasties [258] *de quibus.*[11]

Second course. Hare stew and eel soup, broad bean coulis, salt meat, joints *scilicet* of beef and mutton.

Third course. Roasted capons, rabbits, veal and partridges, fresh and saltwater fish, *taillis* [237] with glazed meatballs [242, 252, 255].

Fourth course. River mallard à la dodine, tench with sops and bourrey with hot sauce, fatted capon pasties with sops of fat and parsley.

Fifth course. *Bouli lardé* [90], riz engoulé, reversed eels, roasted salt or freshwater fish, rissoles, crêpes [262] and old sugar.

The 6th and last course as a finish. Sugared tarts and larded milk, medlars, peeled nuts, cooked pears and comfits, hippocras and wafers.

30. Another meat dinner:

First course. Beef pasties [164] and rissoles, black *porée* [52], lampreys with cold sage sauce [244], German meat broth [108], a white fish sauce and an herb omelet [225], joints of beef and mutton.

Second course. Roasted meats, freshwater fish, saltwater fish, a meat *crétonnée* [95], ravioli, a *rosé* of young rabbits and bourreys with heated sauce of young birds

---

10. This seems to be the solid part of a stew, probably served cut and presented in four pieces (see BF/Ueltschi, 551 n. 3, and also ¶ 246).

11. Latin: "of whatever."

[84], Pisan bird tarts (*id est* from Pisa in Lombardy, called Lombard tarts, and there are little birds in the stuffing, and below they will be referred to as Lombard tarts).

Third course. Tench with sops, decorated blancmanger [107], larded milk, croutons, boar's tail with hot sauce [293], capons à la dodine, bream and salmon pasties, poached plaice and *leschefrite,* and *darioles.*

Fourth course. Frumenty [234], venison, roast fish, cold sage, reversed eels, fish in aspic [251], capon pasties with small sops.

31. Another meat dinner:

First course. Norse pasties, *cameline*-flavored meat soup [271], beef marrow beignets, eel soringue, poached loach and cold sage, joints of meat and saltwater fish.

Second course. The best roast to be found and freshwater fish, bouli lardé, meat tile [118], capon pasties and crêpes, bream and eel pasties, and blancmanger.

Third course. Frumenty, venison, lamprey with hot sauce, lechefrites, bream and darioles, sturgeon in aspic.

32. Another meat dinner:

First course. Beef and marrow pasties, hare stew, joints of meat, a white rabbit soup, capons and venison with sops, white porée [50], turnips, salted goose and pork chine.

Second course. The best roast, etc., a rosé of larks, a blancmanger, boar numbles and tail with warm sauce, fat capon pasties, fritters and Norse pasties.

Third course. Frumenty, venison, various types of glazed meats, fat geese and capons à la dodine, cream darioles and sugared lechefrites, bourreys with warm galantine [283]; capon, rabbits, spring chickens, young rabbits and piglets in aspic.

Fourth course. Hippocras and wafers to finish.

33. Another meat dinner:

First course. Shelled beans, cinnamon soup [102], black hare stew, a green eel soup [112, 122], smoked herring [28], joints of meat, turnips [54], tench with sops, salted geese and pork chines, beef marrow rissoles, *hastelets* of beef . . . of pork *ut prima.*[12]

Second course. The best roast to be had, freshwater and saltwater fish, poached plaice, bourreys with heated sauce—prepared like lampreys, lark *gravé* g i g of peach blossom,[13] a decorated blancmanger, Lombard tarts, venison and small bird pasties, Spanish crétonnée, fresh herring.

Third course. Frumenty, venison, glazed meats, fish in aspic, fat capons à la dodine, roasted fish, lechefrites and darioles, reversed eels, crayfish, crêpes and pipe-farces.

---

12. Latin: "as first courses."

13. Probably an abbreviation for *id est gravé,* "that is, gravy/stew." See ¶ 39 for a stew the color of peach blossom.

34. Another meat dinner:

First course. White porée, beef hastelets, joints of meat, veal stew, broth *houssié* [103].

Second course. Roasts of meat, salt and freshwater fish, Lombard raviolis, Spanish crétonnée.

Third course. Lampreys in sauce, a rosé, larded milk and croutons in milk, Pisan *id est* Lombard tarts, cream darioles.

Fourth course. Frumenty, venison, glazed meats, bream and gurnard pasties, reversed eels, fat capons à la dodine.

To close. Hippocras and wafers.

Boutehors.[14] Wine and spices.

35. Another meat dinner:

First course. Joints of meat, Norse pasties, beef marrow beignets, cameline meat soup, eel soringue, poached loach, saltwater fish and cold sage.

Second course. The best roast to be had, meat tile, kid goat bouli lardé, capon pasties, crêpes, bream and eel pasties, and blancmanger.

Third course. Frumenty, venison, glazed meats, lampreys with hot sauce, leschefrites and darioles, roast bream, broth with verjuice, sturgeon in aspic.

36. Another meat dinner:

First course. White leeks, beef pasties, goose with pork chines, hare and rabbit stew, lark *genesté* [114], joints of meat.

Second course. Roasted boar's tail with heated sauce, decorated blancmanger, goose dodines, larded milk and croutons, venison, glazed meats, aspics, croutons in milk à la dodine, capon pasties, cold sage, beef pasties and *talemouse.*

37. Another meat dinner:

First course. Pea coulis, herrings, salted eels, oysters in black stew, almond soup, tile, pike and eel broth, crétonnée, green soup of eels, silver pasties.

Second course. Saltwater and freshwater fish, bream and salmon pasties, reversed eels, brown omelet, tench bouli lardé, a blancmanger, crêpes, lettuces, *lozenges, orillettes* and Norse pasties, stuffed luce and salmon.

Third course. Frumenty, venison, glazed meatballs and Spanish peas and Castillian,[15] roasted fish, aspic, lampreys, congers and turbot with green sauce, bream with verjuice, leschefrites, darioles, and *entremets.*

38. Another dinner:

---

14. Final offering at a formal dinner.

15. Middle French: "chastellier," unidentified word that could mean "from Castile," *chatelain* (of the chateau) *chastaignes/chatengnes* (chestnuts), or it could be a scribal error for *castagnoles/chastelonges* [43], a fish.

First course. Beef pasties and rissoles, black porée, lamprey gravé [128], German meat broth, georgié meat soup [103], white fish sauce, an omelet.

Second course. Roasts of meat, saltwater and freshwater fish, meat crétonnée, raviolis, a rosé of small rabbits and birds, bourreys with heated sauce, Pisan tarts.

Third course. Tench with sops, decorated blancmanger, larded milk and croutons, boar's tails in heated sauce, capons à la dodine, bream and salmon pasties, poached plaice, leschefrites and darioles.

Fourth course. Frumenty, venison, glazed meats, roasted fish, cold sage, reversed eels, fish in aspic, capon pasties.

39. Another dinner:

First course. Shelled beans, cinnamon soup, black stew of hare or a green soup of eels, smoked herrings, joints of meat, turnips, tench with sops, salted geese and pork chines, rissoles of beef marrow.

Second course. The best roast to be had, fresh and saltwater fish, poached plaice, bourreys with heated sauce, shad gravé the color of peach blossom, decorated blancmanger, Lombard tarts, venison and small bird pasties, Spanish crétonnée, fresh herrings.

Third course. Frumenty, venison, glazed meats, fish in aspic, fat capons à la dodine, roasted fish, leschefrites and darioles, reversed eels, crêpes and pipefarces.

40. Another meat dinner:

First course. German broth, cabbages, eel soringue, turnips, beef pasties, joints of meat.

Second course. The best roast to be had, fatted geese à la dodine, freshwater fish, blancmanger, an omelet, Norse pasties, crêpes, larded milk, milk tarts.

Third course. Capon pasties à la dodine, riz engoulé, boar's tail with heated sauce, leschefrites and sugared darioles.

Fourth course. Frumenty, venison, glazed meats, reversed eels, roasted bream and boar's head as entremet.

41. Another meat dinner:

First course. White leeks with capons, goose with pork chines and roast chitterlings, pieces of beef and mutton, a georgié soup of hare, veal, and rabbit.

Second course. Capons, partridges, rabbits, plovers, stuffed pigs, pheasants for lords, fish and meat aspic. Entremet of luce and carp, elevated entremet:[16] swan, peacocks, bitterns, herons, and other things.

The closing. Venison, riz engoulé, capon pasties, cream flans, darioles, reversed eels, fruit, *oublies, estriers,* and clarry.

---

16. Pichon suggests that this deluxe dish may have been placed on a footed platter raised above the main table like a centerpiece. These fancy display dishes appear frequently in manuscript illustrations.

42. Another dinner in 24 dishes in three courses:

First course. Pea coulis, salted eels and herrings, leeks with almonds, joints of meat, yellow soup, *salemine,* saltwater fish, oyster stew [130].

Second course. Roast, freshwater and saltwater fish, Savoy broth [110], larded soup of reversed eels.

Third course. Roasted breams, galantine, stew, pilgrim capons,[17] aspic, decorated blancmanger, poached plaice, turbot *à la soucie* [277], cream darioles, lampreys with hot sauce, glazed meats, riz engoulé, etc.

43. Meat supper[18] in 4 courses:

First course. *Seymé* [128], herbed chicken, soup of verjuice and poultry [111], *espinbesche* [134] of bouli lardé, poached pickerels and loach, mullet, salted *chastelongnes.*

Second course. The best roasts to be had of meat and fish, and bits of venison with parsley and vinegar, fish galantine, white sauce over fish and organ meat.

Third course. Capon pasties, *bécuit* of pike and eels, cos lettuce and an omelet, fish, crêpes and pipefarces.

Fourth course. Aspic, crayfish, poached plaice, bleak[19] and cold sage, numbles with a heated sauce, beef pasties and talemouses.

Pottage as a closing, called a *gellée.*

44. Another meat supper:

First course. Herbed capons, a *comminée* [98, 99], *daguenet* peas,[20] loach in yellow sauce, venison with sops.

Second course. The best roast to be had, aspic, decorated blancmanger, generously sugared cream flans.

Third course. Capon pasties, cold sages, stuffed shoulder of mutton, pickerels in broth, venison in boar's tail sauce, crayfish.

45. Another meat supper:

First course. Three types of pottages: whole capons in white broth, pike chowder [129], venison with sops, topped with loach and sliced eels.

Second course. Roasted capons, rabbits, partridges, plovers, blackbirds, small birds, kid goats, with a blancmanger on top, etc., luce, carp, and bass, etc., reversed eels, pheasants and swans as entremets.

---

17. In Chiquart's *Du fait de cuisine,* recipe no. 45, this dish is made with roast lampreys or eels belted around the capons with dodine sauce. See Elizabeth Cook, translation at http://www.david dfriedman.com/Medieval/Cookbooks/Du_Fait_de_Cuisine/du_fait_de_c_contents.html

18. Supper is usually considered a somewhat lighter meal, with fewer roasts, although these menus do not seem overly light.

19. A kind of fish.

20. Unknown term. BF suggest this is dried peas.

Third course. Venison à la frumenty, dove and lark pasties, tarts, crayfish, fresh herring, fruit, clarry, *nieulles,* medlars, pears, peeled nuts.

46. A fish dinner for Lent:

First course. Cooked apples, roasted large Provençal figs topped with bay leaves, cress and herring with vinegar,[21] pea coulis, salted eels, white herring, thick gravy over fried salt and freshwater fish.

Second course. Carp, luce, sole, mullet, salmon, reversed eels in thick sauce, and an omelet.

Third course. Roasted pimpernels, fried whiting, spiced poached porpoise with frumenty, crêpes and Norse pasties.

The closing. Figs and raisins, hippocras and wafers as above.

47. Another fish dinner:

First course. Pea coulis, vegetable broth, oyster stew, white sauce of pike and perch, a cress porée, herrings, salted whale meat, salted eels, poached loach.

Second course. Fresh and saltwater fish, turbot à la soucie, taillis, bécuit, eels in galantine.

Third course. The most beautiful and best roast [fish] that one can buy, white pasties, *larras,* loach with *waymel* [183], crayfish, perch with parsley and vinegar, tench with sops, aspic.

48. Another fish dinner:

First course. Pea coulis, herrings, porée, salted eels, a pike and carp salemine, and oysters.

Second course. Freshwater fish, eel soringue, Norse pasties and decorated blancmanger, an omelet, pasties, beignets.

Third course. The best roast, riz engoulé, tarts, leschefrites and darioles, salmon and bream pasties, fish chowder.

Fourth course. Taillis, crêpes, pipefarces, water parsnips [161], fried loach,[22] glazed dishes,[23] congers and turbot à la soucie,[24] Lombard tarts, reversed eels.

49. Another fish dinner:

---

21. Terence Scully says this dish, *le soret au vinagre,* is herring soringue in "The Menus of the *Menagier de Paris*," *Le moyen français* 24–25 (1989), 219 n. 9. Yet according to the *Dictionnaire de l'Académie française,* 1st ed. (1694), *saure* (adj.), brownish-yellow, when used with herring was spelled *sor* or *soret* and meant smoked and salted herring. BF suggest this is an herb dish. See ¶ 33 for *harenc sor,* translated as smoked herring, which Scully notes is another variety of soringue.

22. Only in MSS B and C.

23. Middle French: "dorures"; usually these are glazed meats, but as a Lenten dish this must be meatless.

24. MSS A and C have sugar instead of the sauce, but the sauce seems to make more sense for this dish.

First course. Cooked apples, plump figs, Grenache wine, cress and chicken,[25] pea coulis, shad, salted eels, herrings and salted whale meat, white broth over perches, and cuttlefish in a gravé over fritters.

Second course. The best freshwater fish that can be found and saltwater fish, reversed eels, bourreys with heated sauce, tench with sops, crayfish, bream pasties, and poached plaice.

Third course. Porpoise frumenty, Norse pasties and roast mackerel, roasted pimpernels and crêpes, oysters, fried cuttlefish with pickerel bécuit.

50. Another fish dinner:

First course. Pea coulis, herring, salted eels, a black oyster stew, almond soup, a tile, pike, and eel broth, a crétonnée, a green eel soup, silver pasties.

Second course. Salt and freshwater fish, bream and salmon pasties, reversed eels, a brown omelet, tench with bouli lardé, blancmanger, crêpes, lettuces, lozenges, orillettes and Norse pasties, stuffed luce and salmon.

Third course. Porpoise frumenty, glazed meatballs and Spanish peas and Castillian, roasted fish, aspic, lampreys, conger eel and turbot with green sauce, breams with verjuice, leschefrites, darioles and entremets.

Then, dessert, the closing, and boutehors.

Hereinafter follow diverse incidentals likewise appertaining to the same matter:[26]

51. First the preparations that Monseigneur de Lagny made for the dinner he gave in honor of Monseigneur de Paris, the president of the parliament, the king's attorney, his barrister and the other members of his council, amounting to eight platters.[27]

Primo, preparation of tablecloths, tableware and crockery, decorative greenery. To set on the table, ewers and footed *hanaps,*[28] two comfit dishes,[29] silver saltcellars,[30]

---

25. Middle French: "poulez"; this means chicken, but chicken is unlikely to be served for a fish dinner; could be an error for *porée*; also, *pilieux* is wild thyme. See Terence Scully, *The Viandier of Taillevent: An Edition of All Extant Manuscripts* (Ottawa: University of Ottawa Press, 1988): 356.

26. From MS B. This rubric is not in A and C, but we include it to separate the sections.

27. The abbé de Lagny, a member of Parliament, is dining with the bishop of Paris and other dignitaries. Church rules of the fourteenth century forbade ecclesiastics to have extravagant meals of more than soup plus two other courses and entremets, unless there was a very influential guest present who would bring some advantage to the Church. Thus, this elegant meal was justified by the guest list. See BF, n. 182, 34 and Pichon, 2: 104 n. 1. The eight *escuelles/écuelles* (salvers or platters) would indicate a formal dinner for sixteen people, since a platter was shared between two people. At more informal occasions, all diners would share a tureen.

28. A kind of chalice with a lid, of pottery, crystal, or silver ornamented with jewels.

29. Containers for spices and sweetmeats (*dragouers*).

30. Indicative of an elaborate and formal meal, saltcellars were usually costly and made of precious metals.

two-day-old bread, crust removed, used as individual trenchers. For the kitchen: two large pots, two washtubs, and two brooms. *Nota* that Monseigneur de Paris had three squires from his household to serve him, and he was served separately with covered dishes.[31] The president had one squire and was served apart, but not with covered dishes. *Item,* by decree of the president, the king's attorney was seated at table above his barrister.

52. The courses and dishes follow: two half gallons[32] of Grenache wine (that is, a pint for two people, which is too much, for a pint suffices for three, and thus the attendants may have some), hot crisp biscuits, one quartern of red cider apples roasted and topped with white comfits, five quarterns of roasted plump figs, sorrel, cress, and rosemary.

Pottages: a salemine of 6 pike and 6 tench, green porée, a quartern of white herring, 6 freshwater eels salted the day before, and three salted cods soaked for a night. For the pottages: 6 pounds of almonds, half a pound of ginger powder, half an ounce of saffron, 2 ounces minced spices, a quartern of cinnamon powder, half a pound of comfits.

Saltwater fish: sole, gurnard, congers, turbot, salmon. Freshwater fish: luce *fandiz,*[33] two Marne carps *fandisses,* bream.

Entremets: plaice, lamprey in *boue* [185].

Roast (fresh napkins and 16 oranges are appropriate here): porpoise in its sauce, mackerel, sole, bream, shad with a cameline sauce or verjuice, rice topped with fried almonds; one pound sugar for the rice and oranges, little napkins.

For dessert: compote topped with white and red comfits, rissoles, flans, figs, dates, grapes, hazelnuts.

Hippocras and wafers to finish, two half gallons (and this is too much, as is said above) of Grenache wine, 2 hundred oublies and *supplications.* And *nota* that for each platter one takes 8 oublies, 4 supplications, and 4 estriers (and that is generous; the cost per platter is 8 deniers).

Wine and spices are the boutehors.

Next, hand washing, grace, and retiring to the drawing room. Then the servants dine and immediately afterward the wine and spices are offered, and then the guests' departure.

---

31. A precaution against poisoning.

32. In general, we gloss the first occurrence but do not translate units of measure (e.g., septier, queue). However, to avoid confusion in the case of the false cognates *chopine, pinte,* and *quarte,* we offer the modern English equivalents: *chopine,* a "Parisian cup," equals approximately one modern pint; *pinte,* a quart; *quarte,* a half gallon.

33. Unknown word; BF and Pichon do not clarify. It could be an error or a variety of the verb *fondre* (to melt, dissolve, blend), used with glacéed (sugared or buttered) food.

53. The arrangements for the wedding feast that Master Helye will give on a Tuesday in May.[34] A dinner for just twenty platters.[35]

Starters: no butter, because it is a feast day. *Item,* no cherries, because none were available. Because of this, no first course.

Pottages: capons with blancmanger, sprinkled with pomegranates and red comfits.

Roast: on each dish, a quartered kid (a section of kid is better than lamb), a gosling, two spring chickens and sauces for these: orange, cameline, verjuice. Fresh towels and napkins.

Entremets: aspic of crayfish, loach, young rabbits and pig.

Dessert: frumenty and venison.

Closing: hippocras and wafers.

Boutehors: wine and spices.

54. The arrangements for a supper to be held on that day, for 10 platters.

Cold sage of spring chicken halves and goslings prepared in vinegar sauce. And for this same course for this supper, on a plate, a pie of two young rabbits and two peacocks (although some say that there should be darioles served at the wedding feasts of the upper crust), and in another dish, organ meats of kid goats and glazed kids' heads, halved.

Entremets: jelly as above.

Closing: apples and cheese without hippocras, because it is out of season.

Dancing, singing, wine and spices, and torches for lighting.

55. And now to discuss the quantity, appurtenances, and prices of the above-mentioned things: who buys and bargains for them.

From the baker: 10 dozen flat white loaves baked the day before, one denier each. 3 dozen brown trencher breads, half a foot long and 4 fingers wide and high, baked 4 days before—or procure Corbeil bread at the Halles.[36]

Wine cellar: 3 containers of wine.

From the butcher: half a mutton to make sops for the guests and a quarter of bacon fat to lard them; the largest leg bone of beef to cook with the capons, so as to have the broth to make blancmanger; a forequarter of veal to serve in blancmanger for the companions of lower rank;[37] a leg of veal or calves' feet, to prepare broth for the aspic. One square section of venison.

---

34. Master Helye is most likely similar to Master Jehan, a household servant who prepares for the feast but is not the host. The host is later named as Jehan du Chesne.

35. I.e., forty persons.

36. The large public marketplace in Paris (since 1135), where a wide variety of wares and food-stuffs were available.

37. The text calls these folk "the seconds," those of lower rank in the retinue of higher-status persons who would thus be fed a lesser meal. See BF, 319 n. 185, 8–9.

From the oublie maker must be ordered: *primo,* for the bride's service, a dozen and a half cheese-filled waffles, at a cost of 3 sols; a dozen and a half ginger breads, 6 sols; a dozen and a half *portes,* 18 deniers; a dozen and a half estriers, 18 deniers; a hundred sugared *galettes,* 8 deniers. *Item:* this merchant also agreed to provide 20 platters for the wedding dinner and 6 for the servants, at 6 deniers per platter, each having 8 oublies, 4 supplications, and 4 estriers.

From the poulterer: 20 capons at 2 Parisian sols apiece; 5 kid goats, 4 Paris sols; 20 goslings, at 3 Paris sols each; 50 spring chickens, 13 Paris deniers apiece (that is, 40 to be roasted for the dinner, 5 for the aspic, and 5 at supper for the cold sage); 50 young rabbits (that is, 40 roasted for the dinner and 10 for the aspic) at a cost of 20 Paris deniers apiece; a lean pig for the aspic, 4 Paris sols; 12 pairs of pigeons for the supper, at 10 Paris deniers a pair. He is the one you should ask about the venison.

At the Halles: 3 dozen loaves of bread for trenchers; 3 pomegranates for blanc-manger, which will cost . . . ; fifty oranges, which will cost . . . ; 6 new cheeses and one ripe cheese and 3 hundred eggs (that is, each cheese should provide for six tartlets, and you need three eggs for each cheese); sorrel to make verjuice for the chickens; sage and parsley to make the cold sage; 2 hundred blandrell[38] apples; 2 brooms and a pail and some salt.

From the sauce maker: 3 pints of cameline for dinner and a half gallon of sorrel verjuice.

From the spice merchant: 10 pounds of almonds at 14 deniers per pound; 3 pounds of milled wheat, 8 deniers a pound; one pound of powdered Columbine ginger, 11 sols; a quartern of Mecca ginger, 5 sols;[39] a half pound of ground cinnamon, 5 sols; 2 pounds of threshed rice, 2 sols; 2 pounds of lump sugar, 16 sols; one ounce of saffron, 3 sols; a quartern of cloves mixed with grains of paradise, 6 sols; half a quartern of long pepper, 4 sols; half a quartern of galingale, 5 sols; half a quartern of mace, 3 sols and 4 deniers; half a quartern of green bay leaves, 6 deniers; 2 pounds of large and small candles, 3 sols and 4 deniers per pound, which comes to 6 sols 8 deniers; 6 three-pound torches; 6 one-pound flambeaux (at 3 sols a pound, including the 6 deniers per pound that are refunded when the ends are returned). Also from the spicer, spices for the drawing room, namely: 1 pound of candied orange peel, 10 sols; 1 pound of lemons, 12 sols; 1 pound of red anise,

---

38. White.

39. Medieval cookery used three different types of ginger: Mecca, Columbine, and Valadine. Columbine got its name from Kollam on India's west coast; Valadine originally was local to Calcutta. See Andrew Dalby, *Dangerous Tastes: the Story of Spices* (Berkeley: University of California Press, 2000): 24–25. See also John Russell's fifteenth-century *Boke of Nurture,* in Furnivall, *Babees Book,* 129–32, and Scully, *Viandier.* The different gingers will be mentioned in the recipes— Mecca/Mesche ginger has a darker skin and is more tender and more expensive (see 2.5.272).

8 sols; 1 pound of rose-sugar,[40] 10 sols; 3 pounds of white comfits, 10 sols per pound. Also from him, hippocras, 3 half gallons at 10 sols the half gallon; he will procure all of it. The total at this spicery: 12 francs, counting only what was burnt of the torches, and a little was left of the spices; thus half a franc can be allowed per platter.

At the Pierre-au-Lait:[41] a septier[42] of good milk, neither skimmed nor watered, to make frumenty.

In the Place de Grève, a hundred of Burgundy firewood, 13 sols; 2 sacks of coal, 10 sols.

At the Porte-de-Paris: greenery, violets, garlands, a half gallon of white salt, a half gallon of coarse salt, a hundred crayfish, a pint of loach, 2 clay pots—a septier size for the aspic, the other of two half gallons for the cameline.

56. Now we have described: *primo,* the service in general, and second, where the necessary items may be procured. Now it is time, third, to list the stewards and officers responsible for various services.

Primo, a clerk or varlet is needed to purchase greenery, violets, garlands, milk, cheese, eggs, firewood, coal, salt, vats, and washing tubs both for the dining hall and for the pantries, verjuice, vinegar, sorrel, sage, parsley, fresh garlic, 2 brooms, a shovel, and suchlike.

Item, a cook and his assistants, who will cost two francs in wages, not counting their other expenses, but the cook will pay the assistants and porters, and as they say: "the more platters, the more wages."

Item, two servers, one who will cut the crust from the bread and make trenchers and saltcellars of bread; they will carry the salt and the bread and the trenchers to the tables. At the end of the meal, they will bear through the hall two or three large containers in which to toss the large scraps, such as sops, cut or broken bread, trenchers, meat, and similar things; as well as two buckets for disposing of and collecting the remnants of soup, sauces, and liquids.

Item, one or two water servers are needed.

Item, big, strong ushers to guard the door.

Item, two kitchen stewards and two aides for the service of the kitchen, one of whom shall be sent to bargain for the kitchen supplies, pastry, and linen for 6 tables. For 20 platters, you require two large copper pots, two cooking pans, 4 vessels for table scraps, a mortar and a pestle, 6 large cloths for the kitchen, three large earthenware jugs for wine, a large clay pot for pottage, 4 wooden basins and spoons, an iron pan, four large pots with handles, 2 tripods and an iron spoon.

---

40. Rosewater-flavored sweetmeat.
41. Milk market.
42. The sixth part, approximately one gallon.

This servant will also bargain for the pewter vessels; namely, 10 dozen platters, 6 dozen small plates, two and a half dozen large plates, 8 half-gallon-sized vessels, 2 dozen quart-sized vessels,[43] two alms dishes.

Item, concerning the inn: know that the hôtel de Beauvais cost Jehan du Chesne 4 francs; tables, trestles, chairs *et similia,*[44] 5 francs; and the floral decorations cost him 15 francs.

The other kitchen steward or his helper will accompany the cook to the butcher, the poulterer, the spicer, etc., to haggle for and choose the supplies and arrange and pay for delivery. They will have a coffer that locks, in which they will keep the spices etc., distributing them reasonably and in moderation. Afterward, they or their helpers will collect the unused spices and put them all in baskets in a locked coffer for safekeeping, to prevent waste and excess by the servants.

Two other stewards, needed for the service of the dining hall, will distribute and collect spoons, pass out the hanaps, pour whatever wine each guest requests, and collect the tableware.

Two other stewards are needed for the wine cellar, to carry wine to the sideboard, the tables, and elsewhere, and they shall have a varlet to draw the wine.

Two of the most honest and skilled servants will attend the bridegroom and go with him to the dishes.

Two butlers must see that the courses are served and removed in order; one should arrange the seating of the guests; and two servants for each table, to serve, clear the table, place the scraps into the baskets and the sauces and soups into the buckets and pails, and bring the table scraps to the kitchen squires or others designated to take care of them. They are not to carry anything else to any other place.

The main butler's office is to prepare saltcellars for the high table; 4 dozen hanaps; 4 covered golden goblets; 6 ewers; 4 dozen silver spoons; 4 silver half-gallon vessels; 2 alms dishes; 2 comfit dishes.

Item, a florist, who will deliver garlands on the wedding day and on the day after.[45]

The serving women's responsibility is to furnish tapestries, to supervise the order of their hanging, and in particular to decorate the wedding chamber and the bed that will be blessed.

A laundress for braiding.[46]

And *nota* that if the bed is covered with cloth, a coverlet of miniver is necessary; but not if it is covered with serge, embroidery, or a sandal silk counterpane.

---

43. These may be drinking vessels, tankards.
44. Latin: "and similar items."
45. The "jour de regard," on which a feast was usually given by the couple's parents.
46. A kind of clothing decoration.

57. The arrangements for the Hantecourt wedding, for 20 platters, in the month of September.

Starter: Grapes and peaches or little pies.

Pottages: Stew, 4 hares and veal; or for blancmanger, 20 capons, 2 sols 4 deniers apiece, or chickens.

Roast: 5 pigs; 20 young capons, 2 sols 4 deniers apiece; 40 partridges, 2 sols 4 deniers apiece; *morteruel* or . . .

For the aspic: 10 chickens, 12 deniers; 10 young rabbits, one pig; 150 crayfish.

Frumenty, venison, pears and nuts (*nota* that 3 hundred eggs are needed for the frumenty), tartlets and other things.

Hippocras and wafers.

Wine and spices.

58. Supper

Gravé of 12 dozen small birds or 10 ducks, or fresh venison bouli lardé.

Pasties of 40 young hares, 20 spring chickens, 40 pigeons; 40 darioles or 60 tartlets.

Nota that three small birds per platter is enough. Nonetheless, when one has capon gizzards *vel similia*,[47] one places three small birds and half a gizzard on each platter.

59. The quantity of the things stated above:

From the baker: *ut supra*[48] concerning the preceding wedding feast.

From the pastry maker: *ut supra*.

Wine cellar: *ut supra*.

From the butcher, 3 quarters of mutton to make the sops for the guests, a quarter of bacon for larding, a forequarter of veal for the blancmanger, venison for the servants.

From the oublie maker: a dozen and a half cheese-stuffed wafers (that is, made of fine wheat flour kneaded with eggs and strips of cheese placed inside) and 18 other wafers kneaded with eggs but without cheese. *Item*, a dozen and a half ginger breads (that is, flour kneaded with eggs beaten together with ginger powder and placed in a mold the size of a sausage and then set between two irons on the fire). *Item*, a dozen and a half other breads and as many biscuits.

Item, for the previously mentioned party on the day after the wedding, it is necessary to send, over and above the oublie maker's goods, 50 blandrell apples, the garlands, and the minstrels. *Item*, have the oublie maker provide for this wedding day the same dishes *ut supra* the preceding wedding.

From the poulterer: the roasts, poultry, and venison, *ut supra*.

---

47. Latin: "or the like."
48. Latin: "as above."

At the Halles and the Porte-de-Paris: the suitable things, *ut supra.*

From the sauce maker: a half gallon of cameline for the dinner and supper, two half gallons of mustard.

From the spicer: aromatic spices for the chamber: comfits, rose-sugar, sugared nuts, lemon and manus-christi,[49] 4 pounds in all. *Item,* hippocras. Kitchen spices: one pound white powder, half a pound fine powder, half a pound cinnamon powder for blancmanger, 2 ounces of small spices, 3 pounds lump sugar, 3 pomegranates; half a pound white and red comfits, 6 pounds almonds, one pound rice flour, a half gallon of hulled wheat.

From the candle maker: torches and flambeaux were bought at 3 sols the pound, and 2 sols 6 deniers refunded on the return of the ends.

Item, as for the renting of linen, it is needed for 6 tables: 3 large copper pots for 16 dozen platters, 2 cooking pots, 4 containers for table scraps, a mortar and a pestle, 6 large cloths for the kitchen, 3 large clay jugs for wine, a large clay pot for pottage, 4 wooden basins and spoons, an iron pan, 4 large pots with handles, 2 trivets, a pierced iron spoon; for this 56 Paris sols. Pewter dishes: 10 dozen platters, 6 dozen small plates, 2 and a half dozen large plates, 8 half-gallon-sized and 2 dozen quart-sized vessels, 2 alms dishes. For all this: 16 Paris sols.

In the Place de Grève *ut supra* for the other wedding.

Nota that because the couple were widowed, they were wedded in the early morning in their black robes and then donned others.

60. *Nota* the extraordinary expenditures for Jehan du Chesne's wedding: 4 and a half francs for the cook, 1 franc for the helpers and porters (5 and a half francs in all); 4 francs for the concierge of Beauvais; 5 francs for trestles *et similia;* for tables, 4 francs, 15 francs for the garland maker; 20 sols for water; 8 francs for the minstrels, not counting the spoons and other gratuities (and they will do the party for the day after the wedding as well as the other entertainments); 2 francs for sergeants, 8 sols for greenery, 10 francs for flambeaux and torches, 7 francs for kitchen crockery, cloths, towels, and glasses, 4 francs for pewter pots.

---

49. A kind of sweetmeat; for a recipe see Thomas Dawson, *The Good Housewife's Jewell* (London, 1596), http://www.harvestfields.ca/CookBooks/003/07/00.htm.

¶ 2.5 *Recipes*

This is now the place to explain the preparation of the foods named in the above menus.

1. But *primo* you must know several general terms, and you will be able to assemble a complete list by adding others that are here and there throughout this book, that is, regarding the thickener for all pottages,[1] such as bread, eggs, starch, flour, etc.

2. *Item,* to prevent your pottage from burning, you must stir down to the bottom of the pot and watch that the burning logs do not touch the pot. If it has already begun to burn, immediately switch it into another pot. *Item,* to keep milk from turning. *Item,* so that the pot does not boil over onto the fire.

3. You must put well-ground, and not strained, spices into pottage, and only at the last moment. In sauces and in aspic, *secus.*[2]

4. Know your spices, as explained previous to this fifth article.

5. *Item,* to kill pigs. It is said that the season males should be slaughtered is the month of November, and the females in December, as for example when people say "February hens."

6. *Item,* to make boudin,[3] collect the blood of a pig in a suitable basin or pan. When the pig has been butchered and the haslet[4] washed thoroughly and set to cook, while it is cooking, remove the clots of blood from the bottom of the basin and discard them. Next, mix peeled and minced onions, about half the amount as there is blood, with about half as much *entrecerele*—that is, the fat found between the intestines—minced as small as dice. Add some ground salt, and stir the mixture into the blood. Grind together ginger, cloves, and a little pepper. Take the small intestines, wash them well, turn them inside out, and rinse well in running water. To remove the odor, place them in a pan on the fire and stir; then add salt, and do it a second and a 3rd time and then wash them. Turn them, this time outer side out, wash them, and set them to dry on a towel, rubbing and wringing them to remove moisture. (What are called the entrecerele are the large intestines, which have fat inside that is pulled out with a knife.) After you have measured and put in equal portions and quantities (half as much onions as blood and

---

1. Pottages range from thin soups to stews or porridges.
2. Latin: "the contrary."
3. Blood sausage.
4. Pork viscera, defined in ¶ 12.

a quarter as much fat), and when your boudins[5] have been filled with this mixture, cook them in a pan with the haslet broth, and prick them with a pin when they swell; otherwise they will burst. *Nota* that the blood keeps well for two, indeed even 3, days, once the spices are added. Some may use as spices pennyroyal, savory, hyssop, and marjoram, gathered when they are in flower and then dried and ground. As for the haslet, put it in a copper pot to cook on the fire, whole and without salt, and skim the pot along the edges, for haslet will foam. When it is cooked, take it out and save it to make pottage.

To make liver boudin. Take two pieces of liver, two pieces of lung, a piece of fat and put it in an intestine along with some blood, and for the rest do as above.

Nota that good boudin can be made with goose blood, provided that the goose is thin, for thin geese have larger intestines than fat ones.

Queritur: how are the intestines turned inside out to be washed? *Responsio*[6]: by a linen thread and a brass wire[7] as long as a gauger's[8] rod.

7. *Nota* that some folks hang their pigs during the Easter season and the air yellows them; for this reason it is best to keep them in salt as they do in Picardy, although it seems that the flesh is then not as firm. Nonetheless, it is much nicer to serve fair and white lard than yellow, for no matter how good the yellow is, its unappealing color condemns it and discourages its use.

8. To make andouille sausage. *Nota* that andouille sausages are made from rectal guts and other large intestines, which are stuffed full of the other entrails to make sausage. These small intestines, when you want to put them in andouille sausages, are split lengthwise into 4 parts. *Item,* you can make andouille from thinly sliced stomach. *Item,* from the meat beneath the ribs. *Item,* from sweetbreads and other things that are around the "small haste"[9] when you do not wish to use the small haste intact. But first these entrails are deodorized in a pot with salt two or three times, as described above for boudin. The other things explained above, that is, the lower and other guts that must be filled to make andouille sausage, are first pricked and sprinkled with a half ounce of powdered pepper and a sixth of fennel, ground, with a dash of finely ground salt sparingly added to the spices. When each andouille is thus stuffed and filled, you place them to be preserved in salt with lard, on top of the lard.

9. Freshly salted ribs, roasted on the grill.

---

5. The intestines are used as sausage casings.

6. Latin: "Question"; "Response."

7. "Brass" is reading from MS B in hand of corrector, noted in BF as B², which says *fil d'archal* (brass or copper wire), a reading Pichon uses, as does BF/Ueltschi. BF have *arichat* but indicate it is a misreading.

8. Weights and measures official.

9. Spleen; see ¶ 12.

10. Chines and hams are salted 3 days and nights with peas.

11. *Nota* that if a ham is cured for a long time in salt, such as for a month, you must soak it in cold water the evening before, and the next day scrape it and wash it in hot water before cooking it; *primo*, cook in water and wine, then throw out this first liquid and cook it in fresh water.

12. Hereafter follow the names of all the parts of a pig, which are sold at the tripe shop for seven blancs.[10]

Primo, when the pig is butchered, the blood and clots come out first, and if you choose you can make boudin from them. *Item*, the viscera include: *primo* the fat, *secundo* the small haste, 3rd the offal. The fat is that fat between the intestines and the small haste; the haslet are the liver, the lungs, the heart, and the tongue; the small haste is the spleen, and to this is tightly connected half of the liver and the kidneys; the other half of the liver is connected to the entrails between the lungs and the heart. The offal are the bowels called the entrecerele of the intestines, and these include the small intestines from which boudin and sausages are made, and also the stomach.

13. The viscera of sheep include the stomach and the rennet stomach, the 4 feet and the head, and it all costs two parisis at the tripe shop.

14. The entrails extracted from calves includes the head and the innards, the belly and the 4 feet and costs two blancs at the tripe shop. *Nota*, the innards are the rennet stomach, the belly, and the bowels, which the tripe merchants sell cleaned, washed, and prepared, soaked in clear, clean water. But those who purchase them do not rely only on the tripe seller to prepare this material for them. Rather they themselves wash the stuff in hot water 2 or 3 times and then wash them out again with salt, putting it all to cook in water without salt until the water boils off, then adding some mutton broth. Put herbs, some of the cooking water, and saffron on a platter with these innards, eating them like tripe with salt and verjuice.

15. *Nota* here the great variety of terms: what one calls viscera of a pig are liver, lungs, and heart; what one calls the viscera of sheep are the head, the stomach, the rennet stomach, and the 4 feet; and what we call the viscera of a calf are the head, the guts, the stomach, and the 4 feet; and what we call the viscera of a cow are the stomach, the omasum, the rennet stomach,[11] the spleen, the lungs, and the liver and the four feet. And for venison, different parts, different names. *Queritur* the cause of this diversity concerning this one word "viscera."

16. Venison of stag or any other. If you wish to salt it in the summer, you must

---

10. A small coin.

11. Middle French: "panse, saultier, franche mule"; modern English: rumen, reticulum, omasum. These are three of the cow's four stomachs.

salt it in a washtub or a bathtub with coarsely ground salt and then dry it in the sun. The croup, *id est,* the hindquarters, that has been salted must be boiled first in water with wine to remove the salt. Then throw away the water and wine and set it to finish cooking in meat broth with turnips. Serve the venison on a platter sliced thinly, with its broth. *Item,* if you have young, small turnips, cook them in water without wine for the first boiling, then throw away that water and continue cooking them in water and wine with chestnuts—or if there are no chestnuts, use sage. Serve as above.

17. In June and July, salted beef and mutton pieces should be well boiled in water with scallions and salted from morning to evening, or a day at most.

18. The butchers of Paris hold that, according to their way of speaking, a cow has only 4 principal members: that is, the two shoulders and the two thighs, and the front and back of the body.[12] The shoulders and thighs being removed, the cow is split from the side, making one piece of the front and another of the rear. In this manner the cow's carcass is transported to the market stall, if the cow is small or medium-sized. But if it is large, the front quarters would be split down the back, and the hind piece also, to be carried more easily. Thus we now have 6 pieces of beef, of which the two briskets are removed first, and then the two plates underneath that hold them, which are three good feet long and a half foot wide, coming from below and not from above. And then the front quarter is cut, and next the sirloin, which is hardly more than 2 or 3 fingers thick. Then the tenderloin, which is closest to the spine, as thick as a large fist. Next, the cut called the numbles, which is a good foot long and no more and stretches from the neck at one end to the kidney. This section belongs rightfully to the one who holds the cow's feet during the skinning. He sells it in a small stall that is below the Grande-Boucherie, and it is of little value. *Item,* according to the size of the cows, they are cut into more or fewer portions and sold at the Porte de Paris. I don't know how the bourgeois' tally can justly proportion itself in measure with the butchers'. For one good cow costs 20 pounds, but another costs only 12. *Item,* the beef extractions cost 8 sols at the tripe shop—that is, the viscera, in which are the belly, the omasum, the rennet stomach, the spleen, the lungs, the liver, and the 4 feet.

19. *Item,* in Béziers, as of the feast of St. Andrew,[13] which is before Christmas, sheep are salted in quarters, by rubbing and rerubbing more and more, and then placing the quarters one upon another for 8 days and then setting them in the fireplace.

20. If you want to salt beef or mutton flesh in the winter, use coarse salt. Dry

---

12. Pichon (2: 130–31, 105) details the various parts of the cow, derived from the *Délices de la campagne* of Nicholas de Bonnefons, chamberlain of the king (c. 1653).

13. November 30.

the meat very well in the pan, then grind it finely and salt it. *Nota* that in June and July mutton must be soaked before salting.

21. Salted beef tongue. In the proper season for salting, take a quantity of beef tongues and boil them a little; then scrape and peel them. Salt them one atop the other and leave them in salt for 8 or 9 days. Then hang them in the chimney and leave them there for the winter. After that, hang them in a dry place for one or 2 or 3 years.

22. Goose must be salted for 3 days and nights.

23. Coot salted for 2 days are good with cabbage. Wood pigeons also; *nota* that they return every 3 years.

24. If a hare is caught 15 days or three weeks before Easter, or at another time when you want to preserve it, split it and remove the entrails; then slit the skin on the head, tear it, and make an opening in the head to remove the brain. Fill that cavity with salt and sew up the skin. It will keep for a month if it is hung by the ears.

25. *Nota* that one of the best morsels or prime pieces of beef, whether for roasting or for stewing, is the noyau. And *nota* that the noyau of beef is the piece below the neck and shoulders. Additionally, this piece is supremely good sliced and put in pasties. After the pasty is cooked, pour on some lamprey sauce.

26. Eel. Let it die in salt and leave it there for 3 entire days and nights. Then scald it and remove the slime; cut it in slices and salt it, then boil in water with scallions. If, instead, you want to salt it from Vespers until the morning, skim off the foam and gut the eel, then cut it into slices and salt it, rubbing each slice well with coarse salt. And if you wish to expedite it even more, grind some salt and rub the cut sides of the pieces and toss it in salt between two bowls. Cook as above and eat with mustard.

27. Herring *caqué*[14] should be soaked in a large quantity of fresh water for 3 days and 3 nights. At the end of 3 days, the herring need to be washed and the water changed; then soak for another 2 days, changing the water twice each day. Some herrings, due to their nature or small size, require less soaking than others.

28. Smoked herring. Good smoked herring is thin with a thick back, round and green, while the inferior kind is fat and yellow or has a flat and dry back.

Ordinary pottages, unthickened and without spices:

29. *Primo,* old pea pottage. First you must sort and cull the peas and find out from the people of that region the nature of the peas. (For peas commonly do not cook in well water; and in some places they cook just fine in spring water or

---

14. A *caque* is a small barrel; the verb *caquer,* "to barrel," means to salt and put into small barrels—thus, salted and barreled herring.

river water, as in Paris, yet in others they do not cook in spring or river water, as in Béziers.) Once you know the character of the regional peas, wash them in warm water, then put them in a pot of water on the fire and boil them till they burst. Drain off the stock and set it aside; refill the pot of peas with warm water. Set it on the fire to boil, and drain off the cooking water a second time, if you want to have more stock. Then put them back on the fire without water, for they will release enough and will cook in that. Do not put the spoon into the pot once they have been drained, but instead shake the pot and the peas together and little by little add warm or fairly hot water, certainly not cold, and bring them to a boil and cook them thoroughly before you add anything other than hot water, whether meat or something else. Do not include salt or bacon fat or a seasoning until they are fully cooked. You can add bacon stock or meat stock, but do not salt or stir with the spoon until they are well cooked. Nonetheless you can swirl them around in the pot.

On a meat day, after the peas have been drained, enhance the dish with bacon or meat broth, adding it when they are nearly cooked. When you remove the bacon from the peas, rinse it in meat broth, so that it will be more attractive when set in thin slices on the meat and not appear encrusted with peas.

On a fish day, while the peas are cooking, have a pot of onions cooking for just as long and, as with the bacon stock, add the onion broth to the peas and serve them. In a similar way on a fish day, when you have put the peas on the fire in a pot, put the sliced onions separately in another pot, and use the onion water to add to the peas; and when all is cooked, fry the onions and mix half of them into the peas and add the other half to the broth, which is mentioned below, and then some salt. If on this fish day or in Lent there is salted whale meat, substitute it for the bacon used on a meat day.

30. As for new peas,[15] sometimes they are cooked on a meat day with meat stock, with minced parsley to make green pottage for a meat day; and on a fish day, they are cooked in milk with ginger and saffron; and sometimes for a crétonnée, as will be explained below [95].

31. With all these peas, whether old or new, you can make a thin strong coulis using a flour sieve, straining cloth, or sackcloth; but you must yellow old peas with ground saffron. The saffron water should boil the peas, and the saffron is cooked with the pea stock.

32. There are other peas that are prepared in their pods with bacon added.

33. *Item*, new pea crétonnée, you will find in the next chapter.

34. On a meat day, you need not worry about the pea stock. On a fish day and

---

15. Not the young tender peas we now call "new," but mature, starchy peas (or beans), probably picked fresh.

in Lent, fry onions as is spoken of above, and mix the fried onions and the oil in which they were fried with breadcrumbs, ginger, cloves, and grains of paradise that have been ground and moistened with vinegar and wine. You then add a little saffron; then prepare sops in the bowl.

Item, with the stock you can make a stew on a fish day; so do not stir it at all, and remove it quickly from the fire and put it into another pot. *Item,* thin a chard purée with the stock, and this will make a very good Lenten pottage, provided that you do not add any other water.

35. *Nota* that all pottages on the fire will overflow and spill over onto the fire until you add salt and fat to the pot, and then they will not.

36. *Item, nota* that the best bouillon is from beef cheeks washed in hot water 2 or three times, then boiled and well skimmed.

37. *Nota,* if you notice that your pottage is burning, add some liquid (it burns because it is too thick) and stir constantly whatever is burning in the bottom of the pot before you add anything else. Before your pottage sticks to the pan and burns, and so that it does not scorch, stir it often, scraping your spoon on the bottom to keep the pottage from sticking. Keep in mind that peas or beans rarely stick to the pan if the burning logs do not touch the bottom of the pot while it is over the fire.

38. Here is how onions are cooked: boil in water quite a while before adding the peas, and in such a way that the water completely evaporates. Then you add the pea stock to complete the cooking and remove the taste of the water.

39. Similarly, oysters are first washed in warm water, then boiled so that their flavor remains in the stock, but they are not skimmed. Then remove the oysters and fry them, if you wish, and place some of them in the bowls and with the rest make another dish.

40. Old beans that are to be cooked in their pods must be soaked and placed on the fire in a pot the evening before and left all night. Then toss out the water, add clean water, and cook them. Drain as for peas to remove that first strong flavor; then boil in meat stock with lard, as is described above in the pea stock recipe, or on a fish day use fresh water, adding afterward some oil. Or cook in onion stock, with the onions, and if you want to make a coulis, do as with the peas.

Item, beans are shelled in this way at Easter: you must sort and wash them, but not soak them. Place the beans in their shells in water to simmer on the fire, and let them boil until the shell wrinkles and bursts. Then push them to the back of the fire and scoop them up with a spoon. Skin and shell them one spoonful at a time while they are hot, then bathe them in cold water. After this wash them in warm water as for peas and cook in cold water, and when they have boiled until they split, pour off the liquid and fill the pot with meat stock if it is a meat day, or another liquid if it is a fish day. Season the beans with oil and well-cooked onions, then fry, or dress them with butter. They can be made green again using fresh ground-up bean leaves, soaked in hot water and strained. Next proceed as with the other peas, either with bacon on a meat day or as on a fish day.

41. *Item,* crétonnée of new beans is prepared as you find in the next chapter.

42. *Item,* if you care to eat beans all year that have the scent and flavor of new beans: plant beans each month, and take a handful of the most tender as they grow up from the soil, grind them, and add them to your other beans. The beans will lighten and will have the color and flavor of new beans.

43. *Item,* new beans must first be cooked until they split, then drained, and afterward in their stock boil large sops of brown bread, two fingers thick; then put in each bowl of beans two of these sops and add salt.

Item, once the beans have split and are strained, they can be fried in bacon grease, then sprinkled lightly with spices.

44. You can recognize bog beans because they are flat, whereas field beans are round. *Item,* they are soft to the tooth, and their pod is tender, unlike the others.

45. *Item,* if you want to shell new beans, you must first cut them lengthwise with a knife, and once everything is cut, peel them by hand.

46. *Nota,* in August one begins to eat coulis of beans and peas with salted meat.

47. *Nota* that a ham must be salted for three days and nights, and then it is at its best.

48. *Nota* also, regarding beans and peas, that crétonée of beans and peas is in the chapter on thick pottages.

49. Porée. Cooks designate three kinds of porée: white porée, green porée, and black porée.

50. White porée is so named because it is made from the white of leeks, pork chine, andouille or ham, in autumn or winter for a meat day. Understand that no other fat besides pork tastes right in it. First, you select, mince, wash, and blanch the leeks—that is, in summertime when the leeks are young, but in the winter when the leeks are older and tougher, they should be boiled instead of just blanched. On a fish day, after doing all that, place them in a pot of hot water, and cook them thus. Likewise, cook minced onions and then fry them. Next, fry the leeks with those onions, then mix together to stew in a pot, with cow's milk if it is a meat day. On a fish day and during Lent, use almond milk. If it is a meat day, when the leeks are blanched in summer, or boiled in the winter, as explained, set them to cook in a pot of salted meat or pork stock and add lard. *Nota,* this leek porée is sometimes thickened with bread.

Item, white porée of chard is made as above, in a stock of mutton and beef, but not with pork; and on a fish day with milk, from almonds or cows.

Item, garden cress during Lent with almond milk. Take the cress and set it to boil with a handful of chopped chard, and then fry it all in oil. Then boil it in almond milk. When meat is allowed, fry it in lard and butter until done, then moisten with meat broth or with cheese, and serve immediately; otherwise it will scorch. However, should you decide to add parsley to it, do not blanch the parsley first.

A variety of greens called spinach has longer leaves, thinner and greener than the ordinary porée. It can also be called *epinoche*,[16] and it is eaten at the beginning of Lent. To cook this, select the new and tender leaves and pick over them, removing the large ribs as one does for cabbage. Without chopping, put the porée in a simmering pot of clear water or broth, with salt. Serve by pouring olive oil or verjuice into the bowl, but no parsley. Sometimes, and most frequently, you fry the spinach, completely raw, and when well fried, add a little water as you do for sops with oil.

Another porée of new chard. Either quickly blanched in the summer when young, or boiled in winter for older greens, depending upon their age. Porée of chard that has been washed then cut up and boiled stays greener than that which is first boiled and then chopped. But still greener and better is that which has been sorted, then washed and cut up very small, then blanched in cold water. You then change the water and soak it all in the fresh water. Then squeeze out the water and shape the greens into little balls and boil in a pot with bouillon of bacon fat and mutton stock. When it has boiled a little and you are ready to serve it, add some parsley, carefully picked, washed, and minced, with a little bit of young fennel, and bring it to a boil once only. Everything considered, the less you boil porée, the greener it stays. Parsley should not be boiled, or for only the briefest time, for in boiling it loses its flavor.

51. Green porée on a fish day. Sort, cut up, and wash the greens in cold water without boiling, then cook with verjuice and a little water, and add some salt, then serve it boiling hot and very thick, without liquid. In the bottom of the serving bowl, underneath the porée, put salted or fresh butter, or cheese, or old verjuice.

Porée of cabbage sprouts is in season from January until Easter and even later.

And *nota* that when preparing porée with almond milk, the milk must not be passed through a sieve, although you do sieve it for some other pottages, and to drink.

52. Black porée is made including slices of grilled salted bacon. Namely, the porée is sorted, washed, then cut up and blanched in boiling water, then fried in bacon fat; then thinned with simmering water. Some say that if it is washed in cold water, it will be blacker and uglier. To serve, place two pieces of bacon on each platter.

---

16. As well as *espinars*.

53. There are five types of cabbage. The best are those that have been touched by the frost; they are tender and cook quickly; and in frosty weather they must not be boiled, although in rainy weather they should be. And this list begins with these because they are the first to grow in the year, *scilicet* from April, and then it proceeds in order, descending toward vine harvest, Christmas, and then Easter.

White cabbages come at the end of August. Cabbage heads are ready at the end of the vine harvest.[17] And after you pick the head of cabbage from the center of the plant, pull up the rest of the cabbage plant and transplant it to new soil, and from it will grow big leaves that spread out. Cabbage takes a lot of space, and such cabbages are called Roman cabbages and are eaten in the winter. If the stumps are replanted, little cabbages called sprouts develop; they are eaten with raw herbs in vinegar. If they are plentiful, they are tasty when sorted, washed in warm water, and boiled whole in a little water. When they are cooked, add some salt and oil and serve them very thick, without broth. In Lent, drizzle olive oil over them. Other cabbages are called Easter cabbages, because they are eaten at Easter time, yet they are sown in August. After these have grown up half a foot, uproot them and transplant them elsewhere. They need to be watered frequently. Indeed, all the cabbages spoken of above are first sown, then transplanted when they are about half a foot in height.

And first concerning cabbage heads, you need to know that once the leaves are stripped off, picked over, and chopped, they need to be boiled very well and long—longer than the other cabbages. The green leaves of Roman cabbages need to be torn into pieces and the yellow, that is the rib or veins, crushed in a mortar; then all blanched together in hot water, then drained well and put in a pot of warm water, if you do not have enough meat bouillon. Serve with the fattiest meat stock. Some cooks add ground bread.

Also recognize that cabbages must be put on the fire quite early in the morning and cooked for a stretch of time, much longer than any other pottage, and over a robust fire. All varieties of cabbage—heads or leaves—should be soaked in beef fat, and no other sort, except for sprouts. Note also that stock of beef and mutton is proper, never pork stock, which is good only with leeks.

If you prepare cabbage on a fish day, boil it, cook it in warm water, and add oil and salt. *Item,* some add meal. *Item,* instead of oil, some put butter in. On a meat day you might add pigeons, sausages and hare, coots and plenty of bacon.

54. Turnips are firm and difficult to cook until they have been through the cold and frost. Cut off the head and tail and other whiskery rootlets or roots. After peeling them, wash in two or three changes of good, hot water; then cook them

---

17. Cabbage was raised both as leaves and as heads, the former seem more predominant. Scully and Scully, *Early French Cookery,* 264.

in steaming meat stock of either pork, beef, or mutton. *Item,* in Beauce after cooking them, they slice them up and fry them in a pan and sprinkle them with spices.

55. Little delicacies. Take gizzards and livers and cook them in wine and water —first the gizzards and afterward the livers. Then place in a dish with minced parsley and pour vinegar over them. *Item,* the feet of beef, mutton, and kid.[18]

56. *Gramose* is made with the household's cold meat left over from dinner and with stock made from this leftover meat, in the following manner: *Primo,* beat 4 or 6 eggs (both yolk and white) until they reach the consistency of water, for otherwise they will curdle; add the same amount of verjuice as eggs, and boil it with meat stock. While it cooks, cut the meat into thin slices and put 2 pieces in a bowl. Then pour the soup over it.

57. Impromptu sops. Take parsley and fry it in butter, then pour boiling water over it and bring it all to a boil. Add salt, and prepare sops as with any vegetable stock.

Aliter,[19] if you have cold beef, slice it thinly and then grind a little bread moistened with verjuice and strain through cloth and set it in a dish and sprinkle it with powdered spices. Warm it over the coals. It serves three.

Aliter, on a fish day, simmer some almonds in water; then peel and grind them, moistening with warm water. Strain them and boil them with ginger powder and saffron. Serve with a slice of fried fish in each dish.

Aliter, on a meat day, take broth from the meat cauldron and bread soaked in degreased meat broth, then grind it with 6 eggs, strain, and put in a pot with fatty stock, spices, verjuice, vinegar, and saffron. Bring it to a boil once and serve in bowls.

Item. If you are in a hurry and should you find meat bouillon at an inn and decide to make pottage with it, add spices and bring it to a boil, then trickle in beaten eggs and serve.

Aliter, on a fish day, grind some bread and soak it in water, verjuice, and vinegar; set it on the fire. When it simmers, take it off the fire and add egg yolks. Replace it on the fire and warm it at low heat until it comes to a boil; add powdered spices and make your sops.

Aliter, boil a little bacon in a pot. When it is half done, slice a fresh mackerel and cook it with the bacon. Remove it from the fire and add minced parsley, then bring to a brisk boil and serve.

58. How to recognize a good cheese. Good cheese has six qualities: *Non Argus, nec Helena, nec Maria Magdalena, sed Lazarus, et Martinus, respondens pontifici:*[20]

---

18. Scully and Scully (84) explain that *menuz de piez* (little feet) describes meat delicacies such as gizzards, livers, etc. Here the "feet" of the three animals may be their internal organs.

19. Latin: "alternatively."

20. This mnemonic on assessing the quality of cheese is discussed in Pichon, 2: 146 n. 4.

Not white like Helen,
Nor weeping, like Magdalen,
Not like Argus, but rather all blind,
And also heavy as an ox.
It stands up to the thumb's pressure,
And it should have a scaly rind.
Eyeless and tearless, and not white,
Crusted, firm, and heavy.

59. In July, fresh pork ham cooked in saffroned stock and grain verjuice, with a little ginger and some bread, served with sauce *râppée* [294]. *Item,* at supper, either beef or mutton meat, salted in the morning, cooked in water and scallions.

60. To new peas cooked and eaten in the pod, on a meat day, add some lard. On a fish day, once the peas are cooked, drain and put melted salted butter on top and stir.

Other clear pottages, with spices:

61. *Primo, nota* that all spices for pottages must be well ground and not sieved, except those for an aspic. For all pottages, add the spices as late in the cooking as you can, for the sooner they are put in, the more they lose their flavor. Any bread-crumbs used should be sieved.

62. Pottage for a fish day, *vide pagina proxima precedente.*[21] *Aliter,* take scalded, peeled, and ground almonds mixed into warm water, boil with fine powdered spices and saffron, and in each dish place half a fried sole and pour the pottage over it.

63. Squash. Peel off the skin, for it is the best part. Nevertheless, if you wish to use the inside, remove the seeds, although the skin is better alone.[22] Next you must cut the squash rinds into pieces; boil, then mince well. Cook in beef fat. At the very end, yellow it with saffron, or toss on threads of saffron, one by one, which is what cooks call *frangié.*

64. *Hericot* of mutton. Cut meat into small pieces, bring to a boil, then fry it in bacon fat with cooked onions sliced thinly; thin with beef bouillon. Add mace, parsley, hyssop, and sage and simmer.

65. *Item,* mutton pie in a pot. Take some meat from a leg of lamb, grease or marrow of beef or veal, chopped finely, and minced onions. Boil together in a well-covered pot, with a small amount of meat bouillon or other stock. Put spices in to boil with a little vinegar to sharpen it, then serve on a dish.

---

21. Latin: "see preceeding page."

22. Prior to the introduction of new varieties of squash from the Americas, European *courges* were gourds harvested and eaten at an immature stage when their rind was fleshy, resembling a zucchini; the inside of the immature fruit was not usually eaten.

66. *Item,* if you wish to salt mutton in hot weather, first soak it and then sprinkle it with crushed coarse salt.

67. Auxerre-style mutton. Cut the lamb into pieces; wash and cook in water. Then grind a lot of parsley and some bread, strain, and place into the pot with spices.

68. Mutton with yellow sauce. Cut the meat—it must be flank—into pieces when completely raw. Cook it in water, then grind in a piece of ginger and some saffron and thin it with verjuice, wine, and vinegar.

69. Tripe in yellow sauce. When cooking tripe, do not add salt while cooking, because it will darken it. *Item,* the feet, tail, and rennet stomach, which are black, must be cooked separately from the stomach and other light-colored organs.

70. Leg of beef in yellow sauce must be stewed for quite a while. If you wish, boil well with a chicken killed one or two days before, with herbs, and then add saffron.

71. Gosling pottage. Boil the gosling until well done and then fry it. Next grind ginger, clove, grain of paradise and long pepper, parsley, and a little sage. Stir together with meat or gosling stock and add grated cheese. In each bowl serve three pieces of gosling.

72. Capon soup. Cook the capons in water and wine, then cut into pieces and fry in grease. Mash the flesh and livers with almonds and dissolve in the bouillon and boil. Stir together ginger, cinnamon, clove, galingale, long pepper, and grain of paradise in vinegar and boil. To serve, put the solid part into bowls and pour the pottage on top.

73. Herbed capons or veal. In the winter, kill the capons, moisten them, and then set them in the frost for 6 days. In summertime, after killing them, keep them out of the sun for two days, or wrap them in a coverlet. Cook them in water with some bacon fat to whet the appetite; add parsley, sage, coq, and hyssop, a little bit of verjuice for piquancy, then a dash of ginger, and saffron for color. This pottage suits the cold weather, but if it is warm out, add only the bacon fat and saffron to this capon or veal dish.

74. Gravé of small birds or other meat. Pluck the birds while dry; then cut some pork fat into cubes and set it on the fire in a pan. Remove the pork rinds and fry the birds in the remaining grease, then cook in a pot of meat bouillon. Take bread toasted on the grill or breadcrumbs soaked in meat broth and a little wine, and ginger, clove, grain of paradise, and cassia buds and the livers. Then sieve the bread and broth and grind the spices finely without sieving them, and put it all to boil with the small birds plus a little verjuice. *Item,* if you do not have broth, add some pea stock. *Item,* the soup should not be too thick, but thin. Thus you need only the bread and livers as thickener.

75. Gravé or seymé is a winter pottage. Peel and mince onions and cook them,

then fry them in a pan. Now the chicken must be split down the back and grilled over a coal fire; for veal, do the same. Cut the veal into pieces, or the chicken into quarters, and put the meat with the onions into the pot. Toast white bread on the grill and steep it in the broth of another kind of meat. Then grind ginger, clove, grain of paradise, and long pepper, thin with verjuice and wine without straining, and set aside. Crush the bread and sieve it, and put it into the soup. Strain the entire mixture and boil; then serve. *Nota* that we say "deep fry" when it is in a pot, and if it is in an iron skillet, we say "fry."

76. Crayfish gravé. Boil crayfish, and when finished, shell them as if to eat, and remove the bad part from inside. Then moisten peeled and ground almonds in pea stock and sieve. Also grind and sieve toasted bread or breadcrumbs soaked in vegetable stock. Then grind some ginger, cinnamon, grains of paradise, and clove, and boil everything in a pot with a little bit of vinegar. Serve in bowls, with the crayfish fried in oil and other fried fish in each one.

77. *Item*, if you want to make crayfish tile, proceed in the same way, but grind the shells of the crayfish well. If you wish to take full advantage of the grinding, put the crayfish shells in a pot or in an earthenware pan and dry in the oven; then grind in a spice mortar and pass through your finest muslin strainer. Dry it once more in the oven, grind and strain it, and then add it to the pottage. (I believe that this thickens its texture.)

78. Rabbit *boussac*. First, Garenne coneys can be recognized by the brownish-yellow color on the nape of their neck, that is, from their ears to their shoulders. Their underbelly and the inner side of their four limbs all the way to their feet is also entirely white, but they should have no other spots of white on them. *Item*, you will know they are in their first year because they have a small, pointy bone on the joint of their front legs, close to the foot. Once they are older than one year, the joint is completely smooth. The same is true for hares and dogs. *Item*, you know that rabbits have been freshly caught if their eyes are not sunken, their teeth cannot be pried open, and the carcass can be stood up straight on its feet. On a fresh rabbit, when the stomach is cooked, it does not fall apart. If it is not fresh, it has sunken eyes, the jaw opens easily, you cannot hold it upright, and when it is cooked, the stomach breaks in pieces. In the winter, coneys taken 8 days ago are edible, and in summer 3 days, as long as they have not been in the sun.

When choice hares are obtained and skinned, cut them up into chunks and boil, then soak them in cold water. Put three pieces of bacon fat into each, boil them in water, and afterward in wine. Then grind ginger, grain of paradise, a clove and mix into beef or rabbit bouillon with a little verjuice. Boil in a pot until tender.

79. *Item*, seymé is made the same way, except you add fried onions, a little bit of bread or breadcrumbs to thicken it. Therefore it is a stew.

80. *Item,* a *bouli lardé* of veal, kid, or deer is made the same way.

81. *Item . . .*

82. Hare boussac. *Nota* that the meat of freshly caught hare cooked without delay is more tender than that of hare that has been stored. *Item,* hare taken within 15 days is fine, provided that the sun has not touched it. That is, 15 days in the midst of winter, but 6 days, 8 at most, in the summer and without any sun exposure. *Item,* know that if the hare is eaten freshly caught, it is the most tender. It should not be washed, but grilled or roasted with its blood.

83. Boussac of hare or coney is made this way: grill the hare on a spit or on the grill, then cut it up and fry in grease or lard. Boil with toasted bread or bread-crumbs that have been soaked in beef bouillon and wine and strained. Then take ginger, clove, and grain of paradise and mix into some verjuice. The mixture should be dark brown and not too thick. *Nota* that the spices must be ground before the bread. For coney, it is done the same way, except that the coney is boiled, then returned to cold water, then larded, etc.

84. Rosé of young rabbit, larks, and small birds or chickens. Skin the rabbits, cut up, boil, put back in cold water and lard them. Scald the chickens for plucking, then return to cold water, cut up and larded. The larks and little birds are plucked only and boiled in meat stock. Then take pork fat cut into cubes; put them over the fire in a skillet and remove the rinds but leave the fat; fry whatever meat you use for the soup, or boil it on the coals in a pot with some fat, turning it often. While you do this, take some peeled almonds and mix with beef broth and strain. Then take ginger, clove, and cedar, otherwise called Alixander, mix in some broth, strain, and put it together in the pot with the cooked meat. Boil the mixture along with a generous amount of sugar. Serve in bowls with glazed spices on top. Red cedar is a wood that the spice merchants sell, and it is called "cedar from which knife handles are made."

85. Beef venison. Because this meat is tougher than that of fawn or kid goat, boil it and lard it the whole length of the piece. Cook it in plenty of wine, and at the tail end of the cooking, add ground mace. It should be eaten with cameline sauce [271]. *Item,* to put in a pasty it must be boiled, larded the entire length, and eaten cold with cameline sauce. If you wish to salt it in summer, dissolve coarse salt in water, soak the venison, then dry it in the sun.

86. If you would like to make a piece of beef taste like stag venison—or bear venison if you are in bear country—take numbles or giste of beef, boil and lard it, put it on a spit and roast it. It is eaten with boar's tail sauce [293]. Boil the beef, lard along the length after having cut it into pieces, then pour very hot boar's tail sauce in the dish over your beef, which *primo* has been roasted or tossed into boiling water and immediately removed, because beef is more tender than stag.

87. Beef as bear venison. With the giste of beef, make a black sauce from gin-

ger, clove, long pepper, grain of paradise, etc., and put two strips of meat in each bowl. When eaten, the beef has the flavor of bear.

88. Thin and unthickened boussac of roe deer. Skin the deer and then toss the meat into boiling water, removing it almost immediately because it is more tender than stag. Lard it along its length, then put it to cook in defatted meat stock, if you have some, and otherwise another broth. Add wine, coarsely ground spices, and serve the meat in the broth. *Item,* roe deer meat is prepared the same way as kid goat in the chapter above [80].

89. Fresh boar is prepared in water with wine and eaten with heated sauce. Salted boar is cooked as above and eaten with mustard in the dead of winter, but in the beginning of winter it is eaten with spices and sops.

90. Deer: On the Feast of Our Lady in March[23] begins the rutting season for deer, and in mid-May we say "Mid-May, half head" because the stag then has put out half of his antlers, but the true heart of the rutting season begins with the Feast of the Holy Cross in May,[24] and from then on the stag fattens its venison until the Feast of Magdalene.[25] The stag can then be hunted until the Holy Cross in September,[26] at which point the season is closed.

Item, at the slaughter, first the two choice parts are removed: these are the testicles, with which are the knots,[27] the throat, the true intestines, etc. These delicacies are boiled, then cooked and eaten with warm sauce. *Item,* in a stag there are shoulders, the breast, thighs, the liver, the numbles, the joints, the tail—*scilicet* the croup—the two ribs, and that is all.

Item, pieces of fresh deer meat, it seems, must be placed in boiling water without boiling them thoroughly. Instead, remove them immediately and lard all along; it is boiled, then larded lengthwise, and then boiled again in water; that pottage is called bouli lardé with spices and sops.

Item, the numbles are roasted and served with heated sauce.

Item, the joints, that is the meat between the ribs and the spine, are better in pastry than prepared otherwise.

Item, also fresh deer is served with a warm sauce when it has been roasted.

Item, make a gift of the head and the feet to the lords. These are not edible but show what kind and what age the deer was. For edible gifts, present them with the hindquarters, the breast, and the two ribs.

Item, the tail end is called the croup. If you want to salt it you must first remove

---

23. March 25.

24. May 3.

25. July 22.

26. September 14.

27. BF/Ueltschi (639 n. 4) say "knots" is the flesh between the neck and the shoulder.

all the bones, as many as possible, because it contains a large part of the back-bone.

Item, the breast is the chest and it is good salted; deer venison is salted just like beef.

Item, all the innards, except the liver, are for the dogs' quarry, and they are called the hue.[28]

91. In September one begins hunting the black beasts,[29] until St. Martin's Feast[30] in the winter.

Item, all 4 limbs are called hams, as with pigs.

Item, from a boar comes the head, the ribs, the chine, the numbles, the 4 hams; that is all.

Item, of the entrails only the liver is kept, which seems appropriate to use in a finely made English broth [109].

Item, fresh meat is cooked and prepared in water with spices as for deer. As for the *bourbelier,* it is the numbles, even though around here "numbles" is said in some places, "bourbelier" in others.

Item, salted boar is eaten with frumenty. The head is cooked whole, in half wine and half water. The cheeks are good in slices on the grill.

92. Wild doe in thin boussac without thickeners: skin it, then boil, or toss in boiling water and pull it out immediately because it is more tender than buck. Lard it lengthwise, then set to cook in degreased meat stock, if you have it, or another broth, with some wine and ground spices. Serve the meat accompanied by the broth.

Additional thick meat pottages:

93. Broth of pork tripe[12]. Grind some ginger, cloves, grain of paradise, etc., then mix with vinegar and wine. Take some toasted bread that has been soaked in vinegar, grind it, strain, and mix all together. Then cut the viscera in pieces and fry them in lard. Pour stock of boudin or offal into a pot along with the bread and spice mixture, and boil. Add the pieces of fried viscera, bring to a boil once, and serve.

94. New broad beans. Boil them past the point where they have split. Take plenty of parsley and a little sage and hyssop, and grind them well. Afterward, crush some bread and a handful of these same broad beans that have been peeled, to use for thickening, and strain through a cloth. Then on a meat day fry the rest

---

28. The quarry or *cuiree* ceremony consisted of giving the entrails to the hounds as a reward for a successful hunt. Hue refers to shouting to the hounds or the cry of the hounds as a group.

29. Boars, wolves, and foxes.

30. November 11.

of the beans in bacon fat; on a fish day in oil or butter. On a meat day add the cooked beans to meat stock, or on a fish day, to bean broth.

95. Crétonée of new peas or new broad beans. Cook the legumes until they are mushy and pour off the liquid. Take fresh cow's milk—and direct the woman who sells it to you not to give it to you if she has watered it down, for often they stretch their milk, and if it is not fresh or if there is water in it, it will curdle. Before adding any ingredients to the milk, boil it, for otherwise it will curdle. Grind ginger to whet the appetite and saffron to color it yellow. However, if you want to thicken it with egg yolks, trickle them in. These egg yolks give a satisfactory yellow color, and they also thicken the dish. But milk curdles more quickly with egg yolks than with bread as a thickener and saffron for color. Therefore, if you thicken it with bread, use unleavened and white bread, soak it in a bowl with milk or meat broth, then crush and run through a straining cloth. When the bread has been strained, but not the spices, set it all to boil with the peas. When it is done, then add milk and some saffron. Yet another thickener can be used, that is, peas themselves or beans, ground and then strained. Avail yourself of whichever thickener you prefer. When you thicken with egg yolks, beat and strain them, then pour them in a fine thread into the milk, after it has been thoroughly boiled with the new peas or beans and the spices and taken off the fire. The surest way is to take a little milk and dilute the eggs in the bowl and continue adding milk bit by bit, until the yolks are well mixed with the spoon, using plenty of milk. Next, put it into a pot that is off the fire and the pottage will not curdle. If the pottage becomes too thick, dilute it with meat stock. Having done this, take some quartered chicks, or veal, or a gosling;[31] boil and then fry them. Put 2 or 3 pieces in each bowl and pour the pottage over them.

96. Crétonnée for a fish day. Use fried tench, pike, sole, or dab.

97. Piglet offal, *scilicet* the intestines. Empty them into the river and wash them twice in warm water. Put into a brass pan and rub thoroughly with salt and water, then wash again in warm water. Some wash them in salt and vinegar. When they are thoroughly washed with or without vinegar, as you prefer, chop them up, skewer the pieces on spits, and roast on the grill. Serve with grain verjuice.

To make a pottage from them, cook them whole in a clay pot and drain in a dish; chop them into small pieces and fry in bacon fat. Grind up first bread, then mace, galingale, saffron, ginger, clove, grain of paradise, and cinnamon. Pour in some bouillon and set aside. Then grind toasted bread or breadcrumbs, and mix with caudle and run through a straining cloth, and put into meat stock or its own stock, or

---

31. Redon, Sabban, and Serventi (*Medieval Kitchen*, 53, 114) say that *petite oé* is not gosling but goose giblets and that these are often fried by goose merchants into small crunchy bits as snacks. So here it may be giblets. See ¶ 71, where the context suggests a gosling.

half of one and half of the other, and boil all together with red wine, verjuice, and vinegar. In winter it must be brown and served as above, and in summer thinner and more yellow. Have ready verjuice grain cooked in water in a cloth, or gooseberries. When you prepare the bowls, put in six or eight morsels of the offal, then the soup on top, and then six or eight verjuice grains or gooseberries in each bowl. Some make the pottage with spices and milk as above for crétonnée.

Nota that the salt and vinegar remove the odor. And what is said in the segment above concerns offal eaten in July. Other hastelets, made in December, are from all the parts such as liver, lung, and other varieties of viscera, and this is what the poor folk cook in washbasins in the streets.

98. Poultry *comminée*. Cut the bird into pieces and cook in water with a little wine, then fry it in fat. Soak a little bread in the bouillon. *Primo,* take ginger and cumin, mixed in verjuice, grind and strain and mix with meat or chicken broth, and then color either with saffron or with eggs or egg yolks, run through a straining cloth, and trickle into the pottage, once it is removed from the fire. *Item,* it is best to prepare it with milk—as has already been mentioned—and then to grind the bread after the spices, but first you must boil the milk so that it does not scorch. After the pottage is finished, put the milk into wine and fry the comminée, although this does not seem necessary to me. Many do not fry it, although that way is the most tasty. Bread is the thickener, and then afterward the recipe mentions "eggs," which is another way to thicken it.[32] One or the other should suffice, just as is described in the recipe for crétonée. "Verjuice and wine": if you wish to make your pottage with milk, do not use either wine or verjuice.

99. Comminée for a fish day. Fry the fish, then peel and crush almonds and mix into vegetable or fish stock to make almond milk. But cow's milk is more appetizing, although not at all as healthy for the sick. For the rest, do as above. *Item,* on a meat day, if you cannot have cow's milk, it can be made with almond milk and meat as above.

100. Capon *hardouil.* Cut up the bird in pieces or quarters, cook them in water, then fry in bacon fat. Meanwhile grind ginger, cinnamon, clove, and grain of paradise and mix into some verjuice, but do not strain; rather, toast bread on the grill, grind—after the spices, and soak in verjuice, then strain the bread through the cloth and put it all to boil. To serve, put the solid parts in bowls and pour the hot pottage over it all.

101. Poultry *hochepot* is made in this way, and it should not have a clear juice. Cut up the bird in pieces. Goose is prepared like this when it is tough and skinny, for the fat ones are roasted. *Item,* also for old doves. The same is done with round slices of beef leg.

---

32. Here the author refers to his source, possibly the *Viandier.* See Scully, *Viandier,* 281, no. 12.

102. Cinnamon broth.[33] Cut up your poultry or other meat and cook it in water, adding some wine, then fry it. Combine ground raw unpeeled dried almonds in their whole shells with lots of cinnamon. Mix this into the cooking broth, or use beef broth and boil with the cooked meat or fowl. Then grind ginger, cloves, and grain of paradise, etc., and let the soup be thick and russet-colored.

103. *Georgié* or *houssié* broth. Cut poultry into quarters, or take veal or another meat and cut it into pieces and boil it with bacon fat. Separately, fry finely minced onions in a pot with fat. Also, soak toasted bread in the meat broth with some wine added. Then blend ginger, cinnamon, long pepper, saffron, cloves, and grain of paradise with the livers, grinding them so well that they do not need to be strained, and soak them in verjuice, wine, and vinegar. When the spices are removed from the mortar, grind the bread and then mix it with the liquid in which it was soaking, and run the resulting combination through the straining cloth. Add the spices and parsley leaves if you wish, and boil it all with the fat and onions; then fry the meat. This pottage should be the brown color of fat and as thick as a *soringue* [127].

Nota that you must always grind the spices first, and for pottages do not strain the spices. Afterward you crush and sieve the bread. I do not find that wine or vinegar is necessary.

Nota that only because of the parsley is it called houssié broth, for just as one says frangié with saffron, one says houssié with parsley; this is the cook's jargon.

104. Red broth is made like georgié broth above, except that you do not add saffron or wine or vinegar, but you use far more cinnamon and onion slices.

105. A vinaigrette.[34] Take the spleen of a pig, washed thoroughly in hot water then half roasted on the grill, and mince it. Combine the meat with fat and onion slices in an earthenware pot and set the pot on the fire, stirring it often. When the mixture is well fried or cooked, add beef broth and boil it all together. Then grind toast, ginger, grain of paradise, saffron, etc., and dissolve in wine and vinegar, and boil it all. It should be brown. (Brown? How will it be brown if there is no toast? *Item*, I think it should be thick, for I find it above in the chapter on thick pottages. And for these two reasons I think that it needs toasted bread to thicken it and color it brown).[35]

106. White broth. Take capons, chickens, or chicks killed an appropriate time beforehand, either whole or in halves or quarters, add some pieces of veal, and

---

33. The term used is *brouet,* which can be either a thin broth-like liquid or a thicker soup.

34. See Scully and Scully, *Early French Cookery,* 81, and Scully, *Viandier,* 282, no. 17.

35. The narrator seems to correct the *Viandier* recipe, which does not require toast or any darkening agent, yet reports that the dish will be brown in color.

cook them with bacon in water and wine, and when they are cooked, set them aside. Peel and grind almonds and blend them into stock from poultry—be sure that it is quite clear, without any sediment or cloudiness—and then run it through the strainer. Combine white ginger, peeled or skinned, with grain of paradise moistened as above with broth, and run them through a very fine sieve and mix with almond milk. If it needs thickening, pour in starch or boiled rice and add a drop of verjuice and plenty of white sugar. When you serve it, sprinkle on a spice called red coriander and pomegranate seeds with comfits and set fried almonds around the edge of each bowl. Regarding this, see the next entry for blancmanger.

107. Blancmanger of capons for the sick. Cook the capon in water until it is well done. Then grind plenty of almonds and the capon's flesh, and mix with the broth and run through the strainer. Set it to boil until it is thickened. Then grind peeled white ginger and the other spices included above under white broth [106].

108. German broth. Take rabbit meat, poultry, or veal and cut it into pieces. Parboil it in water and then fry it in bacon fat. Put finely minced onions in a pot on the fire with some fat and stir often. Grind ginger, cinnamon, grain of paradise, nutmegs, livers roasted on a spit on the grill, and some saffron diluted with verjuice. The mixture should be yellowish and thick. And *primo* take bread toasted on the grill, ground, and sieved and set it all to boil together with some parsley and sugar added. To serve, put 3 or 4 pieces of the meat in the bowl and ladle some broth over them, sprinkling sugar on the top. *Nota* that he is in error.[36] For some cooks say that German broth should not be yellow, and this one says that it should. So if it must be yellow, the saffron should not be passed through the strainer, but it ought to be well ground and dissolved and put into the pottage; for saffron that is strained is for coloring; that which is sprinkled on top is called frangié.

109. Refined English broth. Take cooked and peeled chestnuts and the same quantity or more of the yolks of hard-boiled eggs and pork liver. Grind all together, soak in warm water, then run through the strainer. Then grate ginger, cinnamon, cloves, grain of paradise, long pepper, galingale, and saffron to give color and boil them together.

110. Savoy broth. Take capons or hens and boil them with lean bacon and livers. When they are half cooked, take them off the fire and put crustless pieces of bread to soak in the bouillon. Then grind ginger, cinnamon, and saffron and remove them from the mortar. Mash the livers with plenty of parsley, strain, and afterward crush and strain the bread. Boil everything together. *Nota* that the saffron makes the soup yellow and the parsley makes it green. Together they create

---

36. Taillevent; see Scully, *Viandier*, 282, no. 22.

an unfortunate color; but it seems that the color would be more pleasing if the bread were toasted, for toasted bread and saffron make green, and parsley also makes green.

111. Verjuice and poultry broth. This is a summer dish. Cook the poultry in quarters, or veal or chicks, in bouillon or other liquid with bacon, wine, and verjuice, until the taste of the verjuice is gone. Then fry the meat in good lard. Beat well together egg yolks and powdered herbs and run through the sieve; then pour the eggs in a thin thread into the pot of bouillon, stirring briskly with a spoon. The pot should be at the back of the fire. Boil parsley and grain verjuice in the meat stock in your spoon, while the pot is at the back of the fire; otherwise, boil it in another small pan of clear water to remove some of the green color. Serve the meat pieces and pour the pottage over them. Top with the boiled parsley and grain verjuice.

112. Bright-green broth. Cook whatever meat you wish in water or in a little wine, or in meat stock, wine, and salt pork to give flavor. Then fry this meat, and grind ginger, saffron, parsley, and a little sage, if you wish, and raw egg yolks poured in through a slotted spoon to thicken it, or ground bread mixed with stock, and boil it all with verjuice. Some cooks add cheese, and they're right.

113. *Râppé.* Cook meat, then fry it in fat. Mix ground grain of paradise, ginger, etc., with verjuice. Take bread soaked in meat stock, ground and passed through a sieve. Put the spices, bread, and caudle to boil together. Then have grain verjuice or boiled gooseberries that have been passed through a slotted pan or other water or a cloth or sieve or something else to remove the first green color. Then serve the meat in bowls with the pottage over it, and top with the verjuice.

114. *Genesté* is called genesté because it is as yellow as the flowers of broom. It is yellowed with egg yolks and saffron and is made in the summer instead of civet. It is fried as described below, except that there are no onions.

115. Veal civet. Neither washed nor boiled, half cook the veal on the spit or on the grill. Then cut it up and fry in fat with lots of onions you have cooked beforehand. Prepare lightly browned bread or untoasted breadcrumbs, or the color would be too dark for veal civet. This lightly browned bread is good for hare civet, too. Soak the bread in beef stock and a little wine or pea stock. While it soaks, grind ginger, cinnamon, clove, grain of paradise, and plenty of saffron for coloring it yellow, and mix with verjuice, wine, and vinegar. Grind the bread and sieve it. Add the spices and the sieved bread to the caudle, and boil it all together. The color should be more yellow than brown, sharp with vinegar, and moderate with spices. And *nota* that it needs a lot of saffron. Also, avoid adding nutmeg or cinnamon because they will make it too brown.

116. Hare civet. First, split the hare down the breast, and if it is freshly caught, such as one or two days prior, do not wash it, but set it to toast on the grill—*id*

est to grill over a hot coal fire—or on the spit. Cook some onions in fat, and add the hare to the pot piece by piece, frying the pieces on the fire, stirring the pot often, or fry them in a frying pan. Then toast some bread well and soak it in meat broth with vinegar and wine. Prepare ground ginger, grain of paradise, clove, long pepper, nutmeg, and cinnamon to which are added verjuice and vinegar or meat broth; drain the liquid from this mixture and set it aside. Then grind the toast, mix in some broth, and strain the bread, but not the spices, through the strainer. Combine the broth, onions and fat, spices and toasted bread and cook together with the hare. Take care that the civet is brown, sharpened with vinegar, adjusted with salt and spices.

Nota that the age of a hare corresponds to the number of holes under the tail, for there are as many years as there are holes.

117. Rabbit civet, as above.

118. A tile of meat. Take cooked crayfish and remove the meat from the tails. Grind the rest, that is, shells and carcass, thoroughly. Afterward take unpeeled almonds, sort them, and wash them in hot water as for peas. Grind them up with the crayfish shells as well as with crustless bread browned on the grill. Now cut up and quarter capons, chickens, and pullets, or cut up some veal into pieces, and cook the poultry or veal in water, wine, and salt. In the cooking broth, soak and mix the ground blend of shells, almonds, and bread, and then strain. Then repeat: grind, moisten, and strain again. Add ginger, cinnamon, clove, and pepper well-soaked in verjuice without vinegar, then boil it all together. Now the meat solids, in quarters or in chunks, should be cooked in pork fat. Serve this in bowls and pour the pottage over it. On top of the pottage, in each bowl, put 4 or 5 crayfish tails, with sugar sprinkled over it all.

119. Meat *houssébarré* can be hastily put together for an impromptu supper with unexpected guests. For 10 bowls take 20 thin slices of cold meat from dinner and some giste of beef, and the strips should be as thin as bacon. Fry them in fat on the fire in a pan. *Item,* take 6 egg yolks and a little white wine, beat all together until you are tired, then add to some meat stock, with old verjuice, not new, for it would curdle. Boil it all without the meat, and when serving, put two slices of meat into each bowl. When there is a crowd and you are short on meat, some serve the soup in bowls, and using a dish set before 4 people, put five strips of meat and some soup over them.

120. Fish houssébarré. Prepare and wash plaice, then dry by patting between two towels, and fry and put in one dish and two in another, which makes two dishes. *Item,* have two ounces of coriander and unpreserved *cercuis,*[37] which costs

---

37. Seems to be a spice, but unknown in this form. May be a variation or corruption of chervil, in Old French *cerfueil* or variants *cerfoil, cerfeul.*

one blanc per ounce, and grind, soak in wine and verjuice, then boil and sprinkle on the two dishes.

121. Lombard pottage. When the meat is cooked, set it aside and put the stock in another pot, but watch that no sediment or small bones slip in. Then take egg yolks and beat well with verjuice and powdered spices, and trickle into the pot while stirring constantly. Then prepare sops.

Other thick pottages without meat:

122. Light green eel broth. Skin—*id est,* flay or scald—the eels and put them to cook in water with wine, in very small pieces. Then grind parsley and toasted bread, and sieve. Have on hand ground peeled ginger and saffron, and boil it all together, and when almost done, add morsels of cubed cheese.

123. Saracen broth. Skin the eel and cut into very small pieces, then sprinkle with salt and fry in oil. Grind ginger, cinnamon, clove, grain of paradise, galingale, long pepper, and saffron to give color, add some verjuice, and boil with the eels, which themselves will thicken the soup.

124. Green egg and cheese broth. Take parsley and a little cheese and sage, and a tiny bit of saffron, moistened bread, and mix with pea stock or boiled water. Grind and strain. Grind some ginger and mix it with wine and put on to boil. Then add the cheese, and eggs poached in water, and it should be light green in color. *Item,* some do not add bread but substitute bacon.

125. German egg broth. Poach the eggs in oil, then take almonds and peel, grind, and sieve them; slice up onions in rounds—cook them in water, then fry in oil—and put it all to boil. Then grind ginger, cinnamon, clove, and a little saffron mixed with verjuice, and right at the end put the spices into the pottage, and bring it to a rolling boil. It should be quite thick and not too yellow.

126. White broth can be made from pike, carp, and bass, as explained above for poultry.

127. Eel soringue. Scald or skin the eels, then slice them. Fry onion slices and parsley in oil. Grind ginger, cinnamon, clove, grain of paradise, and saffron, and moisten with verjuice and remove them from the mortar. Then take toasted bread ground and soaked in vegetable broth and strain through the cloth, then mix in the vegetable broth and boil it all together. Season with wine, verjuice, and vinegar; it must be a thin sauce.

128. Gravé or seymé—for it is all the same—of loach or other cold or hot fish, either perch or some other of that nature. Fry without flour in oil, and keep the pan before the fire. Prepare and put in a pot toasted bread crushed and soaked in a little wine, boiled water, or vegetable stock and then passed through a sieve. Then shred ginger, cinnamon, clove, grain of paradise, and saffron to give color; blend with vinegar. Chop and cook some onions and fry them in oil. Boil it all to-

gether in a pot with vegetable stock or boiled water—except for the fried loach. Put 6 or 8 loach or more in each bowl with some broth spooned over them. It should not be yellow, but red.

129. Pike chowder. First, to prepare the pike, draw the guts out through the gills, remove the bitter parts, and replace the guts inside. After this, roast the fish on the grill. If the pike is small, roast it whole, and if it is larger, slice it across in several places and thus roast. Take a lot of saffron, long pepper, clove, and grain of paradise, crush all well and mix with verjuice, wine, and a tiny amount of vinegar, almost none; grind and remove from the mortar. Then get toasted bread soaked in pea water or fish stock, or half wine and half verjuice, and grind, then run through the straining cloth, and set all to boil. Pour over the pike in dishes. This sauce should be yellow.

You can make cold fish galantine in the same way, except that you do not add pea stock, because it does not keep long, but instead you use the fat from fish.

130. Oyster civet. Scald and wash the oysters well. Cook them just until they reach a boil, then drain and fry with onion cooked in oil. Soak toasted bread or plenty of breadcrumbs in vegetable stock or in the water the oysters were boiled in, add plain wine, and strain. Grind cinnamon, clove, long pepper, grain of paradise, and saffron for color, and moisten with verjuice and vinegar and set aside. Then grind up toasted bread or breadcrumbs with the vegetable stock or oyster water, and also the oysters, since they will not have been cooked enough.

131. Egg civet. Poach eggs in oil. Cook onions, sliced in rounds, and fry them in the oil; then boil in wine, verjuice, and vinegar, all together. Put 3 or 4 eggs in each bowl; pour your soup over it. It should not be thick.

132. Sops in mustard. Take some of the oil in which you poached eggs, some wine, water, and boil it all together in an iron skillet. Toast bread crusts on the grill, cut them in cubes to make sops, and boil them. Remove the sops and put in a dish to drain and cool. In the bouillon put some mustard and boil. Then put the sops into bowls and pour the bouillon over them.

133. Thickened cow's milk. Select the choicest milk, as is explained earlier in the chapter on pottages [95], bring it to a boil, then remove from the heat. Trickle into it through a sieve a great quantity of egg yolks, removing the germ. Next, grind and add to the mixture a piece of ginger and saffron, and keep it hot by the fire. Poach eggs in water and put 2 or 3 poached eggs in each bowl, then pour the milk over them.

134. Mullet *espinbesche*. Fillet, boil, and roast your mullets. Then take verjuice, cameline powder, and parsley; boil them together and pour over.

135. Yellow pottage or yellow sauce over cold or hot fish. Fry loach, skinned perch, or other fish of this nature in oil without any flour. Grind almonds and blend into a generous quantity of wine and verjuice; strain and set on the fire. Then grind ginger,

clove, grain of paradise, and saffron, diluting them with broth. When the pottage boils, put in the spices. To serve, add sugar; the mixture should be thick.

136. Millet. Wash it in 3 changes of water and then put in an iron skillet to dry over the fire, shaking it well, so that it does not burn. Add it to simmering cow's milk, and do not put the spoon in it until it has boiled well. Take it off the fire, and beat it with the back of the spoon until it is very thick.

137. The nature of milk is such that once it is taken from the cow and put in beautiful and clean vessels of clay or wood or pewter—and not in brass or copper—and kept in these vessels to rest, without moving or changing from one vessel to another, or transporting them here or there, it will keep well for a day and a half, and will not curdle at all when boiled, provided that you stir it as it first begins boiling. You should not add salt to it until you take it off the fire, or at least when you are ready to add sops to it. You can add to it sops of leavened or other bread, for it will not turn so long as the milk is treated as said.

Item, if the milk is not fresh or if you have doubts about its curdling in the pan, add a little flour and stir it well, and then it will not curdle. Should you want to make porridge with it, mix *primo* flour and milk and some salt, then put it on to boil, stirring well. If you want to make pottage with it, for each quart of milk add the yolks of half a quartern of eggs, the germs removed, well beaten together by themselves, and then beaten again with the milk and poured slowly into the pan, while stirring the boiling milk very well. Then make sops. And if you want to add a piece of gingerroot and saffron, *fiat.*

Roasted meat:

138. Fresh beef tongue must be boiled, skinned, larded, roasted, and eaten with cameline sauce. *Item,* know that tongue of old beef cattle is better than that of young ones, or so some say; others say the opposite.

When the weather begins to get cold, the people of Gascony buy tongues, boil and skin them, then salt them one on top of the other in a salting tub and leave them 8 days. Then they hang them in the chimney all winter, and in the summer higher, where it is dry. In this way they keep well for 10 years. They can be cooked in water, or wine if you wish, and eaten with mustard [269].

Aliter, tongue of old cattle must be boiled, skinned, and cleaned, then put on a spit, pricked with cloves, roasted, and eaten with cameline sauce.

139. *Allouyaux* of beef.[38] Make thin slices from the meat of the leg and wrap around some marrow and beef fat; roast on a spit and eat with salt.

140. Lamb roasted in fine salt, verjuice, and vinegar. First put the shoulder on a spit and turn it in front of the fire until all its grease has dripped off. Then lard

---

38. "Little larks," a dish prepared to resemble a small lark (Scully, *Viandier,* gloss, 343).

it with parsley—at that point and not earlier, for if done earlier, the parsley will burn before the shoulder is roasted.

141. Pork. First scald and then roast on a spit. Put some lard in a pan, and using a stick with some feathers at the end, grease the skin or rind of the pig so that it does not burn and harden; otherwise lard it. Do the same to a young pig, or lard it. It is eaten with grain verjuice or old verjuice and scallions.

142. Stuffed piglet. After killing and cutting the throat of the piglet, scald it in boiling water, then skin it. Take the lean meat, remove the fat and entrails of the piglet, and set it to cook in water. Hard-boil 20 eggs, then boil and peel some chestnuts. Taking the yolks of the eggs, the chestnuts, some fine old cheese, and the meat of a cooked leg of pork, chop them, then grind them with plenty of saffron and ginger powder mixed with the meat. If the meat becomes too hard, thin it with egg yolks. Do not slit the pig across the belly but through the side and with the smallest opening possible; then put it on the spit and afterward stuff it with the mixture above, and sew it up with a big needle. It is eaten either with yellow *poivre* [281] in winter or with cameline sauce in summer.

Nota that I have indeed seen larded pig and it is quite good. And that is how it is now done, and pigeons likewise.

143. Rabbits, boiled, larded, roasted, with a cameline sauce. You know for certain if a rabbit is fat by feeling the nerve that is between the shoulders in the neck, for you know that it has thick fat by a big nerve; and you know it is tender by breaking one of its rear legs.

144. Roasted veal. Brown it on the fire on the spit, without washing it, then lard, roast, and eat it with cameline sauce. Some boil, lard, and then spit it. That is how it used to be done.

145. Kids, lambs. Toss into boiling water just briefly. Brown on the spit, then roast and eat with cameline sauce.

146. Boar bourbelier.[39] *Primo*, put it in boiling water and immediately remove it and stick it with cloves; set it to roast and baste it with sauce made of spices— that is, ginger, cinnamon, clove, grain of paradise, long pepper, and nutmeg, thinned in verjuice, wine, and vinegar. Without boiling, baste it with the sauce; and when it is roasted, boil it all together. This sauce is called boar's tail and you will find it hereafter [293]. (There it is thickened with bread, but here not.)

147. To counterfeit bear venison, using a piece of beef. Take the piece of meat near the flank. Cut it up into big pieces as for bouli lardé, then boil, lard, and roast. Then boil a boar's tail sauce, set the meat to simmer, and pour the sauce over it in a dish. Fresh venison is not basted and is always eaten with a cameline sauce [86, 87].

---

39. Boar's numbles; see ¶ 91.

148. Roasted geese, with white garlic sauce [274] in winter, or *à la jance* [286–88].

And *nota* that in August or September, when the goslings are as large as their fathers or mothers, you can recognize the young by pushing your thumb on their beaks; the gosling's beak collapses under the thumb's pressure, but the older birds' do not.

Item, nota that if goslings are placed in a cage when very young, they will fatten for 9 days and afterward they will get thinner, but geese always fatten, without dwindling. In both cases, they must be kept dry and their feet dry, and they must not be placed on damp litter—rather it must be completely dry. Make sure they do not bathe or eat greenery. They should not see any light. Feed them cooked wheat and let them drink skim milk or the water in which the wheat was cooked. Give them no other liquid, and feed them fine oats.

In Paris the goose sellers fatten their geese with flour, not with fine flour or bran but with that which is between the two, which is called *gruyaulx* or *recoppes*. Some put oatmeal with it and mix it all with a little water, so that it becomes a thick paste. They put this food in a trough on 4 feet, with some water aside, and provide fresh litter each day; and in 15 days the birds are fat. And *nota* that the litter keeps their feathers clean.[40]

149. Capons and hens, hung for 2 or 3 days, put on a spit, flambéed, and roasted, are served with verjuice and their rendered fat, or in Poitou style [289], or à la jance.

150. Chicks as fat as young capons in July: kill them 2 days before, roast, flambé, and eat with must—which is made in any season with wine, verjuice, and lots of sugar.

To "hang" them,[41] you must bleed them and immediately put them to die in a bucket of cold water, then right away put them in a second bucket of very cold water; they will be as well aged that same morning as if they had been killed two days before.[42]

151. Small birds. Pluck them while dry, leave the feet on, and put the spit through the body. Between birds put a slender leaf of fat salt pork.

152. River mallards.[43] In winter, when the young are as large as the adults, you can identify the young by the quills of their feathers, which are more tender than those of old birds. *Item,* you can recognize river mallards because they have completely black nails and red feet and farm ducks have yellow ones. *Item,* the crest or

---

40. Repeats 2.4.18.
41. To age capons and hens to enhance flavor.
42. Repeats 2.4.19.
43. I.e., wild mallards.

upper part of the beak is all green, and sometimes the males have a white mark across the nape of the neck, solid plumage, and iridescent feathers atop their heads.

Item, river mallards. Pluck them while dry, then set over the fire,[44] remove the head and throw it away, leave the feet. Put the bird on a spit and place a dripping pan underneath to collect the grease. Put onions in the pan to fry in the grease. When the bird is cooked, add pork fat and parsley to the dripping pan and cook it all together, add toasts, and serve the bird in pieces; eat it with fine salt.

Item, it can be done differently. Put onions in the dripping pan as said, and when the bird is cooked, put into the dripping pan a little verjuice and half wine, half vinegar; boil it all together and after add the toast. This last sauce is called *saupiquet*.

153. Peacock, pheasant, stork, heron, bustard, crane, wild geese, bittern, cormorant: pluck them dry or bleed them like a swan, and, as appropriate for the species, leave the head and tail or head and feet, and for what remains, proceed as for the swan [157].

Item, for pheasant from which the tail has been removed, once it is roasted and arranged, decorate with 2 or 3 of its plumes.

154. Wood pigeons are good in winter. The old ones can be identified by their entirely black flight feathers; and the young ones, in their first year, have ash-colored tips on their flight feathers and the rest black like the others. They are good in a pasty, cold with cameline sauce, or heated in a river bird sauce. Or roasted slowly like beef and eaten with salt or à la dodine, in pieces on a dish, like river birds.

Nota that in Bésiers they sell two types of wood pigeons: small ones that are not the best, for the larger are more flavorsome; the larger birds eat acorns in the woods as do pigs. These are eaten in a boussac like rabbit, quartered; and sometimes in a halbran sauce [292]; and roasted, à la dodine. Or if you want to store them, put them, larded, in pastry. They are in season from St. Andrew's Day until Lent, but they return only every 3 years.

155. Plovers and woodcock. Dry pluck them, sear them, leave the feet on; roast and eat with salt.

And *nota* that there are three types of birds that some cooks roast without cutting through to gut them, *scilicet* larks, turtledoves, and plovers, because their bowels are fatty and without filth. For larks eat only pebbles and sand; turtledoves, juniper seeds and sweet smelling herbs; and plovers, wind.

156. Partridges mate around mid-February and fly off 2 by 2. At Easter, cook them with some beef in briskly boiling water. Then pull them out and roast.

Item, partridges whose feathers are well attached and tight to the flesh and well

---

44. Probably to scorch off the remaining pinfeathers.

ordered and handsome like the feathers of a sparrow hawk are freshly killed. *Item,* you can tell by pulling on the feathers at their base.

Item, partridges are plucked dry and the head and feet cut off. Plunge into boiling water, then prick with venison, if you have it, otherwise with bacon fat, and eat with fine salt, or in cold broth and rose water and a little wine, or in three parts rose water, orange juice and wine for the fourth part.

157. Swan. Pluck it like a chick or a goose, scald it or plunge it into boiling water, put it on a spit, bind it in four places, and roast it whole, with the feet and beak and with the head unplucked. Eat it with yellow poivre. *Item,* if you wish, glaze it. *Item,* when you kill it, split the head to the shoulders. *Item,* sometimes they are skinned and then redressed in their plumage after cooking.

158. Swan redressed in its skin, with all its plumage. Take it and inflate it [242] from between the shoulders and split it the length of the stomach. Then remove the skin from the neck down, after cutting all the way around, near the shoulders, while holding the body by the feet; then put it on a spit, fasten it, and glaze it. When it is cooked, dress it in its skin again; the neck should be straight or stretched out. Eat it with yellow poivre.

Pasties:

159. Spring chickens are put in pastry, on their backs, breast uppermost, with large slices of pork fat laid on the breast, and then covered.

Item, in the Lombard manner. When the spring chickens are plucked and prepared, take eggs (that is, yolks and whites) beaten with verjuice and spice powder and dip the chicks in. Then place them in the pastry with strips of pork fat as above.

160. Mushrooms one night old are the best. They are little and red inside, closed at the top. Peel and then wash them in hot water and boil. If you want to put them in a pasty, add oil, cheese, and powdered spices.

Item, set them between two dishes on the coals and then add a little salt, cheese, and powdered spices. They are found at the end of May and in June.

161. Water parsnips.[45] Wash in two or three changes of hot water, then flour them and fry in oil. *Item,* after this, some put them in a pasty with a generous amount of onions, and slices of herring or eel, and spice powder.

162. *Nota.* Pasties must be large enough to be filled with plenty of meat.

163. Fresh venison pasties. Venison must be boiled and the foam skimmed off, then lard it to make pasties. All fresh venison pasties are made this way, with the meat sliced into big pieces shaped like long sticks of wood, and for this reason it is called *pasté de bouli lardé.*[46]

---

45. Skirret root.

46. A larded boiled meat pie.

164. Beef pasties. Take good, young beef and remove the fat. Cook the lean part in pieces until it reaches a boil, and then take it to the pastry cook to be minced with the fat and beef marrow.

Beef cheeks are sliced thinly and set in a pasty; then, when the pie is cooked, pour halbran sauce on top [292].

165. Mutton pasties. Finely minced, with scallions.

166. Veal pasties. Take the broad end of the leg of veal, cut round, and add to it an almost equal amount of beef fat. With this you can make six good pies for a course.

Freshwater fish:

167. To cook fish, simmer salted water, then add the heads and boil a little; next put in the tails and cook them together, and then add the remainder. All fresh fish feels firm and hard when pressed with the thumb and has red gills. If it has been dead a while, *secus.*

168. Bass is poached and eaten with green sauce [276].

169. Barbel, in summer, is cooked with water and one third part wine, plus a lot of parsley and sorrel. One cooks it a long time to make it firm.

170. Smaller barbels roasted with verjuice. These small ones are used in winter in pottage or fried with jance sauce. *Item,* in winter serve in sharp or yellow poivre, for they are the same.

171. Perch is cooked in water without being scaled, and then skinned: serve with vinegar and parsley; when fried, it is put in stew.

172. Tench is scalded and the slime cleaned off, as with an eel. Then it is poached and eaten with green sauce. Fried, it is used in pottage. Prepared as "reversed," it is roasted and sprinkled with cinnamon powder, then immersed in vinegar and oil while it is roasting, and eaten with cameline sauce. And note that in reversing it, it must be cut along its back, head and all; then turn it inside out, place a lath between the two skins, and truss it up with thread and roast.

173. Bream poached in water is eaten with green sauce; and when roasted, with verjuice.

174. Luce is cooked by simmering it in water with a little wine. Put the head in first and then the tail and bring to a full boil; then add the rest. Serve luce with green sauce when it is cooked in water. Sometimes pottage is made with fried luce. Other times fried luce is eaten with jance sauce. From one luce, you can eat one half cooked in water and the other half salted one, two, or even eight days later, although in that case you need to soak it to remove the salt. Then boil and drain it and fry and eat with jance sauce. When fresh luce is left over from dinner, you can serve it shredded at supper.

175. Pike is good in chowder. Soft roe of pike is valued more than the hard

roe, except for making rissoles, for you grind up the hard roe to make rissoles.

176. Salted shad is cooked in water and eaten with mustard, or in wine and served with scallions. The season for fresh shad begins in March. Clean it through the gills, scald, cook in water, and eat with cameline sauce; if it will be in a pasty, first scale it, then put it into the pastry, and when it is nearly cooked, add a very thin cameline sauce, and bring this sauce to a boil.

Item, shad is prepared as above, without being scaled, then roasted in the oven with parsley and a combination of half verjuice, with the other half wine and vinegar; it is in season from February to June.

177. *Fenes,*[47] just as with shad.

178. Carp. Some prefer the soft-roed to the hard, and *e contrario. Nota* that the sterile is better than either. Carp with white, and not yellow or red, scales is from good water. One with large eyes bulging from the head and a soft and smooth palate and tongue is fat.

Item, if you wish to carry a live carp for an entire day, wrap it in damp hay and carry it belly up in a pouch or sack without exposing it to the air.[48]

Item, to prepare carp, remove the gall right in its gullet, and once this is done you can put the head to cook whole and it will cook well. If the gall were not removed, the head would stay bloody and bitter. That is why, if the gall is not removed intact, without breaking, you need to immediately wash the place and rub with salt. When the gall is removed whole, you need not wash the head or anything else, but you should put the head to boil first and soon afterward the tail, and then afterward the rest, all over a slow fire. Cooked carp is eaten with green sauce; if any is left over, put it in a galantine.

Item, braised carp. *Primo,* put minced onions in a pot to cook with water. When the onions are well cooked, toss in the head and soon afterward the tail, and next the rest of the pieces and cover it well, allowing no steam to escape. When it is cooked, have ready ginger, cinnamon, and saffron, mixed with wine and a little verjuice, that is, one third part, and boil it all together well covered; serve in bowls.

Nota that the Germans say of the French that they take a great risk by eating their carp so undercooked. It has been observed that if Frenchmen and Germans have a French cook who prepares carp for them, in the French style, the Germans will take their portion and send it back to have it cooked much more than before, but the French will not.

179. Trout. The season begins in May. *Item,* their season lasts actually from March until September. The white ones are good in winter, the red

---

47. BF/Ueltschi give "freshwater fish," but unknown name.
48. Repeats 2.4.24.

sort[49] in summer. The best part of the trout is the tail, and of carp, the head. Trout with 2 little black veins on the palate are red.

Cut up trout into chunks about 2 fingers thick and cook in water with a lot of red wine, and eat with cameline sauce. On meat days, in a pasty, they should be covered with wide strips of bacon.

180. Eels. Those with small, pointed heads, fine, shiny, iridescent, and glistening skin, small eyes, fat body, and white belly are fresh. The others have a big head, tan belly, and thick brown skin.[50]

Fresh eels. Skin and slice, cook in water with lots of parsley, then add thinly sliced cheese. Remove the pieces of eel, make sops, and into each bowl put 4 pieces. Otherwise, cook some onions, then cook the eels in the water, along with a little bit of spices and saffron and the onions in a pot, and make sops.

Large eels, cooked in water with parsley, are eaten with white garlic [sauce]. In a pasty, eat with cheese and finely powdered spices. For reversed large eel, serve in hot sauce like lampreys.

If you wish to keep eel, let it die in salt and leave it there for three days and nights. Then scald it, remove the slime, slice it up, cook in water with scallions, and add wine just at the end. If you want to salt it only from morning until evening, prepare it,[51] slice it up, and put the pieces in coarse salt. If you wish further to hurry the process, grind black salt and rub each piece with it, and with this shake the slices in salt between two bowls.

Reversed eel. Take a large eel and skin it, then split it along the back, down the length of the bone on both sides, in such a way that you remove the bone, tail, and head all together in one piece. Then wash and turn it inside out—that is, the flesh outward—and tie it at intervals and cook in red wine. Remove it and cut the thread with a knife or scissors, and set it to cool on a towel. Grind ginger, cinnamon, cloves, powdered cinnamon, grain of paradise, nutmegs and set them aside. Take toasted and well-ground bread and do not strain it, but moisten it with the wine in which the eel has been cooked and boil all together in an iron pan. Add verjuice, wine, and vinegar and pour this over the eel.

181. Pimpernels have gleaming fine skin and are not muddy like eels. They should be scalded and roasted without gutting—*scilicet* the fresh ones—and those that have been dried and salted are roasted and eaten with verjuice.

182. Loach is poached in water with parsley and good cheese and eaten with mustard. Fried, it can be used in a pottage and with green garlic [sauce]. Cooked in water, it is eaten with mustard; and before frying dust it in flour.

---

49. I.e., salmon trout.

50. Repeats 2.4.26.

51. I.e., scald and remove slime.

183. Waymel is poached in water, eaten with mustard or, if you prefer, with green garlic [sauce].

184. Little lampreys are lightly roasted, eaten with warm sauce, as described below for lampreys. If they are cooked in water, they are served with mustard; if they are cooked in pastry, pour the hot sauce over the pasties, and boil.

185. Lampreys. Note that some bleed the lamprey before they skin it and some skin it before they bleed or scald it. To bleed it, first wash your hands well, then split its jaw through the chin—*id est* up to the lower lip—and thrust in your finger and pull out the tongue, and bleed the lamprey into a dish. Stick a small skewer into its mouth to make it bleed better. If your fingers or hands are covered in blood, wash them and likewise the cut in the lamprey with vinegar and let it run into the dish, and keep this blood, for it is the fat. As for skinning it, have it simmering in water on the fire, then skin it like an eel; and with a blunt knife peel and scrape the inside of the mouth and throw away the scrapings. Then skewer and roast until somewhat underdone.

And to make the boue sauce, take ginger, cinnamon, long pepper, grain of paradise, and a nutmeg and grind them and set aside. Toast bread until it is dark. Grind and moisten it with vinegar, then run through the strainer. Put the blood, the spices, and the bread together and bring just to a boil. If the vinegar is too strong, adjust it with wine or verjuice. This, then, is a boue; it is black and just thick enough—but not too thick—with the flavor of vinegar slightly dominant, and a little salty. Pour it hot over the lamprey and let it sweat.[52]

Item, you can make another, quicker sauce: take the blood and some vinegar and salt, and when the lamprey is roasted to a half-done state, bring the sauce just to a boil, and pour it over the lamprey and leave it to sweat between two dishes.

Item, boiled lamprey. Bleed it as said above and retain the blood. Cook the lamprey in vinegar and wine and a little water, and when just barely done, take it off the fire and cool on a towel. Take toasted bread and mix with the bouillon and put through a strainer; then boil with the blood, stirring well so that it does not burn. When it is boiled, pour into a mortar or a clean basin, and keep stirring until it has cooled. Then grind ginger, cinnamon, powdered cinnamon, clove, grain of paradise, nutmegs, and long pepper, and mix with the bouillon, and put in a dish as above; its color should be black.

Item, braised lamprey. Remove the blood from the lamprey as before; then skin it in very hot water. After this, have the sauce mixed and ready to boil, and it should be thin. Put the lamprey in a pot with the sauce over it, covering the pot with a close fitting lid, and then boil. Turn the lamprey over once in the pot

---

52. I.e., let it finish cooking slowly, at a low heat.

while it cooks, and do not overcook. It is no problem if it is not completely immersed in the sauce, as long as the pot is tightly closed. Then place the fish whole on a dish on the table.

186. Crayfish, cooked in water and wine, is eaten with vinegar.

187. Serve bleak cooked in water with parsley, with mustard.

188. Roach and rosse[53] are for frying. They are gutted, then floured and fried. Eat them with green sauce.

189. Chub[54] prepared as above, or roasted without being skinned, and eaten with sorrel verjuice. Know that chub are larger than bleak, and rounder than roach, because roach are flatter.

Saltwater fish:

190. Round saltwater fish are in season in winter, the flat ones in summer. *Nota* that no saltwater fish is good when caught in rainy or damp weather.

191. Brett is prepared like mullet, cooked and skinned like a ray, and eaten with cameline sauce. Brett is like dogfish, but smaller, milder, and better. Some say that it is the female of the dogfish and that it is brown on the back whereas the dog is red.

192. Dogfish, like brett. *Nota* that the liver of either fish works well in a pasty using fine spice powder; some add cheese, and that makes it nice.

193. Mullet is called *mungon* in Languedoc. Scale it the way you would a carp, then split it lengthwise along the belly, cook in water with parsley, then cool it in its bouillon. Serve with green sauce, or better, with orange sauce. *Item*, it is good in a pasty.

194. They don't say cod in Tournai, unless it is salted, for there the fresh fish is called *cableaux*, but yet they cook and eat it as will be explained here for cod. *Item*, when it is caught just off the coast and one intends to keep it for 10 or 12 years, it is gutted and its head removed, then dried in the air and sun, and certainly not near a fire or smoke. This preparation is called "stockfish." After keeping it a long while, when it is to be eaten, it must be beaten with a wooden hammer for a full hour, and then soaked in warm water for a good 12 hours or more. Then it may be cooked and skimmed very well as one does for beef and eaten with mustard or dipped in butter. If there are leftovers, in the evening fry them in small shreds and top with spice powder. Likewise if any fresh cod is left over for the evening or the next day, shred it and fry it in a little butter. Then remove it from the pan, drain the butter so that none remains, and continue to fry the fish dry and drizzle beaten eggs over it. Put onto platters or dishes and sprinkle fine powdered spices over it. Even without eggs, it is still a good meal.

---

53. Rosse is a small, red-tailed fish like a minnow (Cotgrave).

54. Or dace.

Prepare and cook fresh cod like gurnard, with white wine, and eat à la jance; and salt cod is eaten with butter or mustard.

When salted fish is not adequately soaked, it tastes too salty; yet soak it too much and it does not taste good; therefore, whoever buys it ought to test it by biting off and tasting a bit.

195. Fresh mackerel is in season in June, although it is found as early as March. Prepare by gutting it through the gills, then dry with a clean rag and roast it without washing it at all. Eat it with cameline sauce or fine salt. Salted mackerel is cooked with wine and shallots or put in pasties with powdered spices on top.

196. Tuna is a fish found in the sea or salt ponds in parts of Languedoc. It has no bones except the spine, and has hard skin, and should be cooked in water and eaten with yellow poivre.

197. Langoustes are large crayfish and are good cooked in water. Plug up with tow the place in the tail through which it was emptied, the jaw and any claws that are broken, and all other places through which liquid might drip from its body, and then cook it in water or in the oven, and eat with vinegar. However, if you want to roast it in the oven, you do not have to plug it up; rather, it is sufficient just to cook it upside down.

198. Conger. Scald and skin like an eel. Then put in the pan and salt it like mullet, and simmer it well like beef; and when it is almost done, boil it with parsley. Then let it rest in its juices. Serve and eat with green sauce. Some people brown it on the grill.

199. *Tumbe*, mullet, gurnard, and grimondin are readied by gutting through the belly and washing thoroughly. Put them in the pan, add salt and then cold water. (That is the method used for saltwater fish, whereas for freshwater fish the water must first be simmering.) Cook over a low fire and remove from the fire; let it cool in its liquid and eat with cameline sauce. However, in summer, grimondin is split along the back from the shoulders, roasted on the grill, drenched with butter, and eaten with verjuice.

Nota that tumbe, the largest fish, is caught in English waters. Gurnard is the next largest, and both species are a tan color. Mullet is the smallest and the reddest, and grimondin is the thinnest of all and is tan, spotted, and varies in color; yet all are from the same species and are similar in flavor.

Item, mullet is good in a verjuice *chaudumée*, with powdered spices and saffron.

200. Carve up fresh salmon, leaving the backbone in for roasting; then cut it into steaks, boil them in water, with wine and salt added during the cooking; eat with yellow poivre or cameline sauce or in pastry, if you like, with powdered spices. If the salmon is salted, eat it with wine and scallion rounds.

201. Haddock is prepared like mullet. It must be left to cool in its cooking water and is served à la jance.

202. Garfish is gutted through the gills, cooked in water, and eaten with cameline sauce. Or cut it up and sprinkle powdered spices and olive oil on the pieces.

203. Sea pig, harbor porpoise, and porpoise are all the same. Split the whole fish through the belly like a pig; make soup and pottage with the liver and entrails, as with a pig.

Item, you can also cut it up and split it along the back, like a pig. Sometimes it is roasted on the spit in its skin and then eaten with heated sauce, like *bruliz*[55] in winter.

Otherwise, cook it in water with some wine, powdered spices, and saffron, and place in a dish in its broth like venison. Then grind ginger, cinnamon, clove, grains of paradise, long pepper, and saffron, and moisten with the bouillon, and remove from the mortar and set aside.

Item, grind browned bread, moisten with the bouillon from the fish, and strain through a sieve, and boil it all together until clear. Serve like venison, and prepare black poivre [282]. Or cook the fish, without washing it, in half water, half wine, put it on a dish, and pour on a sauce such as galantine, and serve. When you want to eat it, take a little of the cooled sauce and add either meat bouillon or its own liquid or vinegar *et similia,* and put on the fire in a dish to warm. Serve the warm sauce over the fish.

204. Stockfish must be cut into square pieces like a checkerboard, soaked for only one night, then taken out of the water and put on a towel to dry. Then put some oil on to boil and fry your pieces of stockfish in a little oil. Eat with mustard or garlic sauce. Stockfish is made, it seems, from cod [194].

205. Sturgeon. Scald, remove the slime, cut off the head, and split into two. And first split it along the belly, as for a pig, then gut it, slice it up, and cook in wine and water. Let the wine dominate; as the wine boils away, keep adding more. The fish is done when the skin may be easily lifted. What you wish to eat hot needs broth and spices as if it were venison; and what you wish to keep, cool and eat with parsley and vinegar.

206. Sturgeon counterfeited by veal. For 6 dishes, the evening before, or early in the morning, take 6 calves' heads, without skinning them, but scald them in hot water as you would a pig, and cook them in wine. Add a pint of vinegar and some salt, and boil until they fall apart from cooking. Then let the heads cool and remove the bones. Take a square of good coarse cloth, and put them all in it, that is, one head on top of the other, pressing them tightly into the smallest space you can. Then sew with good strong thread, like a square pillow, then put it between two good planks and see that it is pressed heavily, leaving it overnight in the cellar. Slice it thinly, with the skin on the outside like venison, and add parsley and

---

55. Possibly a kind of fish.

vinegar. Put only 2 slices on each dish. *Item,* if you cannot find enough heads, this can be done with a skinned calf.

207. *Craspois.* This is salted whale and must be sliced raw and cooked in water like bacon, and served with peas.

208. Salted whiting is good when its fin is whole and its belly white and intact. It is tasty cooked in a chaudumée of butter, verjuice, and mustard. Fresh whiting, fried, à la jance.

209. *Vive*[56] have three places that are dangerous to touch: that is, the spine on the back near the head, and the 2 gills. Touch these parts only with a knife, and dispose of it all, and pull the innards out through the gill flaps. Then incise it crossways in several places. Roast it and eat with verjuice and butter, or verjuice and powdered spices.

Aliter, cook in a little water, then fry it in butter. Boil some verjuice with the remainder of the butter and pour onto the fish.

Flat saltwater fish:

210. Ray is gutted through the navel. Keep the liver and cut the ray into pieces. Then put it on to cook like plaice. Skin it and eat with cameline sauce. Ray is good in September and better in October, because then it eats fresh herring. That which has only one tail is from our waters, and those that have several are not. Another fish similar to the ray is called *tire,* but it has no spikes on its back and is larger and more spotted with black.

Galantine preparation for ray in the summer: Grind almonds and moisten with boiled water, and strain through a sieve; then grind ginger and garlic, and mix into the almond milk and pass through a sieve. Boil it all together and put it atop pieces of cooked ray. When ray is fried in oil without flour and eaten hot with cameline sauce, it is tasty and better than a cold galantine.

Ray must be washed several times, then cooked in a little bouillon, quartered, skinned, and cooled. But some boil it in water without salt, then remove it from the pan, skin and wash it thoroughly, and set it on a good bed of straw. Then they bring some salted water to simmer in a pan and cook the ray over a low fire. If you prefer, fry some of the boiled ray. This ray keeps well for eight days.

211. Plaice and *carrelet* are nearly of the same type. The larger is called plaice, and the small one carrelet, and it is spotted with red on its back. They are good eating at March floodtide but better in the April floodtide. Gut from the back, under the gill; wash well, put in the pan with salt, and cook in water like mullet. Eat with wine and salt. *Item,* carrelet are good fried with flour and eaten with green sauce.

---

56. Quaniner or sea-dragon.

212. Dab are speckled with yellow or russet on their backs and become whiter toward the gills. Fry them in flour and eat with green sauce, or half fried and eaten in a civet or gravé.

213. *Pole* and sole are the same species; though poles have spotted backs. They must be scaled and gutted like plaice, washed, and poached with salt and some water. When nearly done, add more salt; then let them sit in their broth. Eat with green sauce or with butter with some of the hot broth, or in a chaudumée of old verjuice, mustard, and butter heated together.

Item, some roast them on the grill with damp straw between the fish and the grill or fire; these must not be scaled and are eaten with sorrel verjuice.

Item, you must also scale those that are to be fried, and they must be floured, then fried, and eaten with green sauce, and put in a civet or gravé.

214. Turbot is called *ront* in Bésiers. Scald it, prepare it as above, and eat with green sauce, or put in sugar; and it is better cooled two days later.

215. Brill is scaled, prepared, cooked, and eaten as above, for they taste the same and are of the same species, except only that brill is smaller and turbot larger and better.

216. Bream and *barte*[57] are scaled, cooked in water, eaten with cameline sauce, or put in a pasty with powdered spices.

217. Sea tench is poached in water or roasted, and eaten with verjuice.

218. Dory is cleaned down the side lengthwise, poached or roasted, and eaten with verjuice.

219. Anchovies are roasted cut into strips, eaten with mustard; or skinned, then cooked in water just a bit, then floured, fried in oil, and eaten à la jance or with garlic [sauce].

220. Flounder. You can completely disregard these, for they are in season only when the *quarrel*[58] are so plentiful that you trip over them. Unlike the carrelet, this fish does not have red spots on its back, which is quite dark.

221. Cockles. *Nota* that fresh cockles are red and brightly colored and are found piled up together and stay in a heap without scattering or leaving. Stale ones from an old catch do not stick together but lie spread about with dulled color. Select them, then wash thoroughly and scald in 2 or 3 changes of good hot water, and then soak in cold water for a while before drying briefly on a towel by the fire. Fry in oil with cooked onions, and afterward powder with spices and eat with light green garlic sauce, made green from wheat or sorrel or leaves of herb bennet or barbery.

222. Mussels are cooked quickly over a high fire, using very little water and

---

57. A type of bream.
58. Plaice.

wine, without salt, and eaten with vinegar. *Item,* when they are cooked in old ver-juice and parsley, with fresh butter added, it makes a quite decent pottage. Mussels are best at the beginning of the new season in March. Cayeux mussels are red, round across, and rather elongated, while the Normandy mussel is black.

223. Cook crayfish in water and wine—more wine than water—and skim, then add a little salt (although some say not, because the salt darkens them).

Saltwater crayfish, langoustes, must be cooked in the oven. Plug up all the holes, the way a baker does, and eat them sliced up, in vinegar and with scallions.

224. Cleaned cuttlefish is skinned, then cut into pieces, then put in a pan on the fire with salt. Stir often, until it dries out. Place it in a cloth and press it well, and pat it dry here and there with the cloth. Then flour it and fry in lots of oil, with or without onions. Sprinkle it with spices and eat with garlic sauce colored green with wheat.

Item after it is skinned and cut in pieces, some keep it and stir it for a long time in the pan to remove its dampness, pouring off the liquid often. When it renders no more liquid, dry it as above. Then fry it in lots of oil for a long time until it is wrinkled and curled up like pork cracklings. Then put it in a dish, sprinkle with powdered spices, and it is ready to eat. The oil that has remained hot in the pan on the fire has taken on the odor of the fish, which makes it worthless, and you have to throw in cold wine which makes the odor come out with the steam. Only in this way will the oil remain good for pottages, and better than other oils that have not been used for cooking.

Item, if you have no other meat except cuttlefish, fry it with onions as above, then put in two dishes with a good boiled garlic jance sauce on it. This would be quite a passable dish.

Thoroughly wash fresh cuttlefish, then put it in a pan in the oven and cook with water, verjuice, oil, and new scallions; but *primo* remove the bones and the gall.

Various ways of preparing eggs:

225. An *arboulastre* or two of eggs. Take just 2 leaves of coq and less than half that, or none at all, of rue, since it is strong and bitter; four leaves or less of wild celery, tansy, mint, and sage; a little more marjoram, yet more fennel, and even more parsley. As for greens, take chard, violet leaves, spinach and lettuce, and clary in equal amounts, so that in all you have two good handfuls. Cull and wash in cold water, then press to remove all the water. Grind up two pieces of ginger; then put your herbs in a mortar two or three times with the ground ginger, and crush them together. Beat sixteen eggs well, both yolks and whites, and grind and mix them in the mortar with what is already there. Then divide in two and make two thick omelets, which will be fried in the following manner: First, heat the pan

thoroughly with oil, butter, or another grease as you wish, and when it is good and hot all over, especially toward the handle, mix and pour your eggs into the pan and turn them often with a spatula, then sprinkle on some good grated cheese. Know that it needs to be put on top, because if you grind the cheese with the herbs and eggs, when you fry the omelet, the cheese on the bottom would stick to the pan. That is what happens when you mix the eggs with the cheese for an omelet. For this reason, first put the eggs in the pan, and put the cheese on top, and then cover with the edge of the eggs; otherwise it will stick to the pan. And when the herbs are fried in the pan, you can give the arboulastre a square or round shape and serve it neither too hot nor too cold.

226. Lost eggs. Break the shell and pour the yolks and whites on the coals or on very hot embers, and after, clean them off and eat.

227. Helmeted eggs. Break open the egg at the end; remove the white, and with the yolk remaining inside the shell, set the shell on a tile, with the hole facing downward.

228. Fried omelet with sugar. Separate the whites and beat just the yolks, then put some sugar in the frying pan and let it melt; after this, fry the yolks in it, then put on a plate, with sugar on top.

229. Lost eggs. Take 4 egg yolks, beat them, add rock and powdered sugar, and beat it all together very well, then pour through a sieve. Fry in an iron skillet and after that cut in diamond shapes and place these lozenges on a dish with other omelets of poached eggs, and sprinkle finely powdered spices on top.

230. To make a beautiful egg omelet, take 7 eggs and remove the whites from two and put those two yolks in a bowl, and break all the others on top of them. Beat it all together and fry; and it will be yellow.

Aliter, take 10 or 12 eggs and remove the whites and beat the yolks, then fry in oil, making sure that they are well spread out in the pan; cut them in lozenges, and flip each lozenge with a wooden spatula. Then put on the plate half an omelet fried in the usual way with 4 lozenges of these yolks and some sugar fried normally.

231. Arboulastre in a tart cooked in a skillet. Grind herbs and a piece of gingerroot, then mix and beat with eggs, as described above. Have ready some kneaded dough as for the bottom of a tart, and heat a skillet with oil or other grease. Then put the kneaded dough into the bottom of the skillet, and add the tart filling with plenty of grated cheese mixed in. Since the bottom, that is, the pastry that forms the bottom of the tart, will be cooked before the top side is barely heated up, you must have ready another skillet with its bottom well heated, wiped, and cleaned. Fill this pan with hot coals, and put it inside the first skillet, atop and touching the filling, so that it heats up and cooks until dry, and that ensures the filling is at the same level of doneness as the dough.

232. Tansy eggs. Grind a little ginger and some tansy, and mix it with vinegar; strain and put in a dish with whole, peeled hard-boiled eggs.

233. *Nota* about the nature of eggs. Cook them in boiling water and the yolk will not harden, in any circumstance, if you have not first put them in cold water. But if you put them in cold water and then immediately into boiling water, they will harden well. *Item,* if you put them in simmering water and leave them on the fire, they will get hard at once. *Item,* hard or soft, as soon as they are cooked, put them in cold water: they will be easier to peel.

Entremets, fried dishes, and glazed dishes:

234. Frumenty. First, hull the wheat just as you would barley. For 10 bowls you need a pound of hulled wheat, and you may sometimes find it at the spice merchant's shop already hulled for one blanc per pound. Cull it and cook it in water in the evening, then cover it and leave by the fire all night in lukewarm water. Later, remove the cover and pick over the wheat to remove any foreign matter from it. Next, boil some milk in a pan—without stirring it, for it would curdle. Right after it boils, put it into a pot so that it does not pick up the taste of brass. Also, once it is cold, take the cream off the top so that the cream does not cause the frumenty to turn. Boil the milk once more with a very scant amount of wheat, hardly any. Pour the egg yolks in, using for each septier of milk, one hundred eggs. Then take the boiling milk, and beat the eggs into it. Move the pot from the fire, add the eggs, and then set it elsewhere. If you see that it is about to curdle, set the pot in a full pan of water. On fish days, use milk; on meat days, use meat broth. Add saffron if the eggs do not seem yellow enough. *Item,* half a piece of ginger.

235. *Faux grenon.*[59] In water and wine, cook poultry livers and gizzards, or a piece of veal or leg of pork or mutton, then mince it very finely and fry in bacon fat. Then crush ginger, cinnamon, clove, grain of paradise, wine, verjuice, beef bouillon, or the broth from whatever meat you use, and plenty of egg yolks. Pour this mixture over the meat and boil well together. Some add saffron, for it should be a yellowish color. Some add browned bread, ground and sieved, in order to thicken it with the eggs and bread. It should taste sour from the verjuice. When serving, sprinkle cinnamon powder over each bowl.

236. *Mortereul* is made like faux grenon, except that the meat is ground in the mortar with cinnamon spice and there is no bread, but cinnamon powder is sprinkled on top.

237. *Taillis* to serve in Lent. Take fine grapes, boiled almond milk, *eschaudés,*[60]

---

59. Possibly from *grenu,* grained, or full of seed (Cotgrave); a "mock porridge" made of minced meat, like grain.

60. A type of pastry.

galettes, and crusts of white bread and apples cut in small cubes, and boil milk with saffron to give it color, and some sugar. Then mix all together until it is thick enough to be cut. It is served in Lent instead of rice.

238. Stuffed chicks. A chick must be suffocated while it is still alive, and do this at the neck. Bind its neck and let it die: then scald, pluck, gut, let it soak a while in water, and then stuff.

Item, otherwise, when the bird is all ready to put on the spit, in the opening where it was gutted, separate with your finger the skin from the flesh. Then push the stuffing in with the end of your finger; after which, sew the skin back to the flesh at the opening with an overcast seam, and put the bird on the spit.

And *nota* that the stuffing is made of parsley and a little sage with hard-boiled eggs and butter, all minced together and mixed with powdered spices. For each chick you need three eggs, whites and all.

239. To fatten chicks, cage them in a dark place, wash out their basin or drinking trough 9 or 10 times a day, and each time give them fresh food and clean fresh water. For their food give them beaten oats, which are called oatmeal, soaked in a little milk or curdled milk. Keep their feet dry for 9 days.

240. To fatten a goose in three days, feed it warm breadcrumbs soaked in curds or whey.

241. To serve young chicks that look like young partridges, you need small pullets. Kill them a day or two beforehand, then clean them and chop off the feet and necks, eviscerate them, and throw out the giblets. Break the carcass and press the thighs and legs to make the flesh on them shorter, then prick with cloves and roast, and eat with salt like partridge.

242. Poultry stuffed another way. Take hens and cut their throats, then scald and pluck, being careful not to tear the skin while plucking them; then refresh them by soaking in water awhile. Take a reed and thrust it between the flesh and the skin, and blow into it. Next, split it between the shoulders—and do not make too large a hole—and pull out the entrails. Leave the skin on the legs, wings, from the neck to the whole head, and the feet. To make the stuffing, take mutton, veal and pork, and chicken meat minced together when raw. Then grind in a mortar with raw eggs, rich harvest-time cheese, good powdered spices, a bit of saffron, and salt to taste. Then stuff the chickens and sew up the hole, and from the remainder of the stuffing make balls like woad cakes[61] and cook in beef bouillon or in good beef broth, with plenty of saffron, but do not boil them so vigorously that they fall apart. Then skewer them on a very slender spit, and to make them golden, take lots of egg yolks, beat them well with a little ground saffron, and glaze them. And if you want to glaze them green, grind up green herbs and then lots of well-

---

61. Woad was a blue dye sold in cake form.

beaten egg yolks passed through the sieve on account of the greens, and glaze your poultry with it when it is cooked along with the meatballs. Set the spit atop the pot of glaze, and pour glaze all along it, and put it back on the fire 2 or three times, until the glaze solidifies on the birds and meatballs. Keep the glaze far enough from the fire so that it does not burn.

243. Riz engoulé for a meat day. Pick over the rice and wash in 2 or 3 changes of hot water, and let it dry over the fire. Put it into simmering cow's milk, add saffron to color it yellow, and thin with more milk. Then add fat from beef bouillon.

Aliter, rice. Pick it over and wash in 2 or 3 changes of hot water until the water remains clear. Then cook it halfway. Strain off the water and put the rice on trenchers in dishes to drain and dry in front of the fire. Then simmer it until quite thick, using beef fat stock and saffron, if this is a meat day. If it is a fish day, rather than meat broth, add well-ground almonds, unsieved; then add sugar, but no saffron.

244. To make a cold sage, quarter poultry and cook in water with salt, then cool. Grind well some ginger, cassia buds, grains of paradise, and cloves, and do not strain. Then grind bread moistened with the broth from the chicken, plenty of parsley, some sage, and a little saffron among the greens to make them bright green, and sieve (and some sieve hard-boiled egg yolks with this). Add some good vinegar and ladle over the cooked poultry. Place quartered hard-boiled eggs atop the poultry, and pour the sauce over it.

Aliter, pluck the chicken, then boil it with salt until done. Take it from the pot, quarter it, and let it cool. Hard-boil some eggs in water; soak some bread in equal amounts of wine and verjuice or vinegar. Then take parsley and sage, with ground-up ginger and grains of paradise, and pass through a strainer. Also, sieve the egg yolks. Place quartered hard-boiled eggs upon the chicks, and then spoon the sauce over them.

245. Piglet souse is prepared the same way as a cold sage, but without eggs, sage, or bread. It is made with the snout, ears, tail, short hocks, and the 4 trotters, well cooked and hairs removed, then put in a sauce of ground parsley, vinegar and spices.

246. *Pottage parti,* faux grenon. Thoroughly cook a leg of mutton, or chicken livers and gizzards, in water and wine, and cut them into squares. Then grind ginger, cinnamon, clove, a little saffron, and grains of paradise, and mix in wine, verjuice, and meat bouillon—the same the meat has cooked in. Remove from the mortar and have ready toasted bread soaked in wine and verjuice. Grind this well and sieve, and boil it all together. Fry the meat in fat and add to it the bread; then add sieved egg yolk to thicken it. Serve in bowls, and sprinkle with powdered cinnamon and sugar, but only on half the contents of the bowl and not on the other; and thus it is called "pottage parti."

247. Flans for Lent. Prepare and skin eels; then cook them in water so hot that you can remove the flesh without the bones. Remove also the head and the tail, and only take the flesh. Grind saffron in the mortar, then mash the eel flesh over it; moisten with white wine, and with this make your flans. Sprinkle sugar on the top.

Item, flans have the taste of cheese when you make them with the soft roe of pike or carp, ground almonds or starch, with saffron soaked in wine, and put lots of sugar on top.

Item, can also be made with tench, pike, carp, and starch, with saffron mixed in white wine with sugar on top.

248. Jacobin tart.[62] Scald eels, cut into small pieces no thicker than half a finger, and take gingerroot, crumbled harvest-time cheese, and bring this to the baker to have a tart made of it. Sprinkle it with cheese at the bottom, and then put the eel on top of that, and then a layer of cheese, and then a layer of crayfish tails, and alternating layers like this as long as the ingredients last. Boil some milk, then grind[63] some saffron and ginger, grain of paradise and clove; mix this mixture with the milk, and then add it to the tart after it has been in the oven a bit. Be sure to add salt to the milk. Do not cover it. Fan out the crayfish tails decoratively and prepare a pretty crust separately, to cover it once it is baked.

249. Another tart. *Nota* that with pig stuffing you can make a covered tart, but the stuffing must be well made.

250. To make a tart. Take 4 handfuls of chard, 2 handfuls of parsley, one handful of chervil, a sprig of fennel, and two handfuls of spinach. Pick them over and wash in cold water, then chop very small. Then crush up two kinds of cheese, one soft and one medium, and mix together with eggs, both yolk and white. Add the herbs to the mortar and mash everything, and mix in some powdered spices. Or instead first grind two pieces of ginger in your mortar, and then grind in the cheeses, eggs, and herbs. Then toss some grated aged hard cheese, or another kind, onto the herbs. Carry to the oven to have it made into a tart and eat it hot.

251. 4 dishes of meat aspic. Take a pig and 4 calf's feet and have two chicks plucked and two lean young rabbits skinned, and remove the fat; then while they are raw, split them all lengthwise—except the pig which is cut into pieces. Mix in a pan 3 half gallons of white wine or claret, a quart of vinegar, a pint of verjuice; boil and skim well. To give it an amber color, add a quarter ounce of saffron enclosed in a small, fine cloth, and boil that together with everything, plus a little salt. Then take 10 or 12 pieces of white ginger, 5 or 6 of galingale, half an ounce of

---

62. Scully and Scully (*Early French Cookery,* 106) explain that "Jacobin" was associated with the hearty eating habits of certain Dominican friars in the rue St. Jacques.

63. MS says *Boulez* (boil), but BF and Pichon agree on *broyez* (grind).

grains of paradise, 3 or 4 pieces of mace leaf, two blancs' worth of zedoary, 3 blancs' worth of cubeb and nard,[64] bay leaves, and 6 nutmegs. Then crush them in a mortar, put in a bag, and boil with the meat until it is cooked. After it is all done, remove and set it to drain on a white cloth. Then take the feet, the snout, and the ears for the best plate, and use the rest for the others. Stretch a fine cloth between two trestles and pour your whole potful through it, except for the spices, which you remove, and strain it for pottage, but do not stir, so that the liquid remains clear. But if it does not strain well, light a fire now and then to keep it hot so it will strain better, and strain it 2 or 3 times until it becomes clear, or pour through a cloth folded three times. Then take the dishes and arrange the meat in them, and place some cooked crayfish legs and tails on top of the meat. Reheat the aspic and pour enough of it over the meat until the meat is covered and bathes in it, for there should be only a little meat showing. Then put in the cellar overnight to cool, and in the morning stick in it cloves and bay leaves and cinnamon powder, and sprinkle with red anise.

Nota that to make it in two hours, you need quince seed, *philicon*,[65] and cherry-tree gum. Crush this all together and put in a linen bag to boil along with the meat.

Item, on fish days, you make the aspic dishes as above, with pike, tench, bream, eels, crayfish, and loach. And when the fish is cooked, put it to drain and dry on a fine white cloth, skin it, and clean thoroughly, throwing the skins into the bouillon.

252. *Item*, to make a blue aspic, take some of the same bouillon, either fish or meat, and place it in a fair-sized pan and boil it again on the fire. Procure from a spice merchant two ounces of tournesoc,[66] and set it to boil in the bouillon, until it takes on a good color, then squeeze it out and remove it. Take a quart of loach and cook it in another pan. Skin the loach on the dishes, pour the bouillon over it as described above, and let it cool.

Item, in this way a blue jelly is made. If you wish to decorate the jelly with your coat of arms, take gold or silver, whichever you prefer, and with the white of one egg draw the design with a small feather, and place the gold on it with a pair of tweezers.

253. *Aliter*, for 20 jellied dishes you need 10 skinny young rabbits, ten skinny chicks, a pint of loach which is worth about 3 sols, one hundred crayfish that are

---

64. Cubeb and nard are spices.

65. Pichon suggests *filicule*, an astringent plant of the fern family. It was used as a medicine, but we find no references to its culinary use.

66. Tournesoc is an orchil lichen (Scully and Scully, *Early French Cookery*, 23); also known as archil or dyer's moss (Redon, Sabban, and Serventi, *Medieval Kitchen*, 26).

not from the Marne, 6 sols; a skinny pig, 3 sols, 8 deniers—and although it is thin, you still must remove the fat from between the skin and the flesh, and cube it; 3 shoulders of veal, 4 sols; 8 half gallons of wine to cook the veal completely in wine; 2 half gallons of vinegar; half an ell of linen cloth, 2 sols.

Item, the veal is cooked completely in wine and vinegar. Skim it and add salt, then remove it and cook the rabbits and chicks, skim, and put half a bay leaf and some saffron in linen or a little pouch to cook with it. Mix in spices finely ground in a stone mortar. When everything is cooked, strain it through the sieve and cloth, until it is clear. Then cook the loach and crayfish separately and take the crayfish tails and prepare your plates, each with half a rabbit, half a chick, 4 loaches, and 4 crayfish tails; put them in the cave or cellar, and taking care to place the dishes so that they are level, pour the aspic on top, filling them well. The next day, put on each plate a white violet, pomegranate seeds, red *dragees,* and four bay leaves.

254. Summer andouille. Take the tripe of a lamb or kid and remove the membrane, cook the remainder in water with a little salt, and when it is cooked, mince it finely or grind it. Beat 6 egg yolks and a tablespoon of fine powdered spices together in a bowl; then add and mix in the tripe. Next, spread it all on the intestinal membrane and roll up as for sausages. Tie loosely with thread lengthwise and then tightly crosswise; and then roast on the grill. Remove the thread before serving. *Vel sic:*[67] make into balls, that is, using the membrane itself, and fry these balls in lard.

255. Meatballs. Take lean meat from a raw leg of mutton and the same from a lean pork leg. Chop it all together finely, then in a mortar grind ginger, grains of paradise, clove, and sprinkle this over the ground chopped meat. Mix in some egg white, but no yolk. Using the palms of your hands, form the raw meat and spices into the shape of apples. When the mix is all well shaped, cook them in water with some salt. When done, remove them and spit them on skewers of hazelnut branches to roast. As they start to brown, have ready some ground and sieved parsley mixed together with flour, neither too thinly nor too thickly. Take the meatballs off the fire and put a dish under them, and holding the spit over the dish, turn it and coat the balls well. Put them back over the fire as many times as needed for them to turn quite green.

256. Frogs. Catch them using a line and hook with a bait of meat or red cloth. Cut them across the body near the legs and empty out the area near the anus. Separate the two legs, remove the feet, and skin the legs raw. Then wash them in cold water; keeping the legs overnight in cold water will render them even better and more tender. After soaking like this, wash them in warm water and dry in a

---

67. Latin: "Or this way."

towel. Roll the clean and dried legs in flour and then fry in oil, fat, or other liquid, and put them in a bowl with powdered spices on top.

257. Snails, called *escargots,* are best if caught in the morning. Take young, small, dark-shelled snails, from vines or elder bushes. Wash them in water until they give off no more slime. Then wash them once in salt and vinegar and cook them in water. Extract the snails from their shells with the end of a pin or needle and then remove their tails, which are black, because that is their excrement. Wash and boil in water, and then set them in a dish or in a bowl, to be eaten with bread. Some say also that they are better fried in oil and onion or other liquid after they have been cooked as explained above. They are eaten with powdered spices, and are for rich people.

258. Norse pasties are prepared from cod liver, sometimes with minced fish added. First you must boil it a little, then mince and put into small pasties of the size that costs 3 deniers, with powdered spices on top. When the pastry cook takes them uncooked to the baking shop, they are fried whole in oil, and this is for a fish day. On a meat day, they are made of reconstituted beef marrow, that is, the marrow has been put in a pierced spoon, and this spoon with the marrow put into the pot of meat bouillon, and left there as long as you would leave a plucked chick in hot water to plump it; then put it in cold water. Then cut the marrow and roll it into large pebble shapes[68] or like small cannonballs. Then take to the pastry cook, who puts them 4 by 4 or 3 in each pasty with powdered spices on top. Without baking in the oven, they are deep-fried in fat. You can also make marrow beignets; prepare them in the same manner, then take flour and egg yolks and make dough. Take each piece of marrow and fry it in fat. As for the beignets, inquire about the rest.

Other entremets:

259. Larded milk. Simmer cow's or sheep's milk and add bits of diced bacon and saffron. Take whole eggs, *scilicet* the white and yolks, beat well and pour in all at once, without stirring, boiling all together. Remove from the fire and let it curdle; or without eggs, use verjuice to make it curdle. When it is cool, fasten it tightly in a piece of linen or cheesecloth and give it whatever shape you wish, either flat or long, and weight it with a large rock, leaving it to cool all night on a sideboard. The next day, open it up and fry in an iron skillet—it needs no added grease, but you can add some if you wish—and place it on plates or in bowls like slices of bacon and stick it with cloves and pine nuts. Should you want a green color, use tournesoc.

---

68. Middle French: "jabetz." Not known; Pichon offers "jalet," pebble or ammunition unit (BF 328 n. 254, 20).

260. Rissoles for a fish day. Cook chestnuts over a low fire and peel them. Mince them together with hard-boiled eggs and peeled cheese. Then pour in egg whites, and mix it all with powdered spices and a little fine salt, and make your rissoles. Fry them in lots of oil and sugar them. And *nota*, in Lent, instead of eggs and cheese, use whiting and cooked water parsnips, chopped very small, or the flesh of pike or eels, and chopped figs and dates. *Item*, commonly rissoles are made of figs, grapes, roasted apples and shelled nuts to imitate pine nuts, and powdered spices; and the dough should be very well saffroned. Then fry them in oil. If it needs a thickener, starch binds and rice also. *Item*, the flesh of langouste is a good substitute for meat.

261. Rissoles for a meat day are in season from the Feast of St. Remy.[69] Take a pork leg and remove the fat. Then put this lean meat in a pot with plenty of salt, and when it is almost cooked, remove it. Chop up hard-boiled eggs, whites and yolks, and separately mince the meat very small, and mix the eggs in, and sprinkle powdered spices on top. Then wrap in dough and fry in its own grease. *Nota* that this is an appropriate stuffing for pig. Sometimes cooks buy it from the roasters[70] to stuff pigs; however, it is good to add some nice aged cheese to use when stuffing pigs. *Item*, at the courts of lords like Monseigneur de Berry, when they kill a beef cow they make rissoles with the marrow.

262. Crêpes. Take flour and stir together with eggs, both yolks and whites, but remove the germ, and thin with water, adding some salt and wine, and beat together for a long time. Then put some lard on the fire in a small iron skillet, or half lard and half fresh butter. When it sizzles, pour some of the batter into a bowl pierced with a hole the size of your pinkie finger, and let it run out into the pan, starting in the center and then pouring it all around. Set the finished crêpe on a plate and top with powdered sugar. And the iron or brass skillet should hold three pints, have sides half a finger tall, and be as wide at the top as at the bottom, neither more nor less, because of the way you have to cook the crêpes.

263. Crêpes Tournai style. *Primo*, you need to have a brass skillet that holds one half gallon, of which the top and bottom are of the same diameter or thereabouts, and the edges should be 4 fingers tall, or at least 3 and a half. *Item*, melt salted butter, skim and clarify it, and then pour it into another pan, leaving behind all the salt, and add fresh grease to the butter, very clear, as much as there is of liquid butter. Remove the white from half of your eggs, beat this together with the rest of the eggs, whites and yolks, and then fry them. Take a third or a fourth measure of warm white wine and mix it all together. Adding the best wheat flour

---

69. October 1.

70. MS has cookie makers (*oubloyers*), but Pichon and BF agree that it must be an error for meat roasters (*oyers*). See BF 328, n. 255, 20.

you can procure, beat the mixture so much and so long—enough to tire out one or two people! The batter should be neither thin nor thick, but such that it runs easily through a hole as big as a little finger. Then put butter and grease on the fire together, in equal amounts until sizzling. Fill a bowl or a large pierced wooden spoon with the batter, and trickle it into the grease, first into the middle of the pan, then circling around until the bottom is covered; and keep beating the batter continuously to make more crêpes. The crêpe in the pan should be lifted with a little skewer or small spatula of wood and flipped to cook on the other side; then remove it, put it on a dish, and start another. Keep stirring and beating that batter without stopping.

264. Pipefarces. Take egg yolks, fine flour, salt, and a little wine, and beat together vigorously. Then roll slices of cheese in the batter and fry in an iron skillet with lard. You can also make these with beef marrow.

265. A meat arboulastre for 4 people. If you have killed a kid goat, you can make a dish of the stomach, rennet stomach or abomasum, the omasum, etc., in yellow sauce with bacon and liver, lungs, viscera, and other tripe. Cook them very well in water, then mince with two knives as for purée, have them minced finely by a pastry cook, or grind them in a mortar with sage or mint, etc., as above.

Nota that with kid goat the bowels are not included with the viscera as they are with pork. The reason is that pig intestines are large and can be washed and turned inside out in the river, but not those of a goat. But all the other things are used as with the pig—the head, the throat and the neck, the liver, the lights or lungs, for it is the same thing, the spleen and the heart—and all together it is called the viscera, all the same as with pigs.

266. *Item,* when people speak of spit-roasted pork entrails that are eaten in July, washed in salt and vinegar, these are the intestines that are fat, sliced in pieces 4 fingers long, and eaten with new verjuice.

267. Water parsnip. The best are the newest taken from the ground and freshly pulled, harvested in January, February, etc. The freshest are recognized because they snap when you break them, whereas those not freshly pulled from the ground will bend. Scrape them and remove any bad parts with a knife as for turnips. Then wash them thoroughly in warm water, boil slightly, and dry on a towel. Then flour them and fry, then serve nicely arranged on little plates, and sprinkle sugar on top.

Item, if you wish to make pasties with them, do as above up to the frying, and then put them in pastry, breaking them in two pieces if too long, and instead of sugar as said above, you put small pieces of figs and grapes.

268. Pike egg beignets. Put the eggs in water with salt and cook well. Let cool, then cut in pieces and wrap in pastry and eggs, and fry in oil.

Sauces not boiled:

269. Mustard. If you want to make a stock of mustard to keep for a long time, do it at harvest time, in mild must. Some say that the must should be boiled.

Item, if you want to make mustard hastily in a village, grind some mustard seed in a mortar and mix in some vinegar, and pour through a straining cloth. If you want it to be ready immediately, put it in a pot in front of the fire. *Item,* should you want to take your time and make excellent mustard, put the mustard seed to soak overnight in decent vinegar, then grind it well in a mill, and then little by little add vinegar. If you have some spices left over from making aspic, clarry, hippocras, or sauces, grind them up with it, and then let it steep.

270. Sorrel verjuice. Grind the sorrel very fine without the stems and add aged, white verjuice; do not strain the sorrel, but grind it well. *Vel sic:* grind parsley and sorrel or wheat leaves. *Item,* young and tender vine shoots, without stems.

271. Cameline. *Nota* that in Tournai, to make cameline, they grind ginger, cinnamon, saffron, and half a nutmeg; mix with wine, then take it out of the mortar. In a mortar, grind untoasted white breadcrumbs that have been soaked in cold water, add wine, and strain. Then boil it all, and at the end add red sugar;[71] and that makes winter cameline. In summer, they prepare it the same way, except that it is not boiled. In truth, to my taste, the winter one tastes fine, but the following one is much better: grind a little ginger and lots of cinnamon, remove from the mortar, and add a quantity of toasted bread or breadcrumbs, moistened in vinegar and strained.

272. *Nota* that there are three differences between Mecca ginger and Columbine ginger: Mecca ginger has darker skin and is more tender to the knife, and whiter inside than the other. *Item,* Mecca ginger is better and always more costly.

The best galingale is bright magenta when cut. The heaviest nutmegs, firmest when cut, are the best. It's the same for heavy galingale—firm to cut—since some that is spoiled and rotten is light as dead wood and will be no good. The one that is heavy and firm to the knife like a walnut is the one to use.

273. Garlic cameline for skate. Grind ginger, garlic, and vinegar-soaked white bread crusts or toast. And it tastes better if you add liver.

274. White or green garlic sauce for gosling or beef. Grind a clove of garlic and untoasted white breadcrumbs, and moisten with white verjuice. If you want it green for fish, grind some parsley and sorrel, or one of the two, or rosemary.

275. Garlic and must sauce for fresh herring. Crush the garlic—only slightly—without peeling it, and mix with must, and serve it with the peels.

---

71. This sugar is "red" because it may have been colored with spices as in ¶ 290. Scully and Scully (*Early French Cookery*) call it "brown sugar," which is its modern French translation.

276. Green spice sauce. Finely grind ginger, clove, grain of paradise, and remove from the mortar. Then grind parsley or herb bennet, sorrel, marjoram, or one or two of the four, and white breadcrumbs moistened with verjuice, and strain and grind again very well. Then strain again, combine it all, and season with vinegar. *Nota* that it makes a good *soutié* [277], but without the breadcrumbs. *Nota* that to spice it, many put in only rosemary leaves.

277. A bright green soutié for preserving saltwater fish. Strain parsley, sage, herb bennet, and vinegar; but beforehand grind coq, hyssop, whole sorrel, marjoram, ginger, cassia buds, long pepper, clove, grain of paradise, and remove from the mortar. When it is all strained, pour it over the fish, and it will be bright green. Some also use herb bennet with its root.

Nota that the word *soutié* is from souse, because it is made like piglet souse [245]. For freshwater fish, make a chaudumée in the same way, except do not use any herbs; in place of them, use saffron, nutmegs, and verjuice. It should be a fine yellow, and boiled and then poured hot onto the cold fish. Cut it crosswise, put it on the spit, and roast on the grill.

278. A sauce for roasted capon. Cut up the bird and put on the pieces a mixture of salt, verjuice, and one-third wine (either white or red). Press the flesh well together as for chicken [241].

Item, in summer, the sauce for a roasted chicken is half vinegar, half rose water, and press well, etc. *Item,* orange juice is good.

Boiled sauces:

279. *Nota* that in July old verjuice is quite weak, yet new verjuice is too green. Therefore, at vine-harvest time, a verjuice mix of half old and half new is best. *Item,* in pottage, dilute it with broth, but in January, February, etc., the new verjuice is better.

280. Tournai-style cameline: look in the preceding chapter [271].

281. Yellow or sharp poivre. Take ginger and saffron, then take toasted bread moistened with meat broth—or even better, thin cabbage broth—then boil, and when it boils, add vinegar.

282. Black poivre. Grind finely some cloves, a little pepper, and ginger. Then grind toasted bread soaked in lean meat broth—or cabbage broth, which is actually better. Then set to boil in an iron pan, and when it boils, add vinegar. Then put in a pot on the fire to keep it hot. *Item,* some add cinnamon.

283. Galantine for carp. Grind saffron, ginger, clove, grain of paradise, long pepper, and nutmegs, and mix with the fatty broth in which the carp cooked, and add to it verjuice, wine, and vinegar. Thicken with a little bit of finely ground toasted bread, without sieving it (although it is said that sieved bread makes a nicer sauce). Boil it all and pour over the cooked fish, then serve in dishes. It is

good reheated in a dish on the grill, much better than eating it cold. *Nota* that it is fine and just as tasty without saffron. *Nota,* two pieces of carp and four fried gudgeons[72] suffice per plate.

284. Saupiquet for rabbit, or river birds, or wood pigeons. Fry onions in good fat, or mince them and cook in the dripping pan with beef broth. Do not add verjuice or vinegar until it boils, and then add half verjuice, half wine, and a little vinegar, letting the spices be the dominant taste. Then take half wine, half verjuice, and a little vinegar, and put it all in the dripping pan under the rabbit, pigeon, or river bird. When they are cooked, boil the sauce, and put some toasted bread with the bird.

285. *Calimafrée,* or lazy sauce. Take mustard, powdered ginger, a little vinegar, and the fat from carp broth, and boil together. If the sauce is to be used for a capon, instead of using carp fat and broth, add verjuice, vinegar, and capon grease.

286. Cow's milk jance. Grind ginger and raw egg yolks without germs, and pass them through the sieve with cow's milk; or, or if you fear it might curdle, cook the egg yolks before grinding and passing through the sieve. Then mix with cow's milk, and boil it well.

287. Garlic jance. Grind ginger, garlic, and almonds, mix with good verjuice, and then boil; some use a third of white wine.

288. Jance is made as follows: put almonds in hot water, peel, and grind together with two pieces of gingerroot (or powdered ginger), a little garlic, untoasted white bread—a little more of this than almonds—and mix with white verjuice and a quarter part of white wine. Strain, then boil very well, and serve in bowls. Serve more generously than you would other sauces.

289. Poitevine sauce. Grind ginger, clove, grain of paradise, and some livers, and remove from the mortar. Grind toasted bread, wine and verjuice and water, one third of each, and boil with some fat from the roast. Pour over the roast or into bowls.

290. Must sauce for young capons. Crush new black grapes in a mortar, bring to a boil, and then strain through a sieve and sprinkle on a little powdered ginger and more cinnamon, or cinnamon alone *quia melior,*[73] and stir a bit with a silver spoon. Toss in crusts or toasted bread or eggs or chestnuts to thicken it, along with some red sugar, and serve.

Item, on this subject, know that the spice alkanet[74] colors things red and is also like galingale; it is soaked in wine and meat broth, then ground.

---

72. A kind of fish.

73. Latin: "which is better."

74. Or bugloss, a dye still in use as a food coloring. It was also employed to disguise poor grades of wine by deepening the color or to darken the corks of port to make it look well aged. Here it may be to color the sugar.

Item, if you care to make this must sauce as early as St. John's Day,[75] before grapes are available, you can do so with cherries, wild cherries, morello cherries, mulberry wine, by using powdered cinnamon, but no ginger, or only a little. Boil as above, then put sugar on it.

Item, after grapes can no longer be found, *scilicet* in November, a must sauce is made with wild plums. Remove the pits, then grind or crush in the mortar, boil with the skins, then pass through a sieve, add powdered spices, and the rest as above.

291. Quick sauce for capons. Put nice clean water in a dripping pan under the capon while it is roasting and sprinkle the capon with it continuously. Grind up a clove of garlic, add to this water, and boil. Serve like jance sauce. You can make do with this if you have nothing better.

292. Sauce to boil pasties of halbran, duck, young rabbits, or wild rabbits. Finely grind lots of good cinnamon, ginger, clove, half a nutmeg, mace, and galingale, and mix with half verjuice and half vinegar. The sauce should be thin. Once the pasty is just about done, pour this sauce into it and put it back into the oven until it bubbles. *Nota* that halbran are young duck that cannot fly before the August rain. And *nota*, in winter add more ginger so it will be spicier, for in winter all sauces should be stronger than in summer.

293. Boar's tail sauce. Take pork numbles, hares, and river birds and put them on the spit, with a dripping pan beneath containing wine and vinegar. Grind grain of paradise, ginger, clove, nutmeg, long pepper, and cinnamon; remove from the mortar. Then crush toasted bread soaked in true wine and strain. Pour everything from the dripping pan plus the spices and bread into an iron skillet or a pot; add liquid from the meat. Prick with cloves whatever meat you roasted, then add it to the pot. This is how to prepare a sauce for breast of wild boar. *Nota* that nutmeg, mace, and galingale cause headaches.

294. Sauce râppée. Scald three or four bunches of verjuice grapes, crush part of them, and remove the sediment from this verjuice. Then grind ginger and mix with the liquid and put in a bowl. Grind up the grape skins, soak in verjuice, and strain. Combine everything in the bowl. Serve with some seeds on top. *Nota,* in July, when the verjuice crop is maturing and abundant, use this sauce with ham or pig's feet.

295. Sauce for a capon or hen. Soak some crustless white bread in verjuice and saffron. Grind it, then put it in a dripping pan with 4 parts verjuice and one part of grease from the capon or hen—and no more, for any more would be too much. Boil it in the dripping pan and serve in bowls.

296. Sauce for eggs poached in oil. Cook and boil onions a long time, as for

---

75. June 24.

cabbage, and then fry them. Empty a skillet in which you have fried some eggs so that nothing is left in it; add water and the onions and a quarter of vinegar—that is, the vinegar should make up one quarter of the whole. Boil and pour it over your eggs.

Beverages for the sick:

297. Sweet tisane. Boil water, then for each septier of water add one generous bowl of barley—it doesn't matter if it is all hulled—and two parisis' worth of licorice; *item*, also figs. Boil until the barley bursts, then strain through two or three pieces of linen. Put plenty of rock sugar in each goblet. The barley that remains can be fed to poultry to fatten them. *Nota* that the youngest licorice is the best; when cut it is bright green, while the older is more faded and dead and dry.

298. Bouillon. To make 4 septiers of bouillon, you need a portion of yeast risen for three days[76] about the size of half a one-denier loaf of brown bread; *item*, a generous quarter bushel of bran. Put 5 septiers of water in a pan, and when it simmers, put the bran in the water and boil until it is reduced by a 5th or more. Let it cool until it is just warm, then strain through a sieve or cloth. Soak the yeast in the liquid, put it all in a cask, and leave it for 2 or 3 three days to ferment. Put in the cellar and let it clear, and then drink. *Item*, if you want to make it better, add a quart of well-boiled, well-skimmed honey.

299. *Bochet.* To make 6 septiers of bochet, take 6 quarts of fine, mild honey and put it in a cauldron on the fire to boil. Keep stirring until it stops swelling and it has bubbles like small blisters that burst, giving off a little blackish steam. Then add 7 septiers of water and boil until it all reduces to six septiers, stirring constantly. Put it in a tub to cool to lukewarm, and strain through a cloth. Decant into a keg and add one pint of brewer's yeast,[77] for that is what makes it piquant—although if you use bread leaven, the flavor is just as good, but the color will be paler. Cover well and warmly so that it ferments. And for an even better version, add an ounce of ginger, long pepper, grains of paradise, and cloves in equal amounts, except for the cloves of which there should be less; put them in a linen bag and toss into the keg. Two or three days later, when the bochet smells spicy and is tangy enough, remove the spice sachet, wring it out, and put it in another barrel you have underway. Thus you can reuse these spices up to 3 or 4 times.

Item, another bochet which keeps for 4 years, and you can make a whole queue[78] or more or less at one time if you wish. Combine three parts water and a 4th part honey, boil and skim until reduced by a 10th, and then pour into a con-

---

76. A sourdough sponge with its yeast fermenting.

77. Brewer's yeast.

78. Barrel or cask; also a unit of measure.

tainer. Refill the cauldron and do the same again, until you have the amount you want. Let it cool and then fill a queue. The bochet will then give off something like must that will ferment. Keep the container full so that it keeps fermenting. After six weeks or seven months,[79] you must draw out all the bochet, up to the lees, and put it in a vat or other vessel. Then break apart the first container and remove the lees. Scald it, wash, reassemble it, and fill it with the liquid you set aside, and store it. It does not matter if it is tapped. Crush four and a half ounces of clove and one of grain of paradise, put in a linen bag, and hang inside the keg by a cord from the bung.

Nota for each pot of foam skimmed off, add twelve pots of water and boil together; this will make a nice bochet for the household staff. *Item,* using other honey rather than the skim, make it in the same proportions.

300. Beverage of red capon broth. Put a capon or hen in a very clean, newly leaded pot, well covered, so that nothing can escape. Place the pot in a pan full of water and boil until the capon or hen in the pot is cooked. Remove the capon or hen, and give the broth in the pot to a sick person to drink.

301. Hazelnut beverage. Boil and peel the nuts, mix in cold water, then grind them and thin with boiled water and strain. Do this, grind and strain, twice. Then put in the cellar to cool; it is quite a bit better than a tisane.

302. Beverage of almond milk as above.

Pottage for the sick:

303. Flemish caudle. Put a little water on to boil, Then for each bowl, use 4 egg yolks beaten with white wine, trickle them into the water and stir well, and add salt as needed. When it has boiled well, pull it to the back of the fire. *Nota,* if making only one bowl for a sick person, put in five yolks.

304. Hulled barley or barley gruel. Soak the barley in a basin for about half an hour. Pour off the water, put it in a copper mortar, and crush with a wooden pestle. Then set it to dry, and when it is dry, winnow it. When you want to make pottage, cook it in a little pot with water, and when it is about to split, pour off the water and boil it with almond milk. Some then strain it. *Item,* add plenty of sugar.

305. Almond milk. Boil and peel almonds, put them in cold water, then grind and mix with onion bouillon and strain through a sieve. Fry some onions, adding a little salt, and then boil on the fire. Add sops. If you make almond milk for sick people, do not put in any onions, and in place of the onion broth to soak the almonds as said above, soak them in clean warm water and boil, and do not add salt, but plenty of sugar. If you want to make it suitable for drinking, strain it

---

79. More likely two months, though all MSS say seven (BF 328).

through a sieve or through two pieces of linen, and add lots of sugar just before drinking.

306. Chicken coulis. Cook the chicken until it falls apart and grind it with all its bones in a mortar. Then mix it with its own bouillon, strain, and add sugar. *Nota* that the bones must be ground first[80] and removed from the mortar. Strain them and clean the mortar. Then grind the flesh and add plenty of sugar.

307. Perch, tench, sole, or crayfish coulis. Cook it in water and retain the liquid. Then grind almonds with the perch and add the broth, then strain and boil it all. Serve the perch with sugar on top. It should be a clear broth, and use plenty of sugar.

308. The best coulis for a meat day are made from the necks of chickens and chicks. Grind up the necks, heads, and bones, and then grind again very thoroughly. Mix this with broth from beef cheek or giste of beef, and strain.

309. *Nota* that after the great heat of June, spice pottages come into season, and after St. Remy's Feast stews of veal, hare, oysters, etc.

310. Gruel is cooked until it bursts, then strained and cooked with almond milk as said above in the recipe for hulled barley, and use lots of sugar.

311. Rice. Cull it and wash it in two or three changes of warm water, until the water remains completely clear. Partially cook it, then strain and put on trenchers in dishes to drip and dry before the fire. When dry, cook with meat-fat broth and saffron until thickened, if it is a meat day. If it is a fish day, don't add meat broth, but instead use almonds finely ground and not strained, then sugar it abundantly, with no saffron.

Some little extras:

312. How to make compote. *Nota* that you must begin on St. John's Day which is the 24th day of June. First, take 5 hundred new walnuts, around that time, and be careful that neither the shell nor the kernel is already formed and that the shell is neither too hard nor too tender, and peel them completely, and then pierce them in three places, right through, or in a cross shape. Then soak them in water from the Seine or a spring, changing it daily. Keep them soaking for 10 to 12 days, until they turn nearly black and have no bitter taste when you bite into them. Then bring them to a boil in fresh water, just for the time it takes to recite a *Miserere*, or boil just until you see none of them will be either too hard or too soft. Empty the water and drain the nuts in a strainer. Melt a septier of honey, or enough to cover all the nuts. Strain and skim the honey. When it has cooled to lukewarm, add the walnuts, leave them there two or three days, and then drain. Take enough honey to soak them in, and put the honey on the fire. Bring it to a

---

80. MS says "boiled"; seems in error for "ground."

good boil, then skim it and remove from the fire. Into the holes you made in each walnut, put a clove at one end and a little piece of ginger at the other. Add the nuts to the honey once it cools to lukewarm. Stir two or three times a day. At the end of 4 days, remove them and reheat the honey, adding more if necessary, boil and skim and boil, then put your walnuts into it; and do this process each week for a month. Then leave them in an earthenware pot or a cask and stir once a week.

Around All Saints' Day,[81] take large turnips, peel, and cut them into quarters, then boil. When they are slightly cooked, remove them and soak in cold water to make them tender. Then drain. Melt honey and proceed the same as with walnuts. Be sure that you do not overcook your turnips.

Item, on All Saints', take as many carrots as you wish, scrape them well, and cut in pieces, then cook them like the turnips. Carrots are red roots that are sold at the Halles by the handful; each handful costs one blanc.

Item, cut choke pears into quarters without peeling them, and cook them exactly the way you do turnips.

Item, when squash are in season, take the ones neither the hardest nor the softest, peel them, remove the seeds and cut into quarters, and prepare the same as for turnips.

Item, when peaches are in season, take the hardest ones, peel, and cut up.

Item, when squash are in season, cut them into quarters, remove the seeds from the center, and proceed the same as for turnips.

Item, around St. Andrew's Day, take roots of parsley and fennel, scrape them, and cut into small pieces. Split the fennel and remove the core, but do not do this with parsley. Proceed exactly the same way as described above, no more, no less.

When all your preserves are ready, you can then go on to the following recipe: First, for 5 hundred walnuts, grind into powder a pound of mustard seed and half a pound of anise, a quartern and a half of fennel or of coriander, and a quartern and a half of caraway seed, a seed eaten in dragees. Grind all these things in a mustard mill and with very good vinegar moisten the mixture, but it should still be quite thick, and put in an earthenware pot. Then take half a pound of horseradish—a root sold by herbalists—and scrape it well, cut it up as small as you can, grind it in a mustard mill, and mix with vinegar, adding it to the pot.

Item, grind into a powder half a quartern of clove stems, half a quartern of cinnamon, half a quartern of pepper, half a quartern of Mecca ginger, half a quartern of nutmeg, and half a quartern of grains of paradise.

Item, take half an ounce of saffron of Ort,[82] dried and crushed, and an ounce

---

81. November 1.

82. This is probably saffron wort (garden saffron); in his notes Pichon tries to identify it as a location.

of red cedar—a wood sold by spice merchants, called "cedar from which knife handles are made." Then take one pound of good honey, hard and white, and melt it on the fire. When it is well cooked and skimmed, let it sit, then strain it and cook again, and if it still foams, strain it again; otherwise let it cool. Then mix mustard with good wine and half as much vinegar and add it to the honey. Mix the powdered spices into some wine and vinegar and add to the honey. Boil the cedar a little in wine and then stir it and the saffron into the other things, plus another handful of coarse salt.

Item, when that is done, get two pounds of the small and seedless Digne grapes —be sure they are fresh—and pound them thoroughly in a mortar and add some good vinegar. Strain and add to the other mixture. *Item,* if you add 4 or 5 quarts of must or fortified wine, the sauce will be better.

313. To make *cotignac,* peel quinces, cut in quarters, and remove the eye and the pips. Cook them in some decent red wine and then strain. Boil some honey for a long time and skim it, then add the quinces and stir thoroughly. Keep boiling until the honey is reduced by at least half; then toss in hippocras powder and stir until is completely cooled. Then cut into pieces and store.

314. Fine spice powder. Take an ounce and a dram of white ginger, a quarter ounce of hand-picked cinnamon, half a quarter ounce each of grain of paradise and clove, and a quarter ounce lump of sugar, and grind to powder.[83]

315. Walnut jam. Before St. John's Day, peel and pierce fresh walnuts and soak in fresh water for 9 days, changing the water every day. Then dry them out and fill the holes with cloves and ginger and boil in honey, and keep them thus as preserves.

316. Water for washing hands at the table. Boil some sage, then strain off the water and cool it until tepid. Instead, you can use camomile and marjoram, or rosemary, and cook with orange peel. Bay leaves also work for this.

317. Hippocras. To make hippocras powder, pound together a quartern of very fine cinnamon, selected by tasting it, half a quartern of choice cassia buds, an ounce of hand-picked, fine white Mecca ginger, an ounce of grains of paradise, and a sixth of an ounce of nutmeg and galingale together. When you want to make hippocras, take a generous half ounce of this powder and two quarterns of sugar, and mix them together with a *quarte* of wine as measured in Paris.[84] And *nota* that the powder and the sugar mixed together make "duke's powder."

---

83. MS A has: "Take I3° of white ginger, 3° of hand-picked cinnamon, half a quarter ounce each of grain of paradise and clove, and 3° lump of sugar." Pichon suggests the above quantities. The 3° symbol is unclear, and MS B has 4°—probably a quarter ounce, note BF. BF/Ueltschi interprets the last two symbols as 3 ounces rather than a quarter ounce.

84. Approximately one half gallon.

To make a quarte or quartern of hippocras by the measure used in Bésiers, Carcassonne, or Montpelier, pulverize 5 drams of choice cinnamon, hand selected and cleaned; 3 drams of white ginger, culled and prepared; one and a fourth drams altogether of clove, grains of paradise, mace, galingale, nutmeg, and nard—more of the first, and of the others less and less of each as you go down the list. Add to this powder a pound and half a quartern, by the heavier measure, of rock sugar, ground and mixed with the above spices. Put some wine and the sugar to melt on a dish on the fire, add the powder, and mix, then put through a straining cloth and strain as many times as needed until it comes out clear and red. *Nota* that the tastes of sugar and cinnamon should dominate.

318. *Saugé.* To make a *poincon*[85] of saugé, remove the stems from two pounds of sage, then put the leaves in the poincon [of wine]. *Item,* hang half an ounce of cloves in a linen bag in the poincon from a cord. *Item,* you can include half an ounce of bay leaves. *Item,* half a quartern of Mecca ginger, half a quartern of long pepper, and half a quartern of bay leaf. To make saugé at the table in winter, have a ewer of sage water and pour it into a hanap of white wine.

319. To make white wine red at the table, in the summer gather red flowers that grow amidst grains, called *perseau* or *neelle* or *passe rose,* and let them dry enough so that they can be made into a powder. Toss it secretly into a glass of wine, and the wine will turn red.[86]

320. If you want to have verjuice from your grape arbor at Christmas, cut off the cluster from the stem as soon as you see it beginning to appear, before it flowers, and after the 3rd time leave it to grow until Christmas. Master Jehan de Hantecourt says that you should trim the vine stock below the cluster, and the bud beneath will sprout a new cluster.

321. If you want to have red choke pears in November and December, cook them with some hay, covering the pot so well that no steam escapes. *Nota,* atop the pears, set fennel seeds boiled in new wine and then dried, or comfits.

322. To make salt white, put a quart of coarse salt and three quarts of water on the fire until it all dissolves. Strain through a cloth, towel, or strainer, then put back on the fire, boil well, and skim. Boil until it is almost dry and the little bubbles that had thrown off water become completely dry. Then take the salt from the pan and spread on a cloth in the sun to dry.

323. To write a letter on paper that stays invisible to everyone unless the paper

---

85. A container the size of a measure by the same name.

86. These plants, perseau (possibly for *percele* [cornflower]), with blue flowers, neelle (corncockle), with reddish-purple flowers, and passe rose (rose-mallow/hollyhock), with flowers of various colors, would seem when ground possibly to impart a reddish color to white wine. BF pose that perseau are red poppies.

is heated, moisten and dissolve some ammonium salt in water, write with this, and let it dry. It will last about eight days.

324. To make birdlime. Peel holly when the sap is rising—this is usually from May to August—and then boil the bark in water until the outer bark separates, then peel it. When the outer bark is peeled away, wrap the remainder in dwarf elder or elder leaves, or other broad leaves, and put in a cold place like a cellar, or in the ground, or in a cold manure heap for 9 days or longer, until it decomposes. Then pound it as for a cabbage purée and shape into little round cakes like woad. Then wash the cakes, one after the other, and break up like wax. Do not wash them too much in the first water or in water that is too hard. After this, break it all up together, knead in running water, put in a pot, and keep well covered. If you want to make birdlime that is waterproof, heat a little oil, mix the birdlime in it, and then smear your line with it. *Item,* another birdlime is made from wheat.

325. If you want to preserve red roses, gather a dozen buds together into a ball, wrap them in linen, and tie with a string just like a ball. Make as many as needed for the amount of roses you want to keep. Then put them in a jug of Beauvais earthen-ware—and not of any other sort—and fill it with verjuice. As the verjuice diminishes, add to it, but use only verjuice that is very mature. When you would like them to open fully, unwrap them, put them in warm water, and let them soak a little.

Item, to keep roses another way, take as many buds as you would like and put as many as can fit into a bottle made of Beauvais clay. Then take the finest sand you can procure and put as much of it into the bottle as there is room for; then plug it so tightly that nothing can get in or out, and put the bottle in a running stream. The roses will keep there the whole year.

326. To make rose water without alembic, take a barber's basin and tie onto it a kerchief stretched across the opening like a drum. Set your roses on the ker-chief, and on top of the roses set the bottom of another basin containing hot ashes and live coals.

To make rose water without either alembic or fire, take two glass bowls and do as explained just above, but in place of ashes and coals, put it all out in the sun, and the rose water will form from the heat of the sun.

327. Roses from Provins are the best to put in clothing, but they must be dried, and in mid-August sifted over a screen so that any worms fall through the holes of the screen, and then spread the roses over your clothing.

328. For Damask rose water, add crushed rose-colored dye to the rose petals. *Vel sic:* pour the water distilled from a first layer of roses onto a second and third and fourth layer; and thus redone four times, it will become red.

329. For red rose water, half fill a glass flask with good rose water, then fill it to the top with red roses, that is, petals of young roses from which the white tips have been cut away. Leave in the sun 9 days and nights, then strain.

330. To make caged birds lay, brood, and raise young. *Nota* that they have never been able to hatch and raise baby birds either in the Hesdin cage, which is the largest in this realm, or in the king's cage at St. Paul, or in the cage of Messire Hugues Aubriot, yet in the Charlot cage they do, *scilicet* lay eggs, brood, hatch young, and raise them. In the first case, the fault is that the young birds are fed on hemp seed, which is hot and dry, and have nothing to drink. In the second case, they give them chickweed or sow thistle, field thistles soaked in water and often changed and always fresh—change it three times a day—in lead vessels that keep it cool. In with the chickweed and green sow thistle, and field thistles whose stems have been soaking in water well beforehand, is mixed hemp seed that has been threshed, sorted, and the hull removed, then moistened and soaked.

Item, put out for the birds in the cage carded wool and feathers to make their nests. Similarly, I have seen turtle doves, linnets, and goldfinches raised in cages laying eggs and multiplying.

Item, also give them caterpillars, small worms, small flies, spiders, grasshoppers, butterflies, and fresh hemp just off the blade, dampened and soaked. *Item,* provide spiders, caterpillars, and such things that are soft to the young bird's tender beak, such as the things peacocks feed their young. Indeed, hens have been seen to brood a peahen's eggs with her own. The eggs all hatch at the same time, but the baby peacocks do not survive for long because their beaks are too tender, and the hen does not seek delicate food for them as their nature requires. Yet her chicks live well on grain or soft animal feed, which is not proper food for peacocks. Furthermore, we have seen hens destroy the very finest, best-sifted wheat in the world, searching for worms or flies.

Item, at the end of April, you must go to the woods to find branches with three forks, and nail them to the wall and cover with other greenery, and there, in this forked stick, they will make their nests.

331. To cure a toothache, take a clay pot with a lid, or one without a lid with a trencher on top, and fill with water and put it on to boil. Then strip and lie down in bed with your head well covered. Have the pot with its cover sealed closed except for one small hole in the middle, or covered by a trencher pierced in the center. Lie with your face held over it, your mouth wide open, so that you can breathe in the steam coming through the hole. Put sage or other herbs in the pot, and keep it well covered.

332. To make sand to put in clocks,[87] take the dust that falls when great tombs are sawed from black marble. Then boil it well in wine like a piece of meat and skim it, then set it out to dry in the sun. After you reboil, skim, and dry 9 times, it will be ready.

---

87. I.e., hourglasses.

333. Poisons to kill deer or boar. Grind in a mortar the root of the electuary herb with blue flowers, put in a bag or wrap in a piece of cloth, and press it, collecting the juice in a basin in the sun. At night keep it covered and dry so that neither water nor other moist liquid can come into contact with it, and keep putting it out in the heat of the sun until it becomes gluey and solidifies like gummed wax. Then close it tightly in a box. When you want to shoot using it, smear it between the barbs and socket of the arrowhead so that when the beast is struck, this part will penetrate the flesh. If you do it otherwise and daub it on the arrowhead differently, when it enters the beast's hide, the ointment will stick only into the hide and the blow will be worthless.

334. Medicine to heal the bite of a dog or other enraged beast. Take a crust of bread and write what follows: *bestera + bestie + nay + brigonay + dictera + sagragan + es + domina + fiat + fiat + fiat.*

335. To make boar meat taste like wild boar, take a boar about two years old and in May or June castrate him; in boar-hunting season hunt it, remove its entrails for the dogs, and butcher it like a wild boar.[88] *Vel sic:* take some pieces of a domesticated pig, sear, and cook in half water, half wine, and serve in a dish some of this bouillon, with some turnips and chestnuts. À la venison, *sic* the third way.

336. *Nota* that a candle put in bran keeps exceptionally. *Nota,* to make a candle, you must first dry the wick very well by the fire.

337. To remove water from wine, put water and wine in a cup, and plunge one end of a cotton thread into the bottom of the cup, the other end hanging out over the edge, below and outside of the cup, and you will see the water dripping, colorless, from this end. When the water has all dripped out, the red wine will begin to drip out. It seems that the same can be done with a barrel of wine.

338. To make fortified wine. Take from the vat or barrel the "mother drop"[89] or the flower of wine—red or white—as much as you want, and put it in an earthenware vessel, and boil it gently and moderately over a fire of very dry wood with a clear flame, without the smallest puff of smoke, and skim with a pierced wooden ladle, not an iron one. If the grapes are green that year, boil until the wine reduces to a third; and if the grapes are ripe, to a fourth. Next, set it to cool in a cask or other clean wooden vessel. When it is cooled, put it in a barrel; it will be better in the third or fourth year than in the first. Store it in a temperate place, neither hot nor cold. Set aside in a small vessel some of this

---

88. This refers to the *fouaille* or entrails of a boar, traditionally grilled and given to the dogs after a hunt, like the "quarry" of a deer. The third alternative recipe may be to make boar taste like venison, as in ¶¶ 86 and 87. See ¶ 91 for the boar-hunting season, September–November 11.

89. Literal translation of Middle French *mergoute/meregoute;* the first juices dropped from the grapes, before treading or pressing, and thus pure, without lees.

boiled wine, to refill the cask in perpetuity, for you know that wine always likes to stay full.

339. To serve tripe in yellow sauce. Choose some tripe either raw or cooked. If raw, cook in a pot with water and without salt, and elsewhere cook a giste of beef, or cheek, without salt. When the two pots are boiling, enrich the tripe pot with the broth from the beef, and cook the tripe longer than the beef. When the tripe is almost cooked, add some bacon and boil and cook together. When it is time to take the tripe out of the pot, add saffron, and when its color is yellow enough, remove the tripe, and salt the broth if you wish. If you use cooked tripe, boil them some more in the giste stock without salt; and for the rest, as above. To cook tripe, do not add salt during the cooking, for it will darken. *Item,* feet, tail, and rennet stomach, which are black, must cook separately, and the stomach and other white things apart.

340. Hedgehog. Cut it by the throat, skin, and gut, then soak in warm water as you would a chick, and dry well by pressing in a towel. Roast it and eat with cameline sauce or in a pasty with halbran sauce. *Nota* that if the hedgehog does not uncurl, put it in hot water, and then it will stretch out.

341. Squirrels are skinned, gutted, allowed to soak like rabbits, roasted, or put in pastry. Eat with cameline sauce or, if in a pasty, with halbran sauce.

342. Turtledoves are good roasted and in pastry and are in season in September, even beginning in August. However, when roasted they toughen up incredibly. If you have plenty of them and wish to raise and keep them, you should clip or pluck feathers at their rump; otherwise their manure will plug them up and from this they will die.

343. Waffles are made in 4 ways:

First, beat eggs in a bowl, then add salt and wine, toss in some flour, and mix them together, then spread the batter a little at a time into two irons, each time as much batter as the size of a slice of cheese. Press it between the two irons, and cook one side; then turn and cook the other. If the finished pastry does not easily come away from the irons, grease them beforehand with a small cloth moistened in oil or fat.

The second way is like the first, but you add cheese. That is, spread the dough as though making a tart or pasty, then put slices of cheese in the middle, and cover it with batter on top. That way the cheese stays between two pieces of dough and then you place it all between two irons.

The third manner is for poured waffles, called "poured" simply because the batter is thinner, like clear broth, made as above. Add finely grated cheese and mix all together.

The fourth manner is with flour kneaded with water, salt, and wine, without eggs or cheese.

344. *Item,* waffle makers prepare another dish called *gros batons,*[90] which are made of flour kneaded with eggs and powdered ginger beaten together, and shaped to be of the size and form of sausages. They are cooked between two irons.

Other miscellaneous odds and ends not needing a chapter:

345. To freshen[91] pottages without adding or removing anything, put a very white cloth on your pot and turn it often; the pot must be away from the fire.

346. To remove a burned taste from pottage, pour the pottage into a clean pot, then take a little leaven and tie it in a white cloth and toss it into your pot, but just briefly.

347. To make a liquid for marking cloth, take axle grease, that is, the black goo at each end of the axle of a cart, and add oak gall and thin with oil and vinegar and boil it all together. Heat up your marker, dip it in, and apply it to your linen.

348. For good kindling to light a fire with a flint, take the froth[92] of a walnut tree more than a year old and put in a pot full of very strong lye, either whole or in pieces the size of two fingers, whichever you prefer, and boil continuously for at least two days and one night. If you do not have lye, take good ashes and add them to the water and make it like *charree,*[93] then boil this foam in it for the time mentioned above and add liquid as needed while it boils. If you boil it in lye, add lye; if you boil it in charree, add water; nonetheless, whatever you boil it in, if you add urine at the end, it will be better for it. Once it has been boiled in this manner, pour off the liquid, then wash in nice clean water to rinse it, then put in the sun to dry, or in the chimney, far from the fire, so it does not burn, for it should dry gradually and smoothly. When it is dry and you want to use it, beat it with a mallet or stick to break it up.[94] When you want to light a fire, take a piece about the size of a pea and put it on a cobblestone, and you immediately can have a fire. All you need are sulphured wicks to light the candle. It must be kept clean and dry.

349. Coot must be very well roasted, and are better cooked in a pottage than roasted, for roasting makes them too dry. Baste coot with its own grease and keep

---

90. Large sticks.

91. This direction *dessaler* means either "to desalt" or "to refresh or make fresh." Used in ¶ 354 it certainly means desalt, but here in reference to pottage, the desired result is unclear.

92. Middle French: *"escume,"* literally "foam," "scum"; it is unclear what part of the tree this refers to, possibly bark, moss, fungus, or sawdust.

93. Wood ash used in washing.

94. This direction is linguistically uncertain. The expression means to beat something until it becomes like an *espurge.* Old French dictionaries give "sponge, purge, alibi" for *espurge,* and Pichon suggests *éponge* (sponge), none of which clarifies this recipe. BF offer Cotgrave's *epurer* (to strain, wring, or squeeze liquids from; to cleanse or purify). Nicot's dictionary, *Thresor de la langue française* (1606), cites *espurge* as an herb, also called Lathyris, Amygdalites, vulgo Cataputia minor.

next to, not too near, the fire. *Item,* it is quite agreeable when fresh and cooked with cabbage. *Item,* put water and onions in a little pot with the coot, then let it boil like a piece of beef. Then grind up some spices[95] and mix them with two parts verjuice and one part vinegar, and you will have a nice pottage. *Item,* coot salted for two days is good in pottage.

350. *Nota* that the croup of venison is the rump and tail. When fresh it is cooked in water and wine, with spices and saffron; it's the same with fresh boar.

351. To make 3 quarts of ink, take 2 ounces each of galls and gum arabic, and 3 ounces of copperas. Break the galls and soak them for 3 days, then boil in three half gallons of rainwater or water from a still pond. And when they have boiled long enough so that nearly half the water has boiled off—that is, there is only about 3 quarts left—take off the fire, and add the copperas and gum, and stir until cool. Store in a cold, damp place. *Nota* that after 3 weeks, it will spoil.

352. To make candied orange peel, cut the peel of one orange into five pieces and scrape off the pith with a knife. Then soak the peels in nice fresh water for 9 days, changing the water every day. After that, bring them just to a boil in fresh water, then spread them on a cloth and let them dry very well. Put them in a pot and cover with honey, and boil over a low fire and skim. To test whether the honey is cooked, drop one drop of hot honey into a bowl of water. If it spreads, it is not cooked; but if the drop of honey holds together in the water without spreading, it is cooked. Draw out the orange peels one at a time and layer them, sprinkling with ginger powder between each layer, *usque in infinitum.*[96] Let season a month or more before eating.

353. To make sausages after killing a pig. Take some meat and chops, first from the part they call the *filet* and then from another area, and some of the finest fat, as much of one as the other, in the amount for the number of sausages you want. Have this finely ground and chopped by a pastry cook. Then grind fennel and a little fine salt. Next, thoroughly mix the fennel with a quarter as much of powdered spices. Combine well the meat, spices, and fennel. Fill the intestines, that is, the small intestines, with this mixture. Know that the guts of an old pig are better than those of a young pig because they are larger. After this, smoke them for four days or more. To eat them, bring once to a boil in hot water and then grill.

354. To desalt butter, put it in a bowl on the fire to melt, and the salt will fall to the bottom of the bowl. This salt is good in pottage. The remainder of the butter stays sweet. Otherwise, put your salted butter into fresh water, knead and pound it, and the salt will stay in the water.

---

95. Middle French: "*menues espices.*" See ¶ 314.
96. Latin: "and so on."

Item, nota that flies do not pursue a horse smeared with butter or old salty grease.

355. Burbot[97] is the same shape as chub, but rather larger. Cook it in water, then skin it like a perch, then boil a cameline or galantine sauce and pour it over; or roast and put in pastry with powdered spices.

356. Pears, at the beginning of the season, *scilicet* in October and November, when freshly picked, are hard and tough, so they need to be cooked in water. When they are choke pears, in order to make them have a nice color, put some hay in the pot while they cook. Next, bake them. But later, when they are dried out and softened from the dampness of the weather, do not cook them in water, but rather only over coals, *scilicet,* in February and March.

357. Magpies, crows, jackdaws are killed with crossbows with large arrows, and those crows that sit on branches can be shot with a weak crossbow, but for those in the nest you need to shoot large arrows to knock down nest and all. Skin them, then boil with bacon and cut in pieces and fry with eggs like *charpie.*

358. Sheep's head should be very well cooked, the bones removed, and the rest finely minced and tossed with powdered spices.

359. To make vinegar to store, empty out the old cask of vinegar, then rinse it thoroughly with very good vinegar and not with water, hot or cold. Next, put that vinegar used for rinsing and any lees into a wooden or clay vessel, not brass or iron. Let this vinegar and lees settle. Then pour off the clear liquid and strain, and put the solids[98] back in the barrel, and fill with more good vinegar. Let it sit in the sun and the heat, the top pierced in 6 places. At night and in fog, plug up all the holes, and when the sun returns, unplug as before.

360. *Rique-manger.* Take two apples as big as two eggs or a little more, peel them, and remove the seeds. Then cut into small pieces, then boil them in an iron pan. Pour off the water and let the rique-manger dry. Then fry it in butter, and while frying, drip two eggs over it, stirring. When everything is fried, sprinkle on powdered spices and saffron threads, and eat with bread in the month of September.

361. Baked hare. I have seen a roasted hare wrapped in that membrane of a pig's viscera known as the caul; it costs 3 blancs. This way, the hare is not larded. *Item,* I have seen it larded.

362. The meat of beef cheek is cut into slices and put in a pasty. When it is cooked, pour on a halbran sauce.

363. Pig spleen needs no preparation except to wash it, put it on a spit, wrap it in its membrane, and cook for a long time.

---

97. Ling cod.
98. I.e., the "mother."

364. Stuffed chickens, colored or gilded. *Primo* blow air into them and remove all the meat inside, then fill with other meat, then color or gild as above. But, really, this dish is too complicated and it is no job for a bourgeois's cook, or even for a simple knight's; therefore I drop the topic.

365. *Item,* for shoulder of mutton, *quia nichil est nisi pena et labor.*[99]

366. *Item,* hedgehogs can be prepared using mutton rennet stomachs; it is very costly and a great amount of work for little praise and profit; therefore, *nichil hic.*[100]

367. *Agmidala rescencia recipe, et ab eis cum gladio remove eciam subtiliter primum corticem, et postea perforetur quodlibet agmidalum uno foramine in medio. Et hiis peractis, dicta agmidala ponantur in aqua dulci, in qua stent per quinque vel sex dies. Sed qualibet die fiat mutacio aque semel en die. Deinde lapsis quinque vel sex diebus, dicta agmidala extrahantur a dicta aqua et ponantur in aliqua aqua ubi stent per unum diem naturalem ad exteandum et removendum vaporem dicte aque. Postea habeatur sufficiens quantitas boni et optimi mellis respectu quantitatis dictarum agmidalarum. Et illud mel buliatur bene et decoquatur sufficienter et decoquendo purgetur, et cum decoctum fuerit et refrigeratum, ponatur in quolibet foramine dicti agmidali unum gariofilum, et respositis omnibus dictis agmidalis in aliquo bono vase terreo, ponatur desuper.*

Item fiat de nucibus conficiendis, sed ille habent stare in aqua per novem dies qualibet die mutanda, dictum mel bene decoctum et dispositum pro mensura coperiente dicta agmidala, elapsis duobus mensibus postea comedantur.[101]

368. Cow's udders are cooked with meat and eaten like meat. *Item,* salted with mustard sauce. *Item,* sometimes cut in strips and roasted on the grill, just after being boiled.

369. Starlings. Pluck dry, eviscerate, cut off the heads and feet, and soak in water. Put into pastry with two strips of bacon over them; or cut the parts into pieces as for a gosling, and make a charpie; that is, cut the leg quarter into three parts, leaving the bone in each piece; the same for the wings and the remaining parts. Then fry in a pan with eggs as for charpie. It seems that they should *primo* cook halfway before being fried.

---

99. "Nothing but pain and labor." May refer to Taillevent's recipe no. 212, which indeed is a complex and time-consuming task (Scully, *Viandier,* 303).

100. Latin: "nothing of this."

101. These two Latin recipes for almonds resemble ¶¶ 312 and 315 for preserved walnut confits. To summarize: Peel the first skin of the almond and pierce each almond, making a hole. Soak them in water for five or six days, changing the water daily, dry, then stuff the holes with cloves. Place in a clay container and completely cover with honey that has been boiled, skimmed, and cooled. Do the same for walnut confit, but they must soak in water for nine days. The almonds must age for two months before they are ready to eat.

370. Roasted larks. Pluck dry, then cut off the heads, and do not gut them. Soak in warm water, and without cutting off the legs, spit them with pieces of bacon between the birds. *Item,* in a crust, cut off the heads and legs, and gut them, and stuff the cavity with fine cheese, and eat them with salt.

371. Hare is boiled, then larded, put in a crust, with powdered spices, and eaten with cameline sauce. It is a summer meat.

372. Rabbit in summer.

373. Pork pasty. Put the meat in a crust with verjuice grain on top.

374. Geese, hens, capons. Cut into pieces and put in pastry, except for the very fat capons, which are not cut up. One goose can make three pasties.

375. River birds in a pasty, with cameline sauce—or even better, put the sauce in the pasty while it is cooked. The head, legs, and feet are arranged on the outside.

376. Pigeon pasty. Heads and feet are cut off, with two slices of bacon on top. Or they are larded if you roast them.

377. To hull barley or wheat to make frumenty. Put the wheat or barley in very hot water and wash and swirl about well and long, then pour off the water and let the wheat or barley dry. Pound it with a wooden pestle, then winnow it in a wash basin.

378. Hazelnut beverage. Scald and peel the nuts, then place in cold water. Then grind well and soak in boiled water, and strain.

379. Sardines. Gut, cook in water, and eat with mustard sauce.

380. New herring season begins in April and lasts until St. Remy's Day when the fresh herring runs begin.[102] Cook in water. Afterward, make generous-sized sops and eat with old verjuice. But as soon as the herring is cooked and removed from the pan, put it into nice fresh water, wash it, and remove the scales, head, and tail.

Hic finit.

---

102. New herring probably refers to the finest Dutch new herring, the first catch of the season, a cause for culinary celebration in Holland and elsewhere in Europe when they were available. "Fresh herring" may be more local fish.

Glossary of Culinary Terms

Sources for the definitions include Scully, *Viandier;* Scully and Scully, *Early French Cookery;* Terence Scully, *The Art of Cookery in the Middle Ages* (London: Boydell, 1995); Scully, "Menus of the *Ménagier de Paris*"; Brereton-Ferrier; Redon, Sabban, and Serventi, *Medieval Kitchen;* the *OED;* and Cotgrave's 1611 French-English dictionary. Numbers in brackets refer to the recipes in article 2.5.

andouille	tripe sausage [8, 254]
arboulastre (arbolastre, arboulaste)	omelet; herbed omelet [225]; an egg dish, frittata, or lean, deep-dish pie; a minced dish [265]
aspic (gellée)	jellied meat, poultry, or fish
bécuit (bescuit)	a fish preparation; possibly a scarlet-colored sauce made of fish juices
beignet	a kind of fritter, here savory [258]
blancmanger	a "white dish," using ground almonds and almond milk, rice and rice flour, boiled chicken, sugar, and mild spices; bland and considered appropriate for the sick [107]
boudin	blood sausage [6]
boue	thick sauce [185]
bouli lardé	a boiled meat or fish dish where the main ingredient is larded, then reboiled [90]
bouree/bourrey	a saltwater fish, perhaps a flying fish
boussac	a type of stew made with rabbit, hare, or venison [78, 82, 83, 88]
bouthors	the last dish, but also a wordplay—*boter* (v.), "to push/shove/nudge," and *hors,* "out," so the dish signals the guests to proceed to another room where the dish is served and then depart.
brouet	soup or broth
cameline	made with ground spices, including ginger and cinnamon [271, 273]
cassia buds	cinnamon
caudle	broth, stock [303]
charpie	a fried hash dish with cut-up meat or fowl and eggs
chastelonges (castagnoles)	a type of fish; sea bream?
chaudumée	a fish stew or fish sauce; "chowder" [277]
chine	a cut of meat that includes part of the backbone
civet (civé)	stew, usually with onions, not too dark in color [115–117; 130, 131]

clarry	a variation of hippocras, using white or red wine and honey
closing (yssue)	the last course, often of spiced wine and nuts or something sweet
cold sage (froide sauge)	an entire dish made with chicken in a sage sauce; sometimes refers to the sauce alone used on meat or fish [244]
comminée	a dish flavored with cumin, can be of poultry [98] or fish [99]
coq	aromatic herb, dittany (mint family) or costmary (tansy family)
coulis (coulez)	a purée, mashed or strained vegetables, usually peas or beans; can also be made with chicken or meat for invalids [306–8]
crétonnée	a vegetable purée with milk served over fried meat or fish [95–6]
darioles	little cheese tarts or almond-milk flans
à la dodine	a milk-based sauce with onions, used with fowl [154]
dorures (doree)	glazes with saffron and egg yolk [242]; noble households often had actual gilding on some dishes at feasts, but the author does not think this extravagant method appropriate for a bourgeois household like his own [364]
dragees	comfits, sweetmeats
droiz	delicate parts of venison, tripe
entremets	literally, "between courses," marking the change from the roast to the dessert part of a meal; fancy, decorated side dishes, sweet or savory; also, the entertainment during a meal; sometimes consisted of extraordinary concoctions of edible sculptures or decorated food, cooked birds reclothed in their plumage; in this book, usually more modest delicacies
espinbesche	fish stew, made with a larded stock [134], the stock of bouli lardé (see above)
estrier	waferlike pastry
flan	different sorts of pies/tarts; custard, sweet (dessert) or savory, usually sprinkled with sugar even if savory
frangié	"fringed" with saffron [63]
frumenty	hulled wheat porridge boiled in milk and seasoned with cinnamon, used as a side dish with venison, like a stuffing or dressing [234]
galantine	a sauce used with fish [129, 283]
galettte	a variety of thin, flat cake
galingale (garingal)	spice also called Siamese ginger or laos root
genesté	a yellow-colored dish
georgié	garnished

giste	long strip of meat
grain	the pieces of meat or fowl in a soup—the solids in a stew; sometimes shortened form of grain of paradise
grain verjuice	the seeds of unripe grapes, preserved in salt; may also be small unripe grapes [as perhaps in 97] (see verjuice)
grain of paradise	spice related to cardamom often substituted for the more pedestrian pepper in affluent households; with different English common names: alligator pepper, Guinea grains, Malegueta pepper, Melegueta pepper; in *Le Ménagier* often called simply "grain"
gravé	soup, gravy, or a thick stew [74, 128]
gramose	dish made with leftover meat, stock, eggs, verjuice [56]
halbran sauce	*halbran* is a young wild duck; this sauce [292] is also used for wood pigeons [154]
hardouil	a type of stew [100]
haslet	pork heart, liver, and lungs
hastelet	small pieces of roasted beef and pork
hericot (hericoc, hericoq, haricocus)	mutton stew [64]
hippocras (ypocras)	spiced wine, as an after-dinner drink [317]
heated sauce	a sauce that is warmed, not necessarily spicy
hochepot	stew or ragout [101]
houssié	garnished
jance	a garlic sauce [286–288]
lard	no distinction is usually made between lard, bacon fat, and pork drippings; "to lard" is piercing meat and poking into the holes small bits of lard to add to the moistness in the (usually meat) dish
larras	a dish prepared for days of fasting, perhaps consisting of fish
leschefrite	fritters made of strips of fried bread or meat; *lesche* is a blade or thin strip
loin	the flank; from part of the neck and cut along the back, could extend from kidney to rump
lozenges	type of pasty, lozenge shaped
menues espices	mixture of cloves and cardamom
morteruel	a dish containing bread and milk; a kind of entremet
nieulles	light pastries, wafers decorated with religious signs and sold at churches
Norse pasties (pastez noirroix)	a deep-fried pie, usually savory, made with chopped fish [258]

numbles (nomblez)	a cut of meat; archaic term also in English; sources differ on what section of the animal it was, whether entrails (especially of a deer), the back and loins, loin of veal, fillet of beef or venison, chine of pork [86]
orillettes	type of small cake, ear-shaped
oublies	slight, waffle-like pastries, decorated with religious symbols and sold in some churches; word also used in Middle French for the host of the Eucharist
pastie	savory pie
pimpernel(s) (pinperneaulx)	small eels
pipefarces	savory pancakes, fried cheese [264]
poivre	sauce [282]
poivre jaunet	a piquant sauce; perhaps a yellow-colored pepper sauce
porée	puree, mash, or mixture of vegetables; often refers to leafy greens themselves, a salad; see coulis and purée [49–52]
porte	type of cake
pottage	dish prepared in a pot or casserole; soup; stew of vegetables and meat, can be thin or thick in consistency
powdered spices (pouldre fine)	commonly used mixture of spices (ginger, cinnamon, cloves, and grains of paradise); it was often kept premixed
purée	a coulis; strained or puréed vegetables, usually peas; also, when used alone, a vegetable stock/broth
quartern	a quarter measure; where the measure is obviously in pounds, we have used "quarter pound," or in ounces, "quarter ounce"
râppé(e)	sauce, soup, or broth made with a mash of fresh grapes [113, 294]
red sugar	sugar made red with spices [271, 290]
reversed eels	eels skinned, slit down the back, deboned, and inverted flesh side out, tied with string and cooked in red wine, and then untied and served; could be called "butterflied eels" [180]
rissoles	small deep-fried turnovers
riz engoulé	spiced rice, savory rice
rosé	pink-colored stew, with color from red cedar; the name of the sauce used to stew the meat or fowl [84]
salemine	fish dish
septier (sextier)	a measure of liquid, approximately one gallon
seymé	winter soup [75, 79, 128]
sirloin (surlonge, seulonge)	not the modern sirloin, but most likely the end of the loin, part of the rump

sops	bread, toasted or untoasted, used to sop up juices as part of the meal; a broth containing bread as thickener
soringue (soringne, seringne)	brown sauce with onions and vinegar; a dish prepared with this sauce, such as with eel or fish [127]
à la soucie	a sauce, usually green; "souse" [245]
spring chicken	a chicken less than ten months old; chick
supplication	type of cake or wafer
taillis (tailliz)	sweet or savory chopped prepared dish
talemouse	flan or cheesecake glazed with egg yolk and dusted with sugar
tile (tile, tuillé, tieules)	named for its tile-like hue, fried ground meat/fish with spices [77, 118]
trencher	piece of (usually) coarse bread used as a plate at meals
tripe	dish made from the viscera of beef or pork or other meat, usually the stomach [12–15]
verjuice	a mash of sour unripe grapes, widely used as a sauce or ingredient, like vinegar; grain verjuice refers to the verjuice grape seeds preserved in salt, rather than the thin sauce itself
vinaigrette	prepared dish where the taste of vinegar predominates; here, a stew of pork spleen [105]

Bibliography

EDITIONS

Le menagier de Paris. Ed. Georgine E. Brereton and Janet M. Ferrier. Foreword by Beryl
   Smalley. Oxford: Oxford University Press, 1981.
*Le Ménagier de Paris, Traité de morale et d'économie domestique composé vers 1393 par un
   bourgeois parisien.* Ed. Jérôme Pichon. 2 vols. Paris: La Société des bibliophiles françois,
   1846–47 ; reprint, Geneva: Slatkine, 1982.

TRANSLATIONS

Power, Eileen. *The Goodman of Paris.* London: Routledge, 1928; reprint, London: Boydell,
   2006.
Ueltschi, Karin. *Le Mesnagier de Paris: texte édité par Georgina [sic] E. Brereton et Janet M.
   Ferrier; traduction et notes par Karin Ueltschi.* Paris: Livre de Poche, 1994.

OTHER WORKS CONSULTED

Aers, David, and Lynn Staley. *The Powers of the Holy: Religion, Politics, and Gender in Late
   Medieval English Culture.* University Park: Pennsylvania State University Press, 2004.
Alfonsus, Petrus. *The Scholar's Guide: A Translation of the Twelfth-Century Disciplina
   Clericalis of Pedro Alfonso.* Trans. Joseph Ramon Jones and John Esten Keller. Toronto:
   Pontifical Institute of Medieval Studies, 1969.
Amt, Emily. *Women's Lives in Medieval Europe: A Sourcebook.* New York: Routledge, 1993.
Archer, Rowena B. "'How ladies . . . who live on their manors ought to manage their
   households and estates': Women as Landholders and Administrators in the Later
   Middle Ages." In *Woman Is a Worthy Wight: Women in English Society, c. 1200–1500,*
   ed. P. J. P. Goldberg, 149–81. Wolfboro Falls, NH: Sutton, 1992.
Arditi, Jorge. *A Genealogy of Manners.* Chicago: University of Chicago Press, 1998.
Ashley, Kathleen. "Medieval Courtesy Literature and Dramatic Mirrors of Female
   Conduct." In *The Ideology of Conduct,* ed. Nancy Armstrong and Leonard
   Tennenhouse, 25–38. New York: Routledge, 1987.
———. "The *Miroir des bonnes femmes*: Not for Women Only?" In *Medieval Conduct,* ed.
   Kathleen Ashley and Robert Clark, 86–105. Minneapolis: University of Minnesota
   Press, 2001.
Ashley, Kathleen, and Robert Clark, eds. *Medieval Conduct.* Minneapolis: University of
   Minnesota Press, 2001.
Askins, William. "*The Tale of Melibee.*" In *Sources and Analogues of the Canterbury Tales,*
   vol. 1, ed. Robert M. Correale and Mary Hamel, 321–408. Cambridge: D. S. Brewer,
   2002.

Austin, Thomas, ed. *Two Fifteenth-Century Cookery-Books.* Early English Text Society 91. London: N. Trübner, 1888.

Bayard, Tania. *A Medieval Home Companion: Housekeeping in the Fourteenth Century.* New York: Harper Perennial, 1991.

Benson, Larry D., ed. *The Riverside Chaucer.* 3rd ed. Boston: Houghton-Mifflin, 1987.

Berners, Juliana. *Boke of Saint Albans. Selections: The boke of hauking huntyng and fysshyng, with all the properties and medecynes that are necessary to be kept.* London: Robert Toye, 1566.

Blamires, Alcuin. *The Case for Women in Medieval Culture.* Oxford: Oxford University Press, 1997.

——, ed. *Woman Defamed and Women Defended: An Anthology of Medieval Texts.* Oxford: Oxford University Press, 1992.

Boffey, Julia. "Bodleian Library, MS Arch. Seldon. B.24 and the Definitions of the 'Household Book.'" In *The Medieval English Book,* ed. A. S. G. Edwards, Ralph Hanna, and Vincent Gillespie, 125–34. London: British Library, 2000.

Bousmanne, Bernard, Frédérique Johan, and Céline van Hoorebeeck, eds. *La Librairie des ducs de Bourgogne: Manuscrits conservés à la Bibliothèque royale de Belgique.* Vol. 2: *Textes didactiques.* Turnhout: Brepols, 2003.

Brereton, Georgine E. "Deux sources du *Ménagier de Paris: Le Roman des sept sages de Rome et Les Moralitez sur le jeu des eschés.*" *Romania* 74 (1953): 338–57.

——. "*Le Ménagier de Paris,* source de la xxxviiie nouvelle de *l'Heptaméron?*" *Bibliothèque d'Humanisme et de Renaissance* 16 (1954): 207.

Brun, Laurent. "Jacques Bruyant." *Archives de littérature du Moyen Age (ARLIMA).* May 1, 2006. <http://www.arlima.net/il/jacques_bruyant.html>.

Bruyant, Jacques. *Jacques Bruyant: Le Livre du Chastel de Labour.* Commentary by Eberhard König and William Lang. Lucerne: Faksimile-Verlag, 2005.

——. *Le livre de Chastel de Labour, par Jean Bruyant. A description of an Illuminated Manuscript of the fifteenth century, belonging to George C. Thomas, Philadelphia, with a short account and synopsis of the Poem.* [Philadelphia?]: Privately published, 1909.

Bryan, W. F., and Germaine Dempster, eds. *Sources and Analogues of Chaucer's Canterbury Tales.* New York: Humanities Press, 1958.

Carroll, Shawn E. "Ancient and Medieval Falconry: Origins and Functions in Medieval England." January–May 1996. Richard III Society, American Branch Web site. <http://www.r3.org/life/articles/falconry.html>.

Carruthers, Mary. "The Wife of Bath and the Painting of Lions." *PMLA* 94 (1979): 209–22.

Catholic Encyclopedia, The (online). New Advent Catholic Web site. Kevin Knight. 2007. <http://www.newadvent.org/cathen/index.html>.

Caxton, William. *The Book of the Knight of the Tower.* Ed. M. Y. Offord. Early English Text Society, S.S. 2. London: Oxford University Press, 1971.

Chiquart. *Du fait de cuisine.* Trans. Elizabeth Cook. October 20, 1988. <http://www.davidd friedman.com/Medieval/Cookbooks/Du_Fait_de_Cuisine/du_fait_de_c_contents.html>.

Christine de Pizan. *The Book of the City of Ladies.* Trans. Earl Jeffrey Richards. New York: Persea, 1982.

——. *A Medieval Woman's Mirror of Honor: The Treasury of the City of Ladies.* Trans. Charity Cannon Willard. Ed. Madeleine Pelner Cosman. New York: Persea, 1989.

Collette, Carolyn P. "Chaucer and the French Tradition Revisited: Philippe de Mézières and the Good Wife." In *Medieval Women: Texts and Contexts in Late Medieval Britain. Essays for Felicity Riddy,* ed. J. Wogan-Browne and R. Voaden, et al., 151–68. Turnhout: Brepols, 2000.

——. "Heeding the Counsel of Prudence: A Context for the *Melibee.*" *Chaucer Review* 29 (1995): 337–49.

Cooper, Helen. *Oxford Guides to Chaucer: The Canterbury Tales.* 2nd ed. Oxford: Oxford University Press, 1996.

Correale, Robert M., and Mary Hamel, eds. *Sources and Analogues of the Canterbury Tales.* Vol. 1. Cambridge: D. S. Brewer, 2002.

Cosman, Madeleine Pelner. *Fabulous Feasts: Medieval Cookery and Ceremony.* New York: George Braziller, 1976.

Cotgrave, Randle. *A Dictionarie of the French and English Tongues.* London: 1611. Greg Lindahl. <http://www.pbm.com/~lindahl/cotgrave/>.

Crane, Susan. *The Performance of Self: Ritual, Clothing, and Identity during the Hundred Years War.* Philadelphia: University of Pennsylvania Press, 2002.

Crossley-Holland, Nicole. *Living and Dining in Medieval Paris: The Household of a Fourteenth-Century Knight.* Cardiff: University of Wales Press, 1999.

Dalby, Andrew. *Dangerous Tastes: The Story of Spices.* Berkeley: University of California Press, 2000.

Dawson, Thomas. *The Good Housewife's Jewell.* London, 1596. <http://www.harvest fields.ca/CookBooks/003/07/00.htm.>

Delany, Sheila. "'Mothers to Think Back Through': Who Are They? The Ambiguous Example of Christine de Pizan." In *Medieval Texts and Contemporary Readers,* ed. Laurie A. Finke and Martin B. Shichtman, 177–97. Ithaca: Cornell University Press, 1987.

Denny-Brown, Andrea. "*Povre* Griselda and the All-Consuming *Archwyves.*" *Studies in the Age of Chaucer* 28 (2006): 77–115.

Dictionnaire de l'Académie Française. 1st ed. Paris, 1694. Project for American and French Research on the Treasury of the French Language (ARTFL). <http://www.lib.uchicago .edu/efts/ARTFL/projects/dicos/>.

Dinshaw, Carolyn. *Chaucer's Sexual Poetics.* Madison: University of Wisconsin Press, 1989.

Dowd, Maureen. *Are Men Necessary? When Sexes Collide.* New York: Putnam, 2005.

Duby, Georges. *The Knight, the Lady, and the Priest: The Making of Modern Marriage in Medieval France.* Trans. B. Bray. New York: Pantheon, 1983.

Elias, Norbert. *The Civilizing Process: The History of Manners and State Formation and Civilization.* Oxford: Oxford University Press, 1994.

Enders, Jody. *The Medieval Theater of Cruelty.* Ithaca: Cornell University Press, 1999.

Epopée des courges: cultures et consommations en Europe, La. Exposition au Potager du roi. September 9–October 9, 2005. Ed. Antoine Jacobsohn. Saint-Épain: Lume; Versailles: École nationale supérieure du paysage, 2005.

Epstein, Steven A. "The Medieval Family: A Place of Refuge and Sorrow." In *Portraits of Medieval and Renaissance Living: Essays in Memory of David Herlihy,* ed. Samuel K. Cohn Jr. and Steven A. Epstein, 149–74. Ann Arbor: University of Michigan Press, 1996.

Farmer, Sharon. "Persuasive Voices: Clerical Images of Medieval Wives." *Speculum* 61, no. 3 (1986): 517–43.

Farrell, Thomas J., and Amy Goodwin. "*The Clerk's Tale.*" In *Sources and Analogues of the Canterbury Tales,* vol. 1, ed. Robert M. Correale and Mary Hamel, 101–67. Cambridge: D. S. Brewer, 2002.

Ferrier, Janet. "'Seulement pour vous endoctriner': The Author's Use of Exempla in *Le Menagier de Paris.*" *Medium Aevum* 48 (1979): 77–89.

Finke, Laurie A. "Towards a Cultural Poetics of the Romance." *Genre* 22 (Summer 1989): 109–27.

Fliegel, Stephen N. et al., eds. *Art from the Court of Burgundy: The Patronage of Phillip the Bold and John the Fearless, 1364–1419.* Exhibition catalog. Cleveland Museum of Art/Musée des Beaux-Arts of Dijon. Cleveland: Cleveland Museum of Art, 2004.

Foucault, Michel. *Discipline and Punish: The Birth of the Prison.* Trans. Alan Sheridan. New York: Vintage, 1995.

Freedman, Paul. "Spices and Late-Medieval European Ideas of Scarcity and Value." *Speculum* 80 (2005): 1209–27.

Furnivall, Frederick J., ed. *The Babees Book.* Early English Text Society, O.S. 32. London: N. Trübner, 1868; reprint, Millwood, N.Y.: Kraus, 1990.

Gillingham, John. "From *Civilitas* to Civility: Codes of Manners in Medieval and Early Modern England." *Transactions of the Royal Historical Society* 12 (2002): 267–89.

Godefroy, Frédéric. *Dictionnaire de l'ancienne langue française et de tous ses dialectes du IXe au XVe siècle.* Paris: F. Viewig, 1880–1902; reprint, Nendeln, Liechtenstein: Kraus, 1969.

Goodwin, Amy. "The Griselda Story in France." In *Sources and Analogues of the Canterbury Tales,* vol. 1, ed. Robert M. Correale and Mary Hamel, 130–67. Cambridge: D. S. Brewer, 2002.

Greco, Gina L. "Court Values in *Jehan de Saintré.*" Paper presented at the International Congress on Medieval Studies, Kalamazoo, MI, May 7, 2006.

Griffiths, Jeremy. *The Tollemache Book of Secrets: A Descriptive Index and Complete Facsimile with an Introduction and Transcriptions together with Catherine Tollemache's Receipts of Pastery, Confectionary & c.* Completed by A. S. G. Edwards. London: Roxburghe Club, 2001.

Grigsby, John L. "*Miroir des bonnes femmes*: A New Fragment of the *Somme le Roi* and a *Miroir des bonnes femmes,* a Hitherto Unnoticed Text." *Romania* 80 (1961): 447–60 and 82 (1962): 458–81.

Gringore, Pierre. *The Castell of Labour.* Trans. Alexander Barclay. Reprinted in facsimile from Wynkyn de Worde's edition of 1506 with the French text of March 31, 1501, and an introduction by A. W. Pollard. Edinburgh: Constable, 1905.

Grossi, Joseph. "The Clerk vs. the Wife of Bath: Nominalism, Carnival, and Chaucer's Last Laugh." In *Literary Nominalism and the Theory of Reading Late Medieval Texts,* ed. Richard J. Utz, 147–78. Lewiston, NY: Edwin Mellen Press, 1999.

Hieatt, Constance, and Sharon Butler. *Pleyn Delit: Medieval Cookery for Modern Cooks.* Toronto: University of Toronto Press, 1979.

Hindley, Alan, Frederick W. Langley, and Brian J. Levy. *Old French-English Dictionary.* Cambridge: Cambridge University Press, 2000.

Horsemanshop.com. 2002–7. <http://www.horsemanshop.com/index.html>.

How the good wijf Tau3t Hir Dou3tir. In *The Babees Book,* ed. Frederick J. Furnivall, 36–47. Early English Text Society, O.S. 32. London: N. Trübner, 1868; reprint, Millwood, N.Y.: Kraus, 1990.

Jankyn's Book of Wikked Wyves. Ed. Ralph Hanna III and Traugott Lawler, using materials collected by Karl Young and Robert Pratt. Athens: University of Georgia Press, 1997.

Johnson, Lesley. "Reincarnations of Griselda: Contexts for the Clerk's Tale?" In *Feminist Readings in Middle English Literature: The Wife of Bath and All Her Sect,* ed. Ruth Evans and Lesley Johnson, 195–220. London: Routledge, 1994.

Krueger, Roberta L. "Identity Begins at Home: Female Conduct and the Failure of Counsel in *Le Menagier de Paris.*" *Essays in Medieval Studies* 22 (2005): 21–39.

——. "Uncovering Griselda, Christine de Pizan, 'une seule chemise,' and the Clerical Tradition: Boccacio, Petrarch, Philippe de Mézières and the Ménagier de Paris." In *Medieval Fabrications: Dress, Textiles, Clothwork and Other Cultural Imaginings,* ed. Jane Chance, 71–88. New York: Palgrave Macmillan, 2004.

Langfors, A. "Jacques Bryant et son poème: *La Voie de povreté et de richesse.*" *Romania* 45 (1918): 49–83.

Latham, Simon. *Lathams New and Second Booke of Faulconry: concerning the ordering and training vp of all such hawkes as was omitted or left vnmentioned in his printed booke of the haggard faulcon and gerfaulcon, namely, the goshawke and tassell, with the sperhawke, and lanner and lanneret, as they are diuided in their generation, the hobby and marlyn in their kindes: teaching approued medicines for all such infirmities and diseases as are incident to them: published for the delight of noble minds, and instruction of yong faulconers in all things pertaining to this art.* London: Thos. Harper for John Harrison, 1633.

Laurent, Friar. *The Book of Vices and Virtues: A Fourteenth Century English Translation of the* Somme le Roi *of Lorens D'Orléans,* ed. W. N. Francis. Early English Text Society, O.S. 217. Oxford: Oxford University Press, 1942.

Lawton, David. "Dullness in the Fifteenth Century." *ELH* 54, no. 4 (Winter 1987): 761–99.

Lewis, Katherine J. "Model Girls? Virgin-Martyrs and the Training of Young Women in Late-Medieval England." In *Young Medieval Women,* ed. K. Lewis, N. Menuge, and K. Phillips, 25–46. New York: St. Martin's Press, 1999.

Littré, Emile. *Dictionnaire de la langue française.* Paris: Hachette, 1863–67. XMLittré. Ed. François Gannaz. <http://francois.gannaz.free.fr/Littre/accueil.php>.

Lynne, Hanne E. DVM, MRCVS, MDNV. *Equine Dentistry.* 2001–6. <http://www.hanne .com/teeth-anatomy.html>.

Manly, John M., and Edith Rickert, eds. *The Text of* The Canterbury Tales, *Studied on the Basis of All Known Manuscripts.* 8 vols. Chicago: University of Chicago Press, 1940.

Meyer, Paul. Review of *Le livre de Chastel de Labour, par Jean Bruyant. A Description. Romania* 39 (1910): 419–20.

Mézières, Philippe de. *Letter to King Richard II.* Ed. and trans. G. W. Coopland. New York: Barnes and Noble, 1976.

———. *Le Livre de la vertu du sacrement de mariage.* Ed. Joan B. Williamson. Washington: Catholic University of America Press, 1993.

Middleton, Anne. "The Clerk and His Tale: Some Literary Contexts." *Studies in the Age of Chaucer* 2 (1980): 121–50.

Miller, Mark. "The *Clerk's Tale* and the Scandal of the Unconditional." Paper presented to the New Chaucer Society, Glasgow, 2004.

Miller, Robert. *Chaucer: Sources and Backgrounds.* Oxford: Oxford University Press, 1977.

Minnis, Alastair. *Magister Amoris: The Roman de la Rose and Vernacular Hermeneutics.* Oxford: Oxford University Press, 2001.

Morey, James H. "Peter Comestor, Biblical Paraphrase, and the Medieval Bible." *Speculum* 68, no. 1 (1993): 6–35.

Morse, Charlotte P. "The Exemplary Griselda." *Studies in the Age of Chaucer* 7 (1985): 51–86.

Morse, Stephen G. "Apply Yourself: Learning while Reading the *Tale of Melibee.*" *Chaucer Review* 38, no. 1 (2003): 83–97.

Nabokov, Vladimir. *Lectures on Literature.* Ed. Fredson Bowers. New York: Harcourt Brace, 1980.

Nicholls, Jonathan. *The Matter of Courtesy: Medieval Courtesy Books and the Gawain-Poet.* Woodbridge, Suffolk: D. S. Brewer, 1985.

Nicot, Jean. *Thresor de la langue françoyse tant ancienne que moderne.* Paris, 1606. Project for American and French Research on the Treasury of the French Language (ARTFL) <http://www.lib.uchicago.edu/efts/ARTFL/projects/dicos/>.

Oggins, Robin S. *The Kings and Their Hawks.* New Haven: Yale University Press, 2004.

Patterson, Lee. *Negotiating the Past.* Madison: University of Wisconsin Press, 1987.

———. "'What Man Artow?' Authorial Self-Definition in the *Tale of Sir Thopas* and the *Tale of Melibee.*" *Studies in the Age of Chaucer* 11 (1989): 117–75.

Paul the Deacon. *History of the Langobards by Paul the Deacon.* Trans. Wm. Dudley Foulke. Philadelphia: University of Pennsylvania Press, 1974.

Pearce, Lynne. "Popular Romance and Its Readers." In *A Companion to Romance: From Classical to Contemporary,* ed. Corinne Saunders, 521–39. Malden, MA: Blackwell, 2000.

Petroff, Elizabeth Alvilda, ed. *Medieval Women's Visionary Literature.* Oxford: Oxford University Press, 1986.

Plant Finder's Encyclopedia, The. The Plant Press. Susan A. Tindall. 2003–6. <http://www.plantpress.com/plant-encyclopedia/>.

Redon, Odile, Françoise Sabban, and Silvano Serventi, eds. *The Medieval Kitchen: Recipes from France and Italy.* Trans. Edward Schneider. Chicago: University of Chicago Press, 2000.

Riddy, Felicity. "'Abject odious': Feminine and Masculine in Henryson's *Testament of Cressid.*" In *The Long Fifteenth Century: Essays for Douglas Gray,* ed. Helen Cooper and Sally Mapstone, 229–48. Oxford: Oxford University Press, 1997.

——. "Looking Closely: Authority and Intimacy in the Late Medieval Urban Home." In *Gendering the Master Narrative: Women and Power in the Middle Ages,* ed. Mary C. Erler and Maryanne Kowaleski, 212–28. Ithaca: Cornell University Press, 2003.

——. "Mother Knows Best: Reading Social Change in a Courtesy Text." *Speculum* 71, no. 1 (1996): 66–86.

Rose, Christine M. "What Every Goodwoman Wants: The Parameters of Desire in *Le Ménagier de Paris / The Goodman of Paris.*" *Studia Anglica Posnaniensia* 38 (2002): 394–410.

——. "Glossing Griselda in a Medieval Conduct Book: Le Ménagier de Paris." *Medieval English Mirror* 4(2008): 81–103.

Russell, John. *John Russell's Boke of Nurture.* In *The Babees Book,* ed. Frederick J. Furnivall, 115–239. Early English Text Society, O.S. 32. London: N. Trübner, 1868; reprint, Millwood, N.Y.: Kraus, 1990.

Scanlon, Larry. "What's the Pope Got to Do with It? Forgery, Didacticism, and Desire in the *Clerk's Tale.*" *New Medieval Literatures* 6 (2003): 129–65.

Scully, D. Eleanor, and Terence Scully. *Early French Cookery: Sources, History, Original Recipes, and Modern Adaptations.* Ann Arbor: University of Michigan Press, 2002.

Scully, Terence. *The Art of Cookery in the Middle Ages.* Woodbridge, Suffolk: Boydell, 1995.

——. "The Menus of the Menagier de Paris." *Le Moyen Francais* 24–25 (1989): 215–42.

——. *The* Viandier *of Taillevent: An Edition of all Extant Manuscripts.* Ottawa: University of Ottawa Press, 1988.

Seven Sages of Rome, The. Ed. Karl Brunner. Early English Text Society 191. London: Oxford University Press, 1933.

Severs, J. Burke. *The Literary Relationships of Chaucer's* Clerk's Tale. New Haven: Yale University Press, 1942; reprint, Archon Books, 1972.

————. "The Tale of Melibee." In *Sources and Analogues of Chaucer's Canterbury Tales,* ed. W. F. Bryan and Germaine Dempster, 560–614. New York: Humanities Press, 1958.

Staley, Lynn. *Languages of Power in the Age of Richard II.* University Park: Pennsylvania State University Press, 2005.

Strohm, Paul. *Hochon's Arrow.* Princeton: Princeton University Press, 1992.

Tanis, James R., ed., with the assistance of Jennifer A. Thompson. *Leaves of Gold: Manuscript Illuminations from Philadelphia Collections.* Philadelphia: Philadelphia Museum of Art, 2001.

Tobler, Adolf, and Erhard Lommatzsch, continued by Hans Helmut Christmann. *Altfranzösisches Wörterbuch.* Weisbaden: Franz Steiner, 1925–.

Turberville, George. *The Booke of Falconrie or Hawking: for the onely delight and pleasure of all noblemen and gentlemen: collected out of the best authors, aswell Italians as Frenchmen, and some English practices withall concerning falconrie.* London: Thomas Purfoot, 1611.

Van Hemelryck, Tania. "Le Mesnagier de Paris." In *La Librairie des ducs de Bourgogne: Manuscrits conservés à la Bibliothèque royale de Belgique,* vol. 2: *Textes didactiques,* ed. Bernard Bousmanne, Frédérique Johan, and Céline van Hoorebeeck, 164–69. Turnhout: Brepols, 2003.

Vecchio, Sylvana. "The Good Wife." In *A History of Women in the West: Silences of the Middle Ages,* vol. 2, ed. Christiane Klapisch-Zuber, 106–35. Cambridge: Harvard University Press, 1992.

Wallace, David. *Chaucerian Polity: Absolutist Lineages and Associational Forms in England and Italy.* Stanford: Stanford University Press, 1997.

Whitelock, Jill, ed. *The Seven Sages of Rome* (Midland Version), edited from Cambridge, University Library, MS Dd.1.17. Early English Text Society. Oxford: Oxford University Press, 2005.

Index

Note: Cooking spices or ingredients are cited here generally when they are major components of a dish. Not every mention is noted. Recipes for many dishes are cross-referenced in the Glossary. Fish and ingredients mentioned only once are not cited unless significant.

Fortune, 71, 81, 100, 108, 110, 131, 160, 164, 167, 186, 193–94; as Destiny, 192–94; gifts of, 63, 67–68

Fraud, 157; in *Chemin* poem, 196–98; Reason on, 200–201

Frogs, 317–18

Frumenty, 258–63, 265, 267, 269, 287, 312, 339

Furs, skins: covering husband, 138–39; restoring, 220–21; and social climbing, 197

Galantine, 258, 261–62, 295, 302, 307–8, 322

Galingale, 266, 283, 288, 291, 294, 315, 321, 323–24, 329–30

Garlic, 205, 298, 303–10, 321–24; aroma disliked by hawks, 252; green garlic sauce, 303–4, 309, 310, 321; white garlic sauce, 298, 303, 321

Ginger, 266, 269; multiple recipes with, 271–336

Glossing: of Griselda by narrator, 42, 118–37; by a wife, 122

Gluttony: sin of, 66, 76–83, 189; and servants, 217; and women, 13, 76–78

Goat, 227, 251, 254, 259, 261, 265–66, 285–86, 297, 320

Good, translation of, 2, 7, 46

Good men: Abraham, 95; concealing wife's adultery, 144–46; Jacob, 98–101

Good women: and chastity, 86; definition, 92, 103; Griselda, 105–18; Jehanne la Quentine, 174–6; Judith, Abigail, Esther, 154; lawyer's wife, 146; Leah and Rachel, 34, 98–101; loyal wives, 87; Lucretia, 90–92; as peacemaker, 169; Prudence, 147–74; queens of France, 92–93; Rebecca, 154; Sarah, 95–98, 105; Susanna, 87–8; woman of Melun, 129–30; woman who saved her husband through adultery, 123–24

Goose, gosling: dishes, 258–60, 265, 272, 275, 283, 288–89, 298–99, 300, 321, 338–39; fattening, 256, 272, 298, 313; market, 266

Gospels, 61, 86, 153

Grafting, 133, 209–10, 213–14

Grain of paradise (spice), 221n

Grapes, 213, 221–22, 264, 269, 312, 319, 320, 323–24, 329–30, 333, 343–45

Gravé, 258, 260, 263, 269, 283–84, 294, 309

Greco, Gina L., 5n

Greens (porée), 209, 212, 257–64, 278–79, 310, 314

Green sauce, 259, 263, 301–2, 305–6, 308–9

Gregory, Saint, 86, 165

Griselda, 3, 4, 8, 10, 24, 26, 28–43, 105–18, 125, 147; advice to wives, 35; and *Clerk's Tale*, 29–33, 37; clothing, 107–9, 114–17; her contract, 108; ideal Christian wife, 8, 31–32; message of story, 30–31; as moral center of work, 8; narrator's glosses, 33–43; narrator's wife's resemblance to, 36–38; sources of tale, 28–29

Gurnard (fish), 259, 264, 306

Halles, the, 265–66, 270, 328

Hawking: composition of treatise, 54; dogs suitable. 233–34; horses suitable, 234; placement of treatise, 229, 232; as sport for women, 11–12, 16, 231; status symbol, 230–31; symbolic quality, 231

Hawks: bathing, 238; best, 235; cages, 236; capturing, 235, 248; distinguished from falcons, 230, 249–50; droppings, 239–40; "feather," 240–47; feeding, 236, 245; goshawk, 251; illness, 232, 240, 250–52; injuries, 243; molting, 247–49, 252; plumage, 238; seeling eyes, 248–49; taming, 240, 248; types, 248, 250–52; weight, 240; resembling women, 231; temperament, 237, 242, 246

Hazelnuts, 264, 317, 326, 339

Hedgehogs, 334, 338

Hell, 56–57, 61, 63, 64, 68, 76, 81, 121, 141, 168

Herring, 258–64, 275, 300, 308, 321, 339

Hieatt, Constance, and Sharon Butler, *Pleyn Delit*, 4n

Hippocras, 267, 269–71, 321, 329–30; in menus, 257–65

Holly, 221

Homosocial bond, 9. *See also* Husband: future husband

Honey, 325–29, 336, 339; for flies, 140; *Melibee*, 54, 156, 163; wolf poison, 219

Honor, reputation, public opinion, 9, 13–16, 20, 22, 36, 39–40, 50, 57–60, 69–71, 86, 92–94, 105, 107, 109, 119, 120, 122–38, 143, 145–46, 168–69, 173, 181–83, 186, 200, 203, 216, 218; and hawks, 236, 243, 248; mistraining dogs, 234; with servants, 216; shame, 16–17, 27, 39, 41–42, 57–60, 65–66, 77, 79, 135, 142. *See also* Jehanne la Quentine; Lucretia; Melibee; Susanna; and other "good" women

Horseradish, 328

Horses, 1, 6–9, 14–15, 52, 62–63, 83, 85, 91–92, 140–41, 179, 223–28; age, 224; characteristics, 223–24; diseases, 224; and flies, 337; gait; 226; for hawking, 235; inspection, 224–26; selling, 226–27; remedies, 227–28; woman as horse, 12

Hot sauce, 257–61, 303–4

Household: etymology, 21; family life, 9, 15–17; husband's role, 20; meat consumption, 253–54; reflects polis, 24, 30, 43; tasks, 218; tyranny, 24; wife's family, 49. *See also* Orderliness

Household books, 1, 21, 22

How the Good Wijf Tau3t Hir Dou3tir, 18, 21, 42

Hunting, game: lark, 243; magpies, 242, 246, 337; seasons, 244, 246

Husband: Balbi on, 17; choosing, 17, 105; compared to horse or dog, 140–41; compared to Marquis Walter, 38, 41; contentment of, 5, 12, 30, 37, 49–50, 121, 127; duties, 20–21; future husband, 2, 7, 9–10, 13, 44, 103–5, 119, 121–22, 129, 137, 139, 178; as lord, 174; new, 183; obligations to wife, 94, 101–3; resentful of female dominance, 147, 174; surveillance by, 27; as teacher, 20–21; testing by wives, 130–41; testing wives, 31, 35, 38, 40–41, 90, 109–18 (Griselda), 126–30, 137; vengeance, 127. *See also* Submission

Hyssop, 212, 272, 282–83, 287, 322

Ink, 336; invisible, 330

Innocent III, Pope, 167

Jacob (Rachel and Leah), 98–101

James, Saint, 155, 165, 173

Jance, 298, 301, 306, 308–10, 323–24

Jehan, Maître (steward): as audience, 9, 15, 44, 215–26; duties, 253–54

Jehanne la Quentine, 26, 40, 51, 174–76

Jerome, Saint, 104, 167

Jesus-Sirach, 152, 155

Jews, 87–88

Job, 150

Judas Machabeus, 169

Judgment Day, 65, 72, 82, 173, 201

Kings, Book II, 169

Krueger, Roberta L., 10n, 29n

Lamb, mutton, sheep: cuts of, 255; dishes, 257, 260–61, 265, 269, 273–75, 278–83, 296–97, 301, 312–14, 317, 337–38; and hawks, 236, 240, 248, 251

Langoustes, 306, 310, 319

La Sale, Antoine de, 5n, 31n

Lasciviousness, 189

Latham, Simon, 229

Laurent, Friar, *Somme le Roy,* 53–54, 67, 79–80

Lavender, 209

Lawton, David, 42

Leah and Rachel, as ideal wives, 35. *See also* Jacob

Learning and literacy, female, 5, 7–8, 13–14, 85; in church, 59; Dame Agnes's recording, 219; female reading, 159; husband's opinion of, 181; letter writing, 93; Lucretia, 90; praise of wise female, 173; and Prudence, 26, 147–74; queens of France, 92

Leeks: culinary use, 259–61, 278, 280; hawks' aversion to, 252; planting, 210, 213

Lettuce, 211, 259, 261, 263, 310

Lewis, Katherine J., 21n

Liver, 273–74, 287; dishes, 272, 281, 283, 286–87, 289–91, 305, 307–8, 312, 314, 318, 320, 323; and hawks, 251

Loach (fish), 258–59, 261–62, 265, 267, 294–95, 303, 316–17

Louens, Renard de, *Melibee* version, 3, 24, 147–48, 155, 157, 163

Luce. *See* Pike

Lucretia, 90–92

Lust, sin of, 66, 78–79, 84; and carnal gaze, 190; of Duchess Raimonde, 90

Macrobius, *Somnium Scipionis,* 142n

Mandrake, 100

Manuscripts, of *Le Ménagier,* 2–4, 6, 11, 28n, 54, 79n, 122, 152, 254, 262n. *See also Castell of Labour; Chemin de Povreté et de Richesse*

Marguerite de Navarre, 174n

Marjoram: cooking with, 272, 310, 322, 329; growing, 209–10

Marking liquid, 335

Marriage: Aristotelian concept of, 20; choosing spouse, 17–18; crucial things, 5; ideal, 35, 38, 121, 124; manuals, 20, 23; model for, 10, 23–24, 28, 31–34, 37, 40–43; old man with young wife, 26, 43, 132–36, 231; paradoxical nature, 14; remarriage, 138 (*see also* Husband); and salvation, 23; and violence, 7–8, 20, 24, 32–33, 38; wife's responsibilities, 15. *See also* Women: natural and divine law of submission

Mary Magdalene, 153; feast day, 212, 286

Mass, 59–81, 85, 91, 175–76

Meat: cuts, 254–55; dinner and supper menus, 257–62; roasted, 296–97; royal household's consumption, 253–54

Meatballs, 257, 259, 263, 314, 317

Melibee, 3–6, 24–26, 42; 147–74; translation, 46. *See also* Chaucer, Geoffrey

Mercy, works of, 186

Mézières, Philippe de, 8, 18–19, 22, 28–29, 31, 115

Milk: dishes, 257–60, 276–78, 288–89, 295–96, 312–15, 318, 323; preserving, 271, 288, 295–96

Minnis, A. J., 28

Misogyny: *Chemin,* 41, 179, 208; female domination, 174; female intellect, 181; female weakness, 13–15; of Melibee, 152–55

Money: and accounts, 28, 40, 102, 122, 197, 215–16, 217, 254, 274; prices, 254–55, 264–70, 273–74, 294, 312, 316–18, 325, 328, 337; and sin (usury, gambling), 76; wagers, 41, 125, 128–30; wages, 206, 215, 222, 228, 267, 270

Morse, Stephen G., 25n

Mullet (fish), 261–62, 295, 305–6, 308

Mussels, 309–10

Mustard, 270, 275, 286, 295–96, 302–9, 321, 323, 328–29, 338–39

Must sauce, 321, 323–24

Nabokov, Vladimir, 30

Narrator, 1; age, 2–3n; and *Chemin,* 5, 183; corrects recipe, 290; disclaims abuse, 118–19; disclaims wife's boredom, 179; interprets Griselda, 33–43; interprets *Melibee,* 149, 174, 218; labor of writing, 27–28; library, 54, 85; shame from wife, 181. *See also* Author; Husband

Nature: *Chemin,* 190–91

Next husband. *See* Husband

Numbles, 241, 248, 258, 261, 274, 285–87, 297, 324

Nutmeg, 291–93, 297, 303–4, 316, 321–24, 328–30

Obedience, definition, 122–23. *See also* Wife

Oggins, Robin S., 229–31

Omelet, 257, 259–63, 310–11

Onion, 271, 276–78, 282–84; assorted recipes, 290–326, 336; hawks dislike, 252

Orache, 211

Orange, 264–66, 300, 305, 322, 329, 336

Orderliness: household, 5, 28, 30; social and political, 31, 40n; wifely, 9, 30

Ovid, *Remedia Amores,* 149, 152, 160, 163

Oysters, 259, 261–63, 277, 295, 327

Pamphilles, 167

Parsley: cooking with, 276, 279, 281–83, 287; growing, 209–12; many other culinary uses, 290–328

Parsnips, water (skirret), 262, 300, 319

Partridges: cooked, 257, 260–61, 299–300,

313; cost, 269; freshness, 256, 299–300; habits, 242, 245–46; hunting, 233, 251–52; mating, 299. *See also* Hawking; Hawks

Pasties, pastries, pies, 275, 257–63, 269, 275, 282, 285, 299–306, 309, 318, 320, 324, 337, 339; poison, 220. *See also* Tarts

Patterson, Lee, 24n, 29

Paul, Saint, 81, 86, 104–5, 123, 144, 150, 163, 165

Peacocks, 206, 260, 265, 299; raising, 332

Pears, 257, 262, 269, 328, 330, 337

Peas: cooking, 275–78, 282, 288, 293, 308; planting, 213

Peonies, 212

Perch (fish), 262–63, 294–95, 301, 327, 337

Pests, ridding of, with poison: ants, 212; cabbage caterpillars, 213; fleas, 139; flies, 140; mosquitoes, 139–40; moths, 220; rats, 219–20; wolves, 219

Petrarch, 29, 35, 37, 43; Griselda story, 105–18

Petrus Comestor, *Bible historiale,* 53, 94–100, 120

Pets, 218. *See also* Birds; Cats; Dogs

Philosopher, the, 152, 168, 170

Pichon, Baron Jerôme, 2–4, 7, 10n, 44, 46, 53–54, 70n, 84n, 88n, 89n, 105n, 122n, 148, 152n, 180, 194n, 229, 253n, 254n, 260n, 274n, 335n

Pierre Alphonse, 152, 155, 157–58, 160, 167

Pierre-au-Lait, 267

Pigeons: buying, 254, 266; dishes, 269, 280, 297, 299, 323, 339; hawking, 235–37, 240–52; identifying, 256, 279, 299; and rape, 89

Pike, luce (fish), 255–57, 259–64, 288, 294–95, 301, 308, 316, 319, 320; roe, 255, 301–2, 315

Place de Grève, 267, 270

Plaice (fish), 256, 258, 260–61, 263–64, 293, 308, 309

Planting, times and dates, 209–14

Taillevent, Maître, *Viandier*, 5, 263n, 266n, 289–91n, 296n, 338n. *See also* Scully, Terence

Tansy, 310, 312

Tarts, 257–62, 266, 269, 311, 315, 334; rat poison, 220. *See also* Pasties

Tench (fish), 257–60, 262–64, 288, 301, 309, 315–16, 327

Testing: husbands by wives, 132–36; Lucretia, 90; wives by husbands, 27, 118, 127–31. *See also* Griselda

Toothache, 332

Tournai, 51, 125, 305, 319, 321–22

Translation: *Chemin*, 177, 183; of conduct books, 20 ; of "good," 2, 46–47; of *Le Ménagier*, 1–6; *Melibee*, 46; de Mézières, 22; Petrarch's Griselda, 29; protocols, 29, 44–46; *Somme le Roy*, 53

Transplanting, 211

Tripe, 273–74, 283, 287, 317, 320, 334

Trout: dishes: 302–3; season, 256

Turberville, George, 229–30

Turbot, 259, 261–64, 309

Turnips, 212, 258, 260, 274, 280, 320, 328, 333

Tyrant, 8, 24, 147; Wrath as, 187. *See also* Griselda; Husband; Melibee

Ueltschi, Karin, 3, 4, 44, 179

Understanding (allegorical figure), against Fraud, 198–99

Van Hemelryck, Tania, 3n

Veal, 257, 259–60, 265, 269, 282–85, 288, 290–93, 297, 301, 307, 312–13, 317, 327

Vecchio, Sylvana, 20n, 42

Venison, 255, 258–62, 265–66, 269, 273–74, 285–87, 297, 300, 307, 333, 336

Verjuice, 273, 279, 281–85, 288–324, 330–31, 336, 339; for stains, 220–21

Viandier, See Scully, Terence; Taillevent, Maître

Vices and remedies in *Chemin*: Avarice, 188; Covetousness, 19; Envy, 187; Pride, 186; Wrath, 187

Vinegar: making, 337, and throughout recipes

Violence. *See* Domestic violence

Violets, 49, 209–11, 267, 310, 317

Virtues, 7, 186; Chastity, 84; Diligence, 82; Friendship, 80; Generosity, 82–83; Humility, 80, 186–87; Kindness, 81, 187; opposed to Deadly Sins, 66–85, esp. 80–85; Temperance (moderation, abstinence), 83, 187–89

Viscera, entrails, offal, intestines, 271, 273–74, 287–89, 313, 320, 337

Waffles, 266, 334–35

Wallace, David, *Chaucerian Polity*, 24–25n, 32n, 43n

Walnuts, 327–29, 335, 338

Walter, Marquis. *See* Griselda

War, 25, entering, 151. *See also* Melibee

Wealth. *See* Riches

Whale (craspois), 262–63, 276, 308

Wheat: in birdlime, 331; in cooking, 266, 269, 319, 339, 342; feeding horses, 226, goslings, 298; to make food green, 309–10, 321; rat poison, 220–21

Whiting (fish), 262, 308, 319

Wife: Balbi's definition of, 17; care of husband's body, 138–41; correct husband through indirection, 147 (*see also* Melibee); devotion, sacrifice, 94–103; duties, 51–52; ideal, 30 (*see also* marriage); keeping secrets, 142–46; mistress of household, 223; mistress of servants, 217; model for servants, 223; obedience, 2, 6–11, 17–18, 19n, 30–

Wife (*continued*)
40, 49, 98, 105–18, 121– 31, 179, 231
(*see also* Submission); orderliness, 9,
30; taming of, 231; training hawks, dogs,
234; ways to husband's happiness, 138–
40

Wine: in cooking, 333–34, and throughout
recipes; maladies and cures, 221–22, 333;
serving, 268; to treat furs, 221; white to
red, 330

Wolf, wolves, 103, 127, 139, 219, 287

Wrath, and remedies, 66, 71–72, 81, 135, 155,
170–71, 184, 187–88. *See also* Anger

Women: advice from, 149–74; as animals,
7, 11–12, 102–3, 127, 231; as birds, 102;
Duby on, 17–18; and gluttony, 76–78;
ideal, 8, 17, 38, 41; natural and divine law
of submission, 18, 27, 33–34, 38, 41–42,
94–95, 104, 118, 120, 126–27; nature of,
154–55, 208; as peacemaker, 169. *See also*
Bad women; Good women; Misogyny;
Prudence; Wife

Worde, Wynkyn de, 45n, 177n

Yellow sauce (yellow *poivre*), 261, 283, 295,
297, 300–301, 306, 320, 322, 334

Library of Congress Cataloging-in-Publication Data

Ménagier de Paris. English.
   The good wife's guide : a medieval household book /
translated, with critical introduction, by Gina L. Greco and
Christine M. Rose.
      p. cm.
   Includes bibliographical references and index.
   ISBN 978-0-8014-4738-9 (cloth : alk. paper) —
ISBN 978-0-8014-7474-3 (pbk. : alk. paper)
   1. Home economics—France—Early works to 1800.
2. Conduct of life—Early works to 1800.   3. Paris (France)—
Social life and customs—Early works to 1800.   4. Cookery,
French—Early works to 1800.   I. Greco, Gina L.   II. Rose,
Christine M., 1949–   III. Title.
   TX17.M3913   2008
   392.3'70944—dc22

                                        2008029678

CPSIA information can be obtained
at www.ICGtesting.com
Printed in the USA
LVHW041549040123
736363LV00005B/121